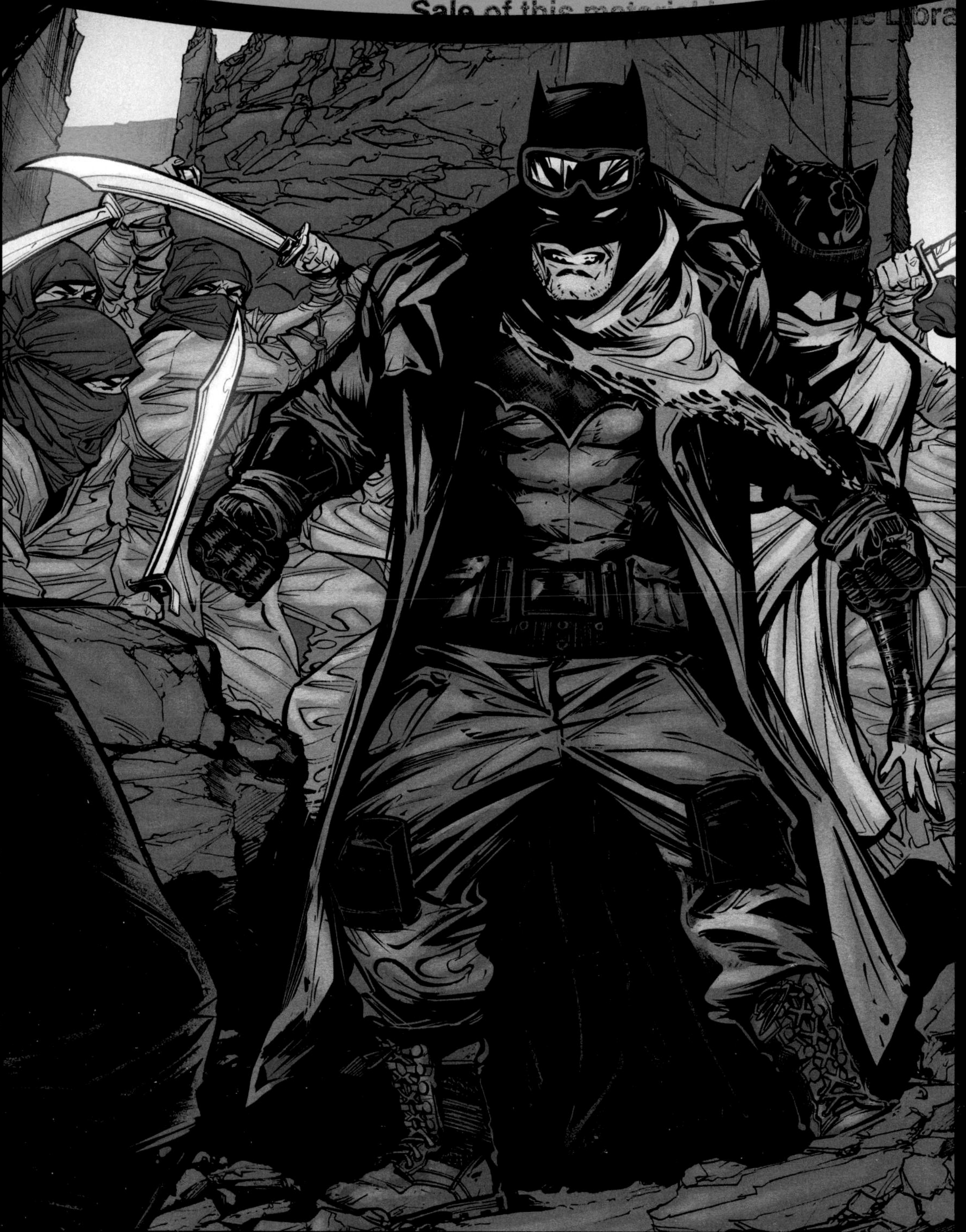

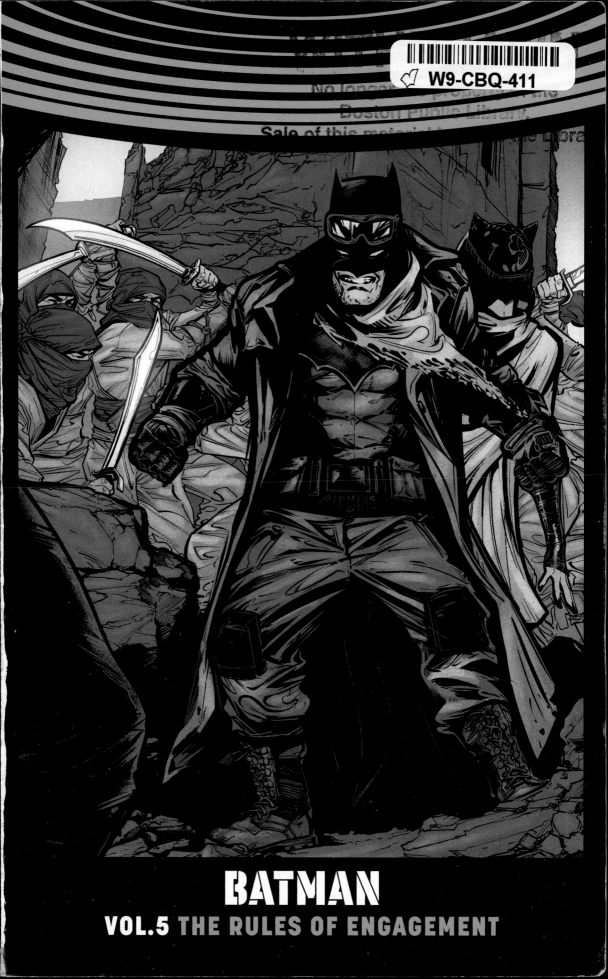

BATMAN

VOL.5 THE RULES OF ENGAGEMENT

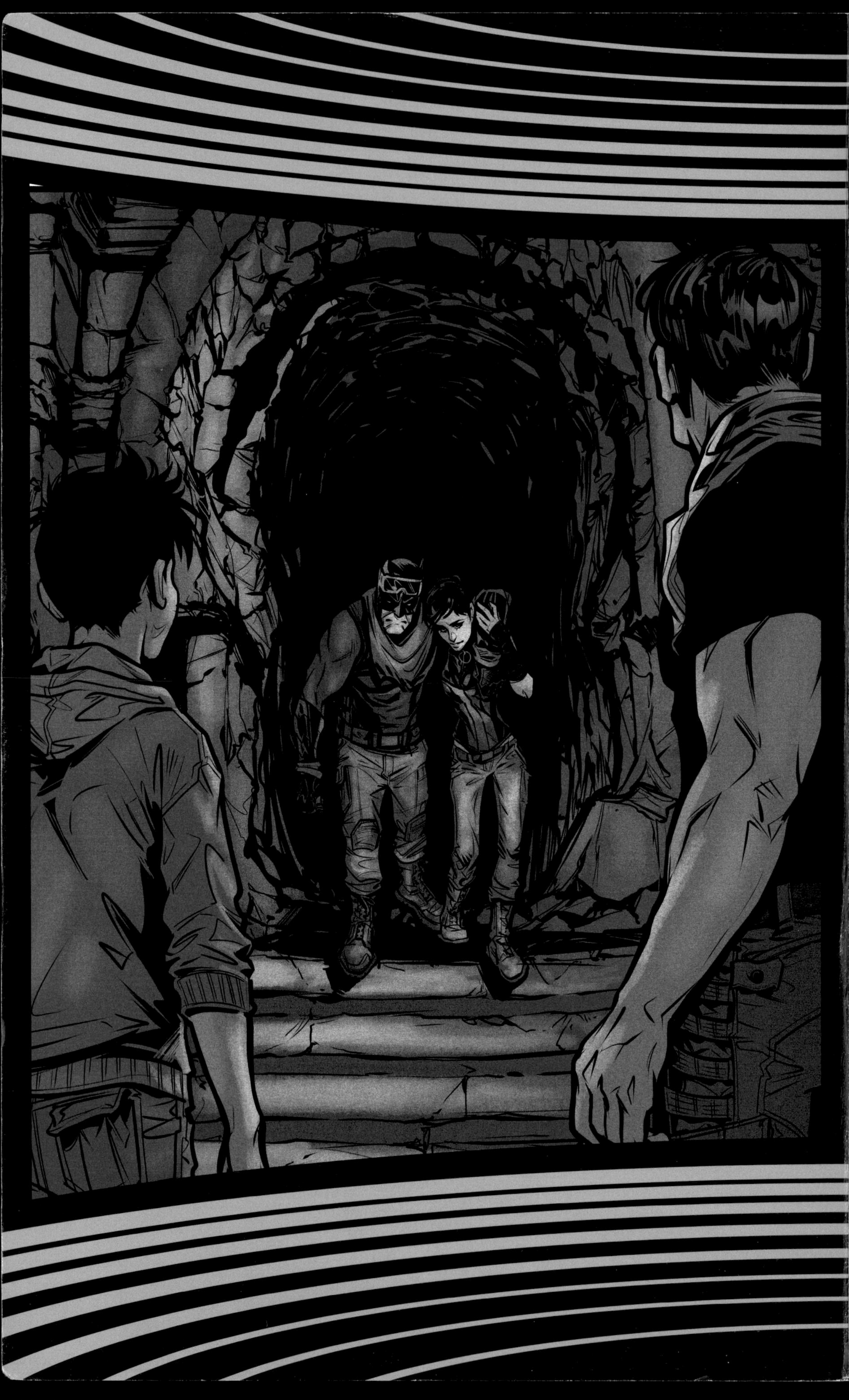

BATMAN

VOL.5 THE RULES OF ENGAGEMENT

TOM KING
writer

JOËLLE JONES
CLAY MANN
LEE WEEKS
MICHAEL LARK
SETH MANN
artists

JORDIE BELLAIRE
ELIZABETH BREITWEISER
JUNE CHUNG
colorists

CLAYTON COWLES
DERON BENNETT
letterers

JOËLLE JONES and **JORDIE BELLAIRE**
collection cover artists

BATMAN created by BOB KANE with BILL FINGER
SUPERMAN created by JERRY SIEGEL and JOE SHUSTER
By special arrangement with the Jerry Siegel family

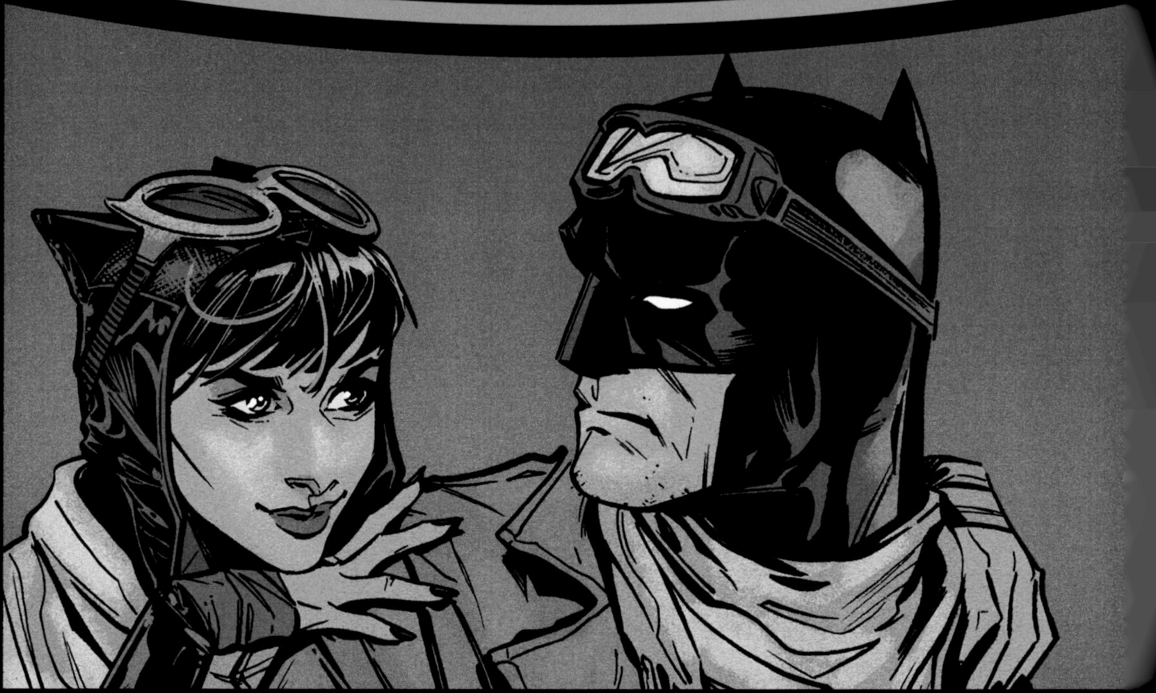

JAMIE S. RICH Editor - Original Series * **MAGGIE HOWELL** Assistant Editor - Original Series
JEB WOODARD Group Editor - Collected Editions * **ROBIN WILDMAN** Editor - Collected Edition
STEVE COOK Design Director - Books * **MEGEN BELLERSEN** Publication Design

BOB HARRAS Senior VP - Editor-in-Chief, DC Comics
PAT McCALLUM Executive Editor, DC Comics

DIANE NELSON President * **DAN DiDIO** Publisher * **JIM LEE** Publisher * **GEOFF JOHNS** President & Chief Creative Officer
AMIT DESAI Executive VP - Business & Marketing Strategy, Direct to Consumer & Global Franchise Management
SAM ADES Senior VP & General Manager, Digital Services * **BOBBIE CHASE** VP & Executive Editor, Young Reader & Talent Development
MARK CHIARELLO Senior VP - Art, Design & Collected Editions * **JOHN CUNNINGHAM** Senior VP - Sales & Trade Marketing
ANNE DePIES Senior VP - Business Strategy, Finance & Administration * **DON FALLETTI** VP - Manufacturing Operations
LAWRENCE GANEM VP - Editorial Administration & Talent Relations * **ALISON GILL** Senior VP - Manufacturing & Operations
HANK KANALZ Senior VP - Editorial Strategy & Administration * **JAY KOGAN** VP - Legal Affairs * **JACK MAHAN** VP - Business Affairs
NICK J. NAPOLITANO VP - Manufacturing Administration * **EDDIE SCANNELL** VP - Consumer Marketing
COURTNEY SIMMONS Senior VP - Publicity & Communications * **JIM (SKI) SOKOLOWSKI** VP - Comic Book Specialty Sales & Trade Marketing
NANCY SPEARS VP - Mass, Book, Digital Sales & Trade Marketing * **MICHELE R. WELLS** VP - Content Strategy

BATMAN VOL. 5: THE RULES OF ENGAGEMENT

DC Comics, 2900 West Alameda Ave., Burbank, CA 91505
Printed by LSC Communications, Kendallville, IN, USA. 3/23/18. First Printing.
ISBN: 978-1-4012-7731-4

Library of Congress Cataloging-in-Publication Data is available.

PEFC Certified
Printed on paper from sustainably managed forests, controlled sources
PEFC
PEFC/29-31-337
www.pefc.org

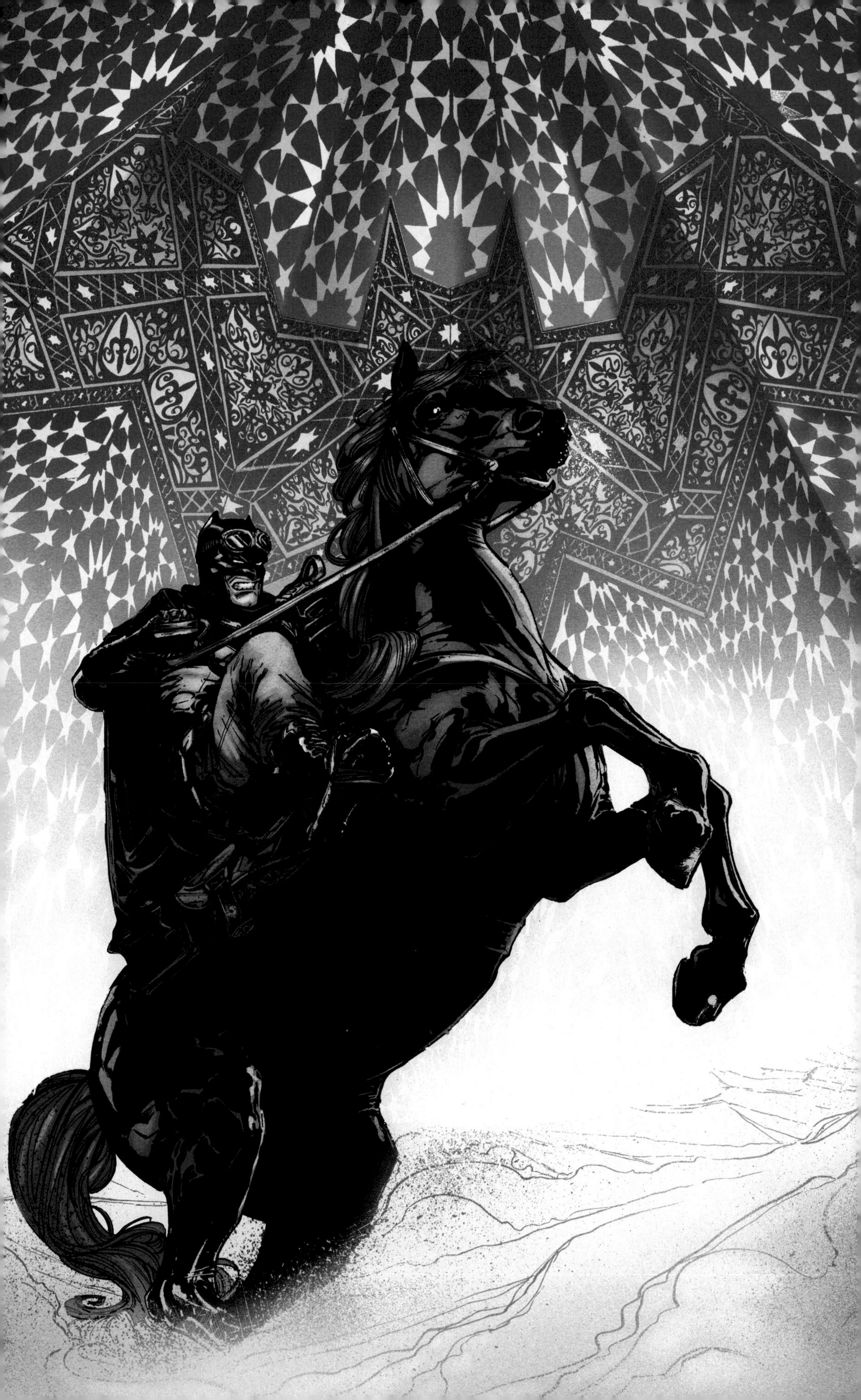

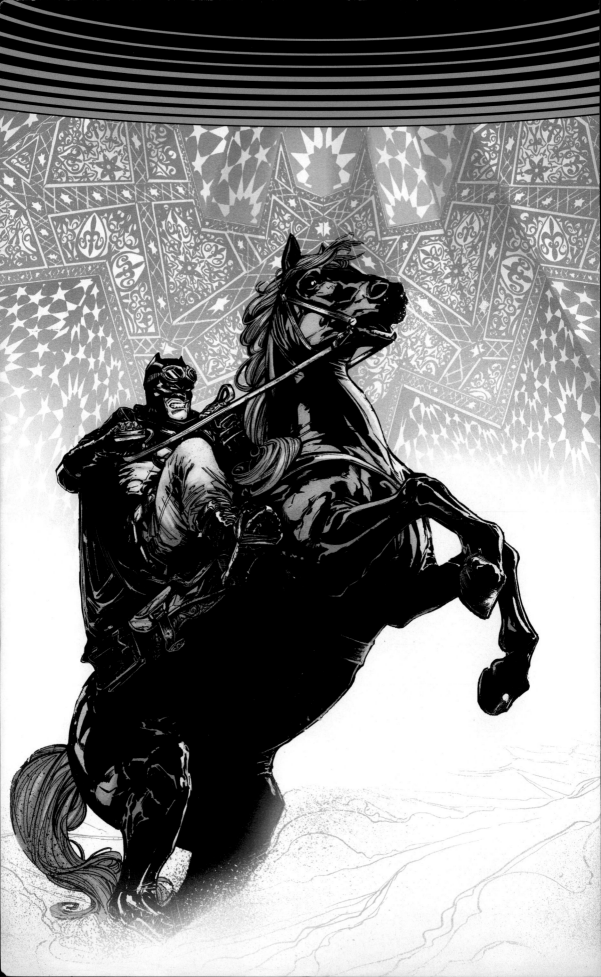

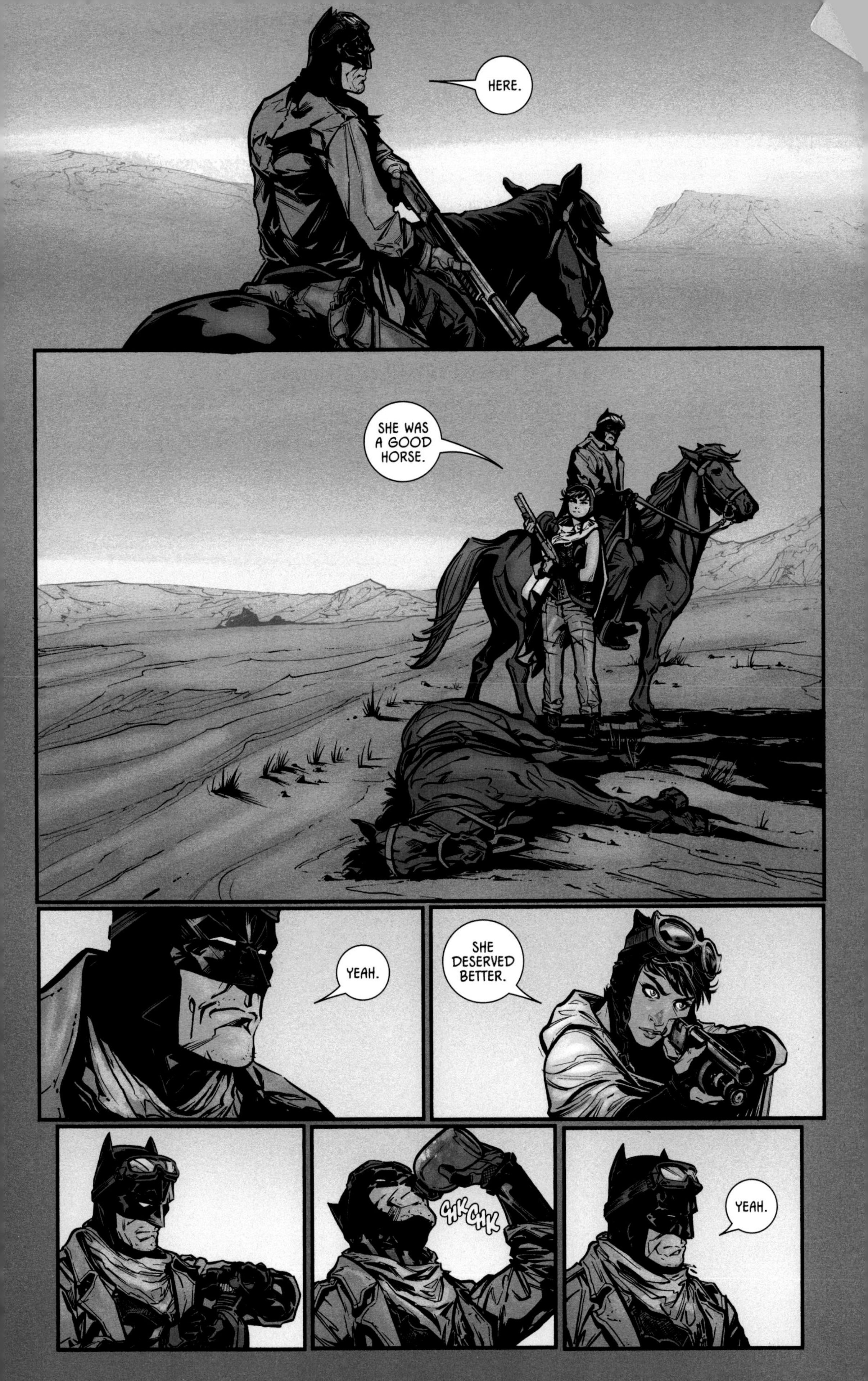
HERE.
SHE WAS A GOOD HORSE.
YEAH.
SHE DESERVED BETTER.
CHK CHK
YEAH.

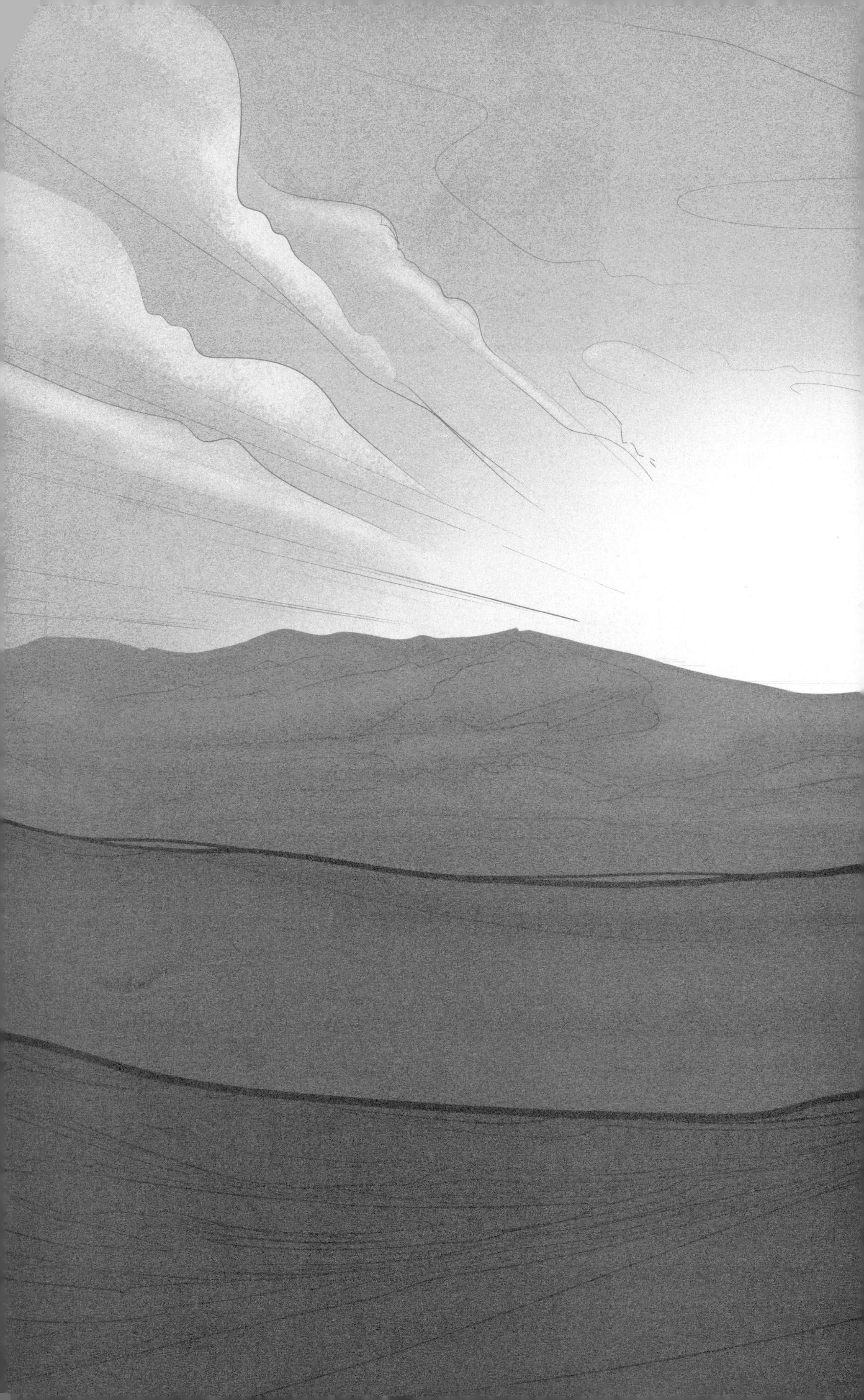

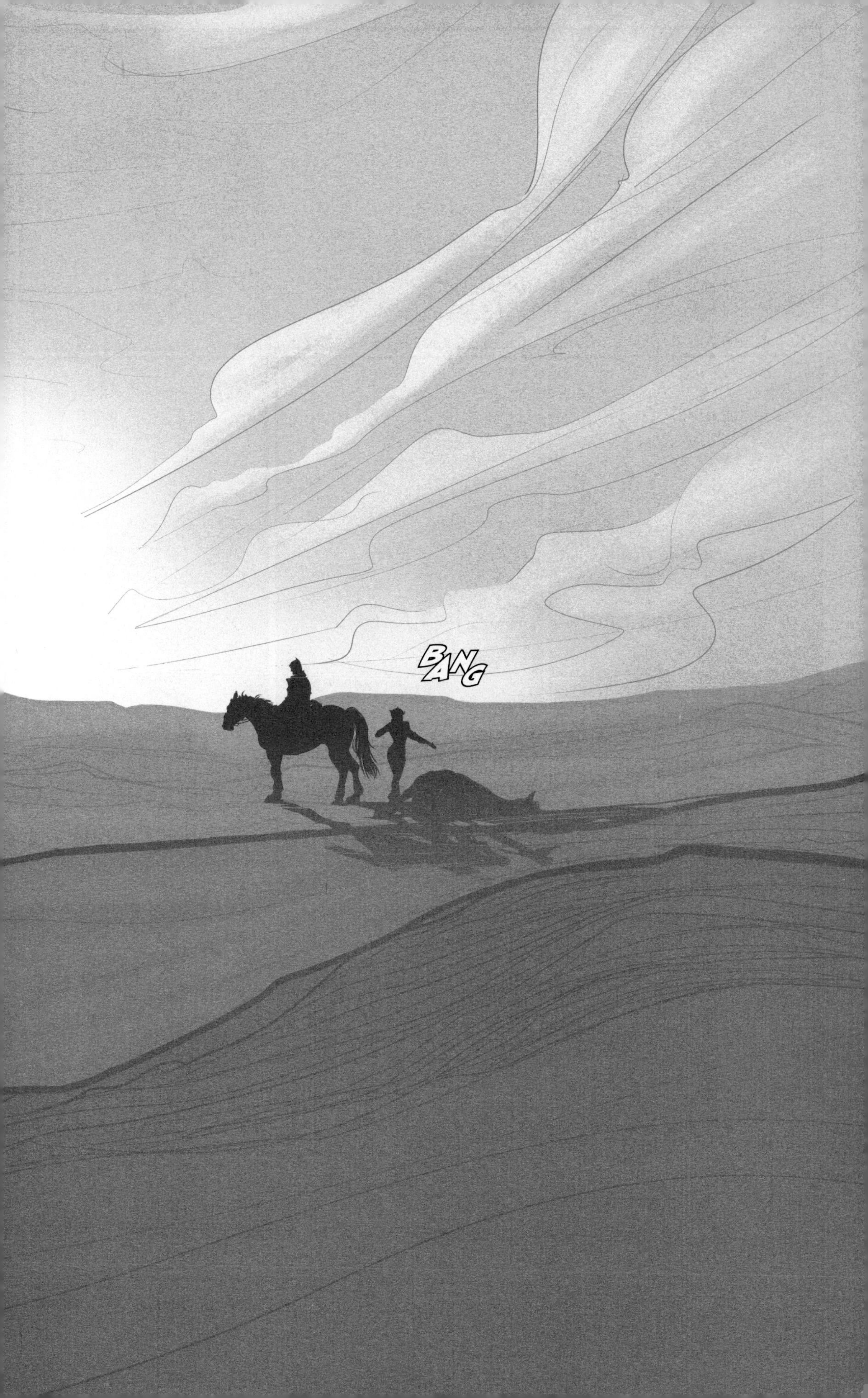
BANG

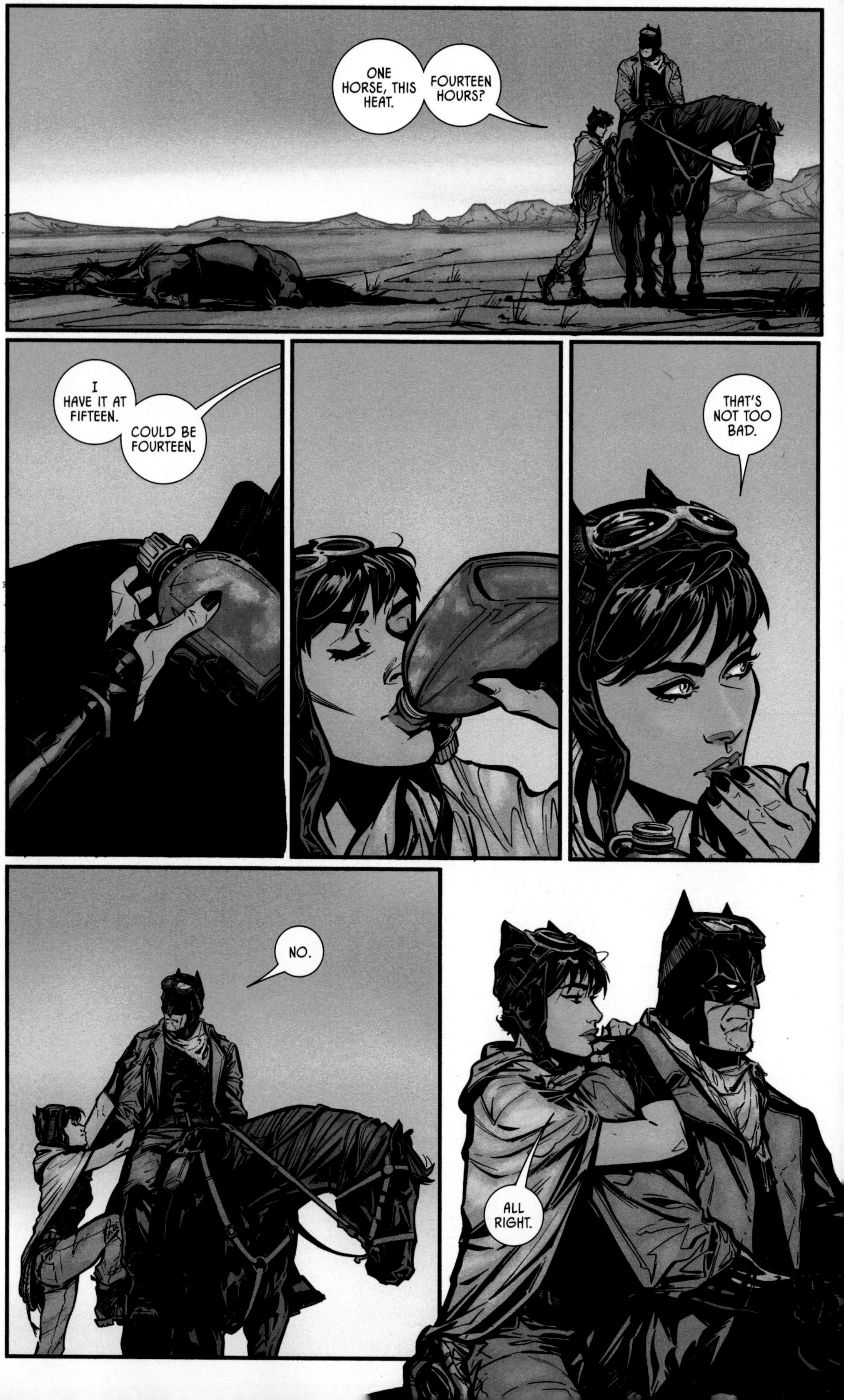
ONE HORSE, THIS HEAT.
FOURTEEN HOURS?
I HAVE IT AT FIFTEEN.
COULD BE FOURTEEN.
THAT'S NOT TOO BAD.
NO.
ALL RIGHT.

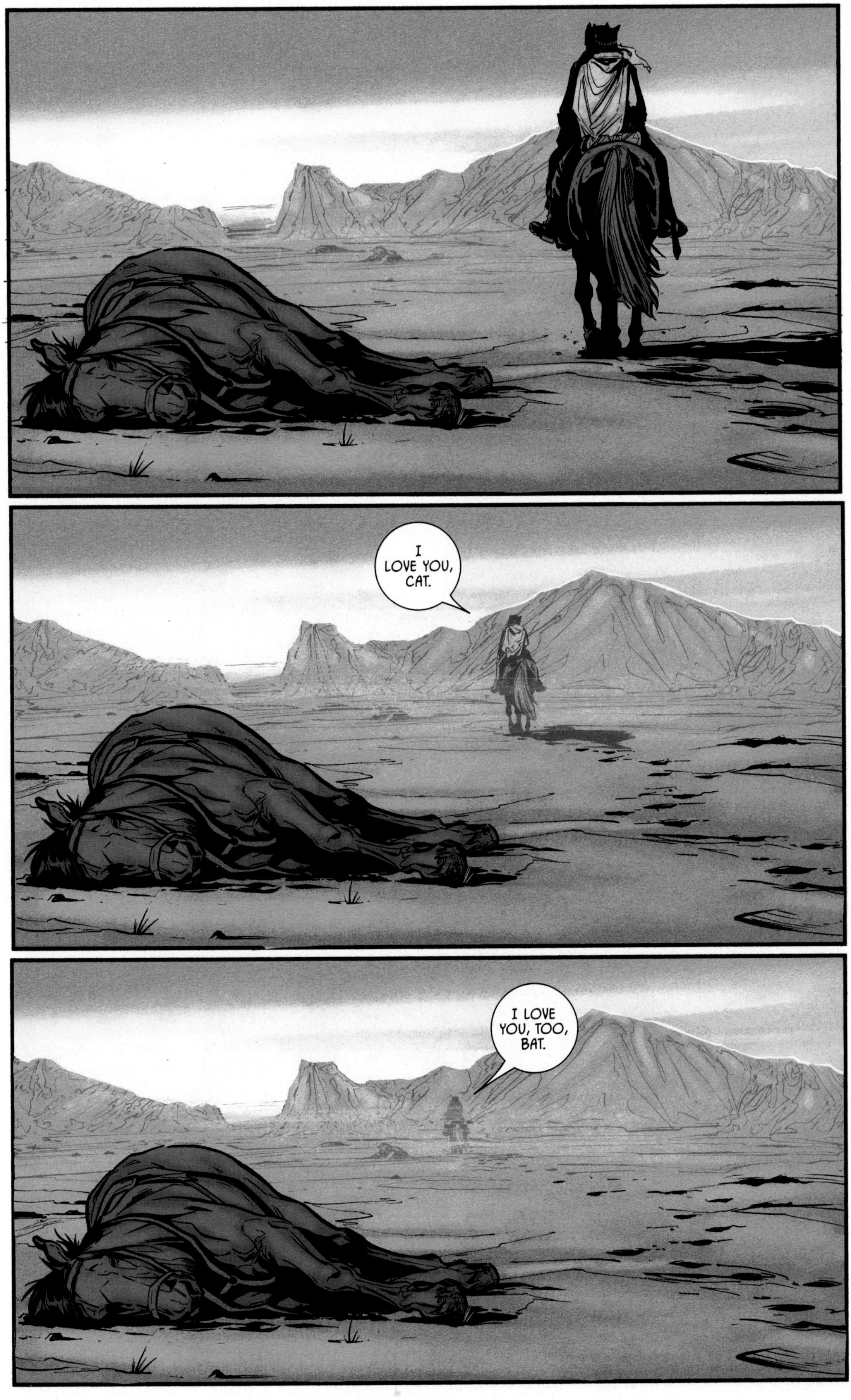
I LOVE YOU, CAT.
I LOVE YOU, TOO, BAT.

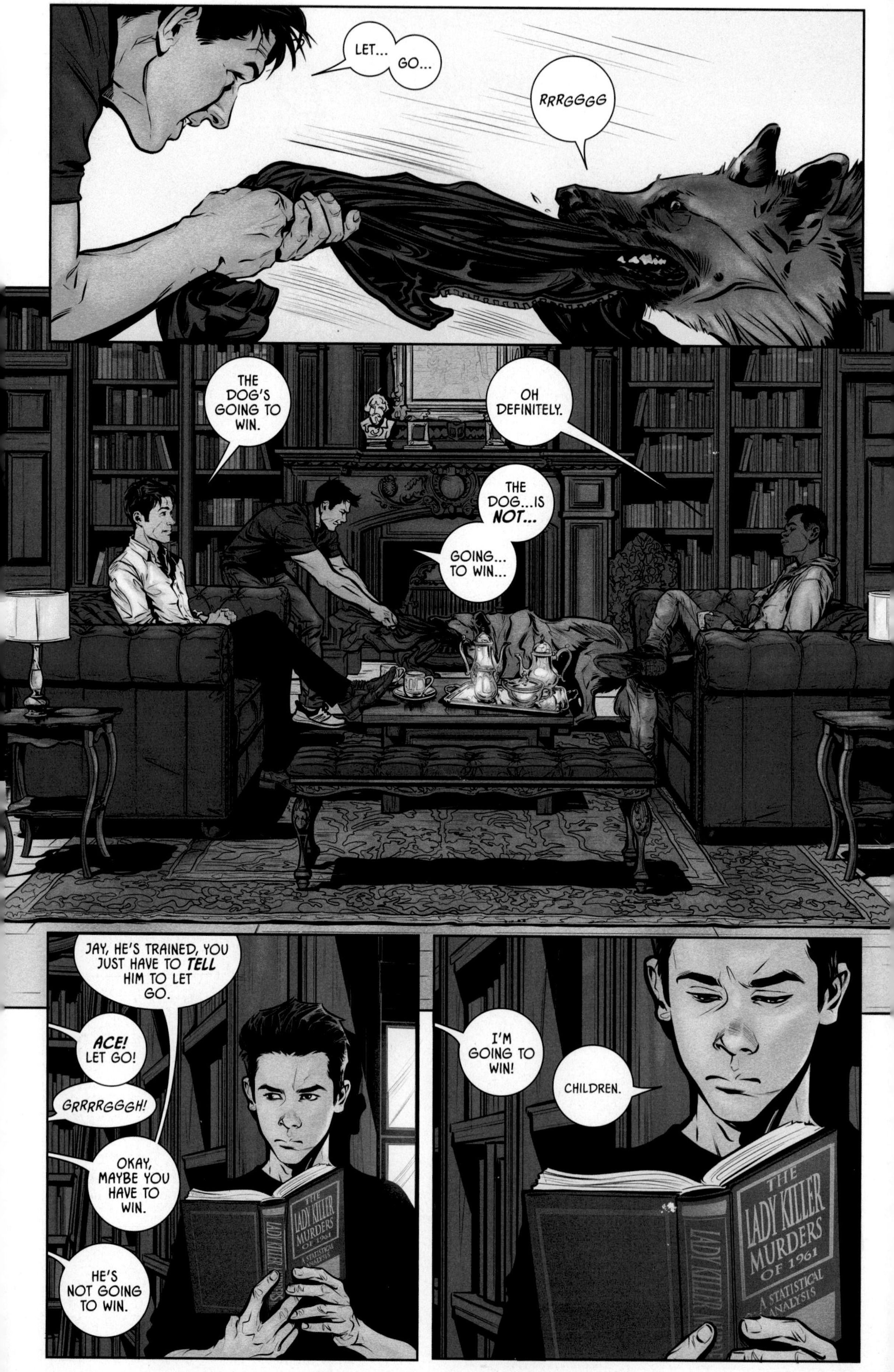
LET... GO...
RRRGGGG
THE DOG'S GOING TO WIN.
OH DEFINITELY.
THE DOG...IS NOT...
GOING... TO WIN...
JAY, HE'S TRAINED, YOU JUST HAVE TO TELL HIM TO LET GO.
ACE! LET GO!
GRRRRGGGH!
OKAY, MAYBE YOU HAVE TO WIN.
HE'S NOT GOING TO WIN.
THE LADY KILLER MURDERS OF 1961 A STATISTICAL ANALYSIS
LADY KILLER
I'M GOING TO WIN!
CHILDREN.
THE LADY KILLER MURDERS OF 1961 A STATISTICAL ANALYSIS
LADY KILLER

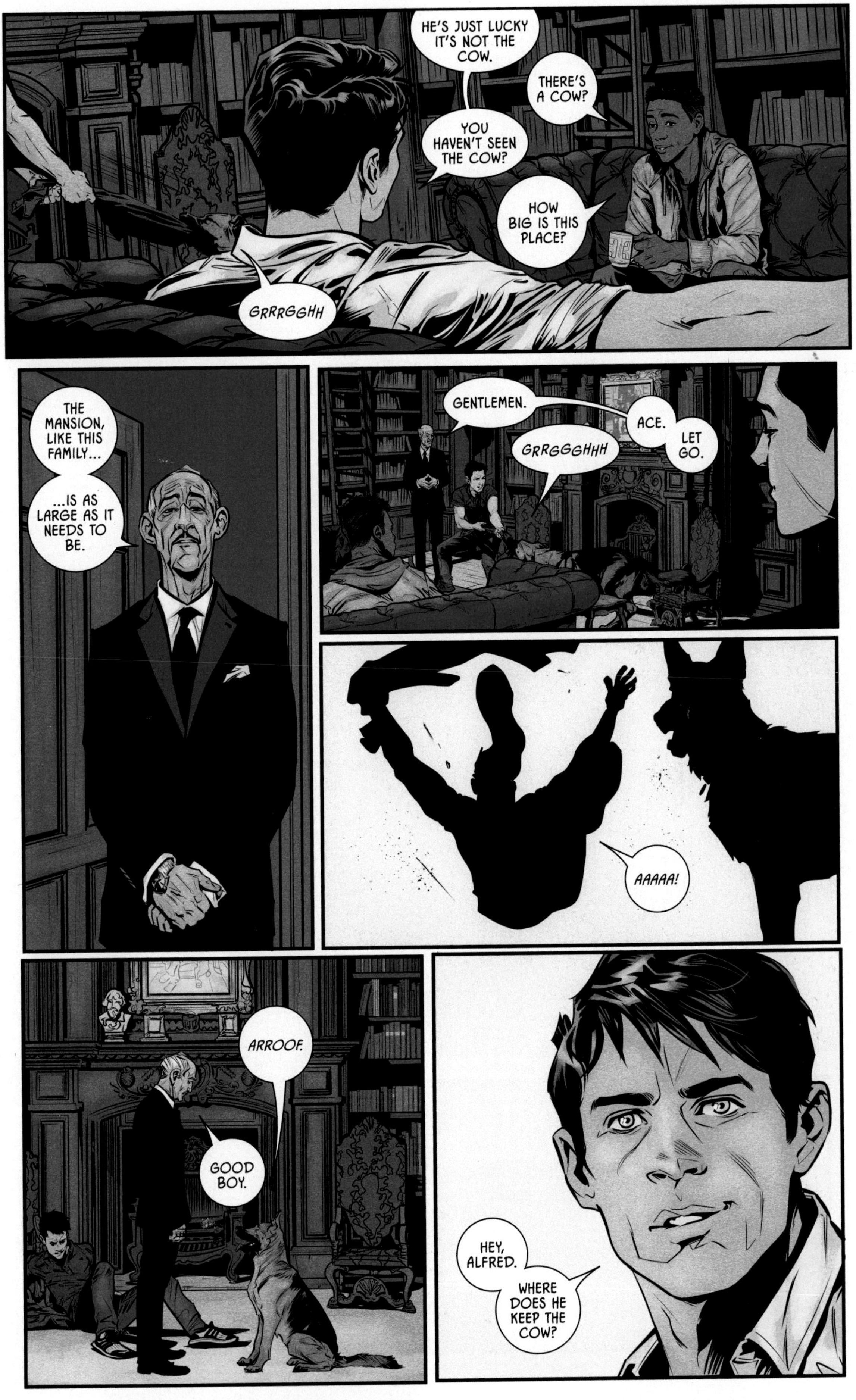
HE'S JUST LUCKY IT'S NOT THE COW.
THERE'S A COW?
YOU HAVEN'T SEEN THE COW?
HOW BIG IS THIS PLACE?
GRRRGGHH
THE MANSION, LIKE THIS FAMILY...
...IS AS LARGE AS IT NEEDS TO BE.
GENTLEMEN.
ACE.
LET GO.
GRRGGGHHH
AAAAA!
ARROOF.
GOOD BOY.
HEY, ALFRED.
WHERE DOES HE KEEP THE COW?

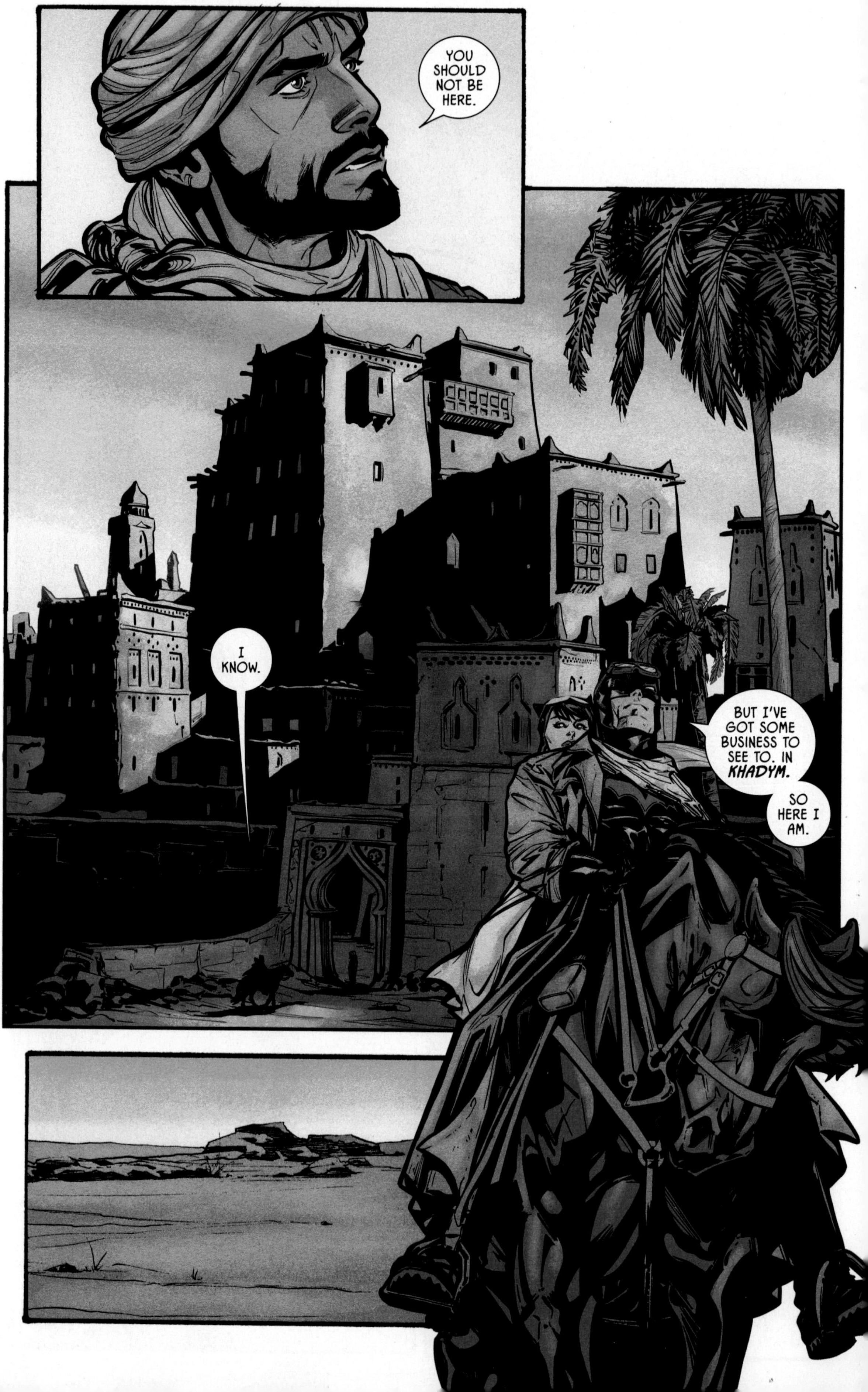
YOU SHOULD NOT BE HERE.
I KNOW.
BUT I'VE GOT SOME BUSINESS TO SEE TO. IN KHADYM.
SO HERE I AM.

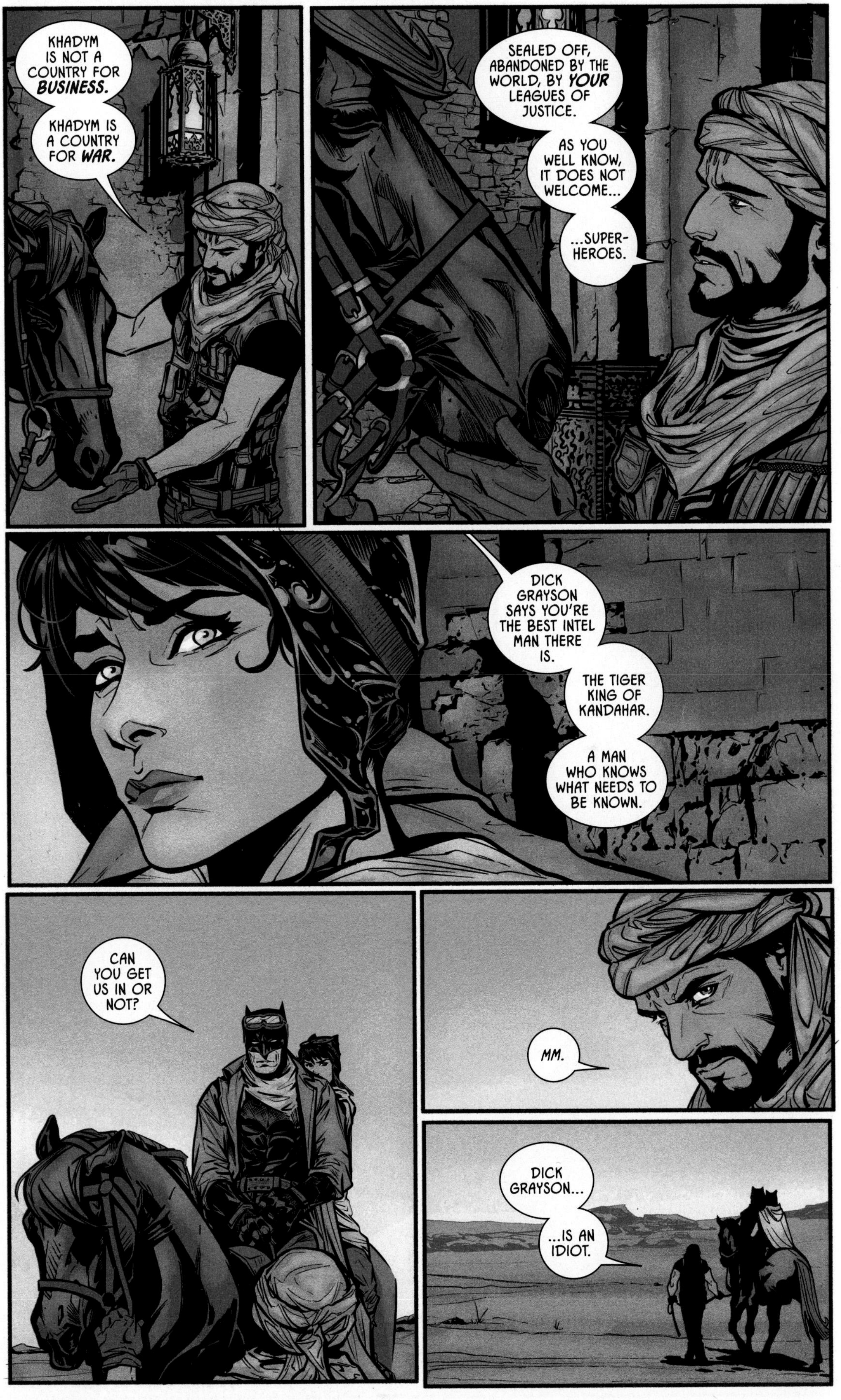
KHADYM IS NOT A COUNTRY FOR BUSINESS.
KHADYM IS A COUNTRY FOR WAR.
SEALED OFF, ABANDONED BY THE WORLD, BY YOUR LEAGUES OF JUSTICE.
AS YOU WELL KNOW, IT DOES NOT WELCOME...
...SUPER-HEROES.
DICK GRAYSON SAYS YOU'RE THE BEST INTEL MAN THERE IS.
THE TIGER KING OF KANDAHAR.
A MAN WHO KNOWS WHAT NEEDS TO BE KNOWN.
CAN YOU GET US IN OR NOT?
MM.
DICK GRAYSON...
...IS AN IDIOT.

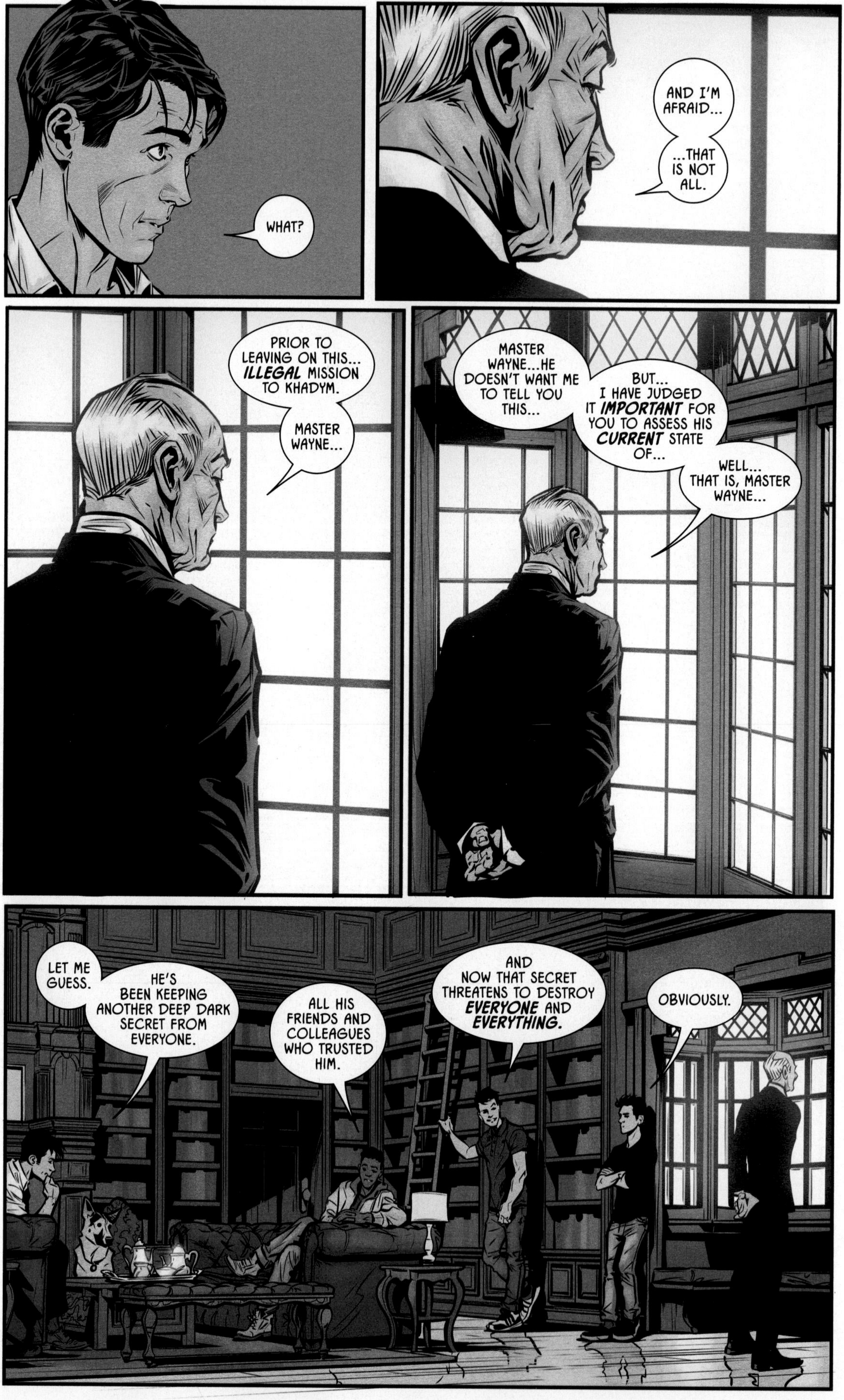
WHAT?
AND I'M AFRAID...
...THAT IS NOT ALL.
PRIOR TO LEAVING ON THIS... ILLEGAL MISSION TO KHADYM.
MASTER WAYNE...
MASTER WAYNE...HE DOESN'T WANT ME TO TELL YOU THIS...
BUT... I HAVE JUDGED IT IMPORTANT FOR YOU TO ASSESS HIS CURRENT STATE OF...
WELL... THAT IS, MASTER WAYNE...
LET ME GUESS.
HE'S BEEN KEEPING ANOTHER DEEP DARK SECRET FROM EVERYONE.
ALL HIS FRIENDS AND COLLEAGUES WHO TRUSTED HIM.
AND NOW THAT SECRET THREATENS TO DESTROY EVERYONE AND EVERYTHING.
OBVIOUSLY.

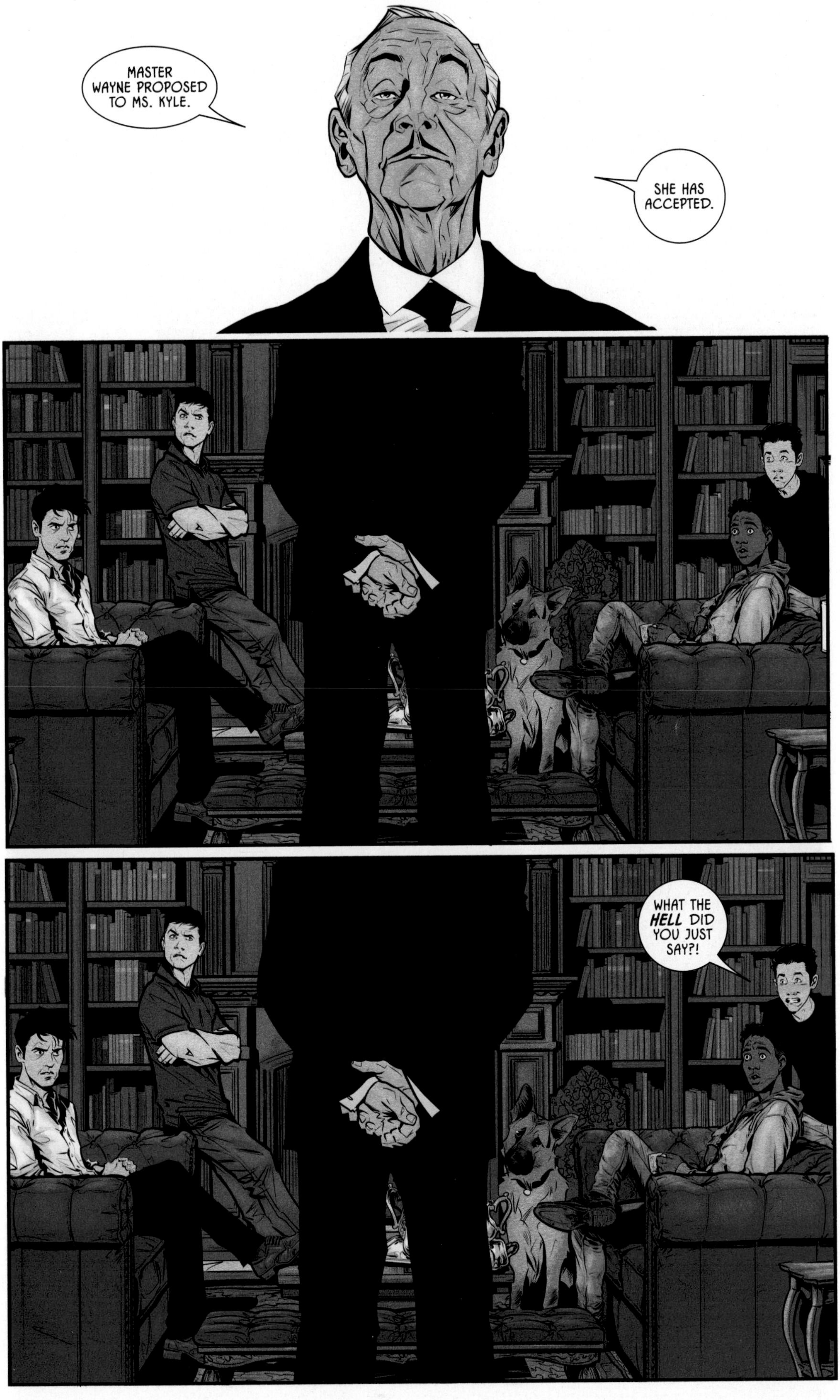
MASTER WAYNE PROPOSED TO MS. KYLE.
SHE HAS ACCEPTED.
WHAT THE HELL DID YOU JUST SAY?!

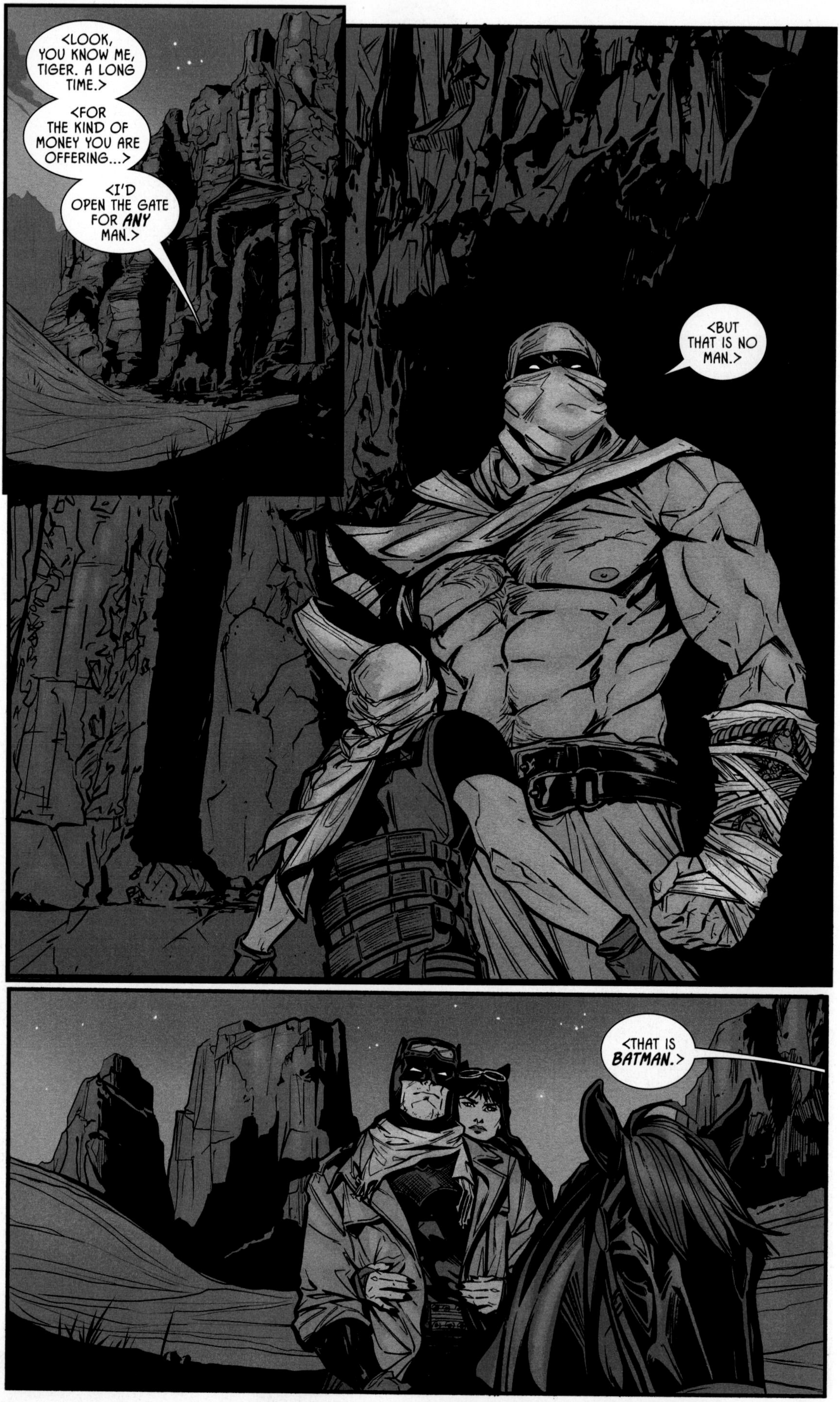
<LOOK, YOU KNOW ME, TIGER. A LONG TIME.>
<FOR THE KIND OF MONEY YOU ARE OFFERING...>
<I'D OPEN THE GATE FOR *ANY* MAN.>
<BUT THAT IS NO MAN.>
<THAT IS *BATMAN.*>

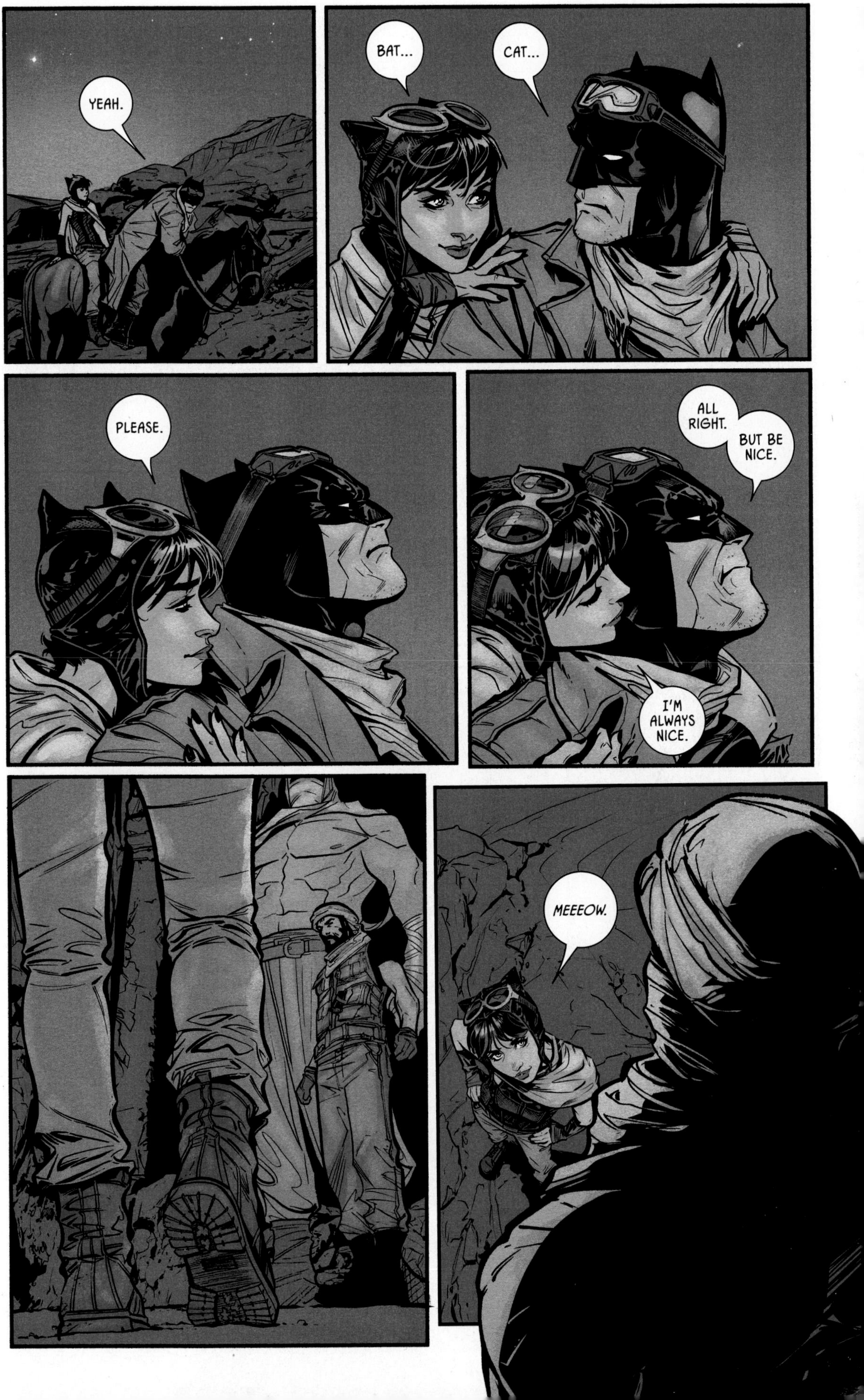
YEAH.
BAT...
CAT...
PLEASE.
ALL RIGHT.
BUT BE NICE.
I'M ALWAYS NICE.
MEEEOW.

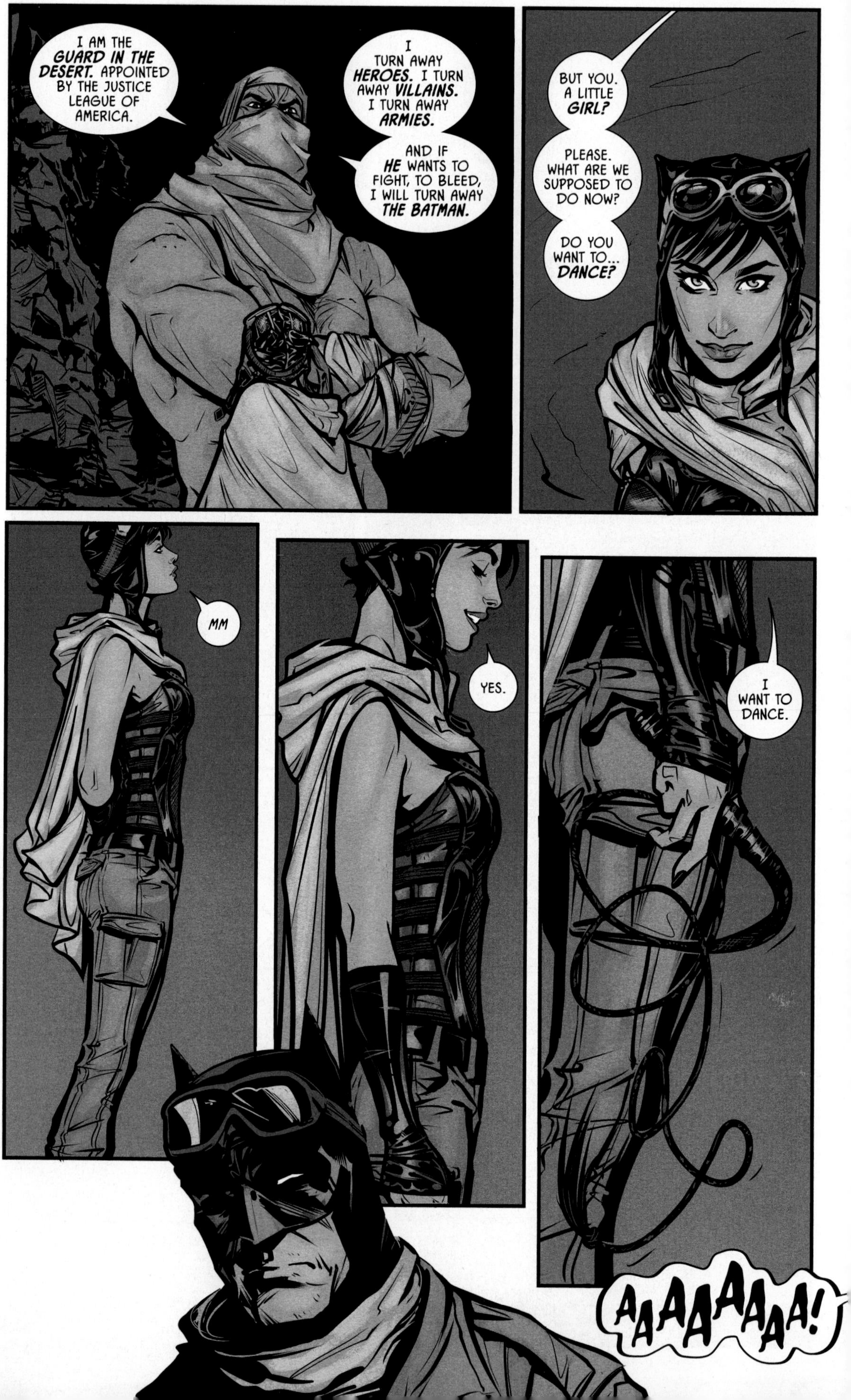
I AM THE GUARD IN THE DESERT. APPOINTED BY THE JUSTICE LEAGUE OF AMERICA.
I TURN AWAY HEROES. I TURN AWAY VILLAINS. I TURN AWAY ARMIES.
AND IF HE WANTS TO FIGHT, TO BLEED, I WILL TURN AWAY THE BATMAN.
BUT YOU. A LITTLE GIRL?
PLEASE. WHAT ARE WE SUPPOSED TO DO NOW?
DO YOU WANT TO... DANCE?
MM
YES.
I WANT TO DANCE.
AAAAAAAA!

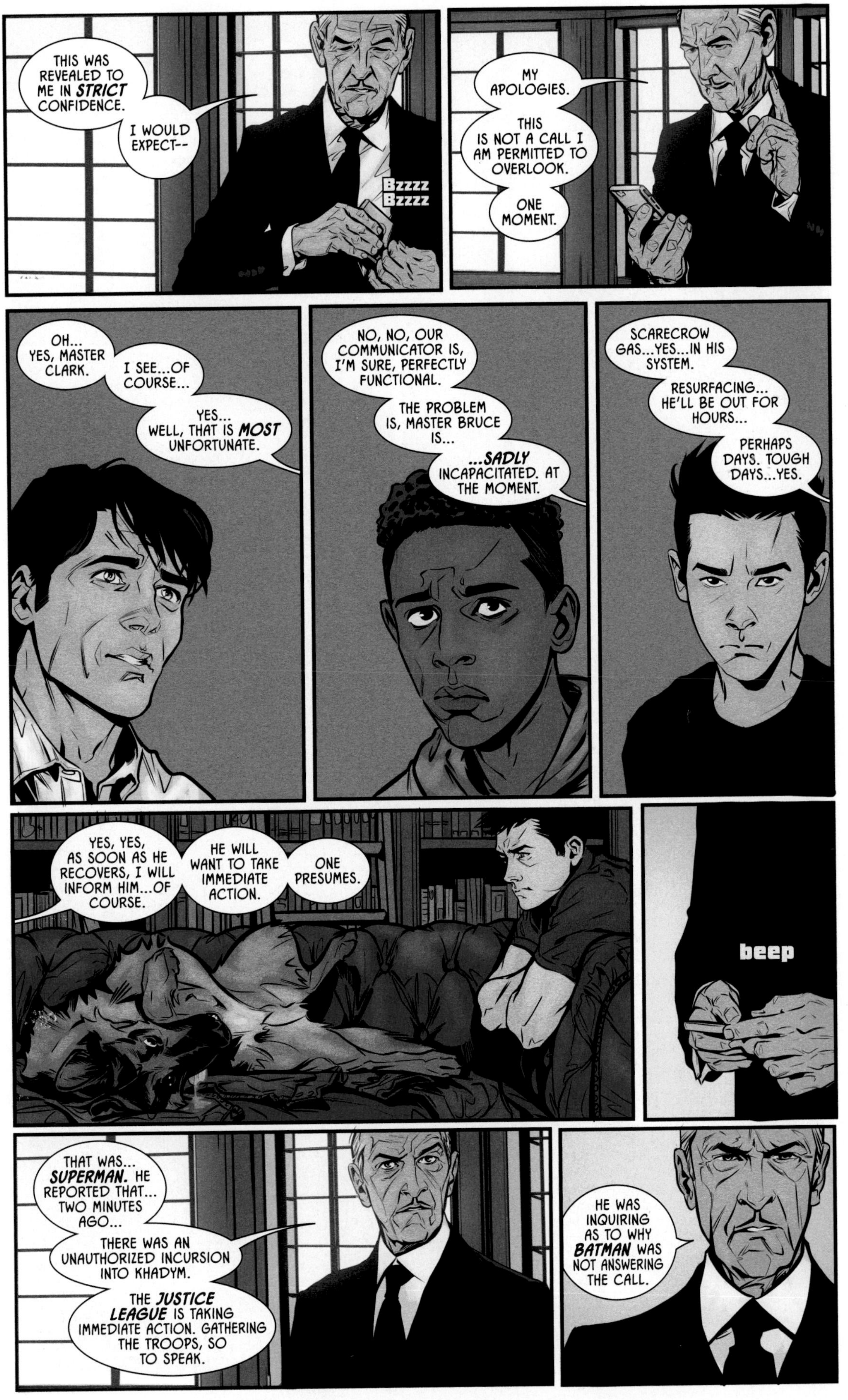

THIS WAS REVEALED TO ME IN STRICT CONFIDENCE.
I WOULD EXPECT--
Bzzzz Bzzzz
MY APOLOGIES.
THIS IS NOT A CALL I AM PERMITTED TO OVERLOOK.
ONE MOMENT.
OH... YES, MASTER CLARK.
I SEE...OF COURSE...
YES... WELL, THAT IS MOST UNFORTUNATE.
NO, NO, OUR COMMUNICATOR IS, I'M SURE, PERFECTLY FUNCTIONAL.
THE PROBLEM IS, MASTER BRUCE IS...
...SADLY INCAPACITATED. AT THE MOMENT.
SCARECROW GAS...YES...IN HIS SYSTEM.
RESURFACING... HE'LL BE OUT FOR HOURS...
PERHAPS DAYS. TOUGH DAYS...YES.
YES, YES, AS SOON AS HE RECOVERS, I WILL INFORM HIM...OF COURSE.
HE WILL WANT TO TAKE IMMEDIATE ACTION.
ONE PRESUMES.
beep
THAT WAS... SUPERMAN. HE REPORTED THAT... TWO MINUTES AGO...
THERE WAS AN UNAUTHORIZED INCURSION INTO KHADYM.
THE JUSTICE LEAGUE IS TAKING IMMEDIATE ACTION. GATHERING THE TROOPS, SO TO SPEAK.
HE WAS INQUIRING AS TO WHY BATMAN WAS NOT ANSWERING THE CALL.

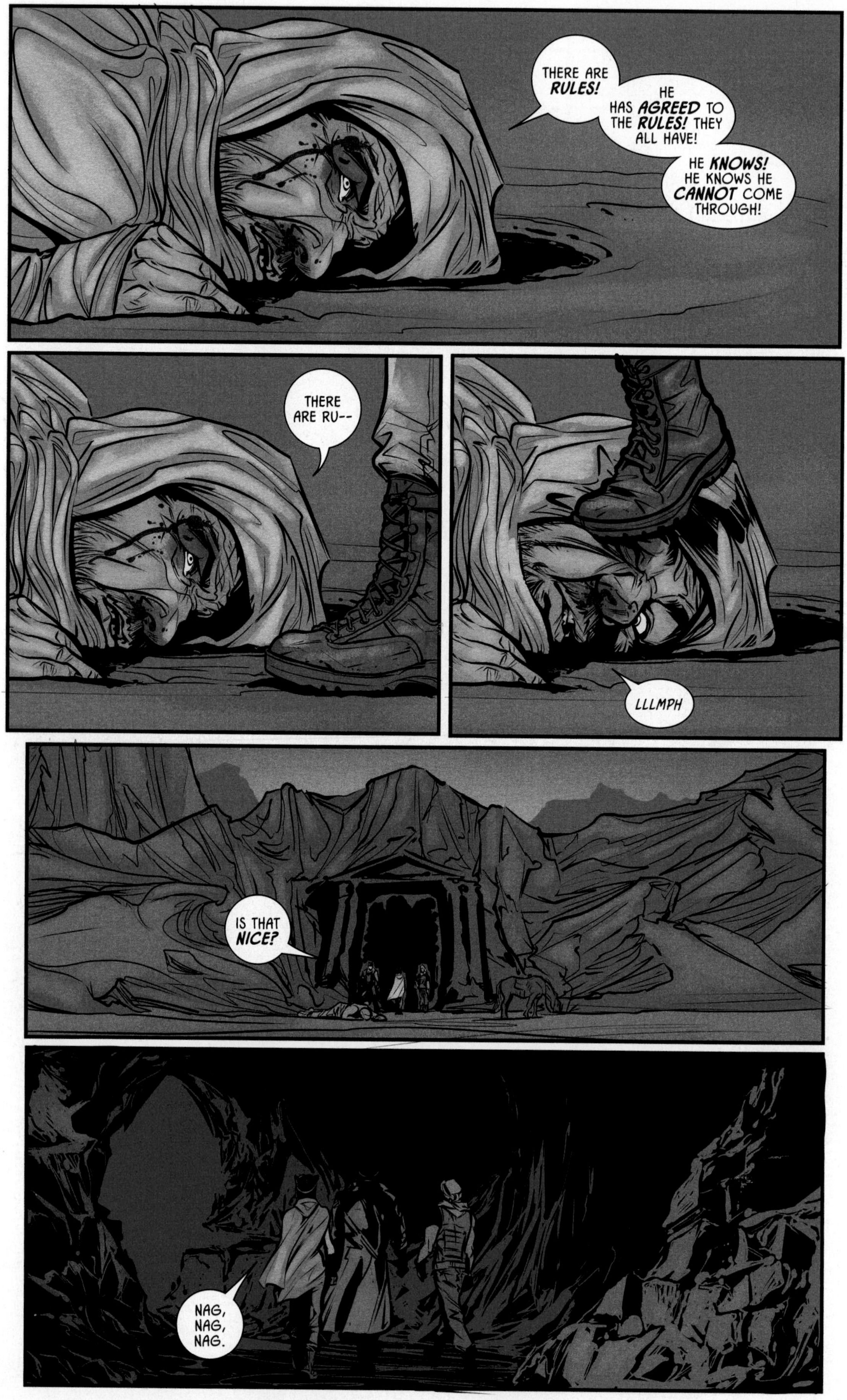
THERE ARE RULES!
HE HAS AGREED TO THE RULES! THEY ALL HAVE!
HE KNOWS! HE KNOWS HE CANNOT COME THROUGH!
THERE ARE RU--
LLLMPH
IS THAT NICE?
NAG, NAG, NAG.

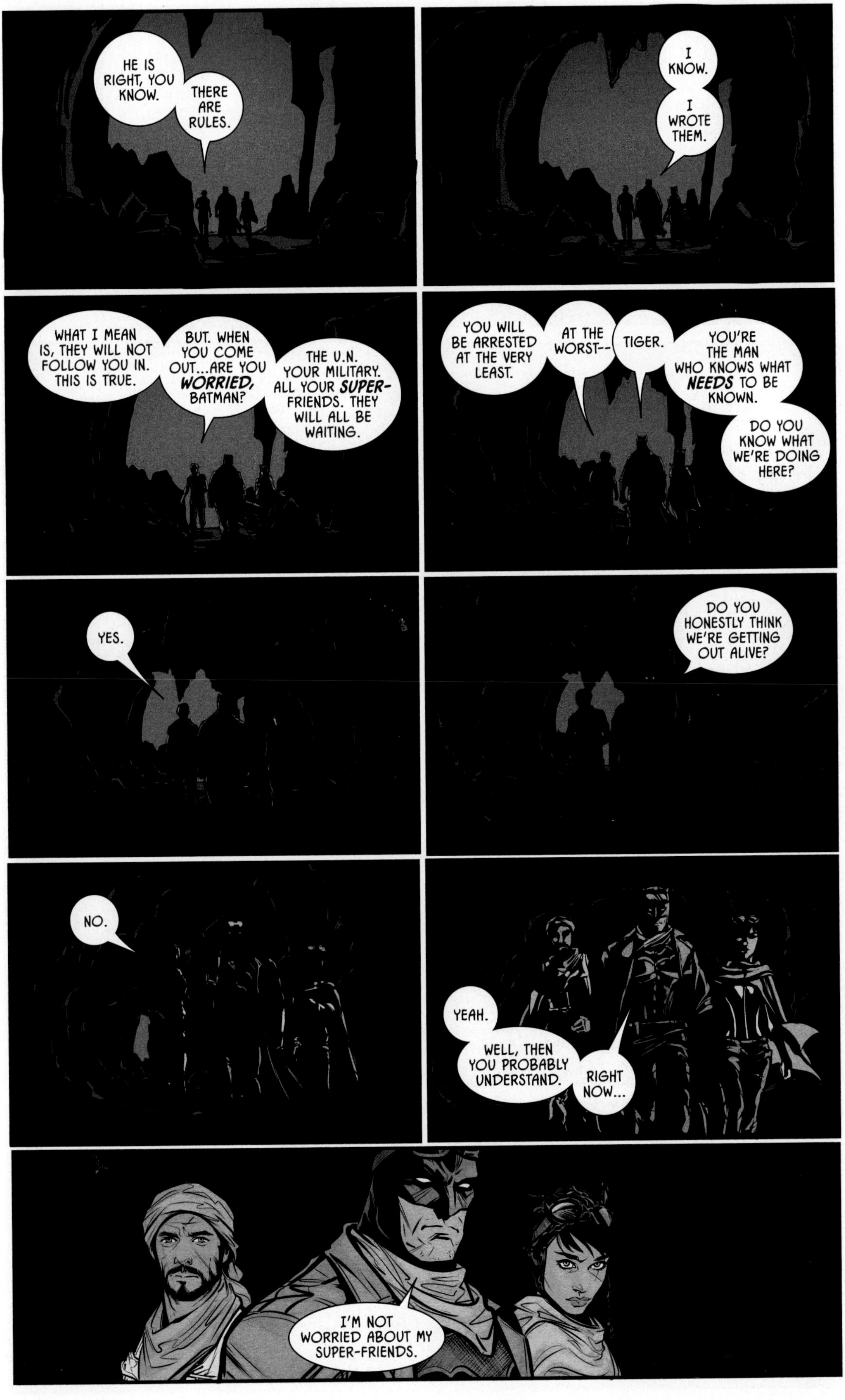
HE IS RIGHT, YOU KNOW.
THERE ARE RULES.
I KNOW.
I WROTE THEM.
WHAT I MEAN IS, THEY WILL NOT FOLLOW YOU IN. THIS IS TRUE.
BUT. WHEN YOU COME OUT...ARE YOU *WORRIED,* BATMAN?
THE U.N. YOUR MILITARY. ALL YOUR *SUPER-*FRIENDS. THEY WILL ALL BE WAITING.
YOU WILL BE ARRESTED AT THE VERY LEAST.
AT THE WORST--
TIGER.
YOU'RE THE MAN WHO KNOWS WHAT *NEEDS* TO BE KNOWN.
DO YOU KNOW WHAT WE'RE DOING HERE?
YES.
DO YOU HONESTLY THINK WE'RE GETTING OUT ALIVE?
NO.
YEAH.
WELL, THEN YOU PROBABLY UNDERSTAND.
RIGHT NOW...
I'M NOT WORRIED ABOUT MY SUPER-FRIENDS.

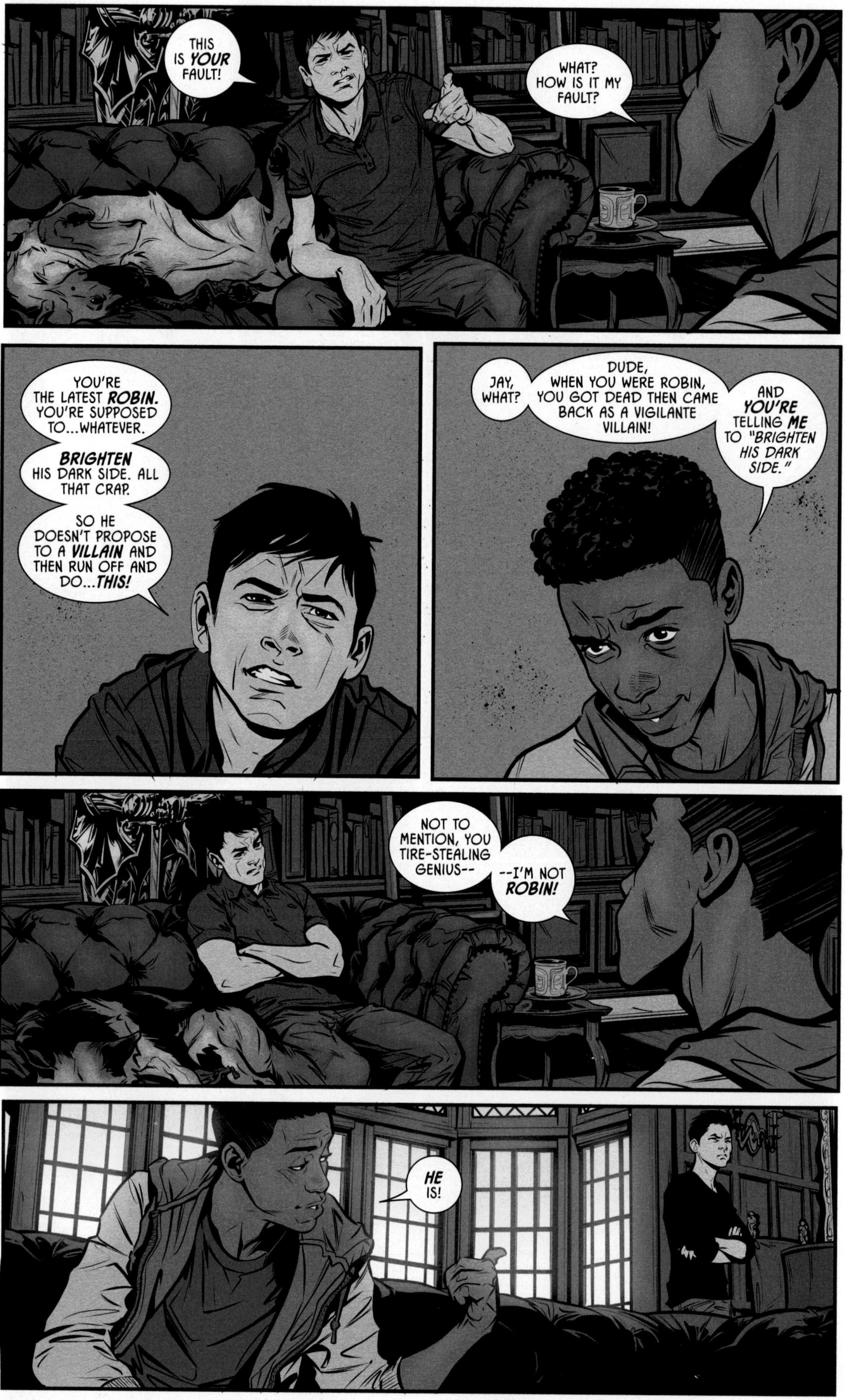
THIS IS *YOUR* FAULT!
WHAT? HOW IS IT MY FAULT?
YOU'RE THE LATEST *ROBIN*. YOU'RE SUPPOSED TO...WHATEVER.
BRIGHTEN HIS DARK SIDE. ALL THAT CRAP.
SO HE DOESN'T PROPOSE TO A *VILLAIN* AND THEN RUN OFF AND DO...*THIS!*
JAY, WHAT?
DUDE, WHEN YOU WERE ROBIN, YOU GOT DEAD THEN CAME BACK AS A VIGILANTE VILLAIN!
AND *YOU'RE* TELLING *ME* TO "BRIGHTEN HIS DARK SIDE."
NOT TO MENTION, YOU TIRE-STEALING GENIUS--
--I'M NOT *ROBIN!*
HE IS!

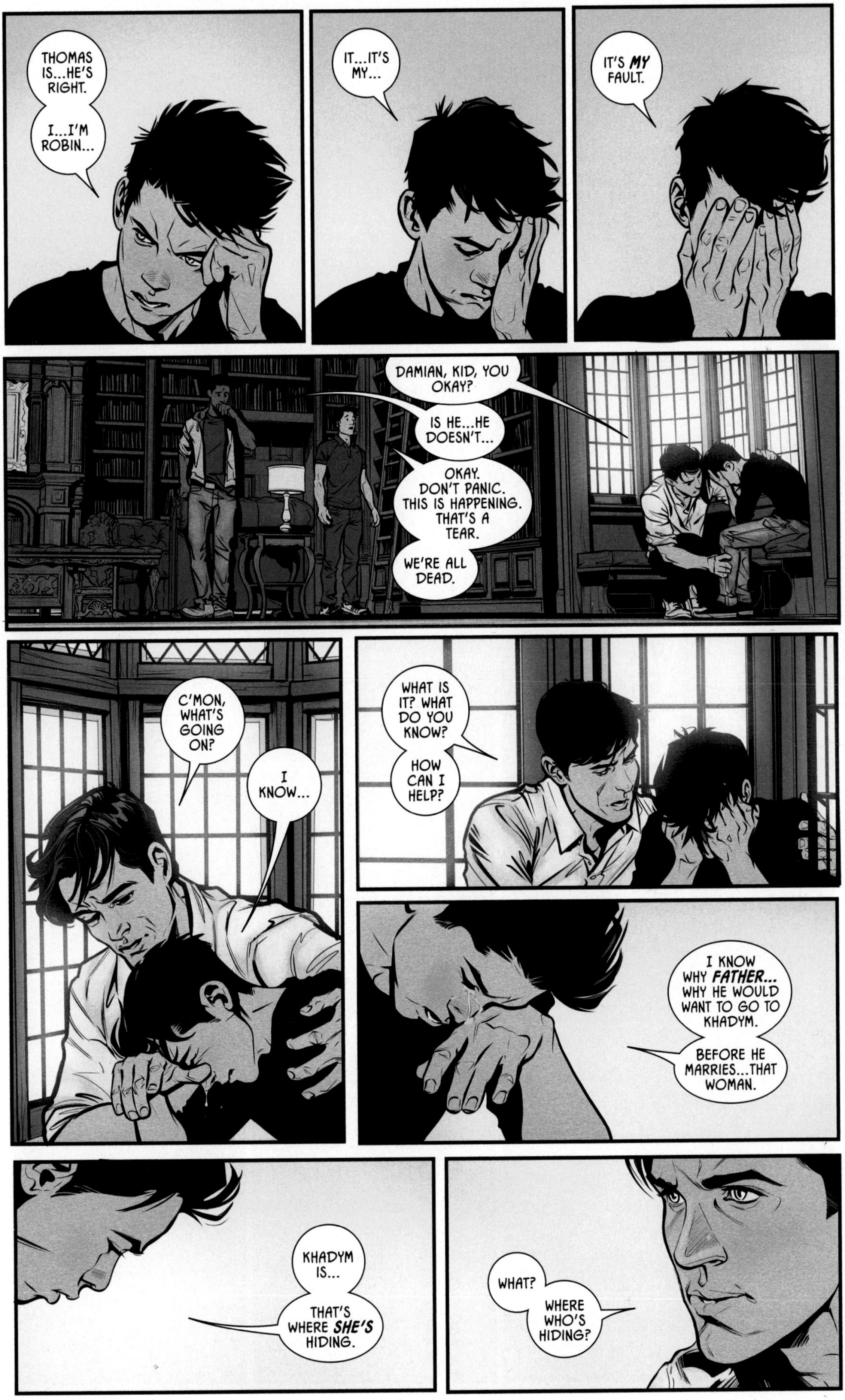
THOMAS IS...HE'S RIGHT.
I...I'M ROBIN...
IT...IT'S MY...
IT'S *MY* FAULT.
DAMIAN, KID, YOU OKAY?
IS HE...HE DOESN'T...
OKAY. DON'T PANIC. THIS IS HAPPENING. THAT'S A TEAR.
WE'RE ALL DEAD.
C'MON, WHAT'S GOING ON?
I KNOW...
WHAT IS IT? WHAT DO YOU KNOW?
HOW CAN I HELP?
I KNOW WHY *FATHER...* WHY HE WOULD WANT TO GO TO KHADYM.
BEFORE HE MARRIES...THAT WOMAN.
KHADYM IS...
THAT'S WHERE *SHE'S* HIDING.
WHAT?
WHERE WHO'S HIDING?

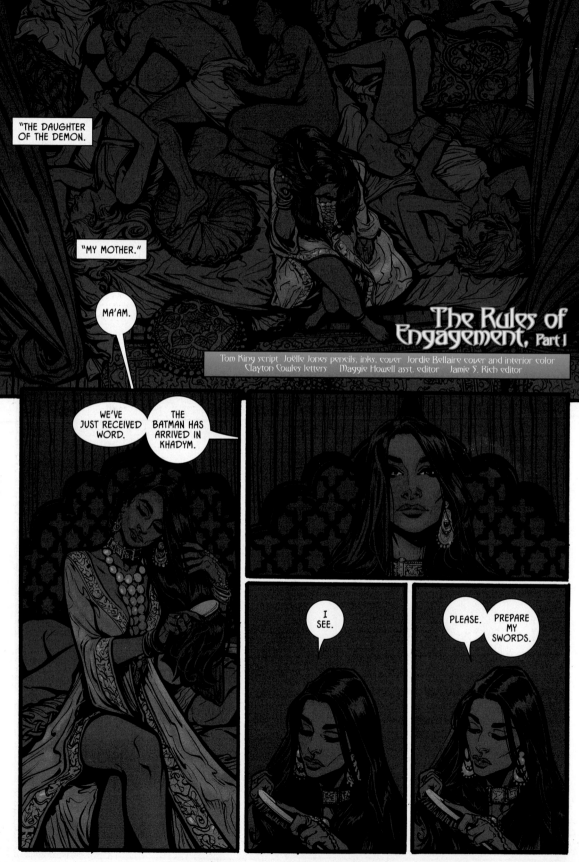

"TALIA AL GHUL.

"THE DAUGHTER OF THE DEMON.

"MY MOTHER."

MA'AM.

The Rules of Engagement, Part 1

Tom King script Joëlle Jones pencils, inks, cover Jordie Bellaire cover and interior color
Clayton Cowles letters Maggie Howell asst. editor Jamie S. Rich editor

WE'VE JUST RECEIVED WORD.

THE BATMAN HAS ARRIVED IN KHADYM.

I SEE.

PLEASE.

PREPARE MY SWORDS.

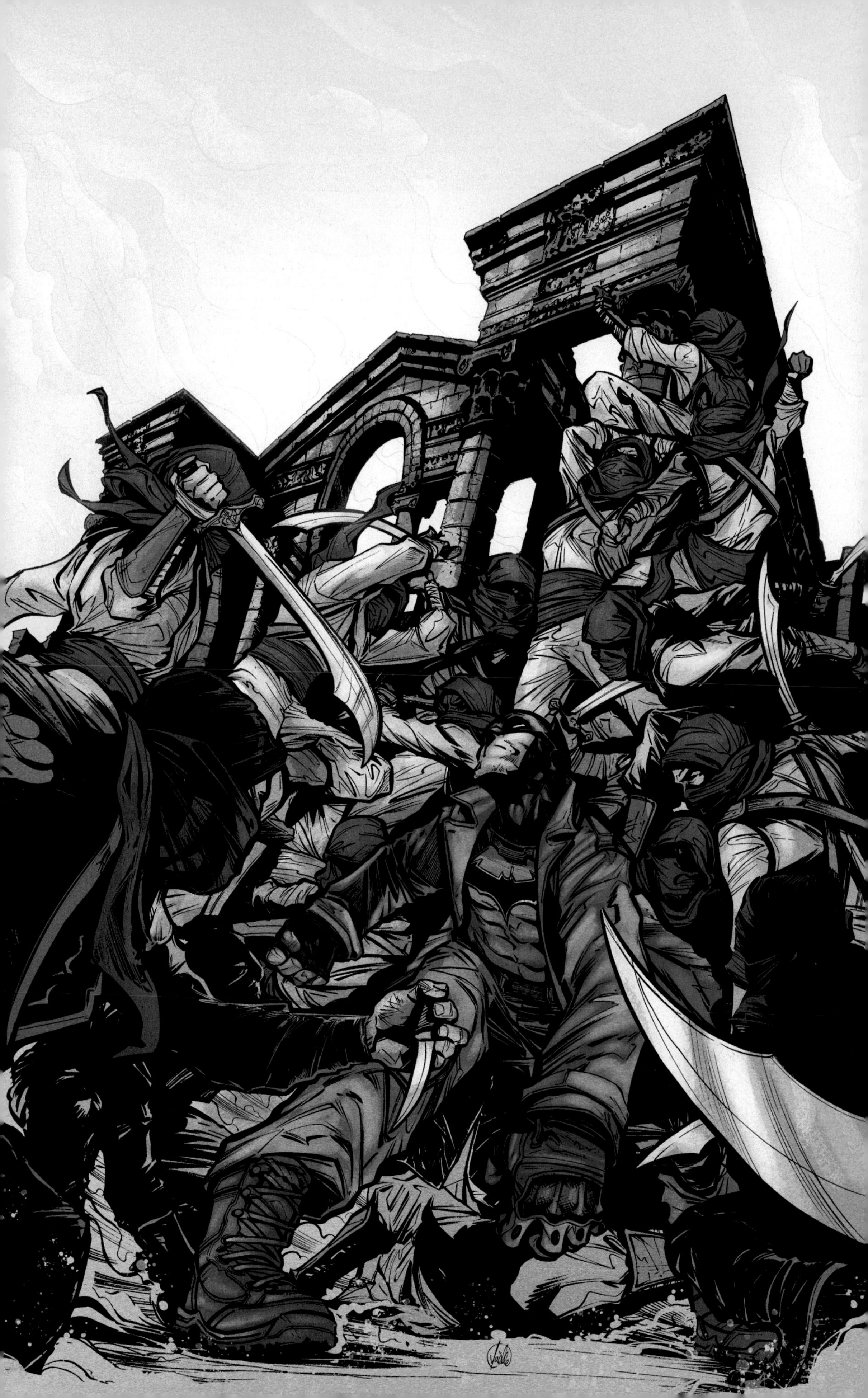

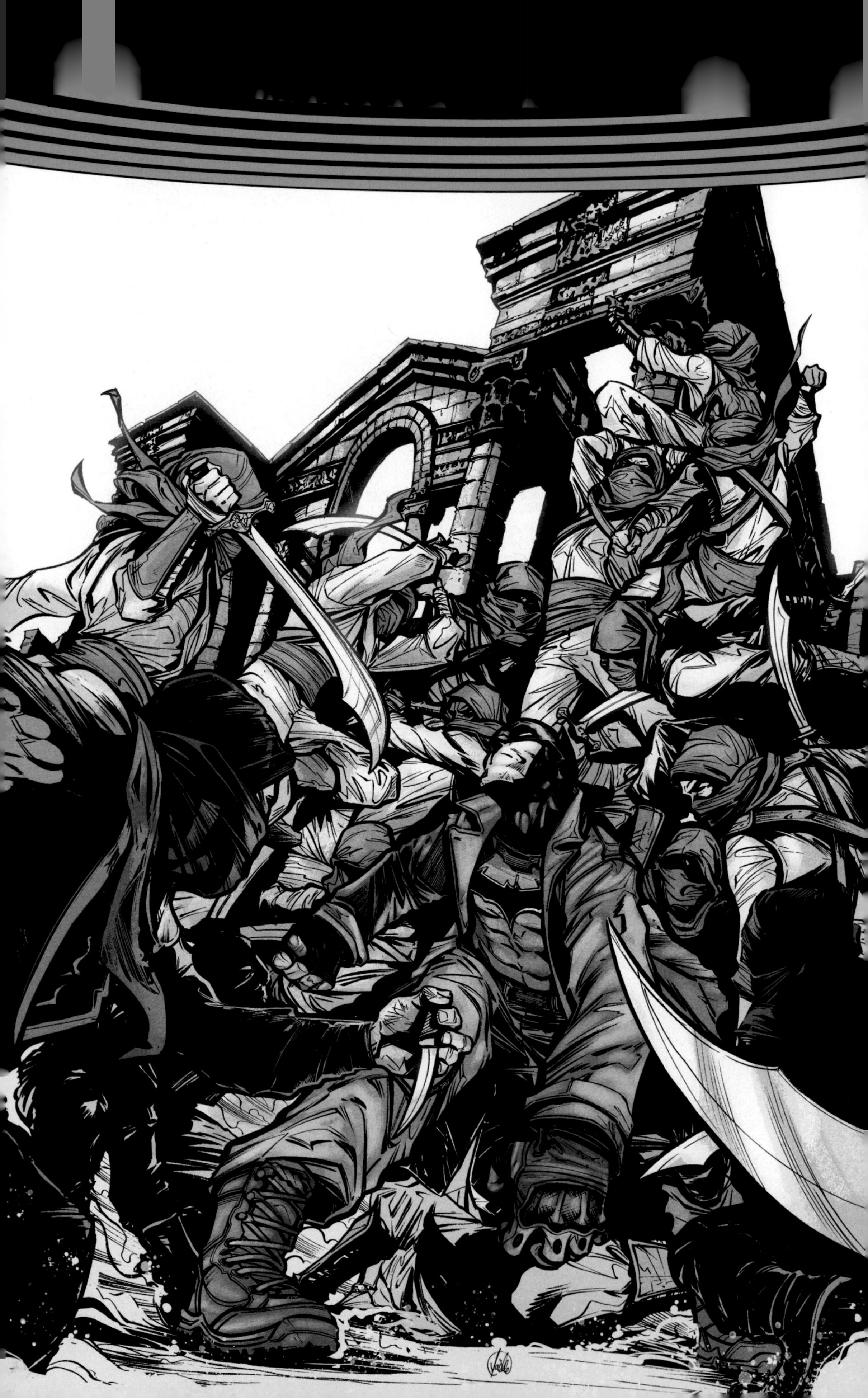

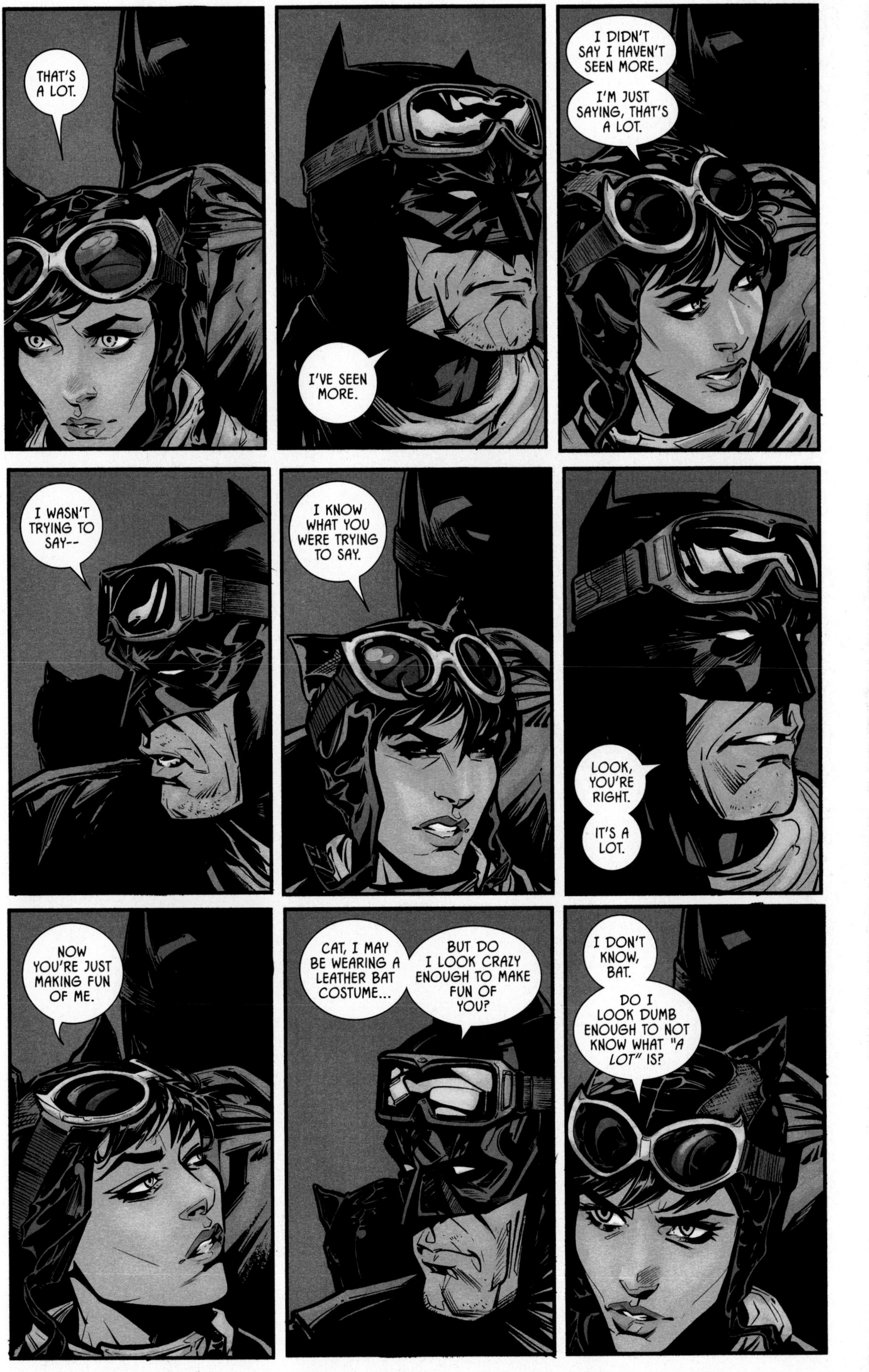
THAT'S A LOT.
I'VE SEEN MORE.
I DIDN'T SAY I HAVEN'T SEEN MORE.
I'M JUST SAYING, THAT'S A LOT.
I WASN'T TRYING TO SAY--
I KNOW WHAT YOU WERE TRYING TO SAY.
LOOK, YOU'RE RIGHT.
IT'S A LOT.
NOW YOU'RE JUST MAKING FUN OF ME.
CAT, I MAY BE WEARING A LEATHER BAT COSTUME...
BUT DO I LOOK CRAZY ENOUGH TO MAKE FUN OF YOU?
I DON'T KNOW, BAT.
DO I LOOK DUMB ENOUGH TO NOT KNOW WHAT "A LOT" IS?

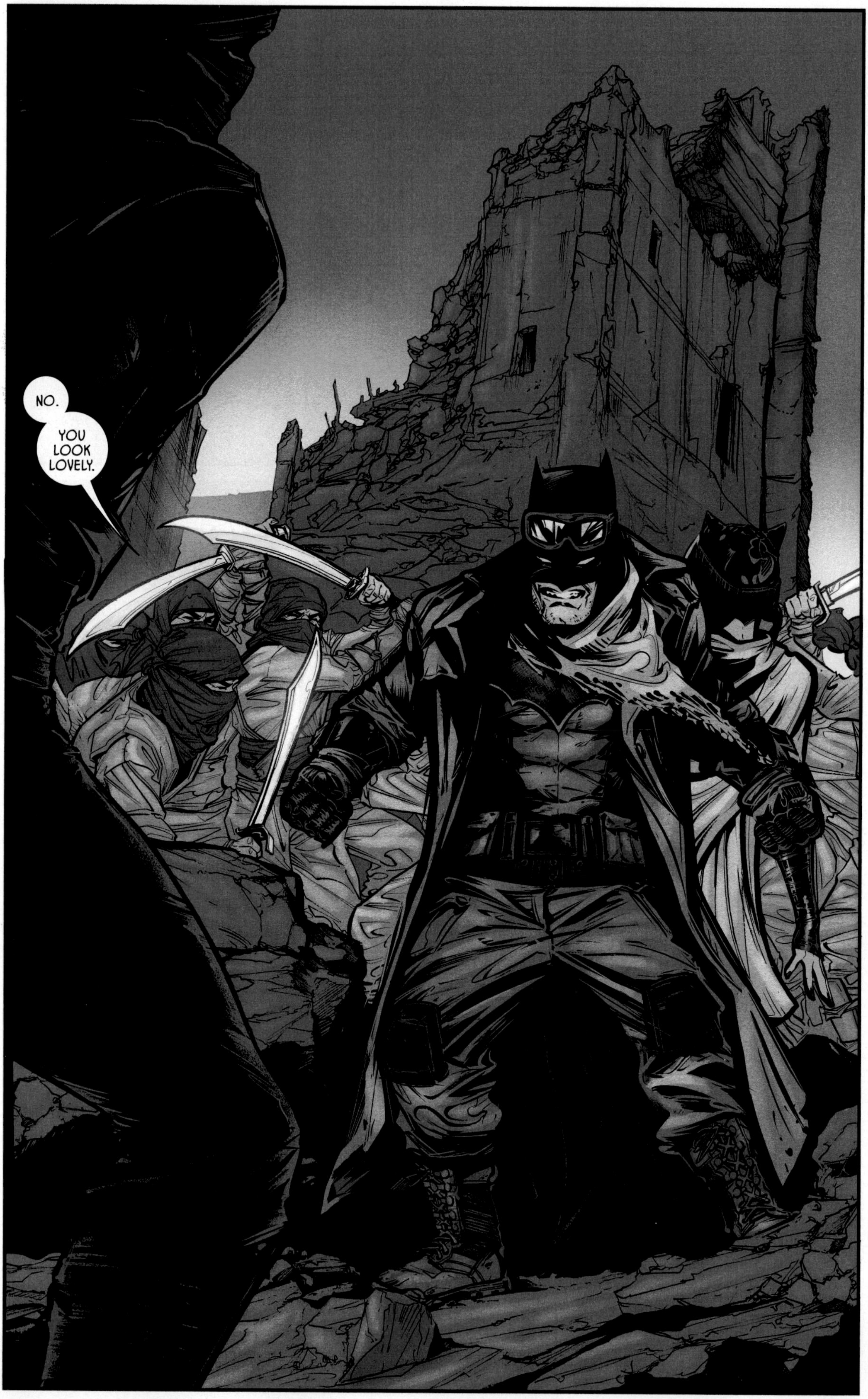
NO.
YOU LOOK LOVELY.

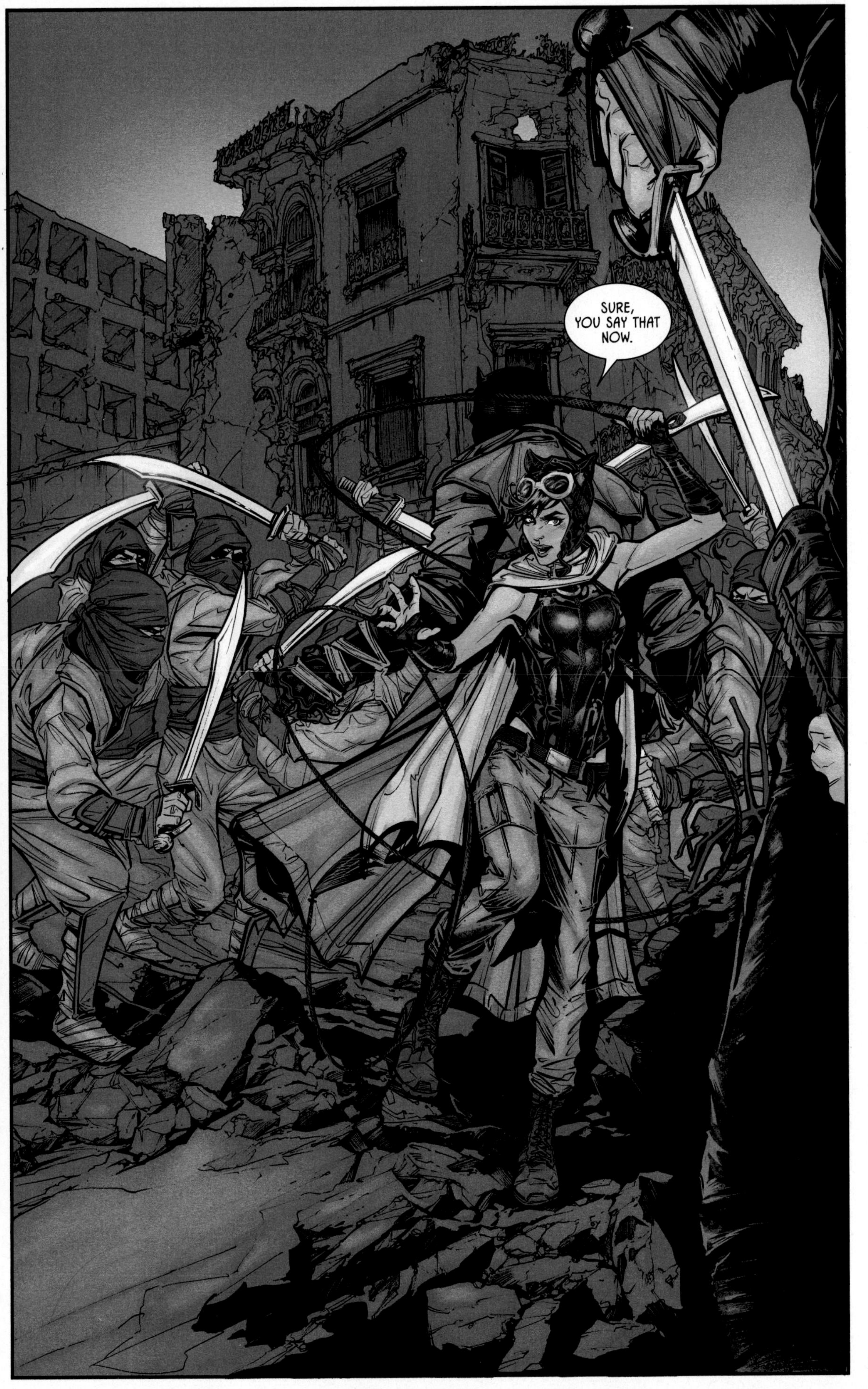
SURE, YOU SAY THAT NOW.

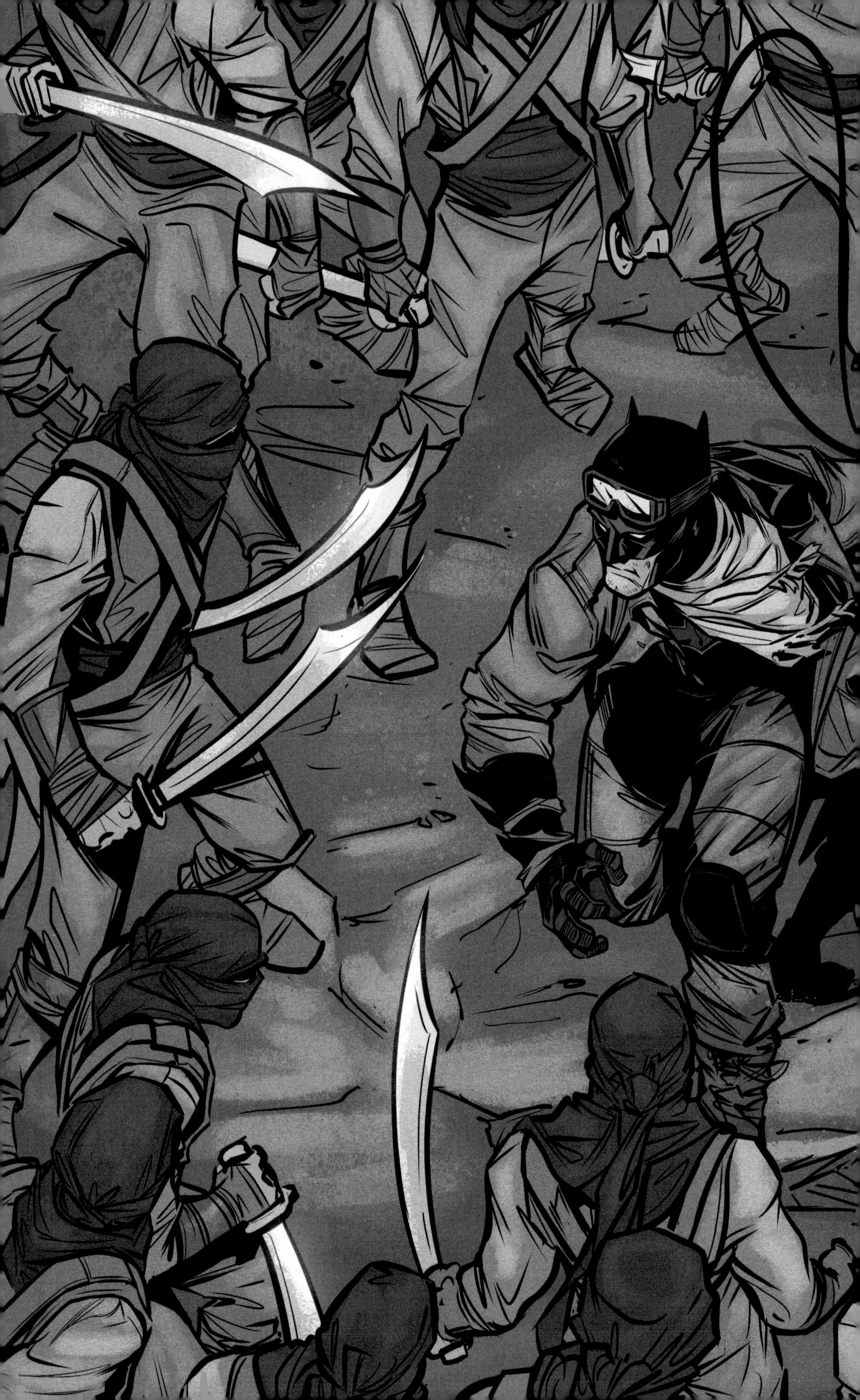

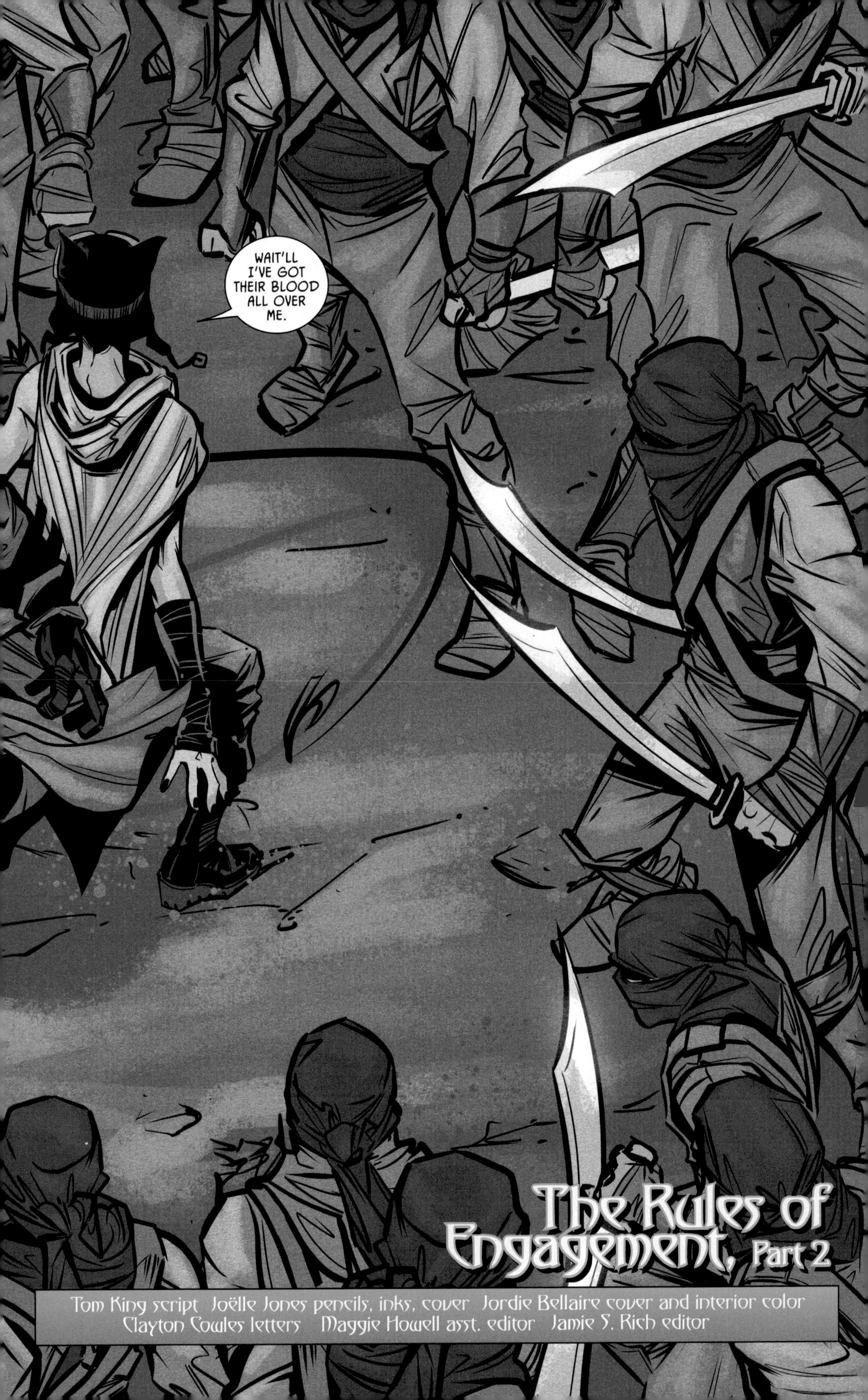
WAIT'LL I'VE GOT THEIR BLOOD ALL OVER ME.
The Rules of Engagement, Part 2
Tom King script Joëlle Jones pencils, inks, cover Jordie Bellaire cover and interior color
Clayton Cowles letters Maggie Howell asst. editor Jamie S. Rich editor

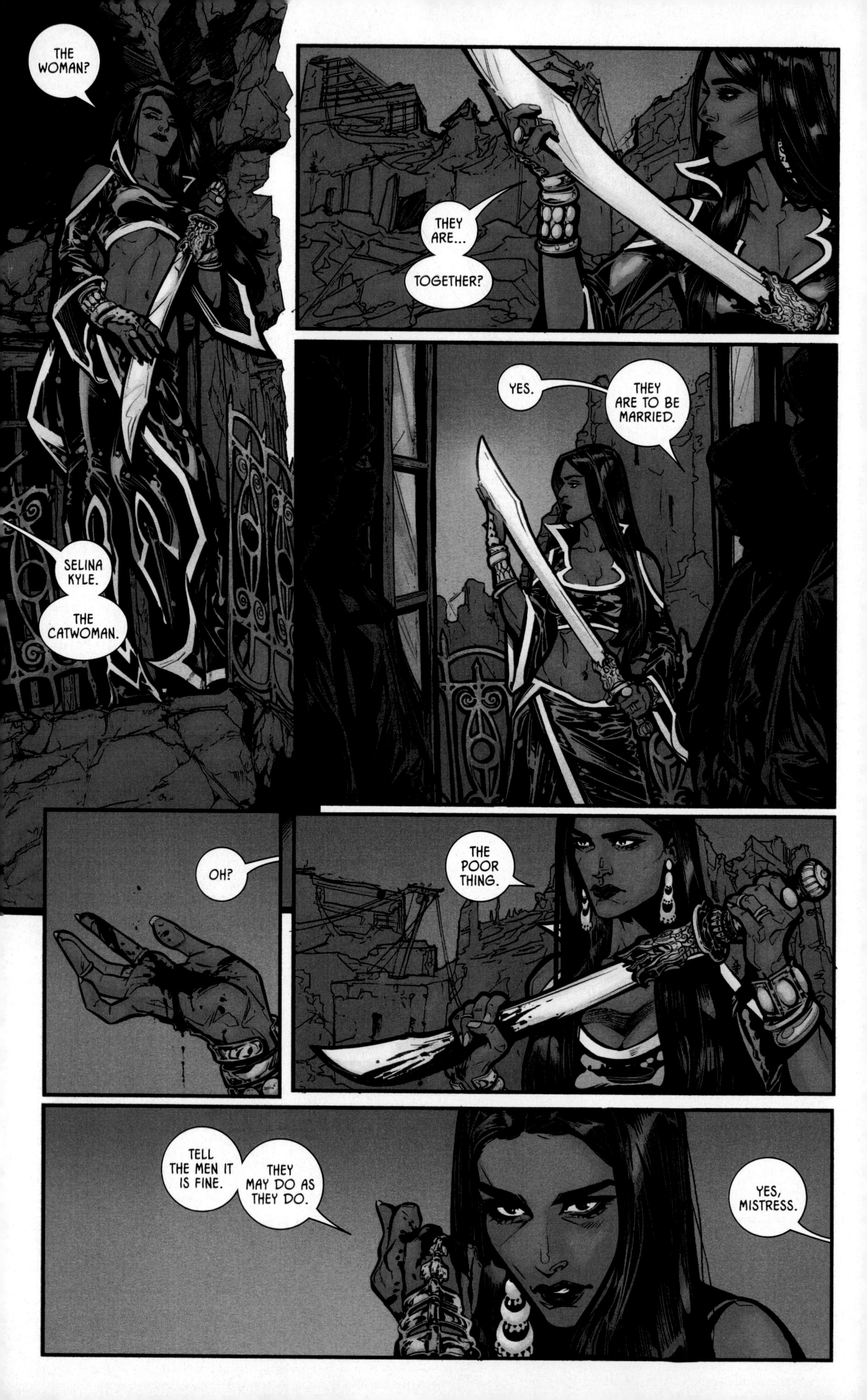
THE WOMAN?
THEY ARE...
TOGETHER?
SELINA KYLE.
THE CATWOMAN.
YES.
THEY ARE TO BE MARRIED.
OH?
THE POOR THING.
TELL THE MEN IT IS FINE.
THEY MAY DO AS THEY DO.
YES, MISTRESS.

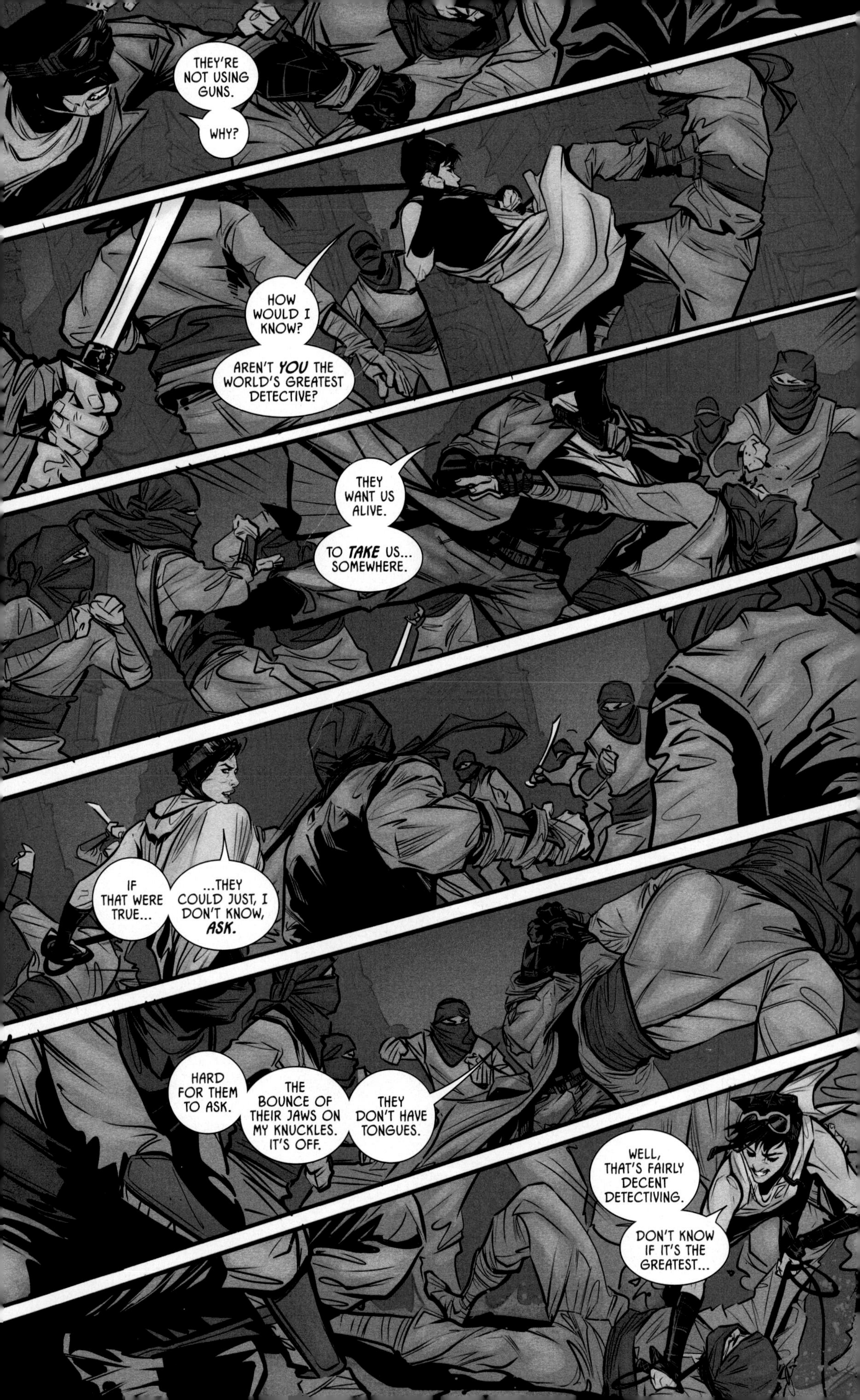
THEY'RE NOT USING GUNS.
WHY?
HOW WOULD I KNOW?
AREN'T YOU THE WORLD'S GREATEST DETECTIVE?
THEY WANT US ALIVE.
TO TAKE US... SOMEWHERE.
IF THAT WERE TRUE...
...THEY COULD JUST, I DON'T KNOW, ASK.
HARD FOR THEM TO ASK.
THE BOUNCE OF THEIR JAWS ON MY KNUCKLES. IT'S OFF.
THEY DON'T HAVE TONGUES.
WELL, THAT'S FAIRLY DECENT DETECTIVING.
DON'T KNOW IF IT'S THE GREATEST...

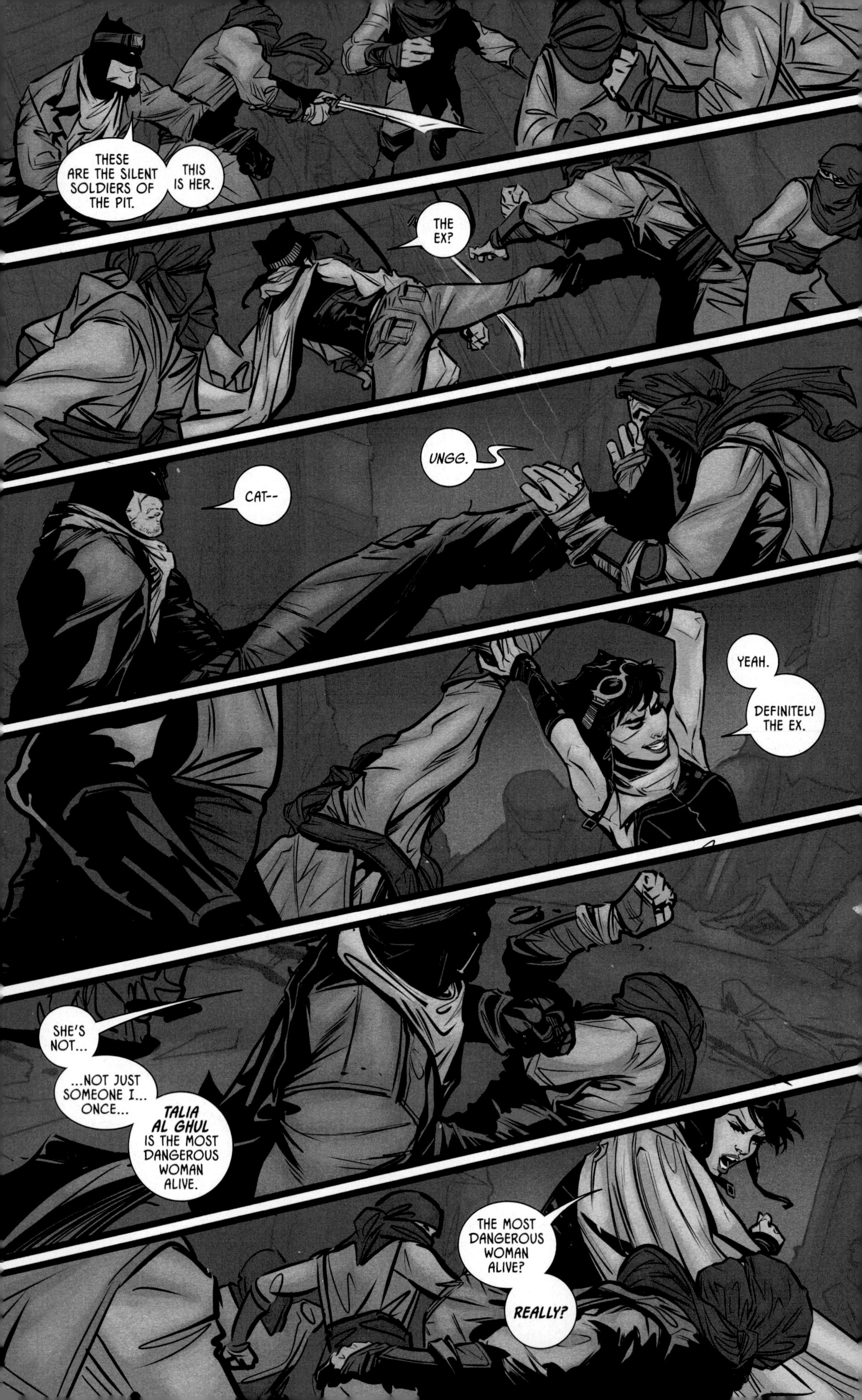
THESE ARE THE SILENT SOLDIERS OF THE PIT.
THIS IS HER.
THE EX?
UNGG.
CAT--
YEAH.
DEFINITELY THE EX.
SHE'S NOT...
...NOT JUST SOMEONE I... ONCE...
TALIA AL GHUL IS THE MOST DANGEROUS WOMAN ALIVE.
THE MOST DANGEROUS WOMAN ALIVE?
REALLY?

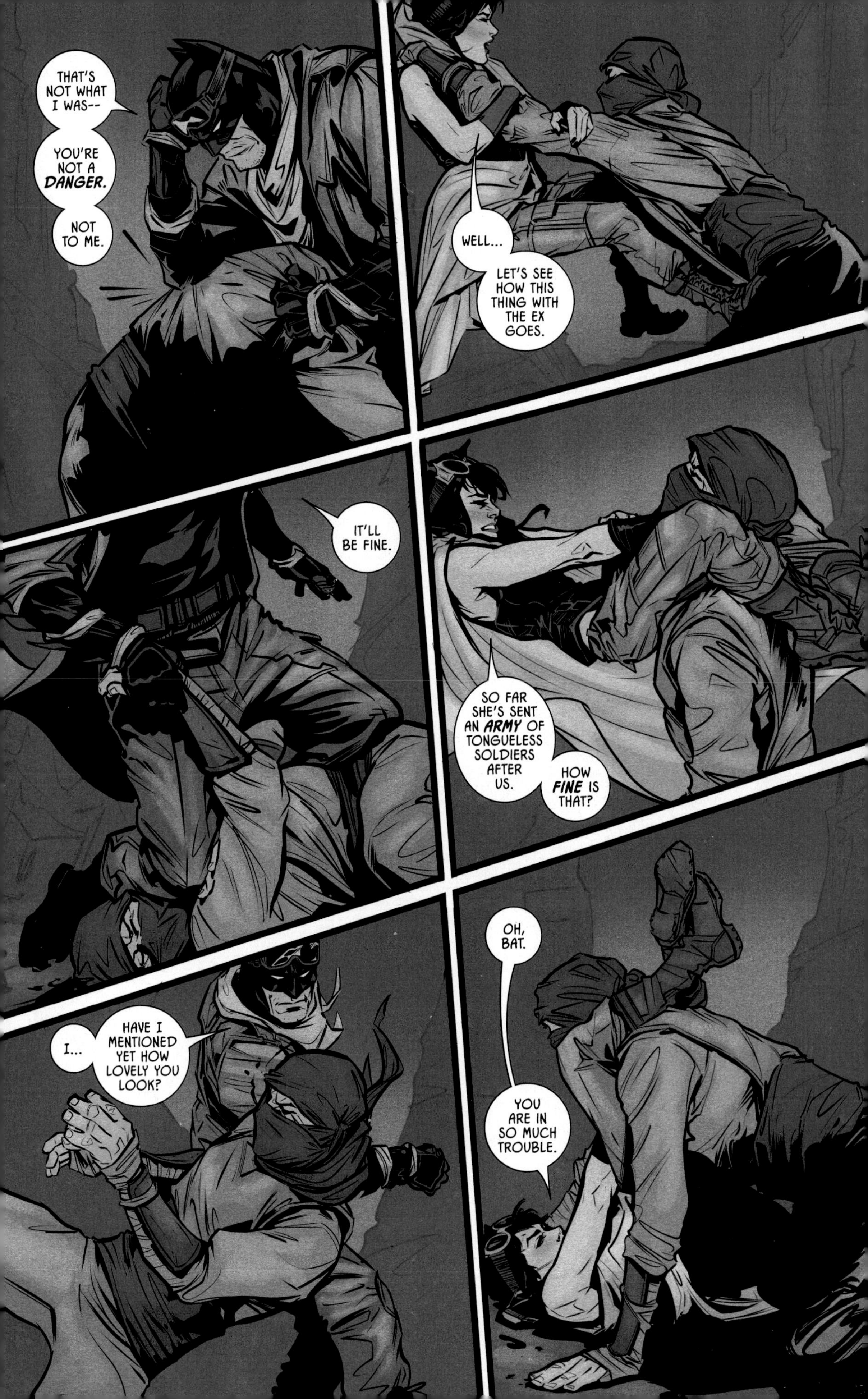
THAT'S NOT WHAT I WAS--
YOU'RE NOT A DANGER.
NOT TO ME.
WELL...
LET'S SEE HOW THIS THING WITH THE EX GOES.
IT'LL BE FINE.
SO FAR SHE'S SENT AN ARMY OF TONGUELESS SOLDIERS AFTER US.
HOW FINE IS THAT?
I...
HAVE I MENTIONED YET HOW LOVELY YOU LOOK?
OH, BAT.
YOU ARE IN SO MUCH TROUBLE.

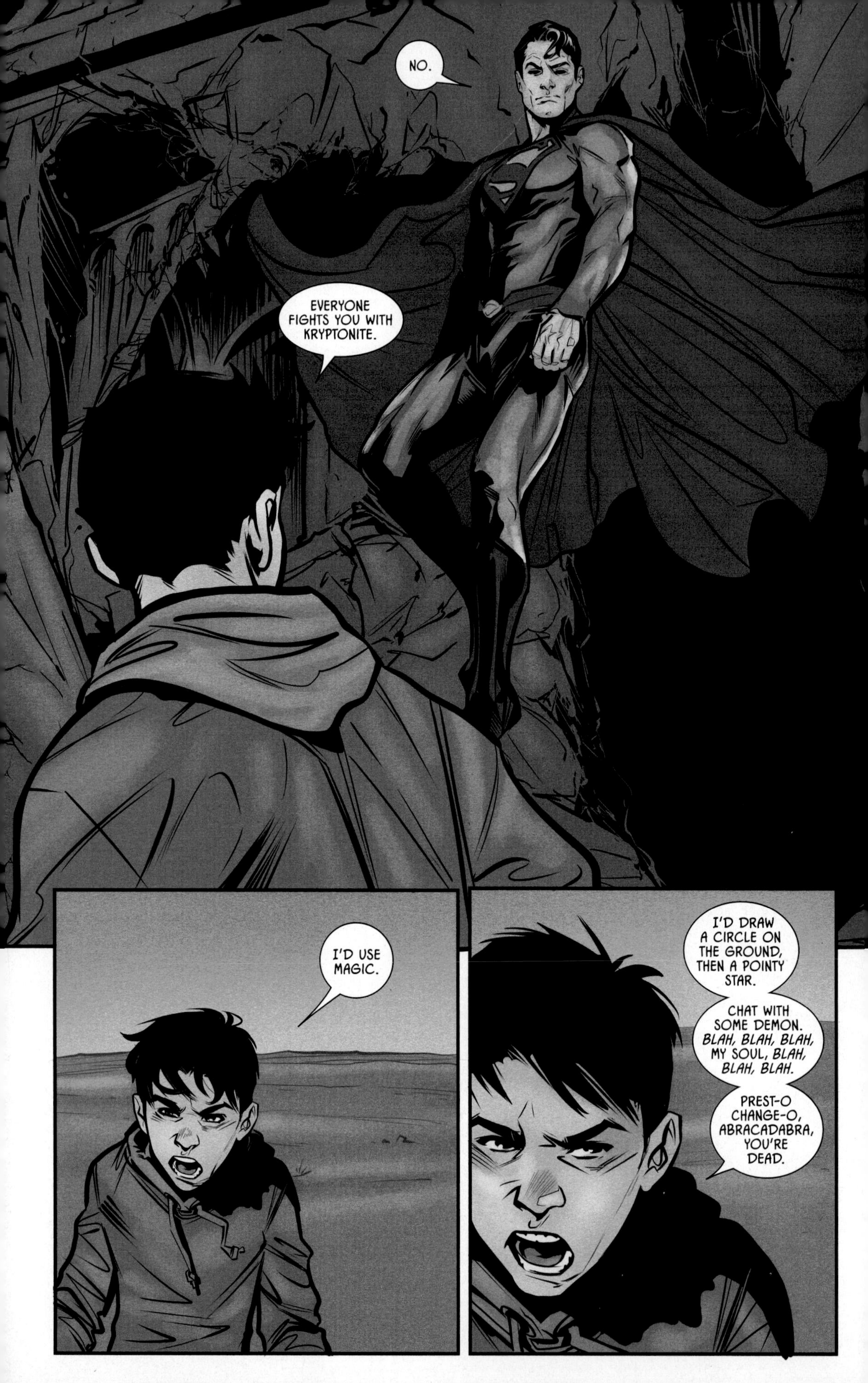
NO.
EVERYONE FIGHTS YOU WITH KRYPTONITE.
I'D USE MAGIC.
I'D DRAW A CIRCLE ON THE GROUND, THEN A POINTY STAR.
CHAT WITH SOME DEMON. *BLAH, BLAH, BLAH,* MY SOUL, *BLAH, BLAH, BLAH.*
PREST-O CHANGE-O, ABRACADABRA, YOU'RE DEAD.

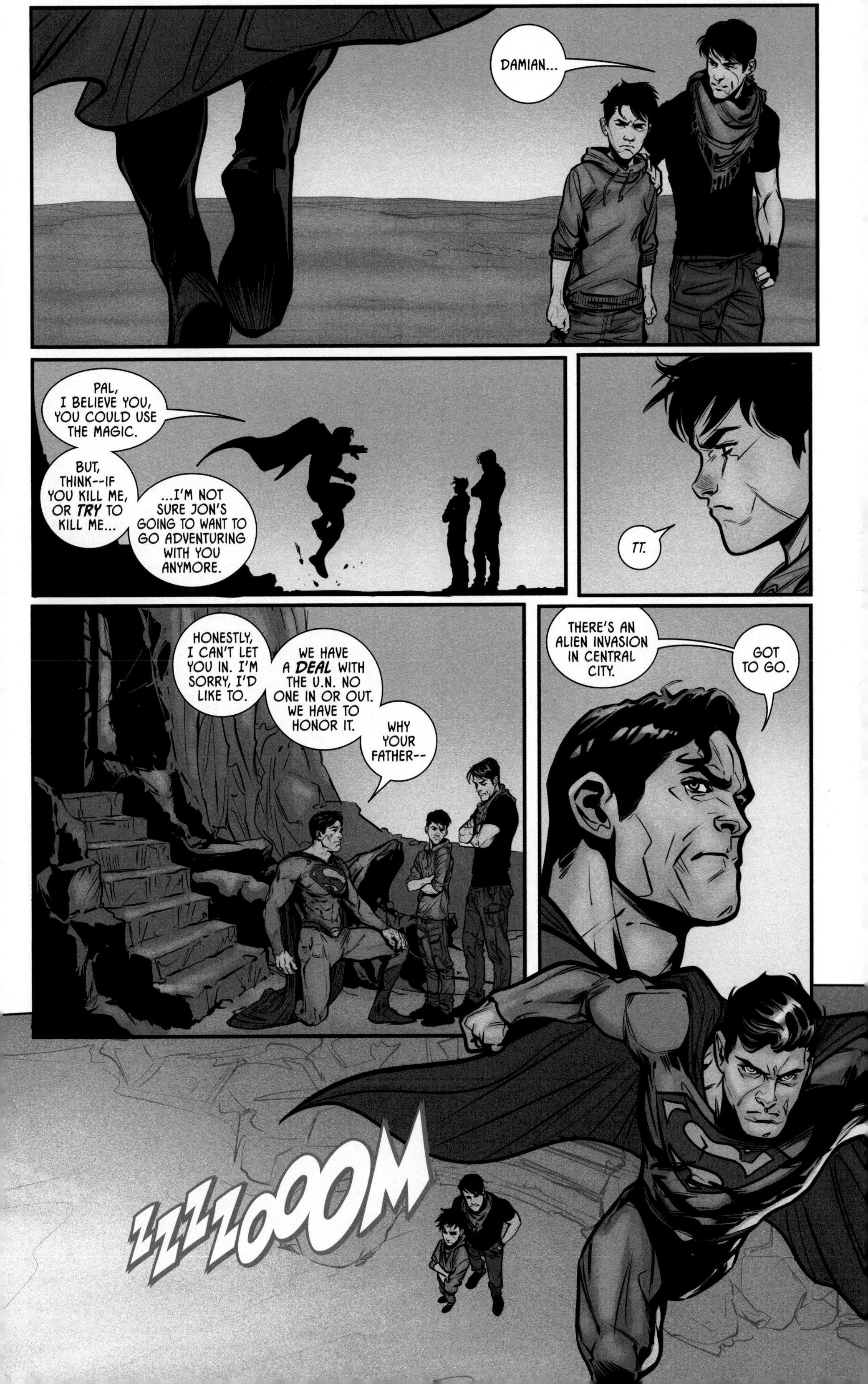
DAMIAN...
PAL, I BELIEVE YOU, YOU COULD USE THE MAGIC.
BUT, THINK--IF YOU KILL ME, OR TRY TO KILL ME...
...I'M NOT SURE JON'S GOING TO WANT TO GO ADVENTURING WITH YOU ANYMORE.
TT.
HONESTLY, I CAN'T LET YOU IN. I'M SORRY, I'D LIKE TO.
WE HAVE A DEAL WITH THE U.N. NO ONE IN OR OUT. WE HAVE TO HONOR IT.
WHY YOUR FATHER--
THERE'S AN ALIEN INVASION IN CENTRAL CITY.
GOT TO GO.
ZZZZOOOM

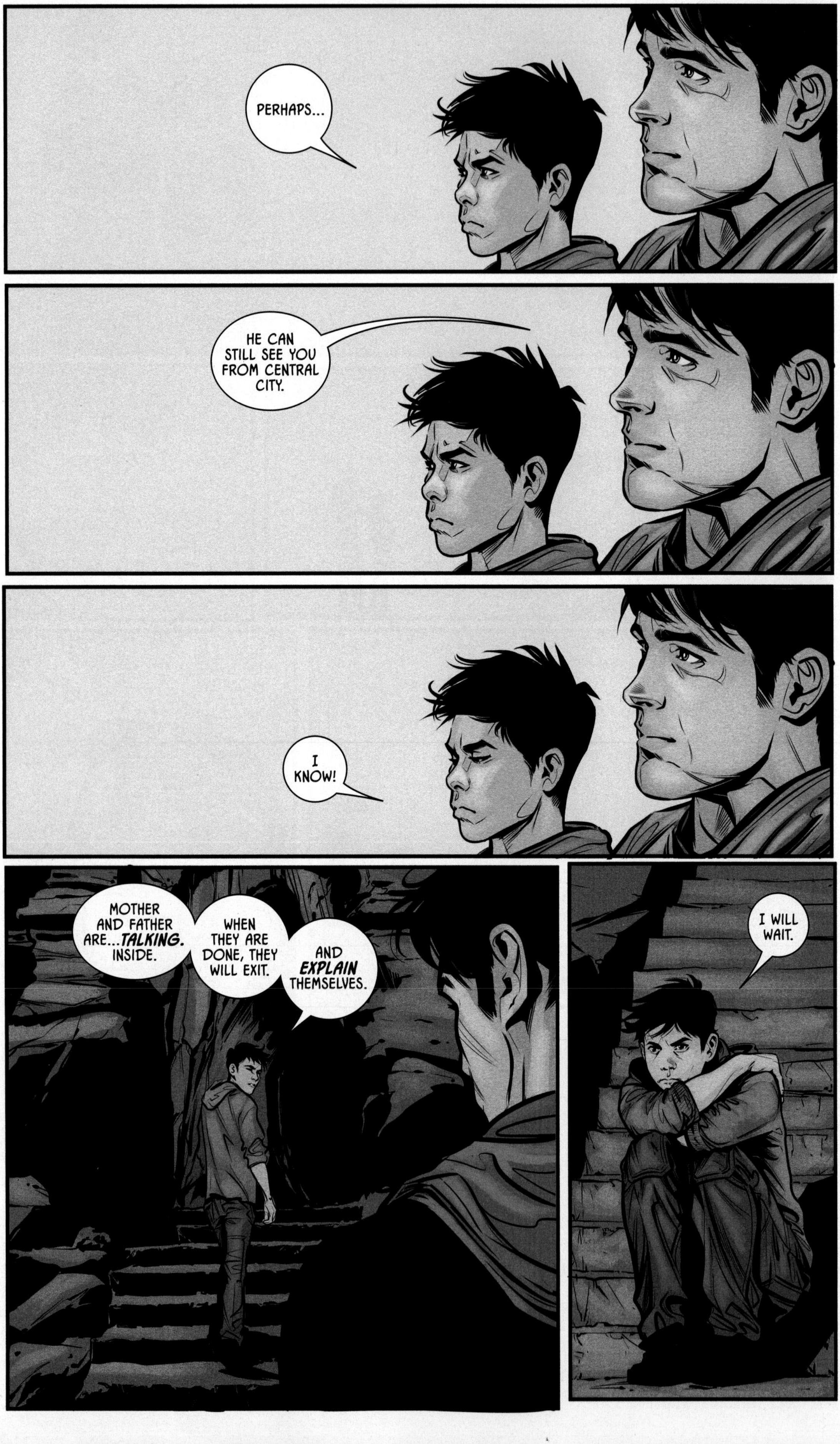
PERHAPS...
HE CAN STILL SEE YOU FROM CENTRAL CITY.
I KNOW!
MOTHER AND FATHER ARE...TALKING. INSIDE.
WHEN THEY ARE DONE, THEY WILL EXIT.
AND EXPLAIN THEMSELVES.
I WILL WAIT.

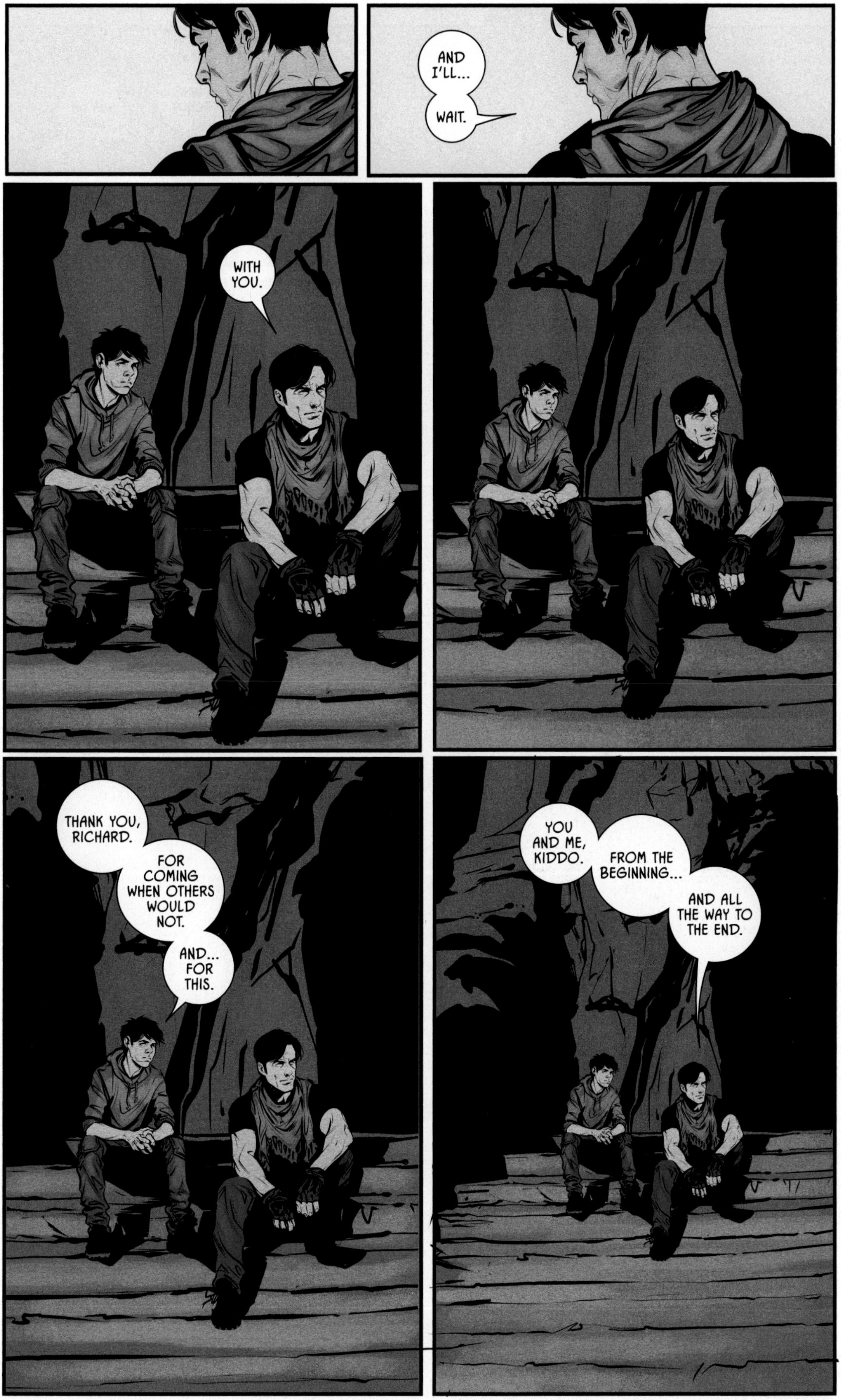
AND I'LL...
WAIT.
WITH YOU.
THANK YOU, RICHARD.
FOR COMING WHEN OTHERS WOULD NOT.
AND... FOR THIS.
YOU AND ME, KIDDO.
FROM THE BEGINNING...
AND ALL THE WAY TO THE END.

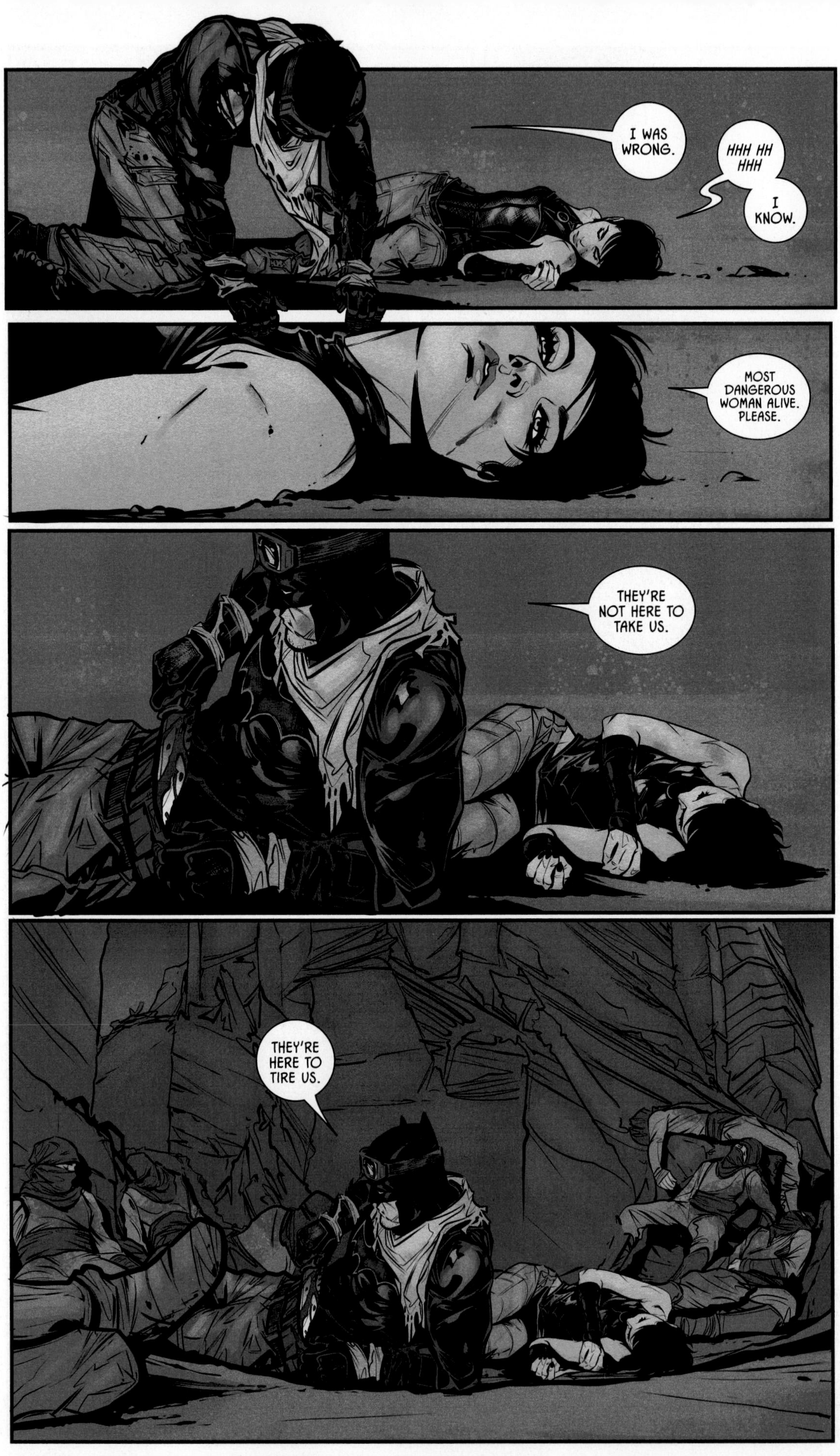
I WAS WRONG.
HHH HH HHH
I KNOW.
MOST DANGEROUS WOMAN ALIVE. PLEASE.
THEY'RE NOT HERE TO TAKE US.
THEY'RE HERE TO TIRE US.

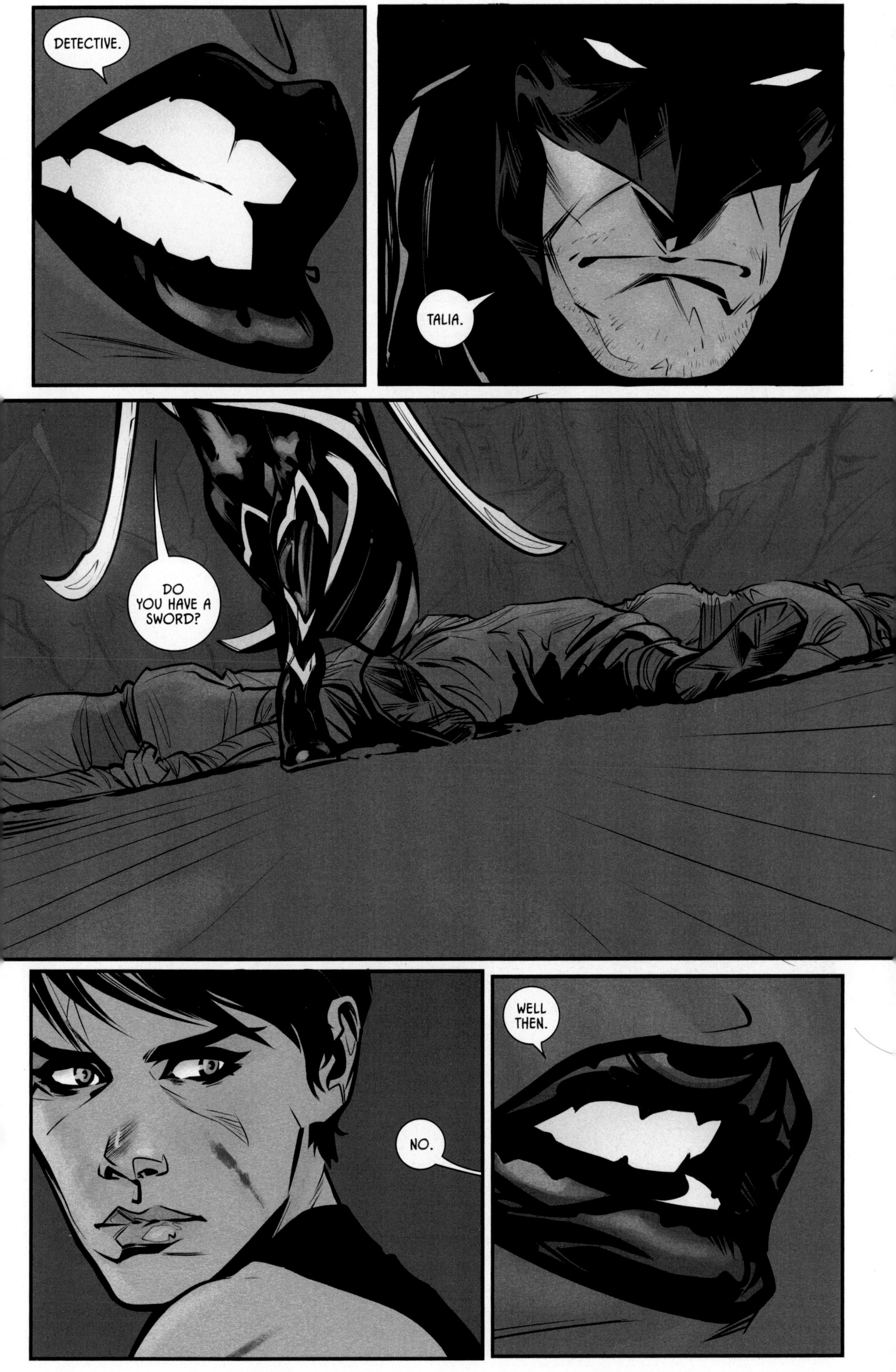
DETECTIVE.
TALIA.
DO YOU HAVE A SWORD?
NO.
WELL THEN.

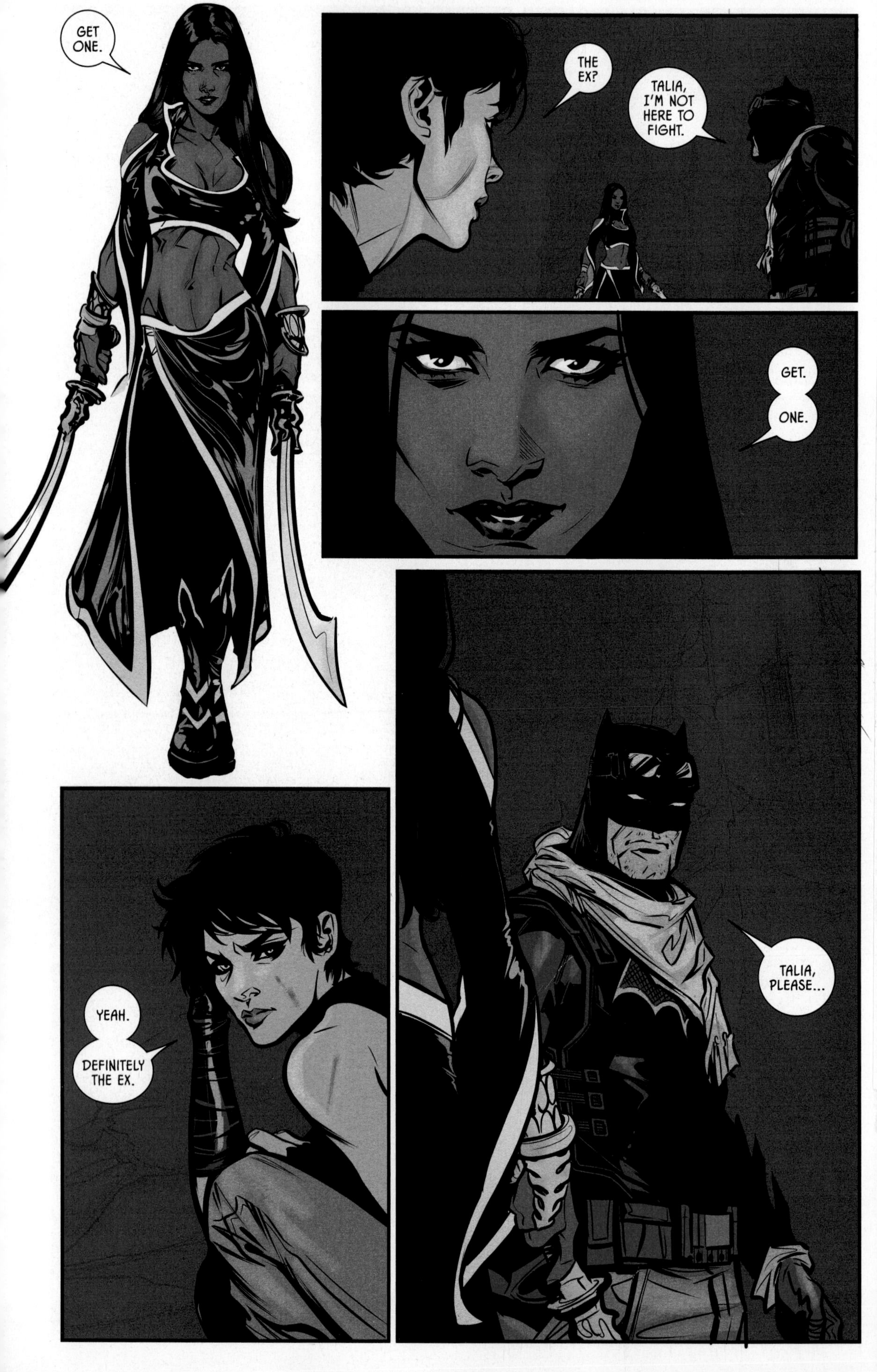
GET ONE.
THE EX?
TALIA, I'M NOT HERE TO FIGHT.
GET.
ONE.
YEAH.
DEFINITELY THE EX.
TALIA, PLEASE...

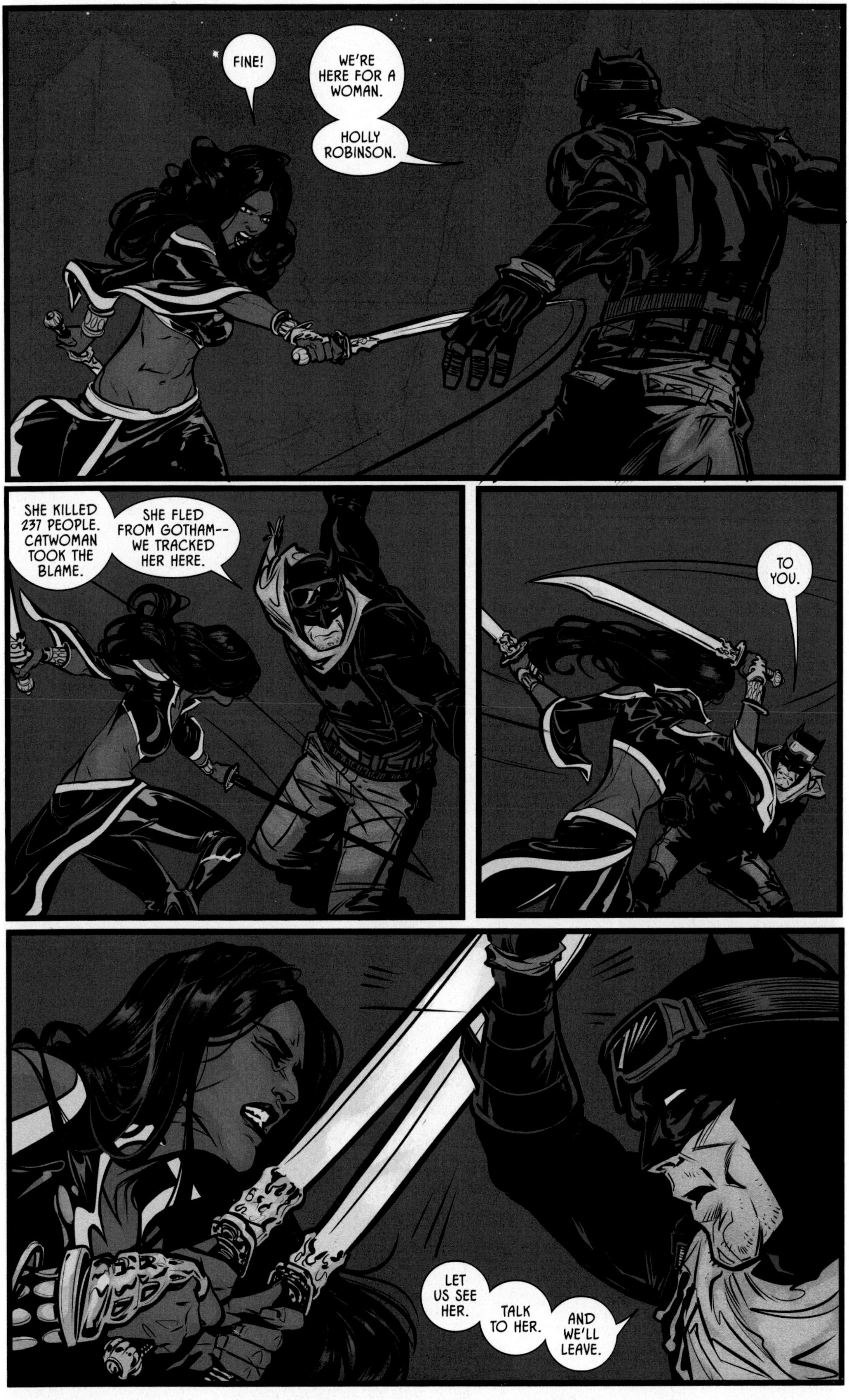
FINE!
WE'RE HERE FOR A WOMAN.
HOLLY ROBINSON.
SHE KILLED 237 PEOPLE. CATWOMAN TOOK THE BLAME.
SHE FLED FROM GOTHAM-- WE TRACKED HER HERE.
TO YOU.
LET US SEE HER.
TALK TO HER.
AND WE'LL LEAVE.

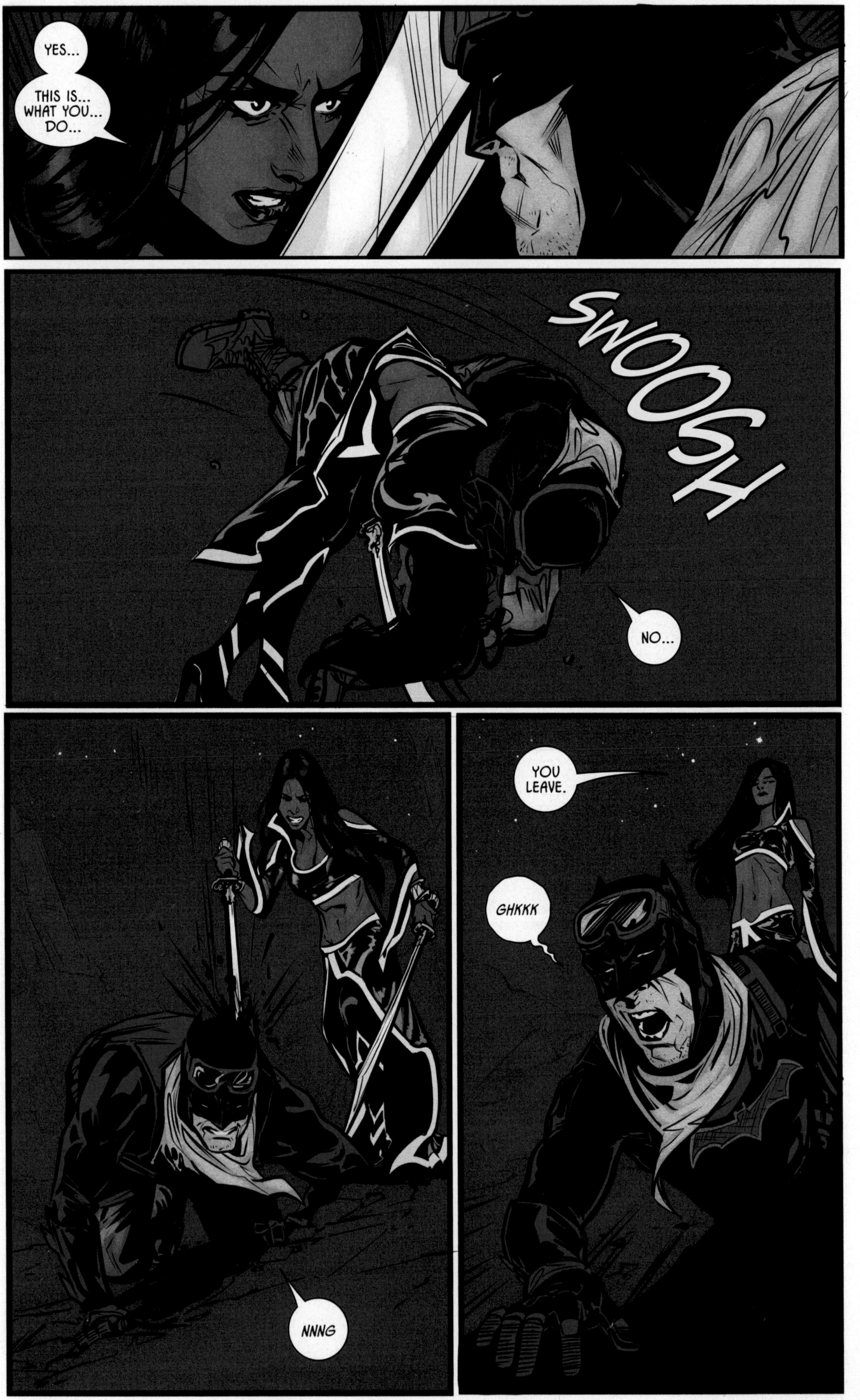
YES...
THIS IS... WHAT YOU... DO...
SWOOSH
NO...
NNNG
YOU LEAVE.
GHKKK

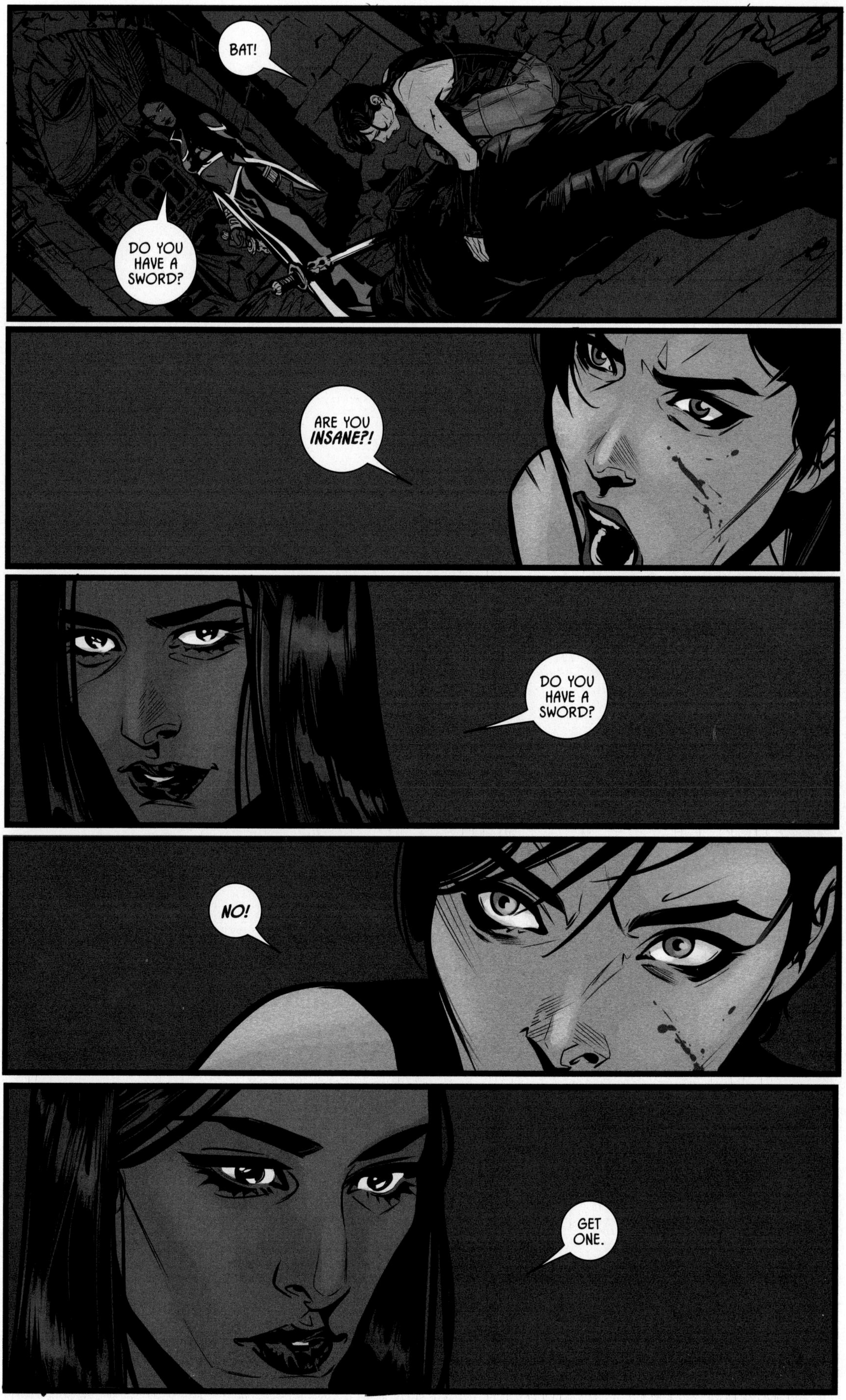
BAT!
DO YOU HAVE A SWORD?
ARE YOU INSANE?!
DO YOU HAVE A SWORD?
NO!
GET ONE.

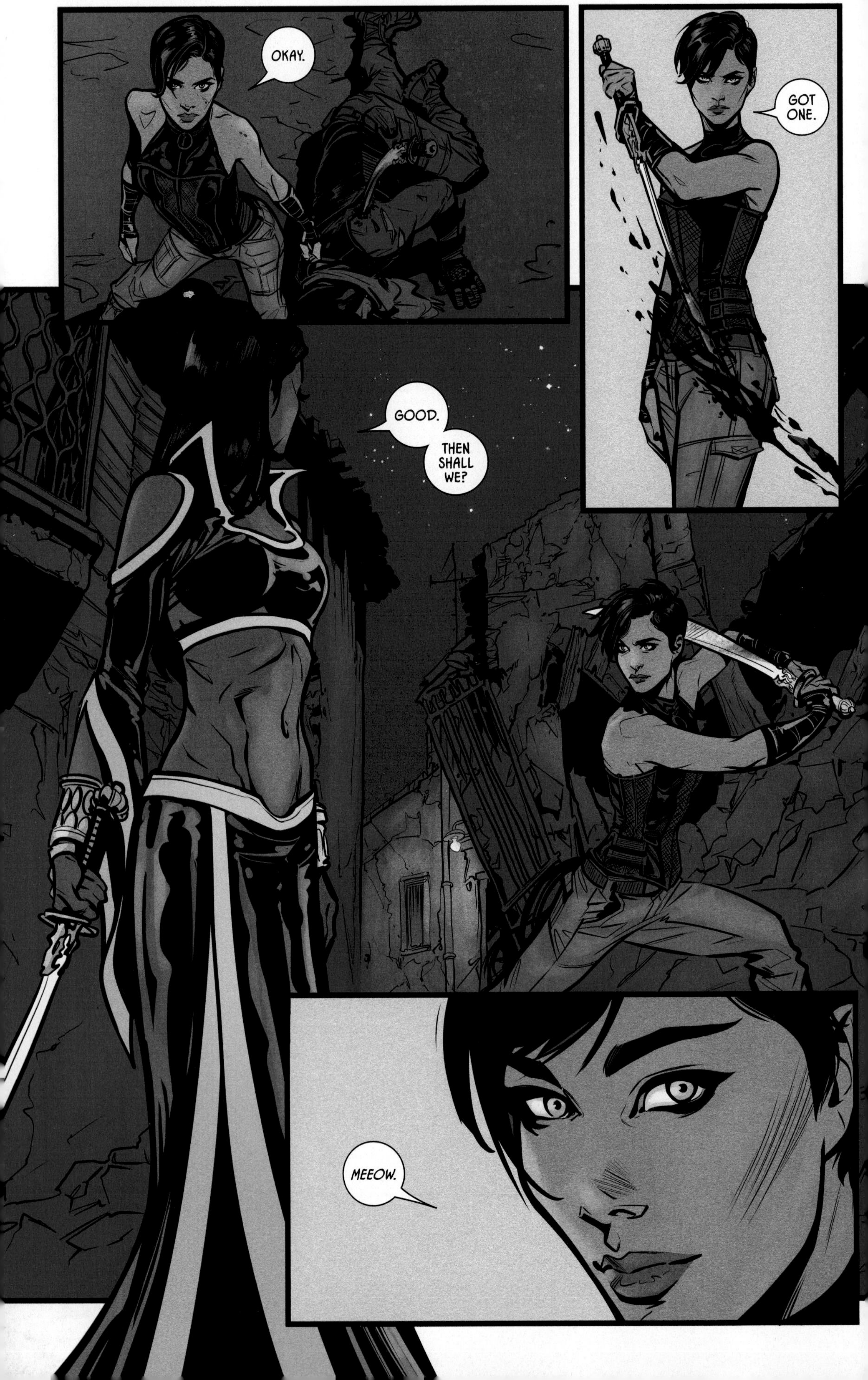
OKAY.
GOT ONE.
GOOD.
THEN SHALL WE?
MEEOW.

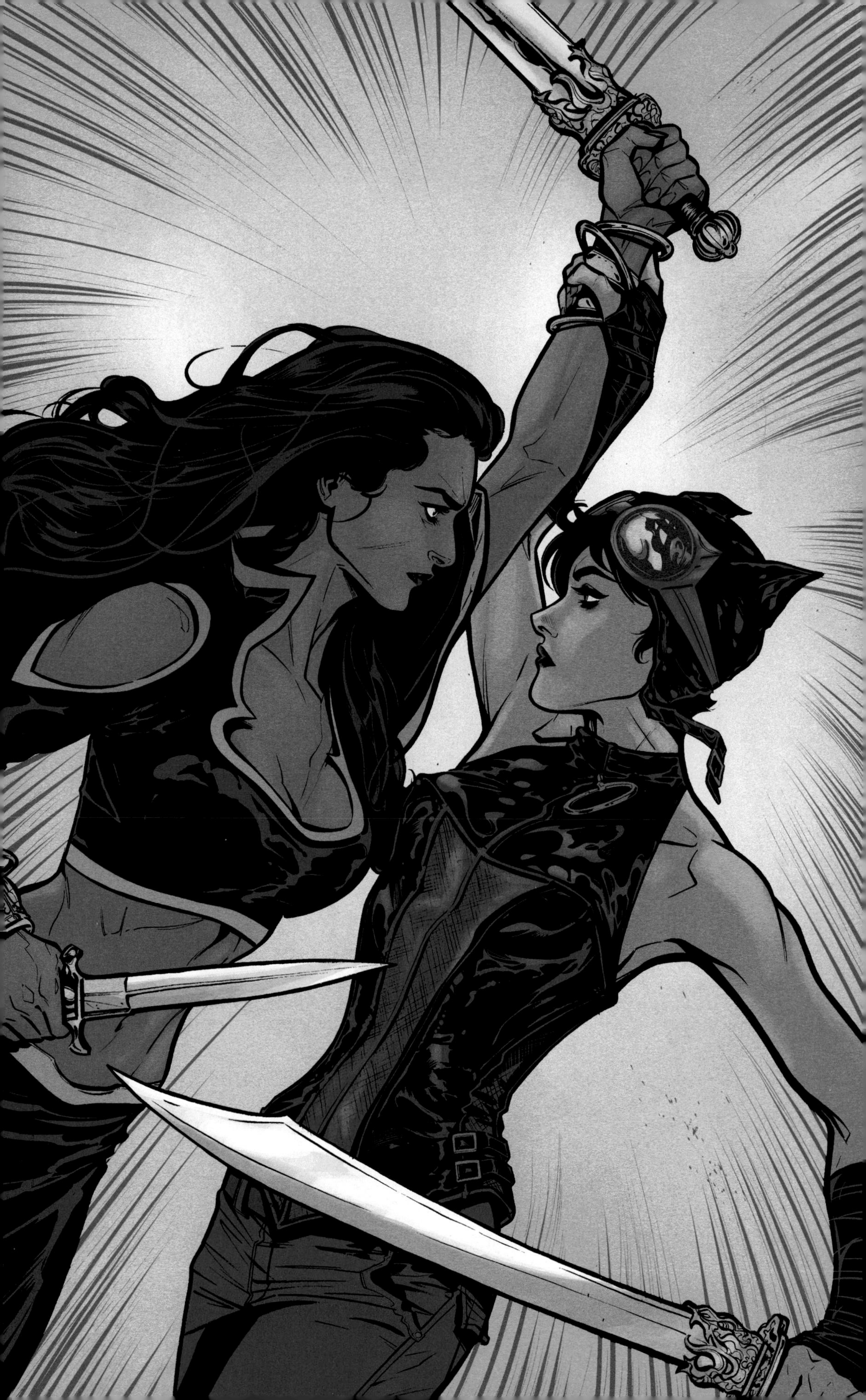

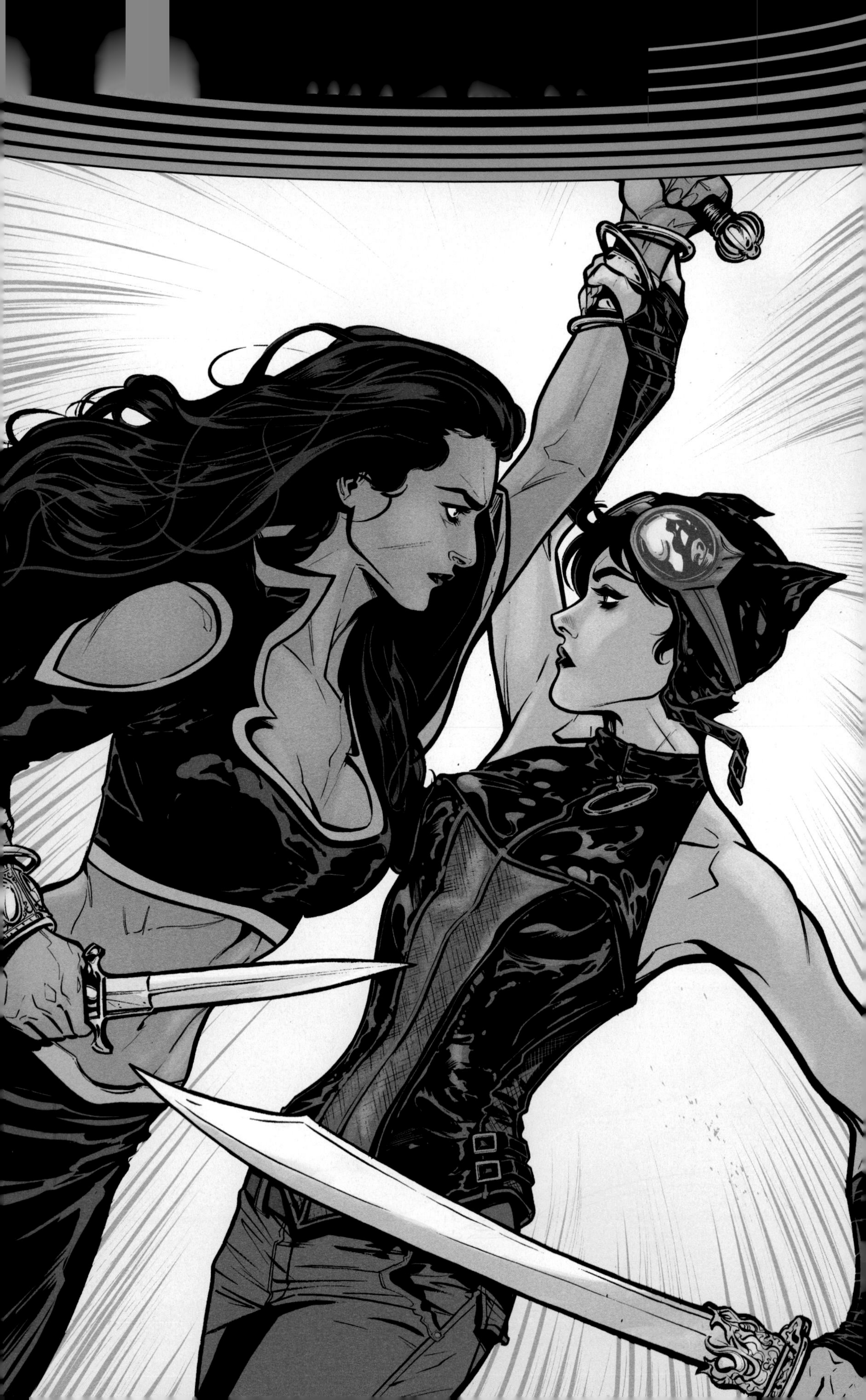

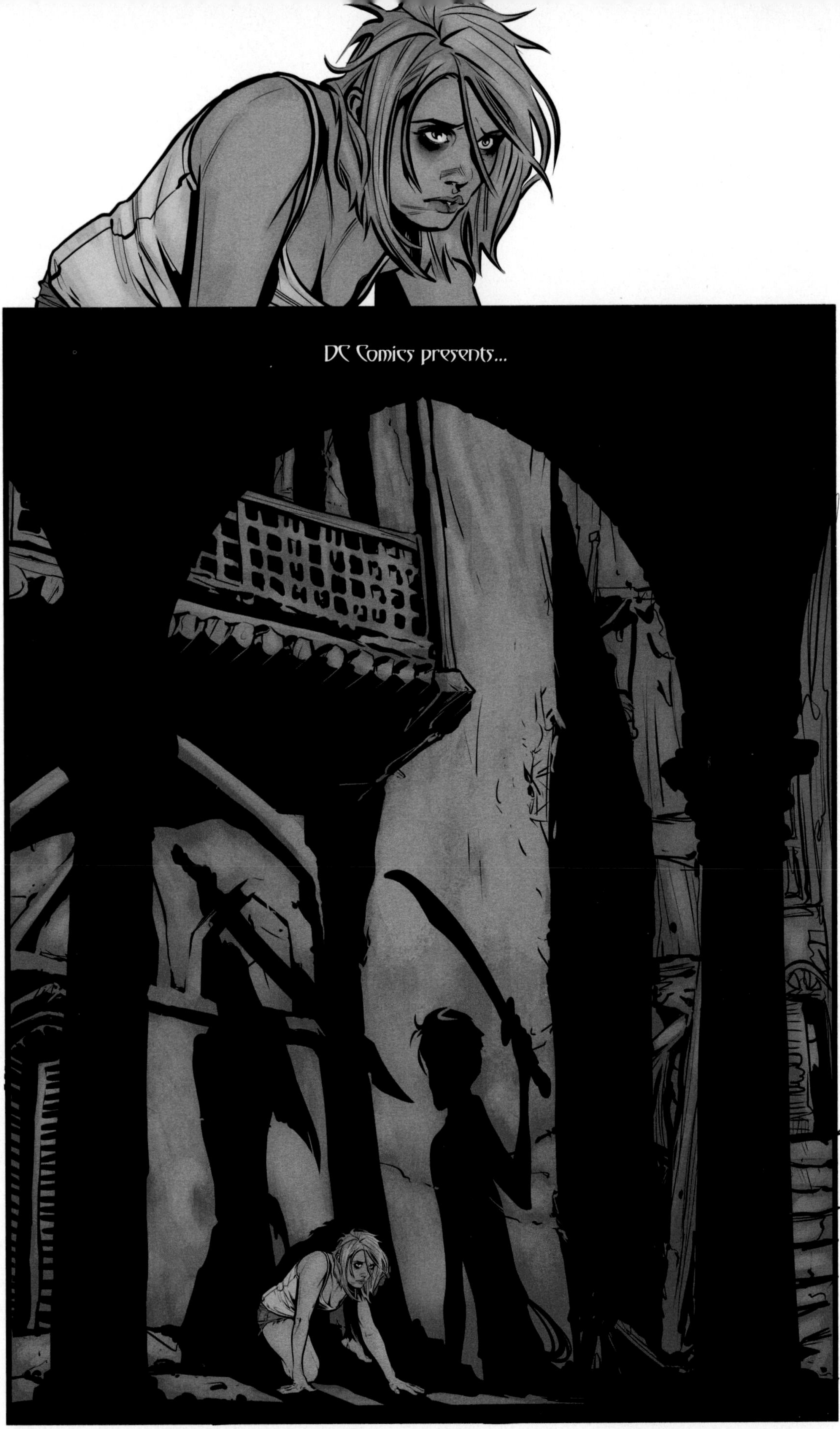
DC Comics presents...

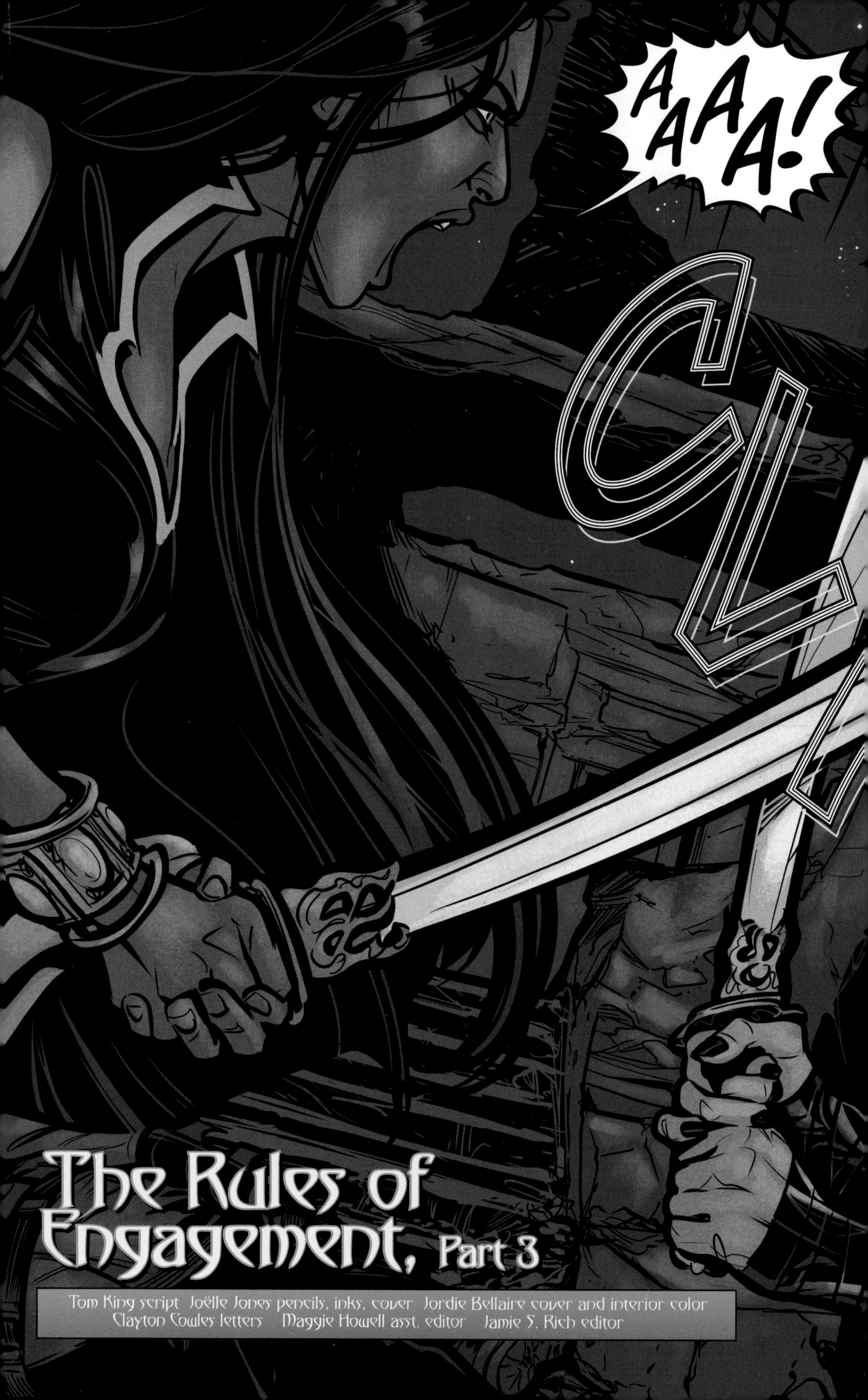
AAAA!
CL
The Rules of Engagement, Part 3
Tom King script Joëlle Jones pencils, inks, cover Jordie Bellaire cover and interior color
Clayton Cowles letters Maggie Howell asst. editor Jamie S. Rich editor

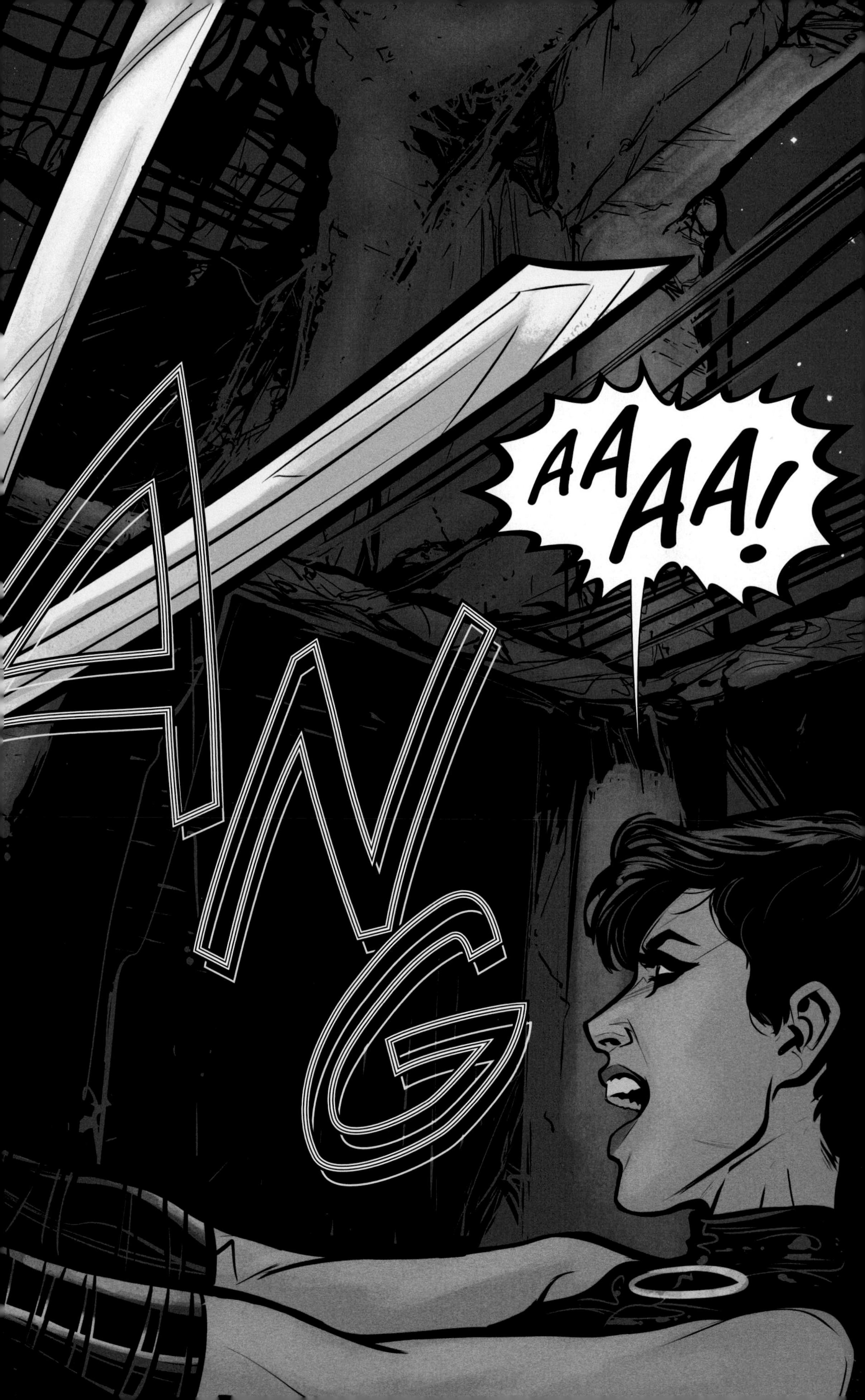
AAAA!
ANG

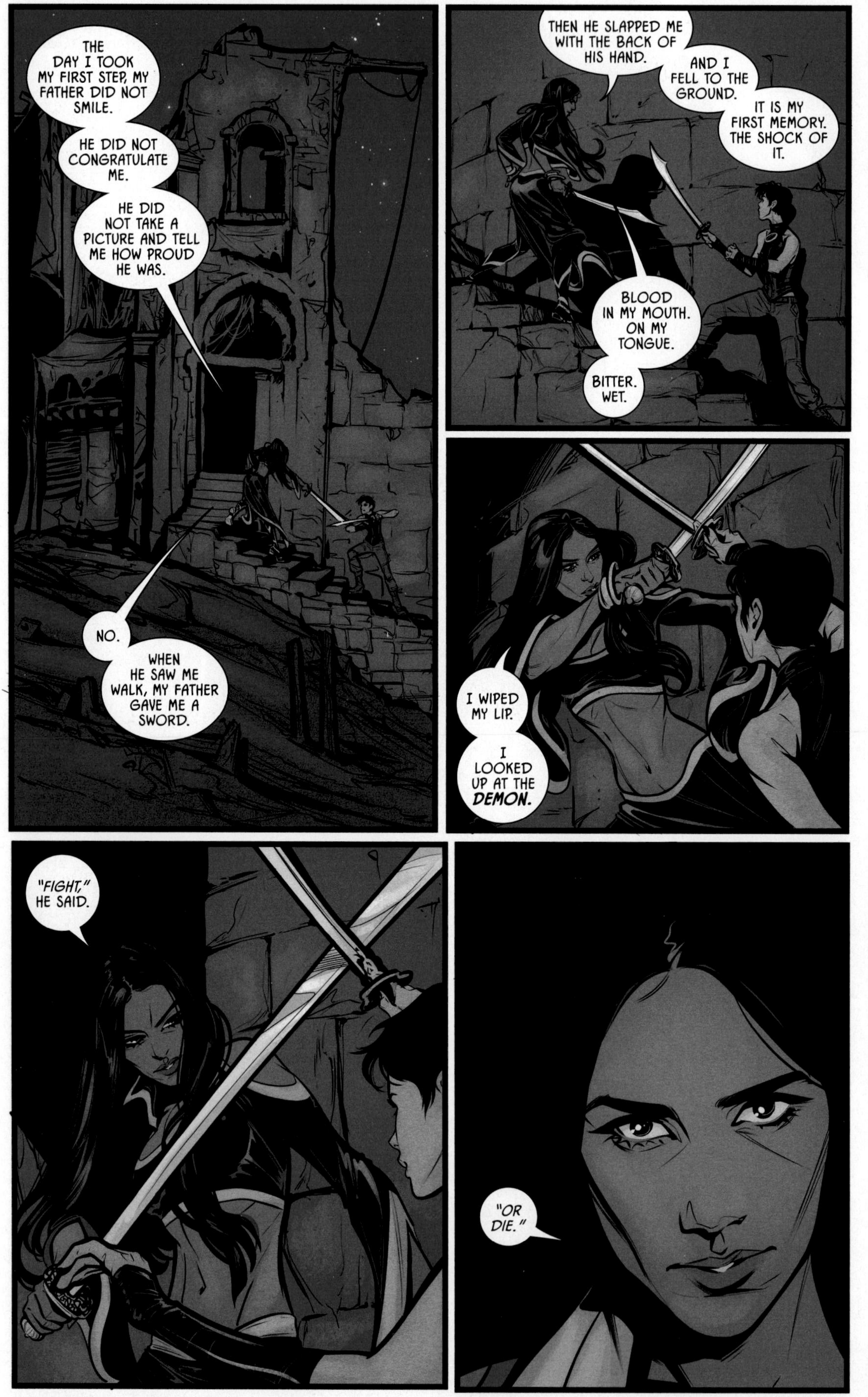
THE DAY I TOOK MY FIRST STEP, MY FATHER DID NOT SMILE.
HE DID NOT CONGRATULATE ME.
HE DID NOT TAKE A PICTURE AND TELL ME HOW PROUD HE WAS.
NO.
WHEN HE SAW ME WALK, MY FATHER GAVE ME A SWORD.
THEN HE SLAPPED ME WITH THE BACK OF HIS HAND.
AND I FELL TO THE GROUND.
IT IS MY FIRST MEMORY. THE SHOCK OF IT.
BLOOD IN MY MOUTH. ON MY TONGUE.
BITTER. WET.
I WIPED MY LIP.
I LOOKED UP AT THE *DEMON.*
"FIGHT," HE SAID.
"OR DIE."

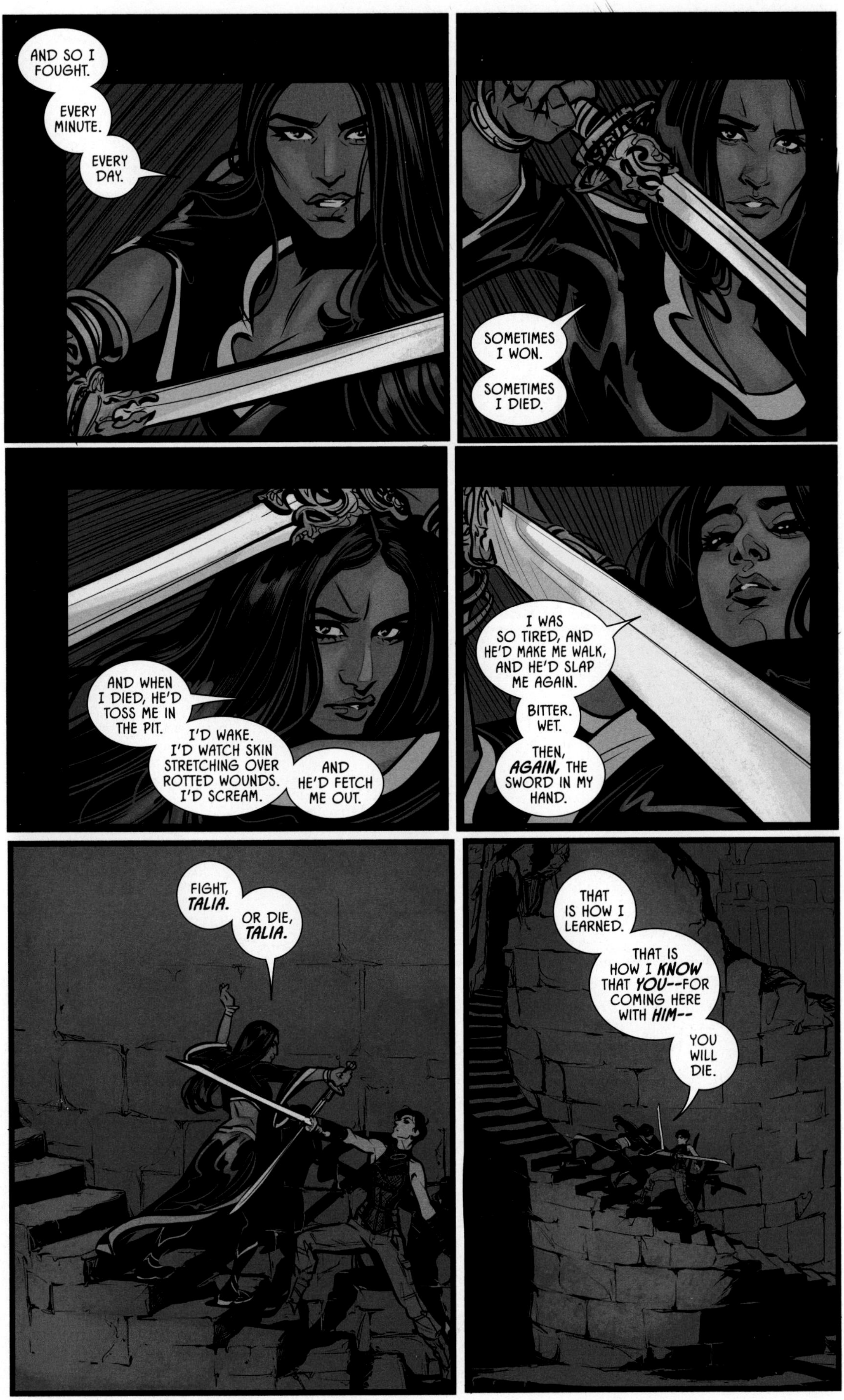
AND SO I FOUGHT.
EVERY MINUTE.
EVERY DAY.
SOMETIMES I WON.
SOMETIMES I DIED.
AND WHEN I DIED, HE'D TOSS ME IN THE PIT.
I'D WAKE. I'D WATCH SKIN STRETCHING OVER ROTTED WOUNDS. I'D SCREAM.
AND HE'D FETCH ME OUT.
I WAS SO TIRED, AND HE'D MAKE ME WALK, AND HE'D SLAP ME AGAIN.
BITTER. WET.
THEN, AGAIN, THE SWORD IN MY HAND.
FIGHT, TALIA.
OR DIE, TALIA.
THAT IS HOW I LEARNED.
THAT IS HOW I KNOW THAT YOU--FOR COMING HERE WITH HIM--
YOU WILL DIE.

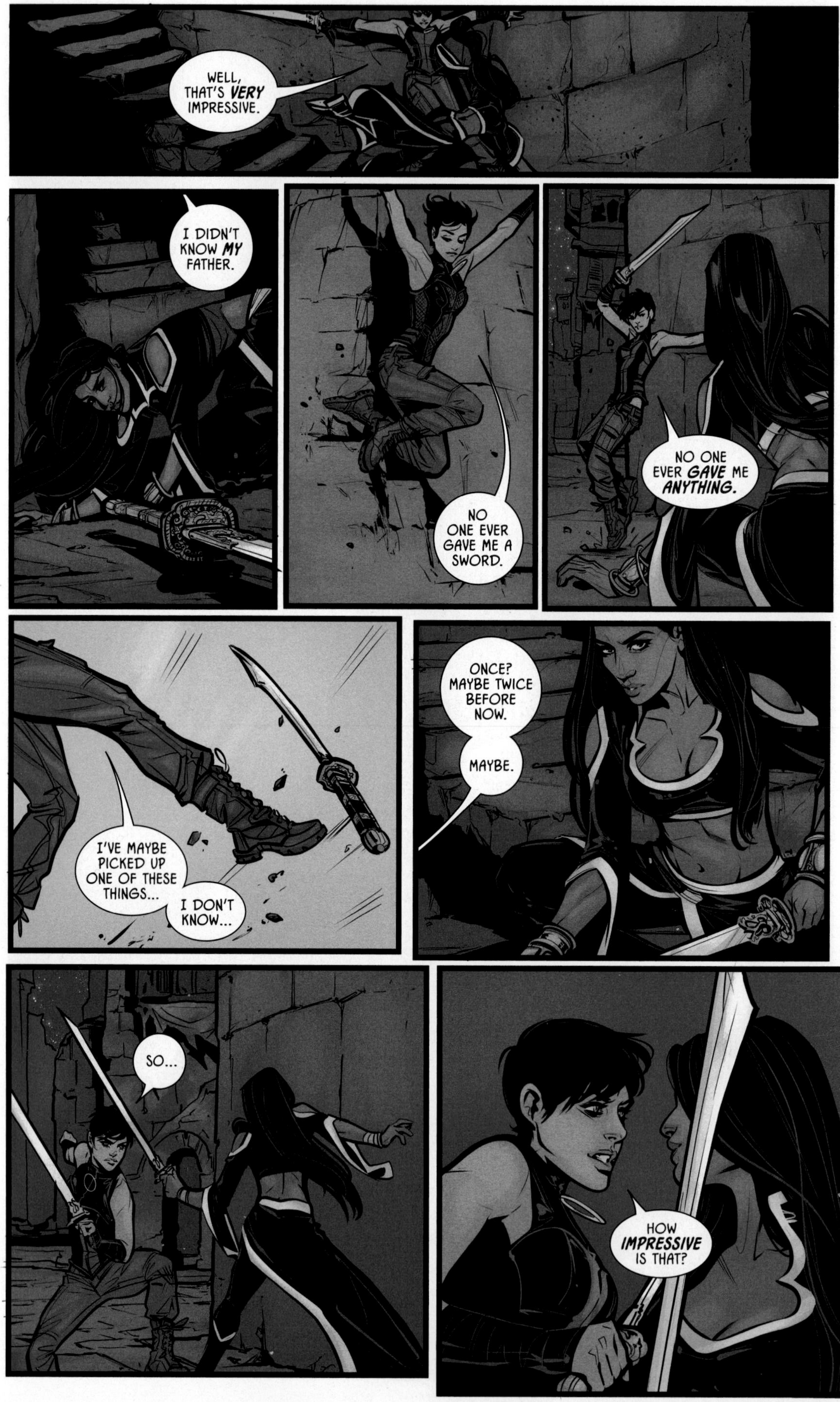
WELL, THAT'S *VERY* IMPRESSIVE.
I DIDN'T KNOW *MY* FATHER.
NO ONE EVER GAVE ME A SWORD.
NO ONE EVER *GAVE* ME *ANYTHING.*
I'VE MAYBE PICKED UP ONE OF THESE THINGS...
I DON'T KNOW...
ONCE? MAYBE TWICE BEFORE NOW.
MAYBE.
SO...
HOW *IMPRESSIVE* IS THAT?

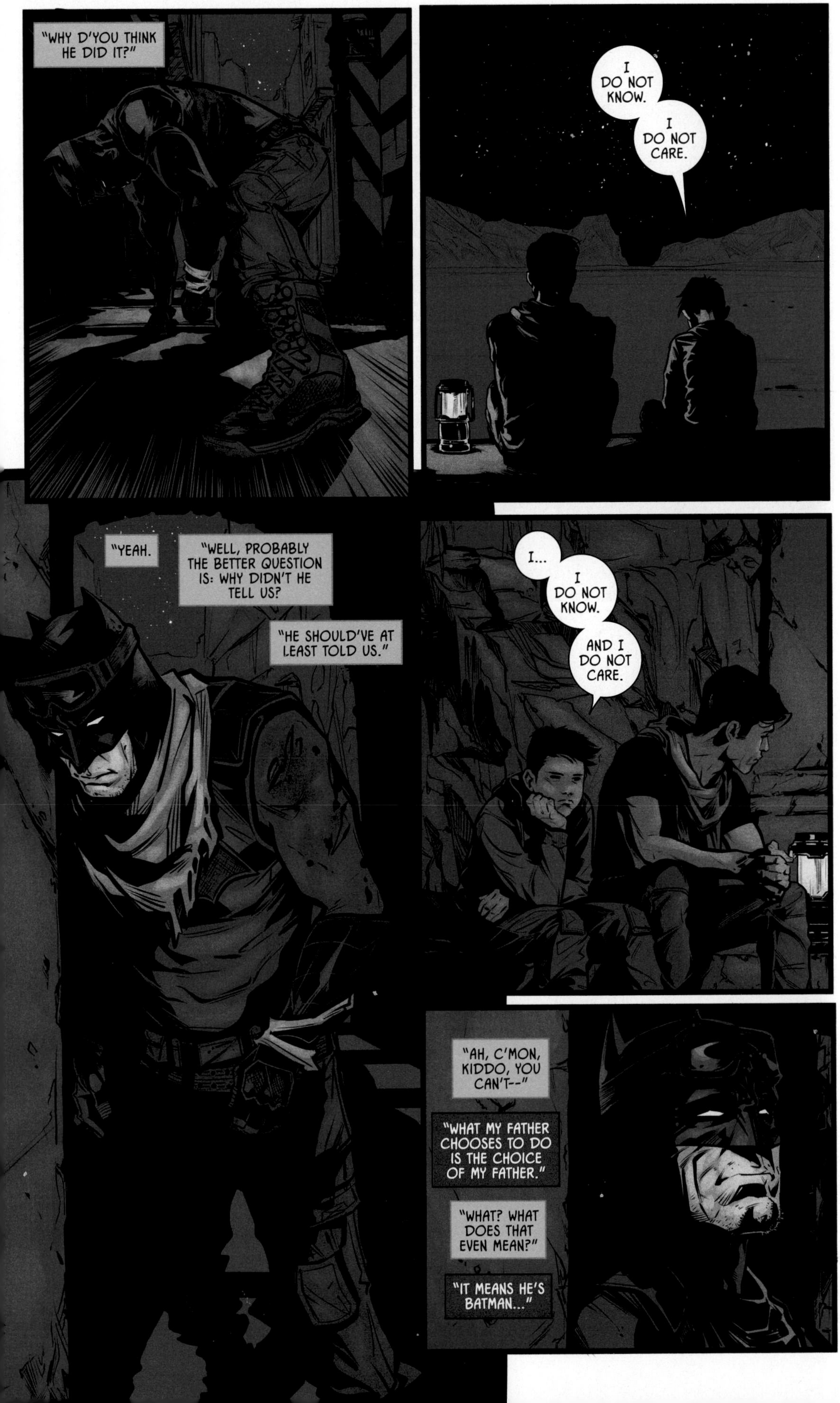
"WHY D'YOU THINK HE DID IT?"
I DO NOT KNOW.
I DO NOT CARE.
"YEAH.
"WELL, PROBABLY THE BETTER QUESTION IS: WHY DIDN'T HE TELL US?
"HE SHOULD'VE AT LEAST TOLD US."
I...
I DO NOT KNOW.
AND I DO NOT CARE.
"AH, C'MON, KIDDO, YOU CAN'T--"
"WHAT MY FATHER CHOOSES TO DO IS THE CHOICE OF MY FATHER."
"WHAT? WHAT DOES THAT EVEN MEAN?"
"IT MEANS HE'S BATMAN..."

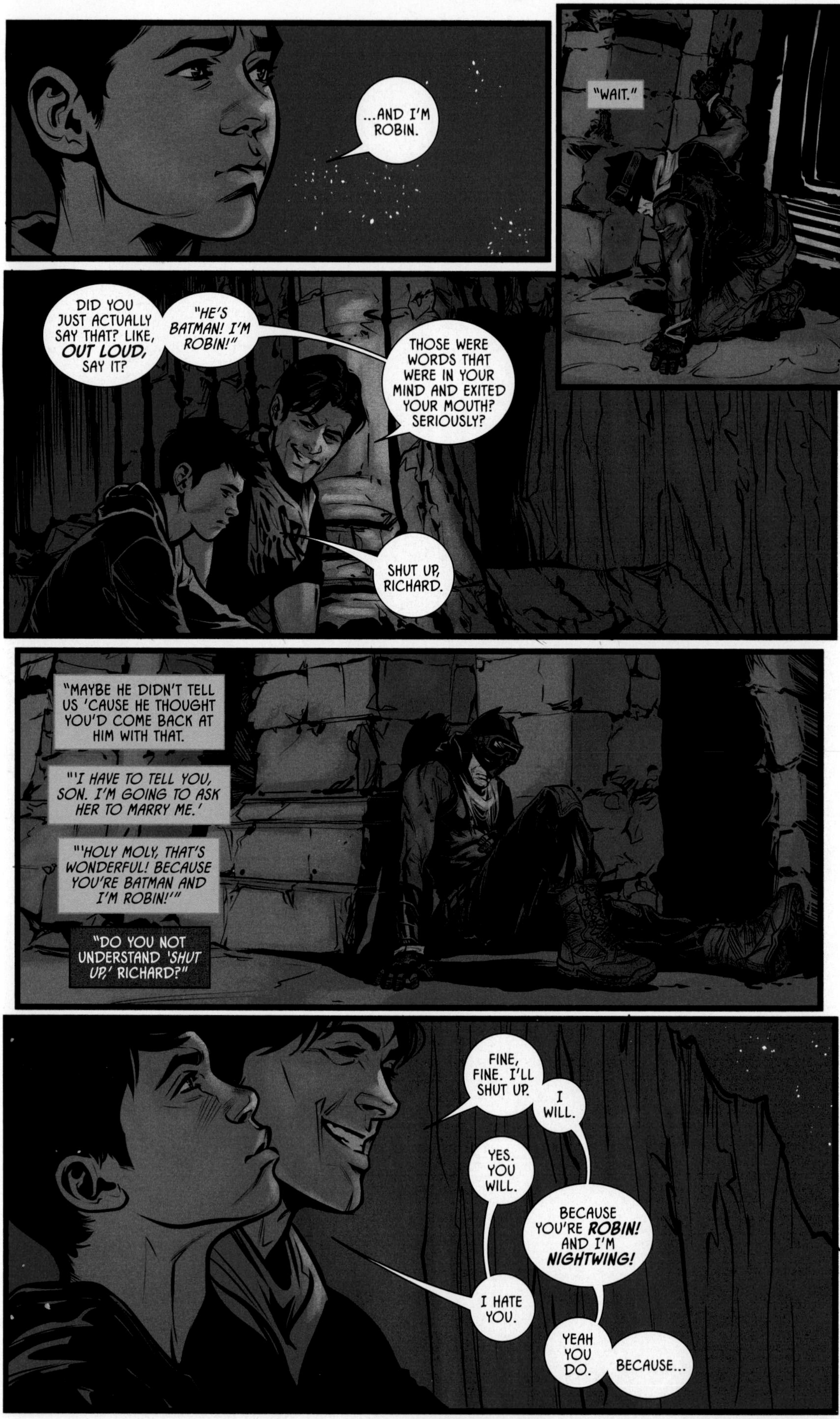
...AND I'M ROBIN.
"WAIT."
DID YOU JUST ACTUALLY SAY THAT? LIKE, OUT LOUD, SAY IT?
"HE'S BATMAN! I'M ROBIN!"
THOSE WERE WORDS THAT WERE IN YOUR MIND AND EXITED YOUR MOUTH? SERIOUSLY?
SHUT UP, RICHARD.
"MAYBE HE DIDN'T TELL US 'CAUSE HE THOUGHT YOU'D COME BACK AT HIM WITH THAT.
"'I HAVE TO TELL YOU, SON. I'M GOING TO ASK HER TO MARRY ME.'
"'HOLY MOLY, THAT'S WONDERFUL! BECAUSE YOU'RE BATMAN AND I'M ROBIN!'"
"DO YOU NOT UNDERSTAND 'SHUT UP,' RICHARD?"
FINE, FINE. I'LL SHUT UP.
I WILL.
YES. YOU WILL.
BECAUSE YOU'RE ROBIN! AND I'M NIGHTWING!
I HATE YOU.
YEAH YOU DO.
BECAUSE...

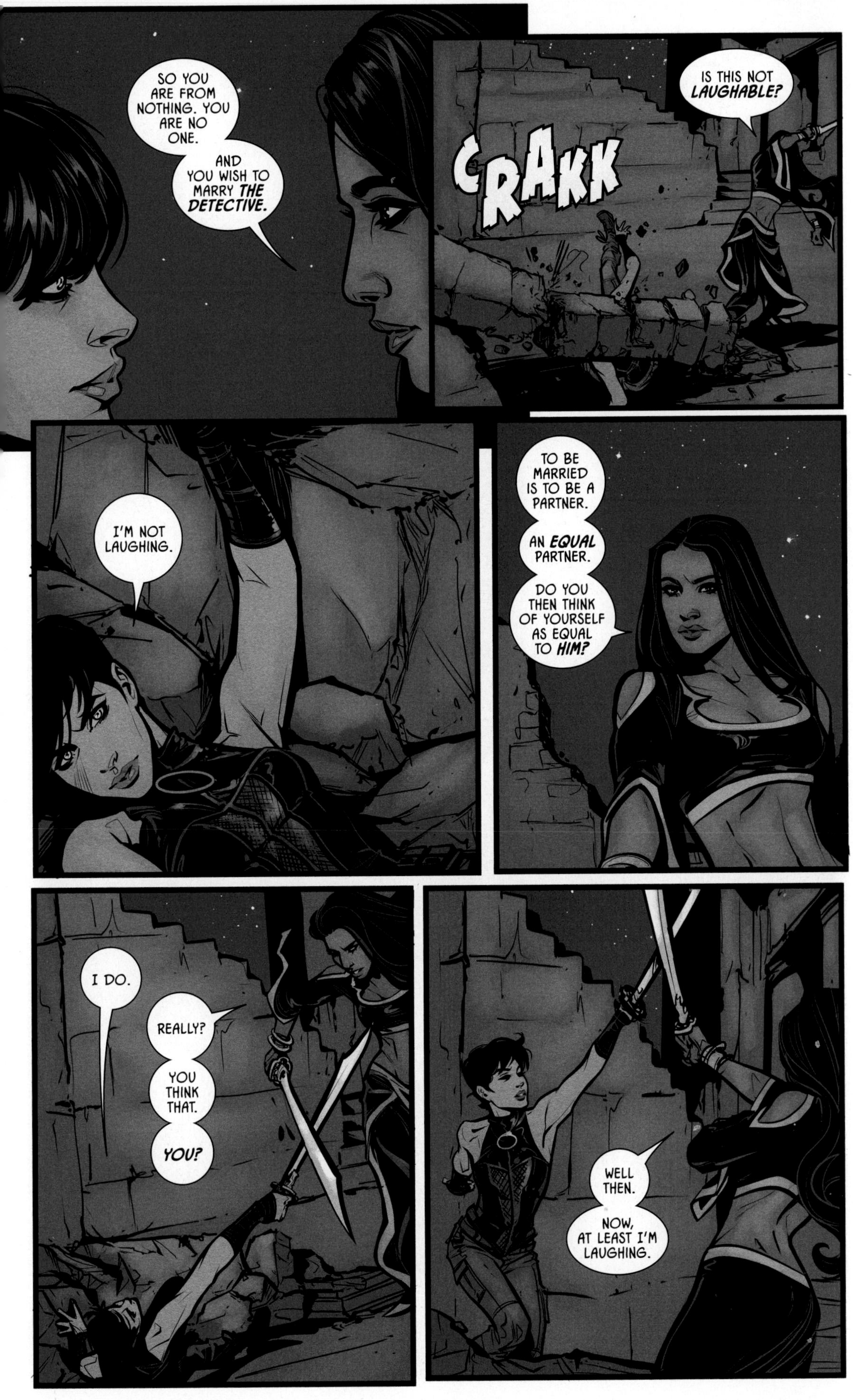
SO YOU ARE FROM NOTHING. YOU ARE NO ONE.
AND YOU WISH TO MARRY *THE DETECTIVE*.
IS THIS NOT *LAUGHABLE?*
CRAKK
I'M NOT LAUGHING.
TO BE MARRIED IS TO BE A PARTNER.
AN *EQUAL* PARTNER.
DO YOU THEN THINK OF YOURSELF AS EQUAL TO *HIM?*
I DO.
REALLY?
YOU THINK THAT.
YOU?
WELL THEN.
NOW, AT LEAST I'M LAUGHING.

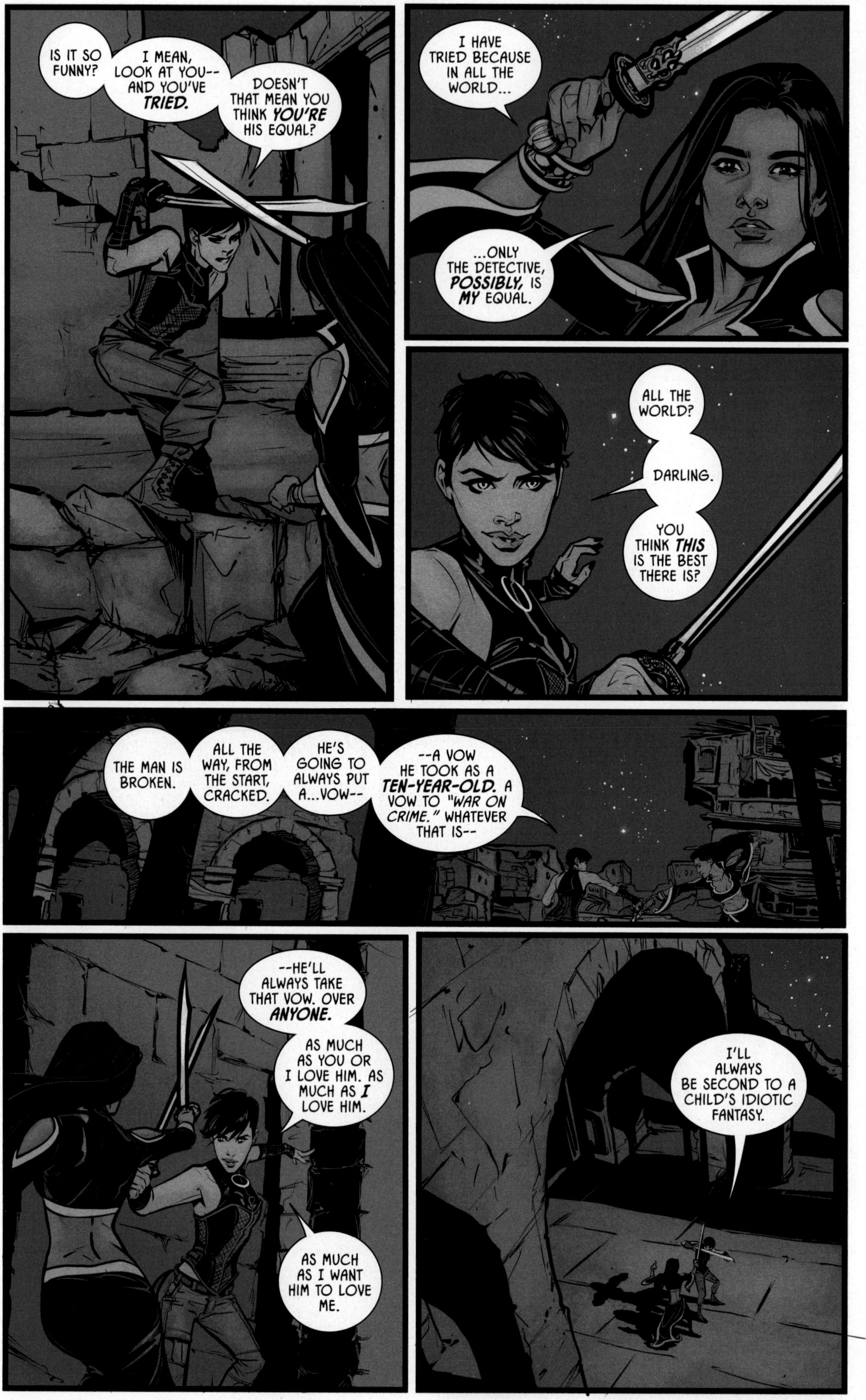
IS IT SO FUNNY?
I MEAN, LOOK AT YOU-- AND YOU'VE ***TRIED.***
DOESN'T THAT MEAN YOU THINK ***YOU'RE*** HIS EQUAL?
I HAVE TRIED BECAUSE IN ALL THE WORLD...
...ONLY THE DETECTIVE, ***POSSIBLY,*** IS ***MY*** EQUAL.
ALL THE WORLD?
DARLING.
YOU THINK ***THIS*** IS THE BEST THERE IS?
THE MAN IS BROKEN.
ALL THE WAY, FROM THE START, CRACKED.
HE'S GOING TO ALWAYS PUT A...VOW--
--A VOW HE TOOK AS A ***TEN-YEAR-OLD.*** A VOW TO "*WAR ON CRIME.*" WHATEVER THAT IS--
--HE'LL ALWAYS TAKE THAT VOW. OVER ***ANYONE.***
AS MUCH AS YOU OR I LOVE HIM. AS MUCH AS ***I*** LOVE HIM.
AS MUCH AS I WANT HIM TO LOVE ME.
I'LL ALWAYS BE SECOND TO A CHILD'S IDIOTIC FANTASY.

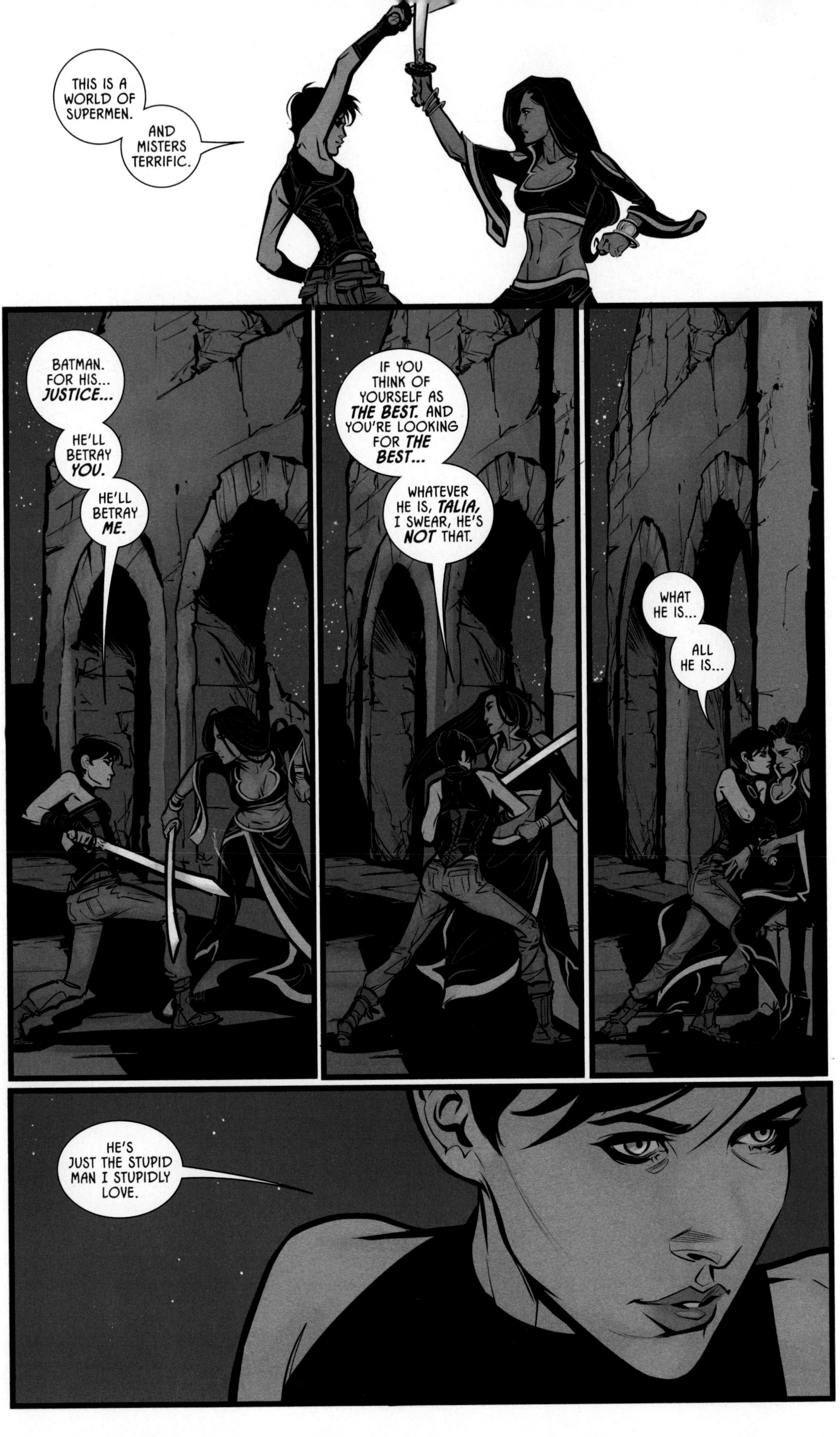
THIS IS A WORLD OF SUPERMEN.
AND MISTERS TERRIFIC.
BATMAN. FOR HIS... JUSTICE...
HE'LL BETRAY YOU.
HE'LL BETRAY ME.
IF YOU THINK OF YOURSELF AS THE BEST. AND YOU'RE LOOKING FOR THE BEST...
WHATEVER HE IS, TALIA, I SWEAR, HE'S NOT THAT.
WHAT HE IS...
ALL HE IS...
HE'S JUST THE STUPID MAN I STUPIDLY LOVE.

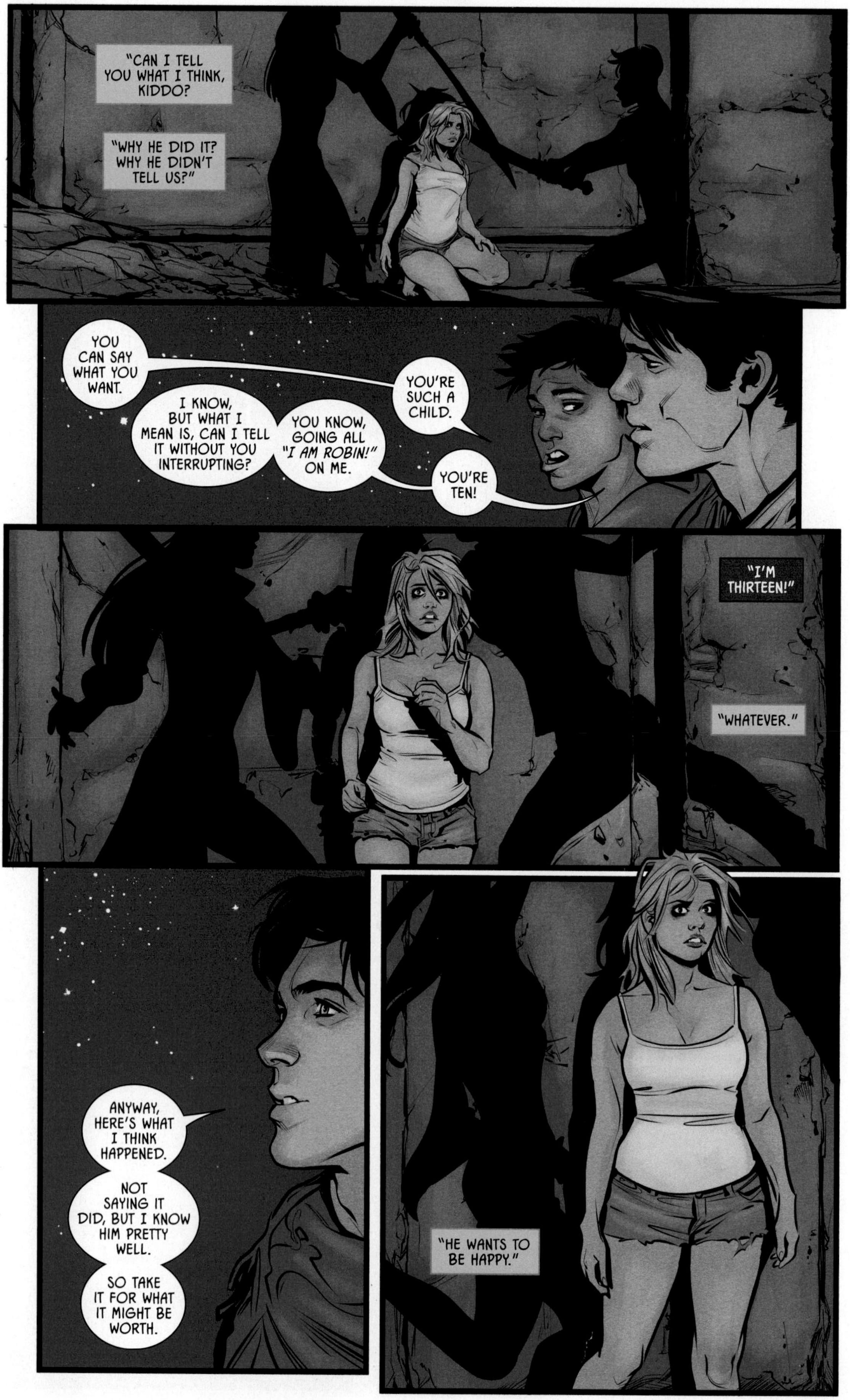
"CAN I TELL YOU WHAT I THINK, KIDDO?
"WHY HE DID IT? WHY HE DIDN'T TELL US?"
YOU CAN SAY WHAT YOU WANT.
YOU'RE SUCH A CHILD.
I KNOW, BUT WHAT I MEAN IS, CAN I TELL IT WITHOUT YOU INTERRUPTING?
YOU KNOW, GOING ALL *"I AM ROBIN!"* ON ME.
YOU'RE TEN!
"I'M THIRTEEN!"
"WHATEVER."
ANYWAY, HERE'S WHAT I THINK HAPPENED.
NOT SAYING IT DID, BUT I KNOW HIM PRETTY WELL.
SO TAKE IT FOR WHAT IT MIGHT BE WORTH.
"HE WANTS TO BE HAPPY."

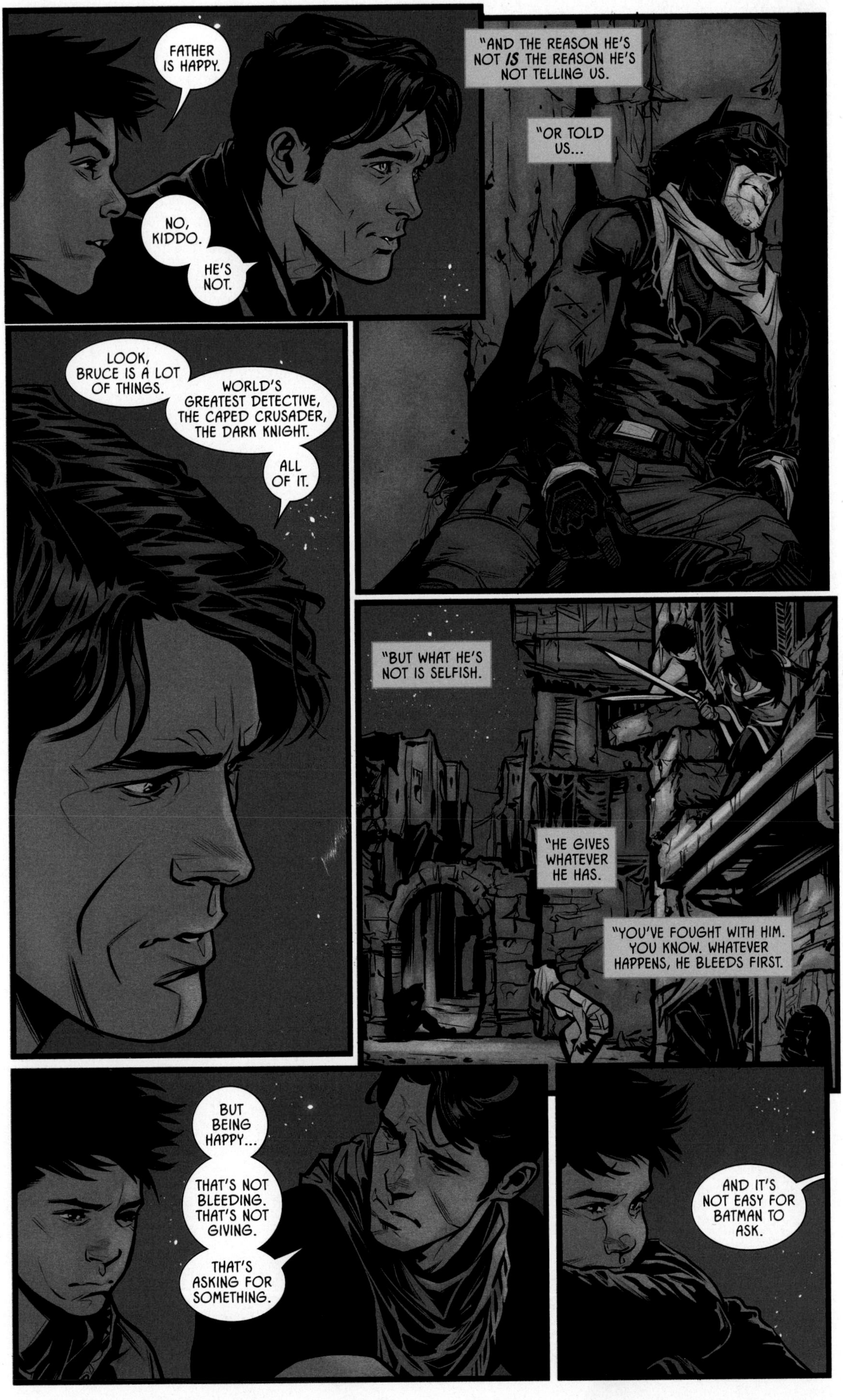
FATHER IS HAPPY.
NO, KIDDO.
HE'S NOT.
"AND THE REASON HE'S NOT *IS* THE REASON HE'S NOT TELLING US.
"OR TOLD US...
LOOK, BRUCE IS A LOT OF THINGS.
WORLD'S GREATEST DETECTIVE, THE CAPED CRUSADER, THE DARK KNIGHT.
ALL OF IT.
"BUT WHAT HE'S NOT IS SELFISH.
"HE GIVES WHATEVER HE HAS.
"YOU'VE FOUGHT WITH HIM. YOU KNOW. WHATEVER HAPPENS, HE BLEEDS FIRST.
BUT BEING HAPPY...
THAT'S NOT BLEEDING. THAT'S NOT GIVING.
THAT'S ASKING FOR SOMETHING.
AND IT'S NOT EASY FOR BATMAN TO ASK.

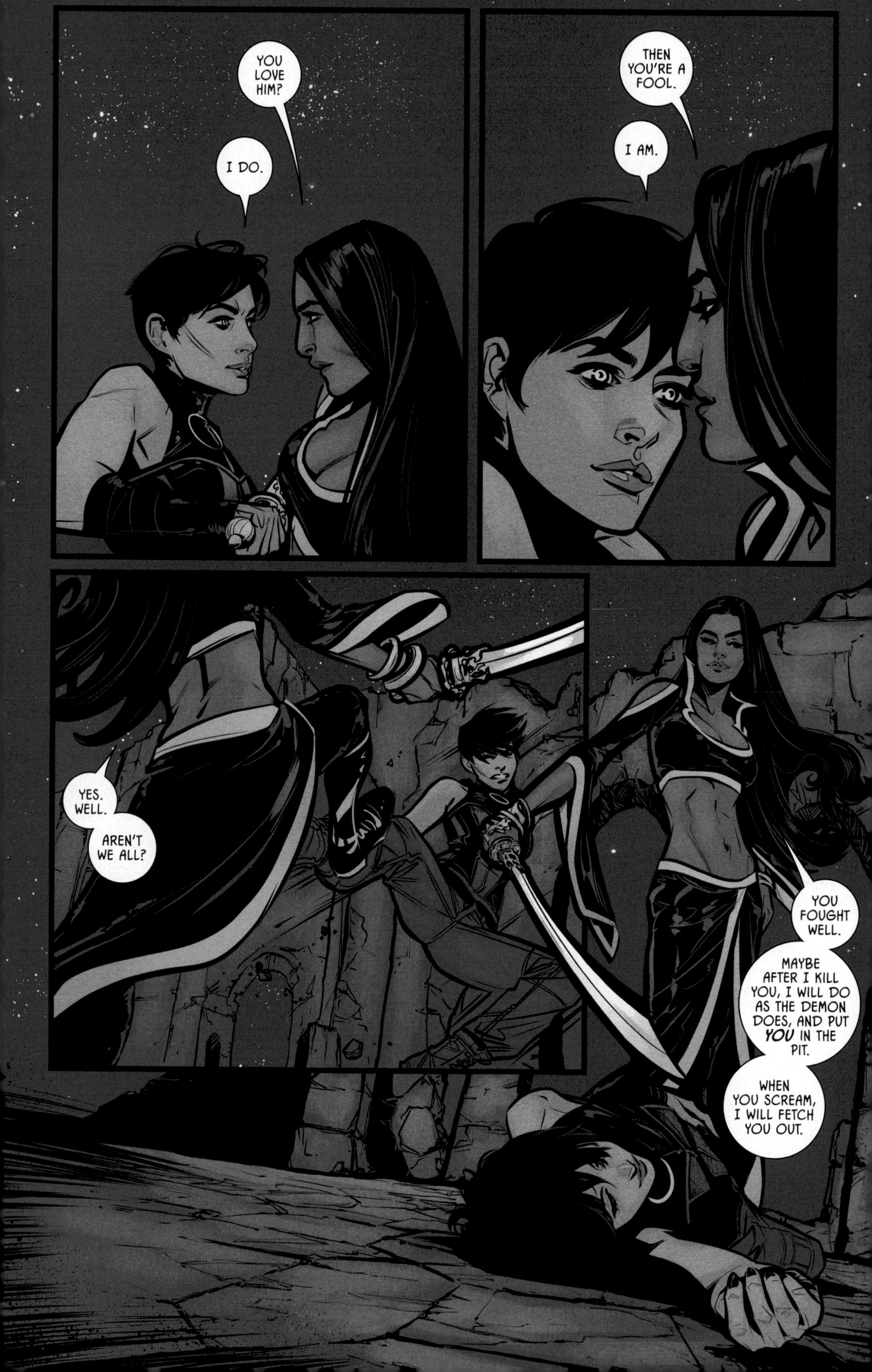

YOU LOVE HIM?
I DO.
THEN YOU'RE A FOOL.
I AM.
YES. WELL.
AREN'T WE ALL?
YOU FOUGHT WELL.
MAYBE AFTER I KILL YOU, I WILL DO AS THE DEMON DOES, AND PUT *YOU* IN THE PIT.
WHEN YOU SCREAM, I WILL FETCH YOU OUT.

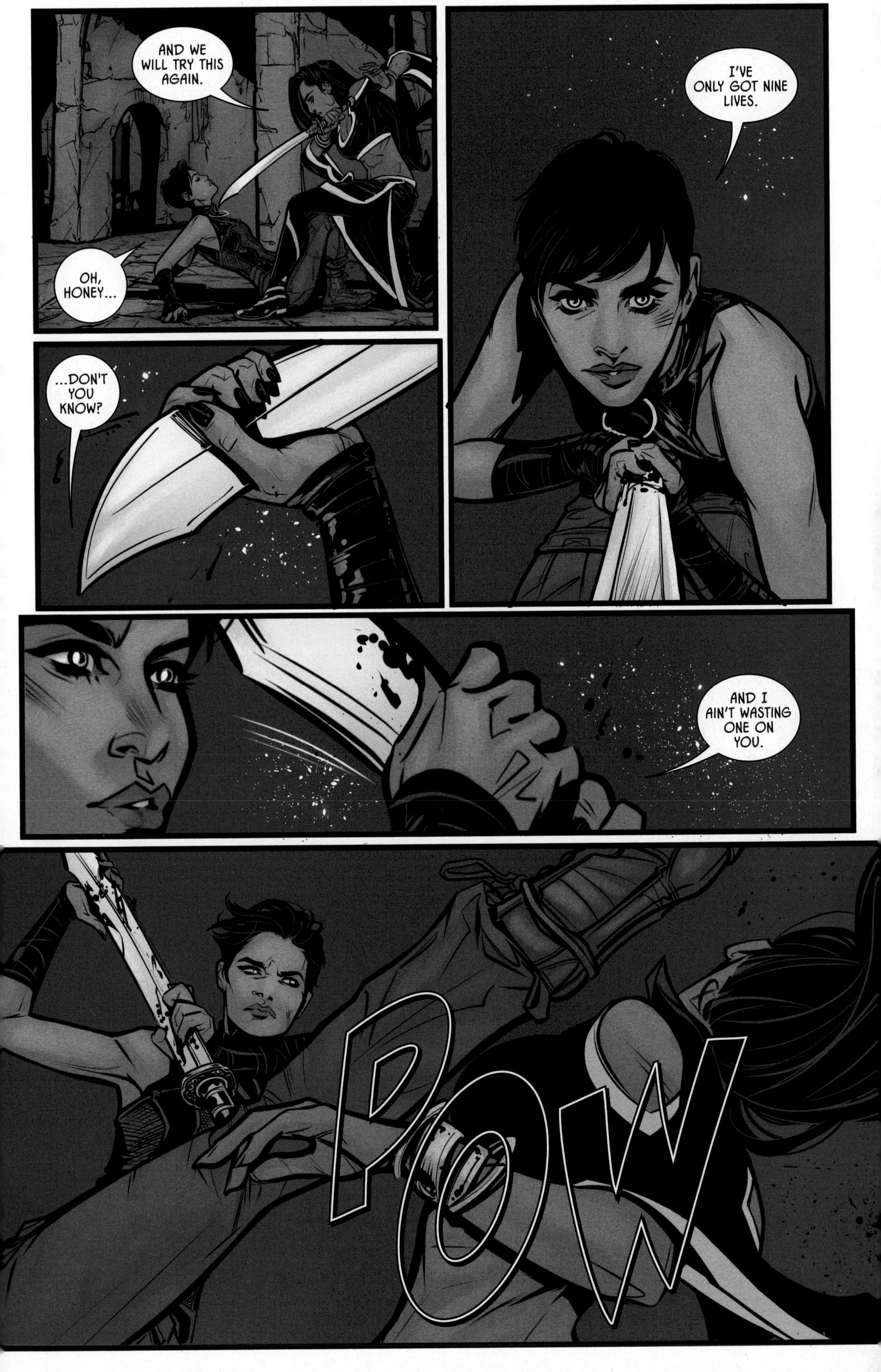
AND WE WILL TRY THIS AGAIN.
OH, HONEY...
I'VE ONLY GOT NINE LIVES.
...DON'T YOU KNOW?
AND I AIN'T WASTING ONE ON YOU.
POW

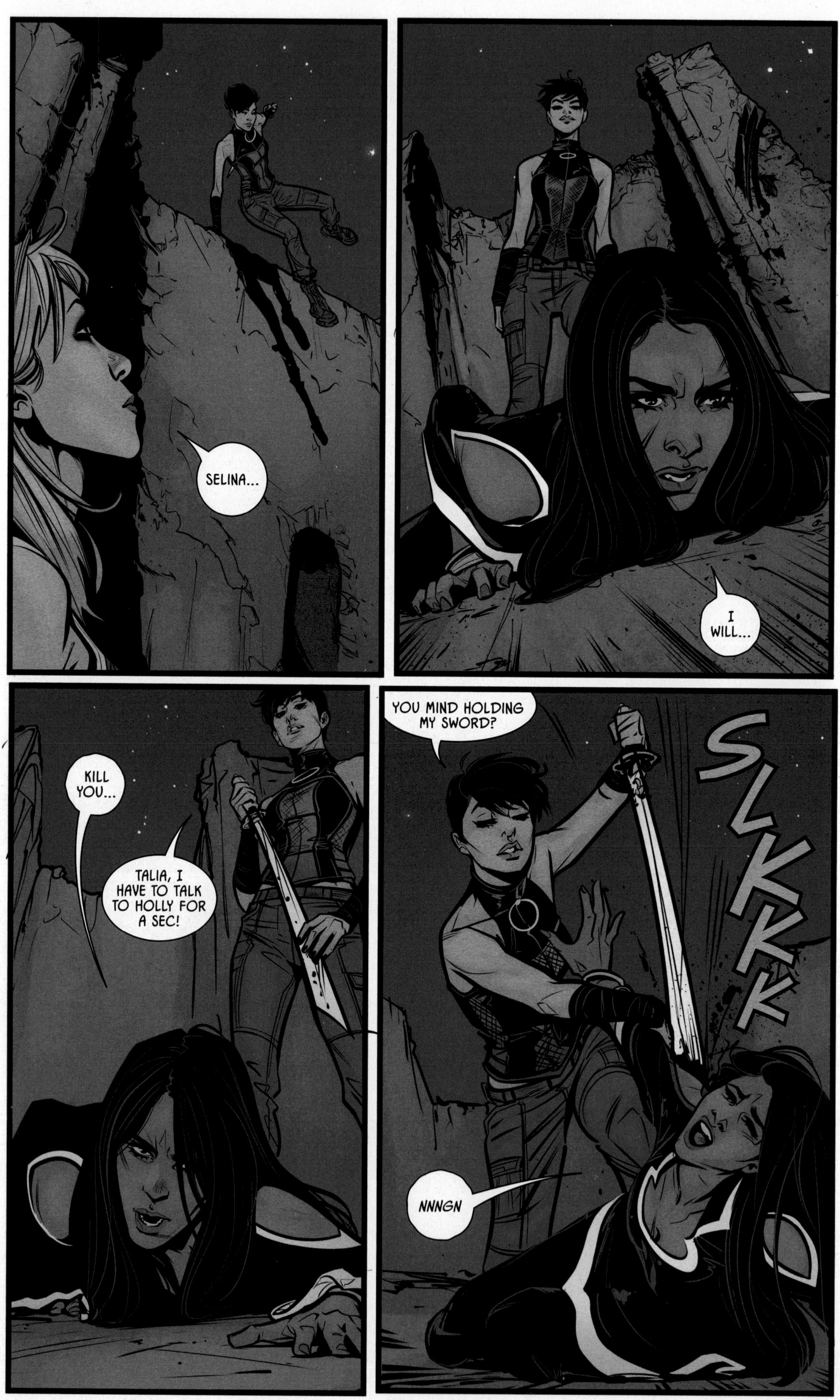
SELINA...
I WILL...
KILL YOU...
TALIA, I HAVE TO TALK TO HOLLY FOR A SEC!
YOU MIND HOLDING MY SWORD?
SLKKK
NNNGN

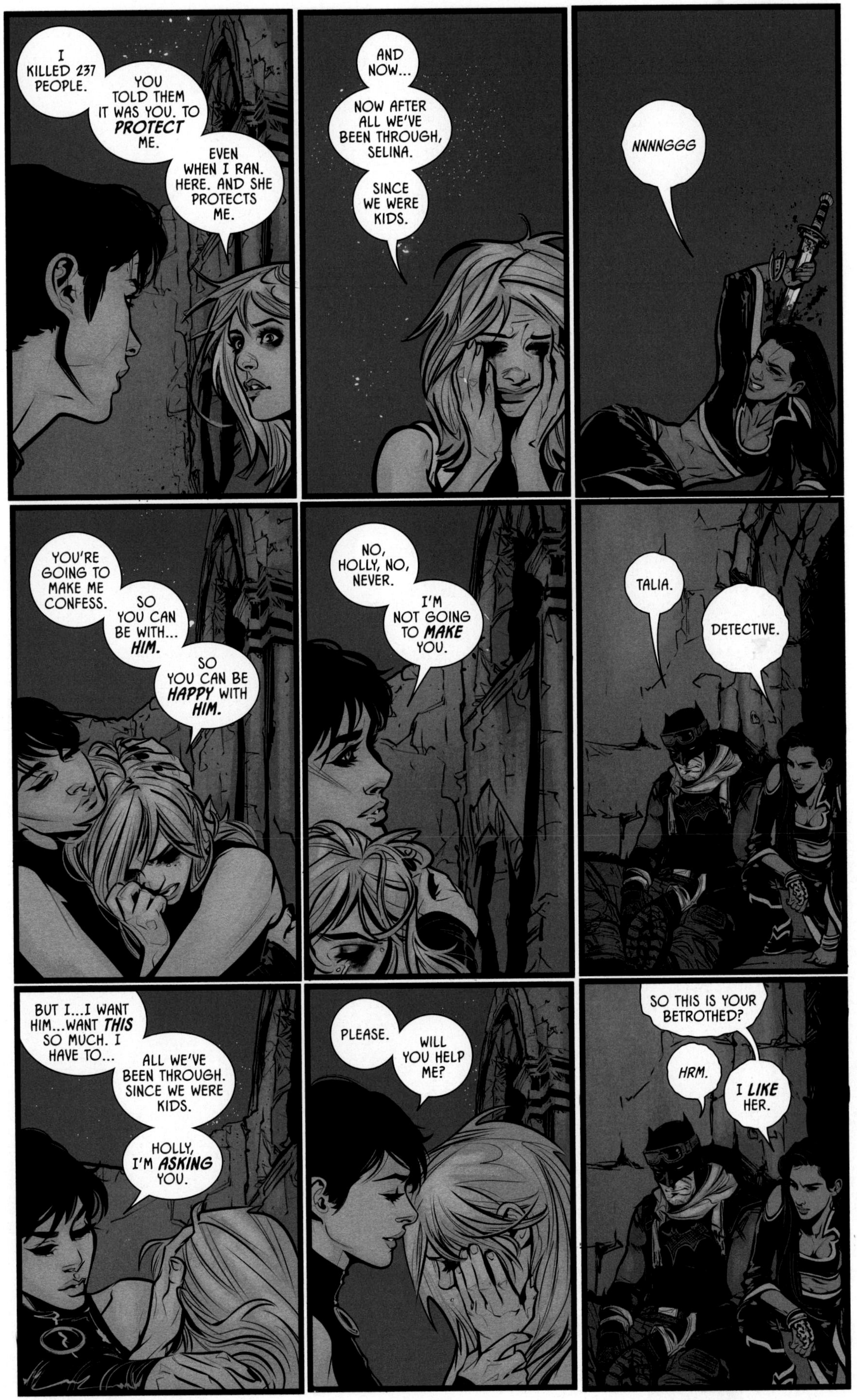
I KILLED 237 PEOPLE.
YOU TOLD THEM IT WAS YOU. TO *PROTECT* ME.
EVEN WHEN I RAN. HERE. AND SHE PROTECTS ME.
AND NOW...
NOW AFTER ALL WE'VE BEEN THROUGH, SELINA.
SINCE WE WERE KIDS.
NNNNGGG
YOU'RE GOING TO MAKE ME CONFESS.
SO YOU CAN BE WITH... *HIM.*
SO YOU CAN BE *HAPPY* WITH *HIM.*
NO, HOLLY, NO, NEVER.
I'M NOT GOING TO *MAKE* YOU.
TALIA.
DETECTIVE.
BUT I...I WANT HIM...WANT *THIS* SO MUCH. I HAVE TO...
ALL WE'VE BEEN THROUGH. SINCE WE WERE KIDS.
HOLLY, I'M *ASKING* YOU.
PLEASE.
WILL YOU HELP ME?
SO THIS IS YOUR BETROTHED?
HRM.
I *LIKE* HER.

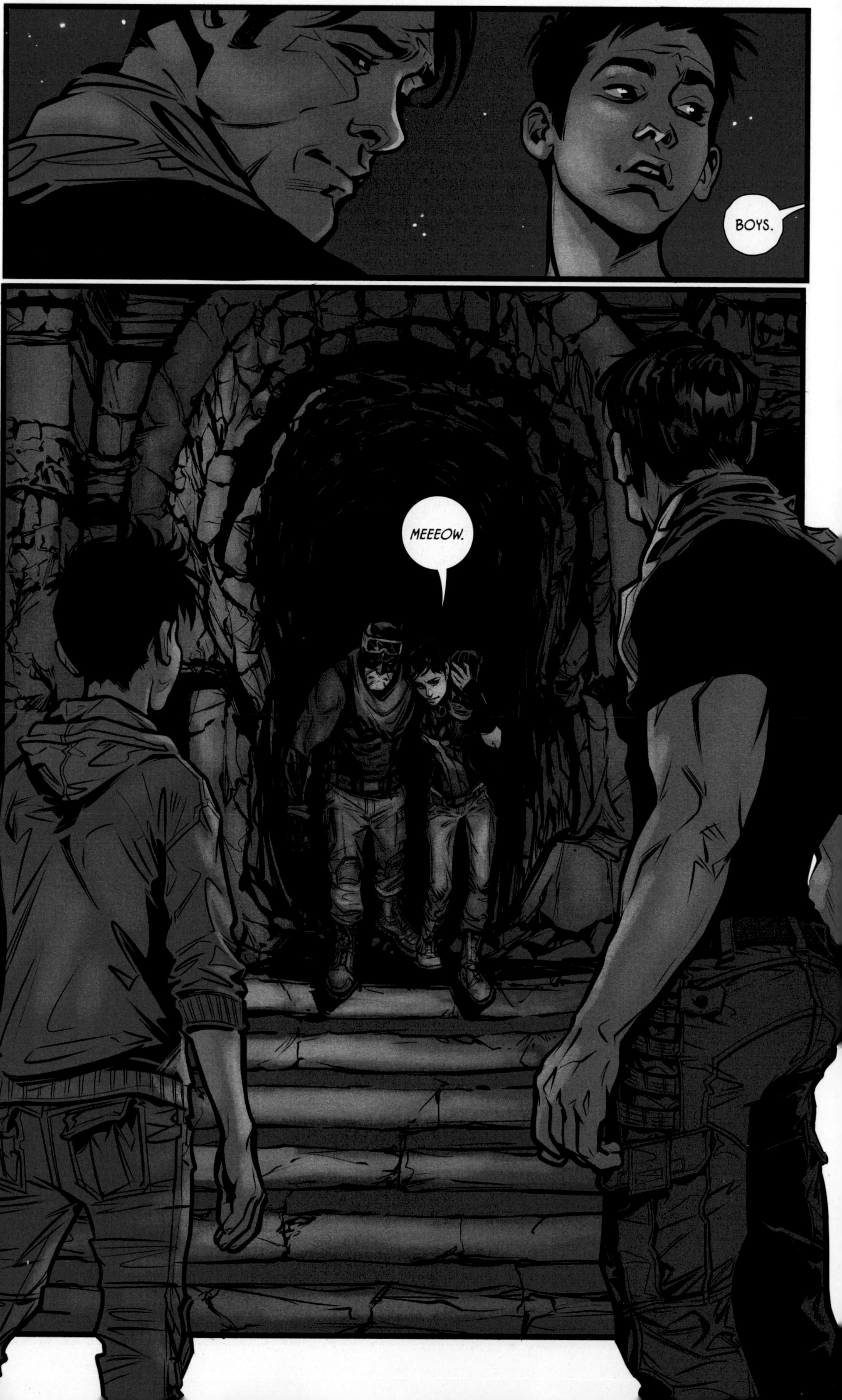
BOYS.
MEEEOW.

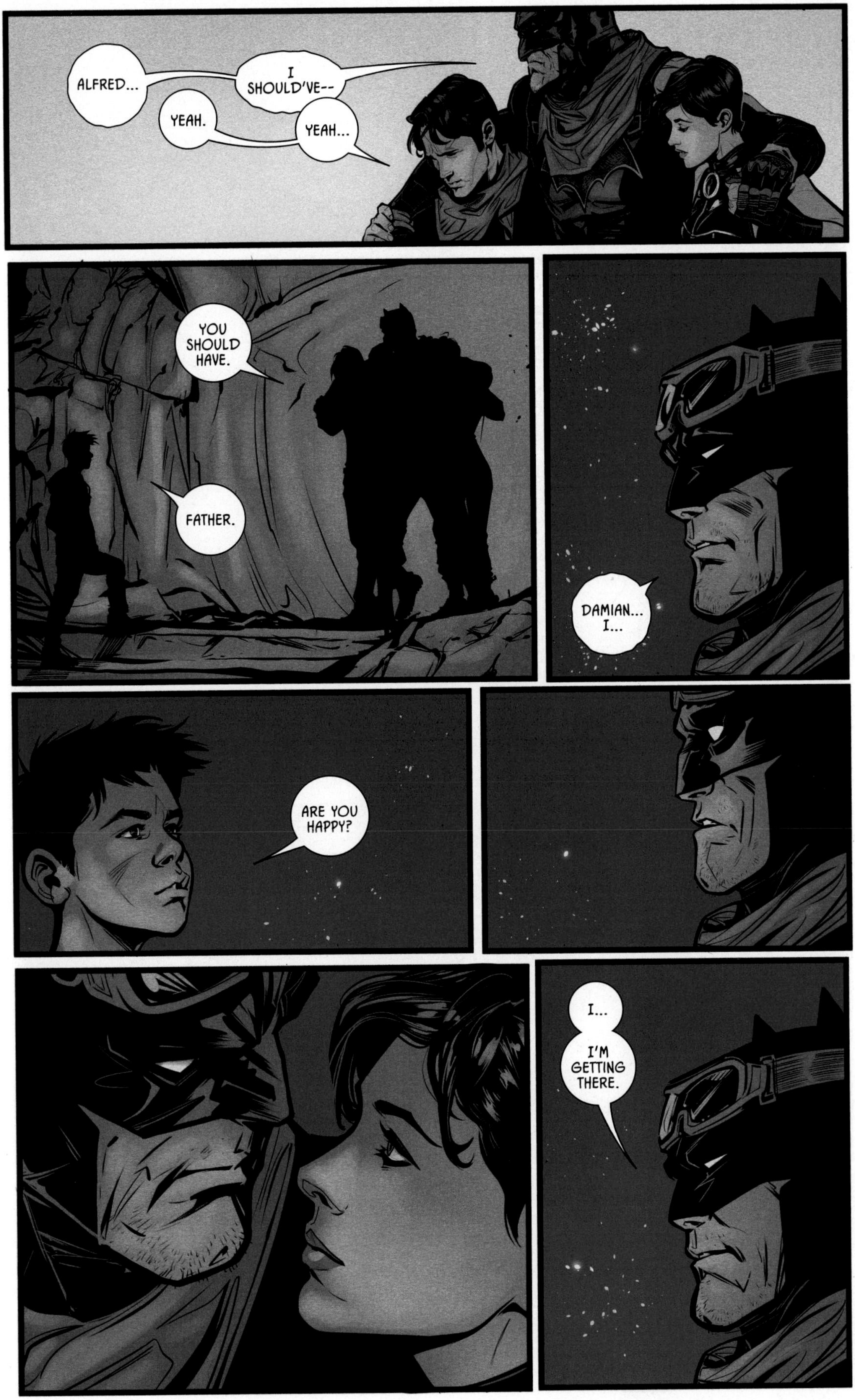
ALFRED...
I SHOULD'VE--
YEAH.
YEAH...
YOU SHOULD HAVE.
FATHER.
DAMIAN... I...
ARE YOU HAPPY?
I...
I'M GETTING THERE.

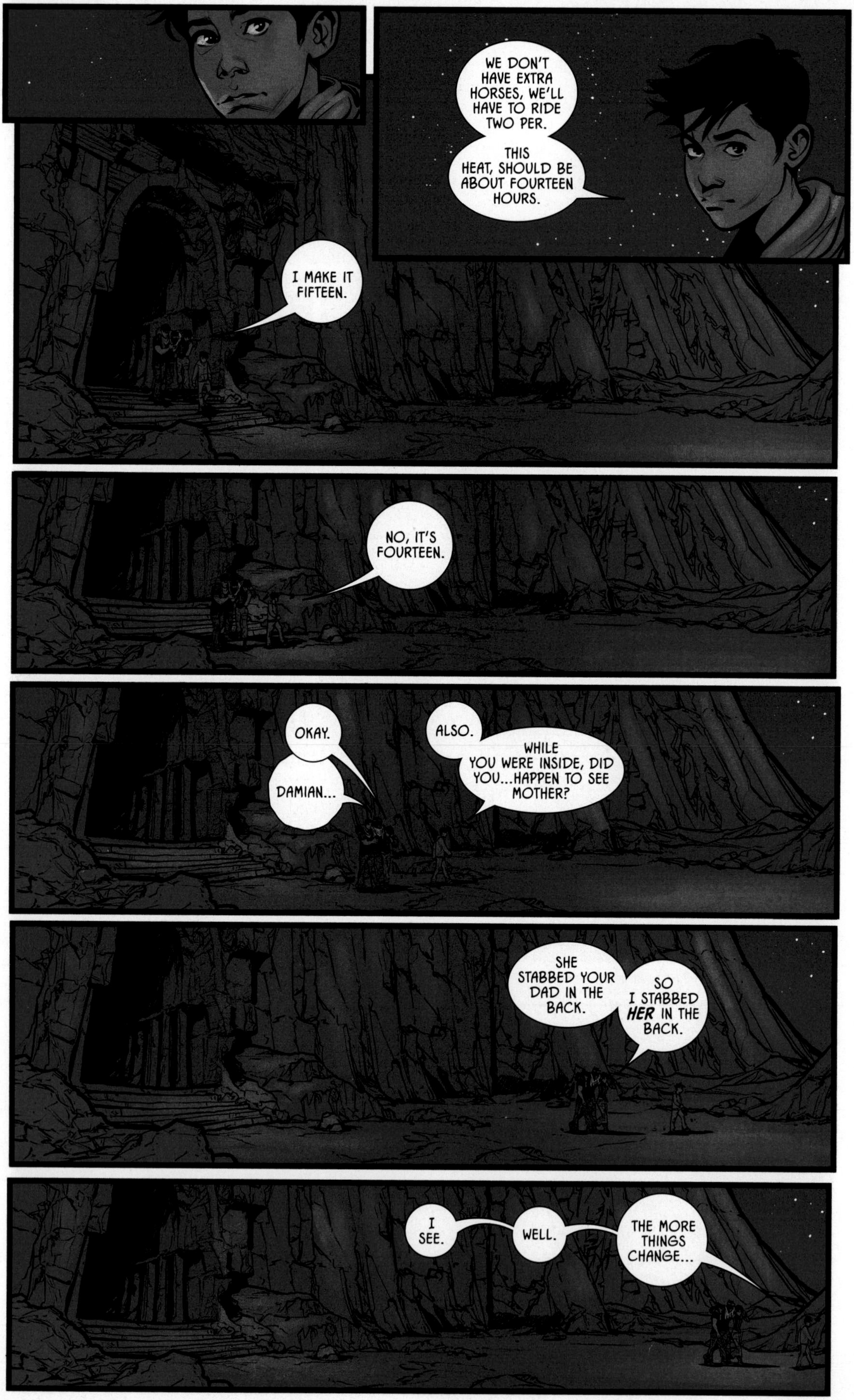
WE DON'T HAVE EXTRA HORSES, WE'LL HAVE TO RIDE TWO PER.
THIS HEAT, SHOULD BE ABOUT FOURTEEN HOURS.
I MAKE IT FIFTEEN.
NO, IT'S FOURTEEN.
OKAY.
DAMIAN...
ALSO.
WHILE YOU WERE INSIDE, DID YOU...HAPPEN TO SEE MOTHER?
SHE STABBED YOUR DAD IN THE BACK.
SO I STABBED **HER** IN THE BACK.
I SEE.
WELL.
THE MORE THINGS CHANGE...

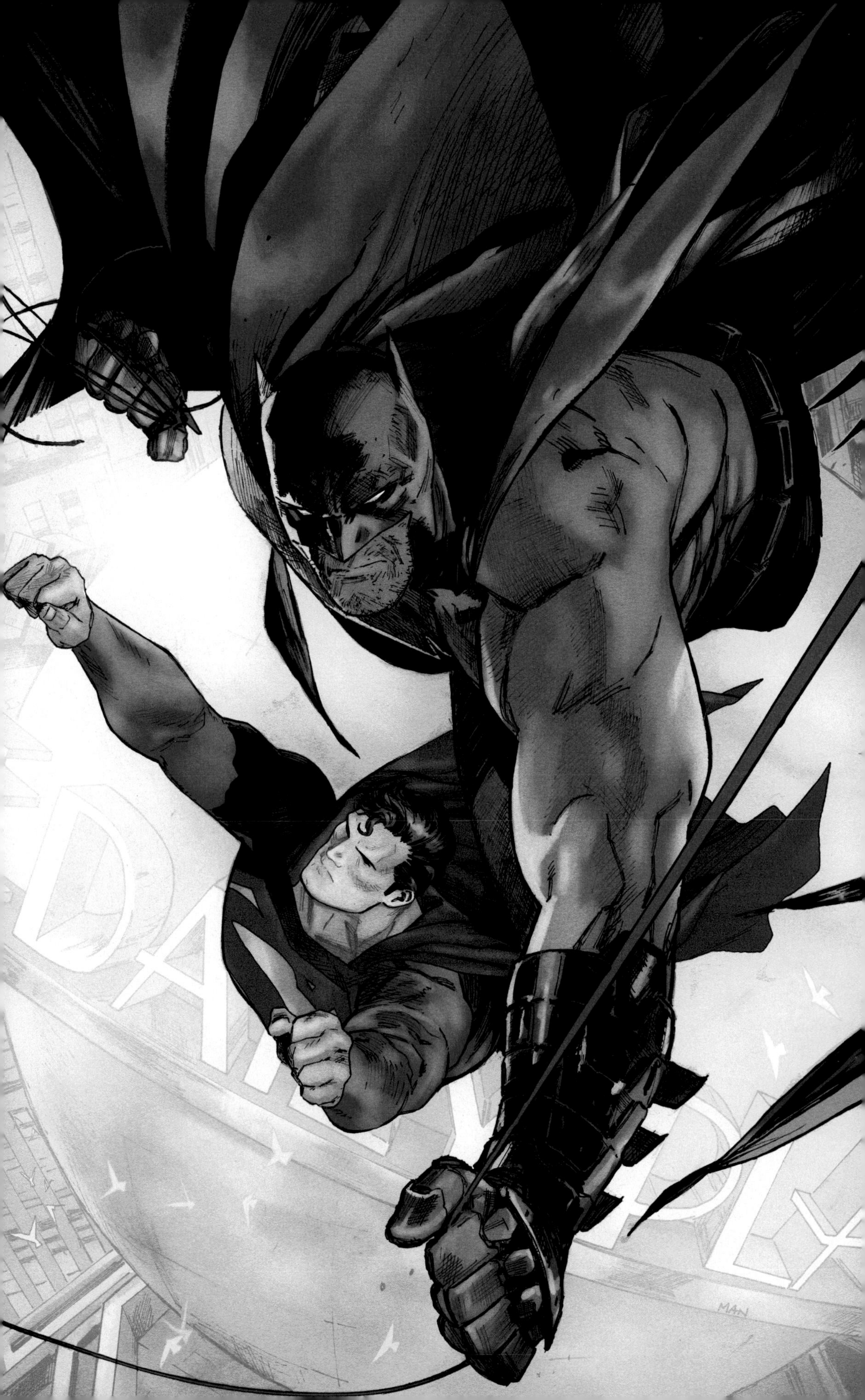

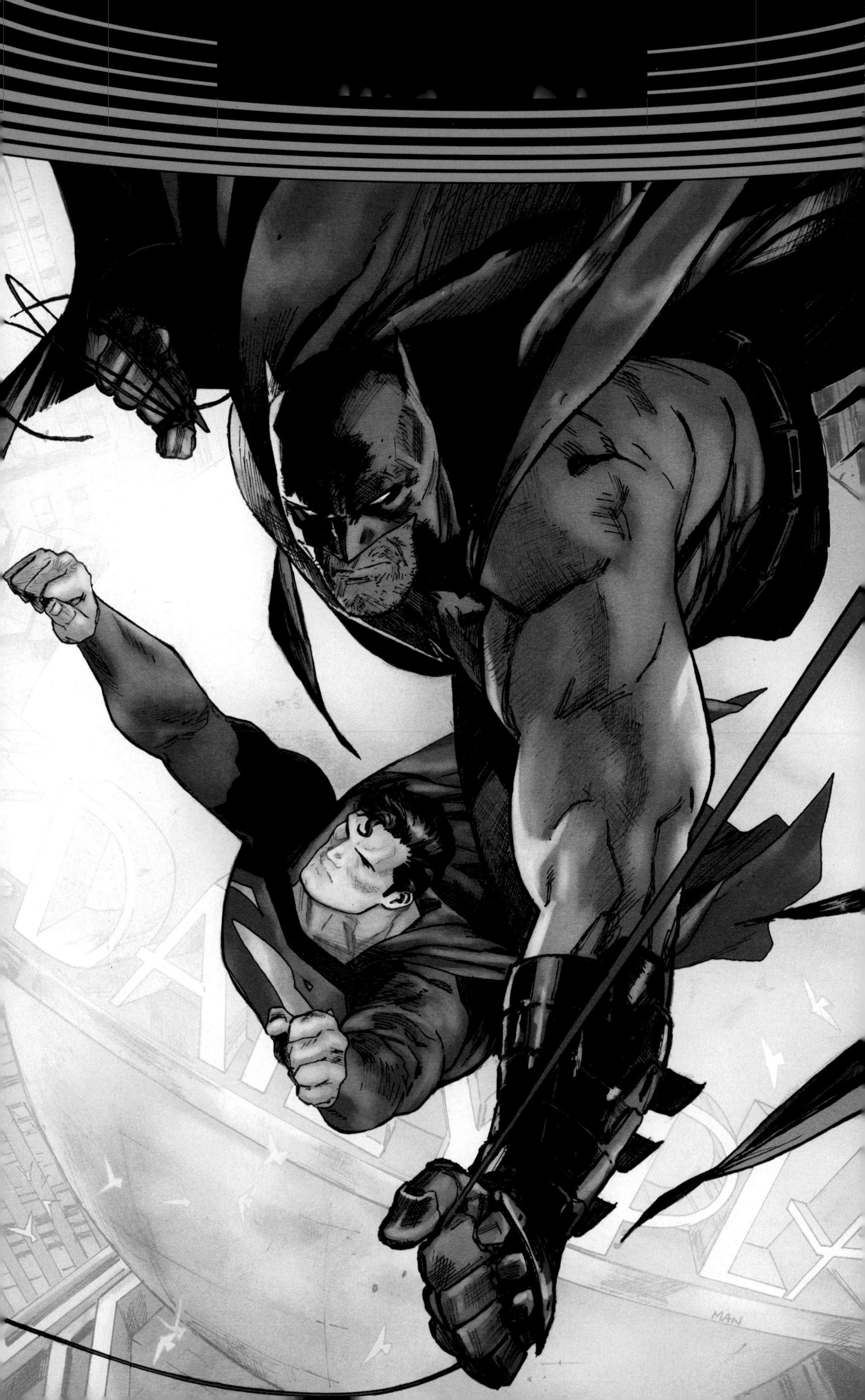

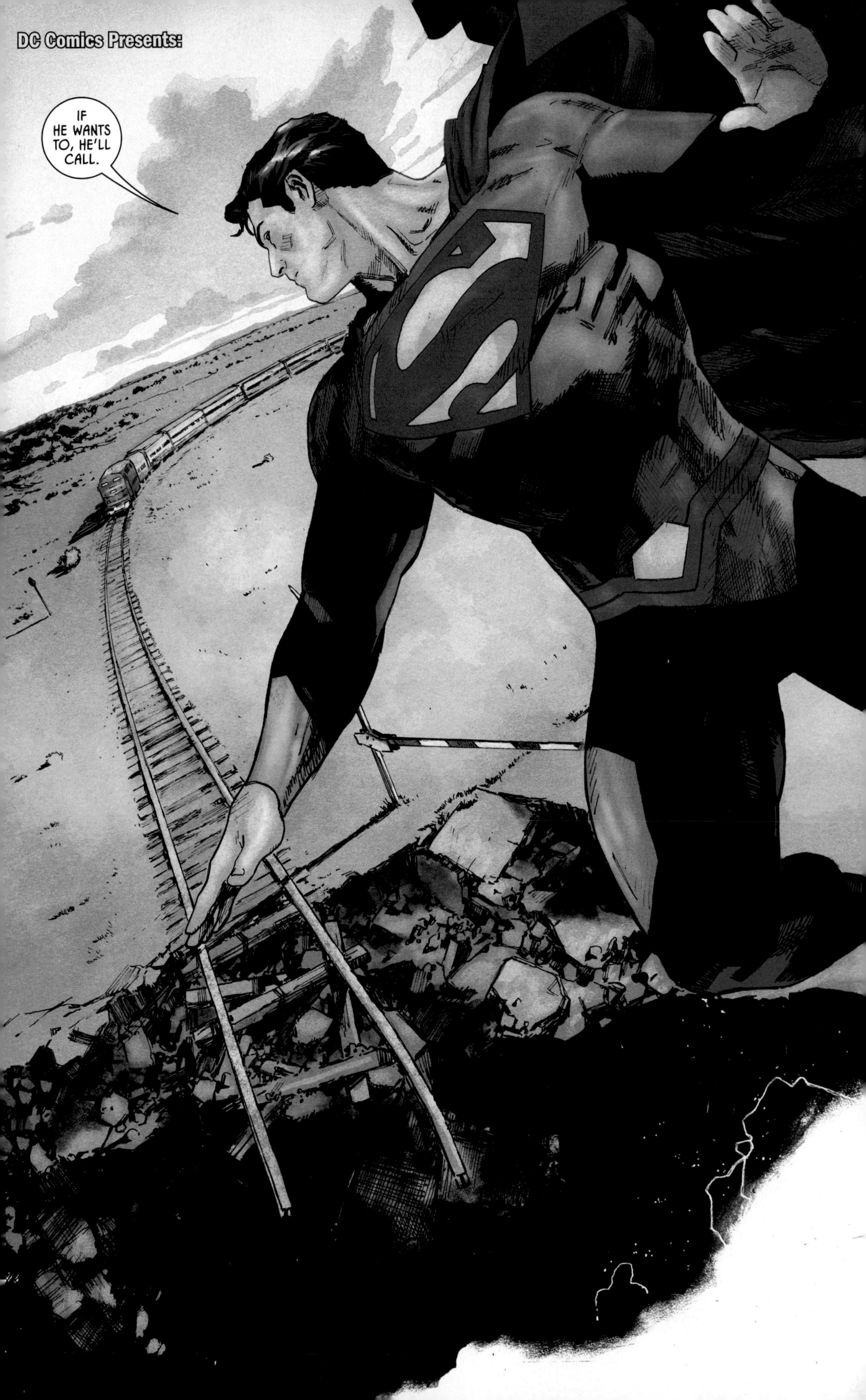
IF HE WANTS TO, HE'LL CALL.

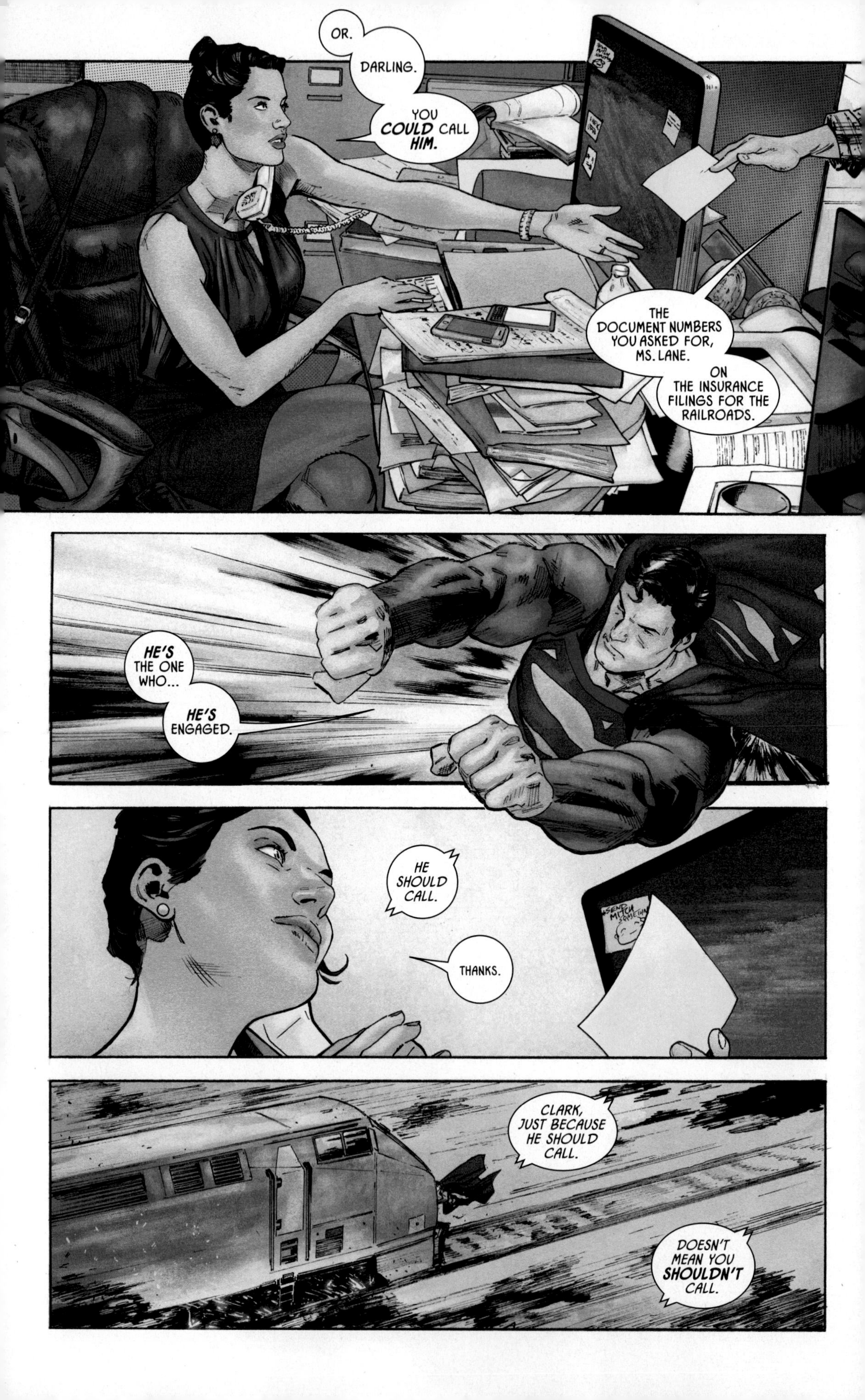
OR.
DARLING.
YOU COULD CALL HIM.
THE DOCUMENT NUMBERS YOU ASKED FOR, MS. LANE.
ON THE INSURANCE FILINGS FOR THE RAILROADS.
HE'S THE ONE WHO...
HE'S ENGAGED.
HE SHOULD CALL.
THANKS.
CLARK, JUST BECAUSE HE SHOULD CALL.
DOESN'T MEAN YOU SHOULDN'T CALL.

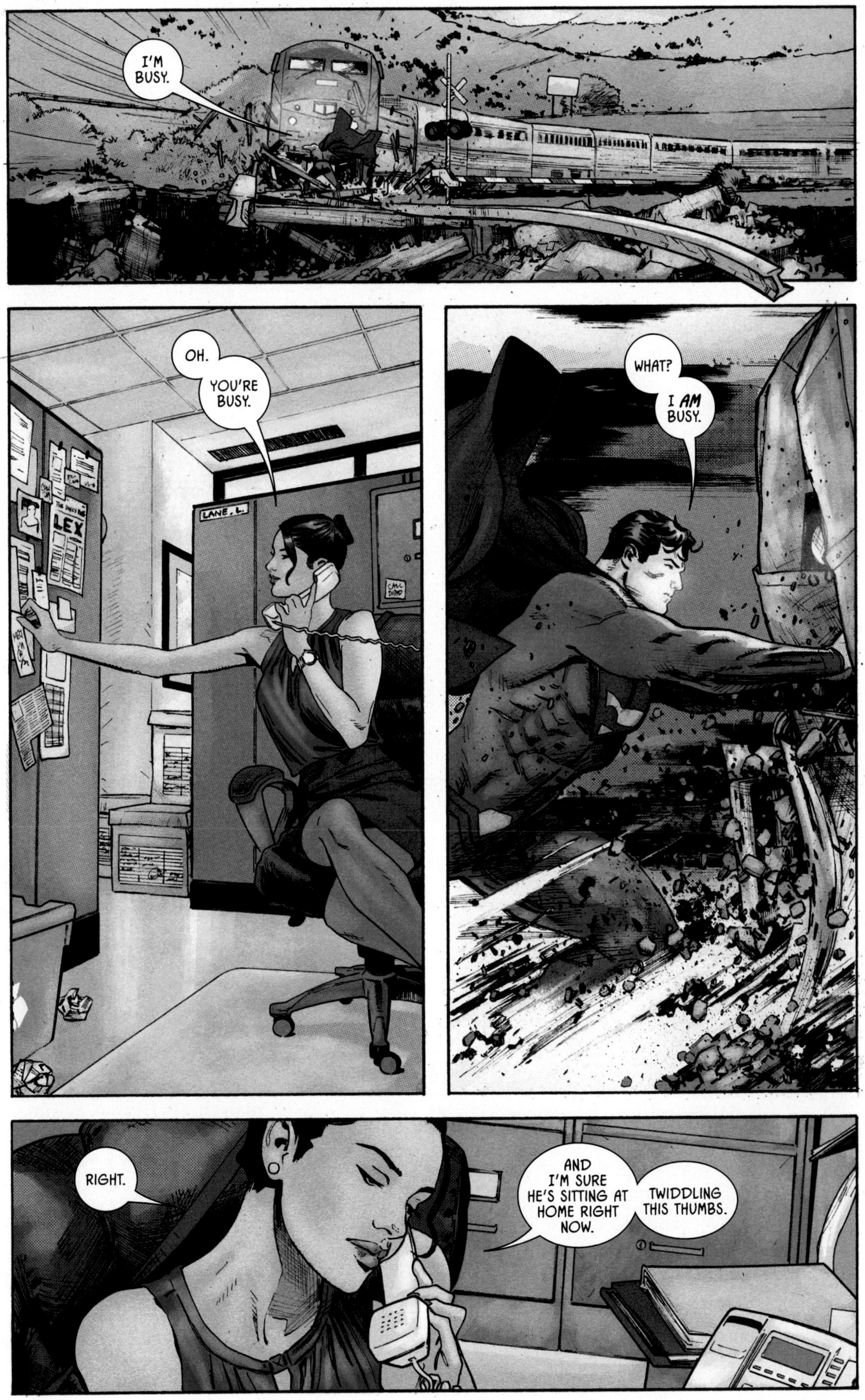
I'M BUSY.
OH.
YOU'RE BUSY.
WHAT?
I *AM* BUSY.
RIGHT.
AND I'M SURE HE'S SITTING AT HOME RIGHT NOW.
TWIDDLING THIS THUMBS.

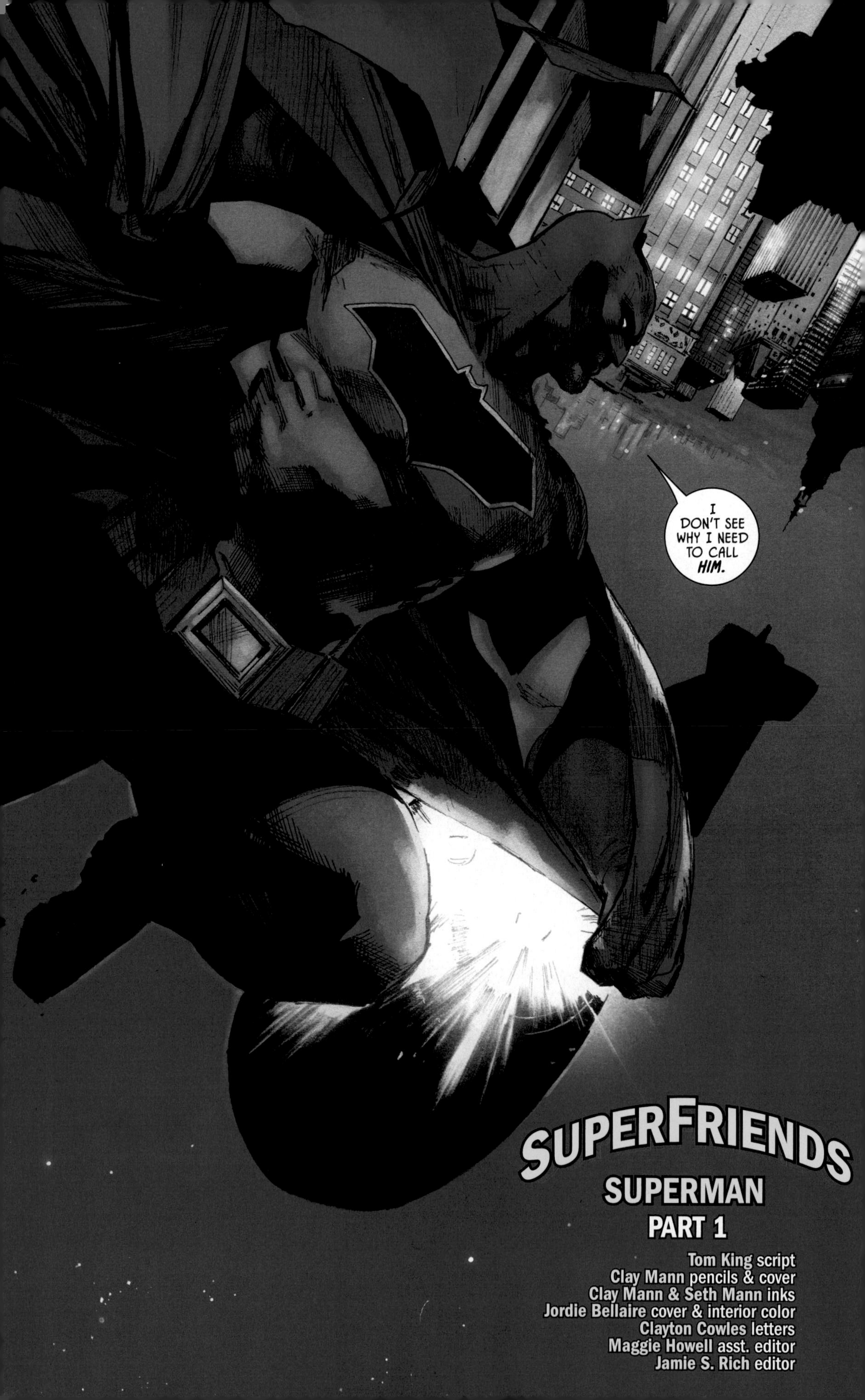
I DON'T SEE WHY I NEED TO CALL *HIM.*

SUPERFRIENDS

SUPERMAN

PART 1

Tom King script
Clay Mann pencils & cover
Clay Mann & Seth Mann inks
Jordie Bellaire cover & interior color
Clayton Cowles letters
Maggie Howell asst. editor
Jamie S. Rich editor

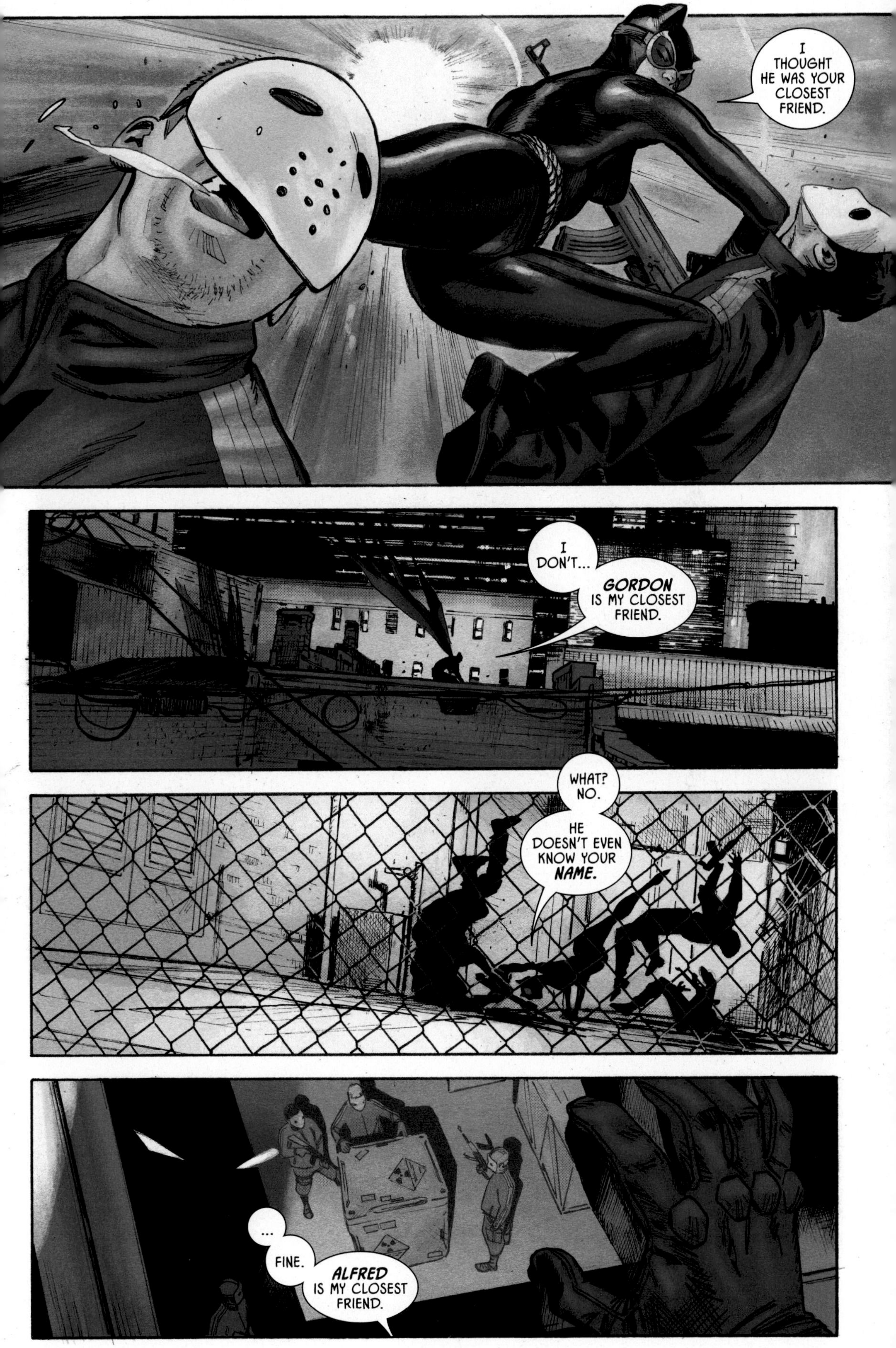
I THOUGHT HE WAS YOUR CLOSEST FRIEND.
I DON'T...
GORDON IS MY CLOSEST FRIEND.
WHAT? NO.
HE DOESN'T EVEN KNOW YOUR NAME.
...
FINE.
ALFRED IS MY CLOSEST FRIEND.

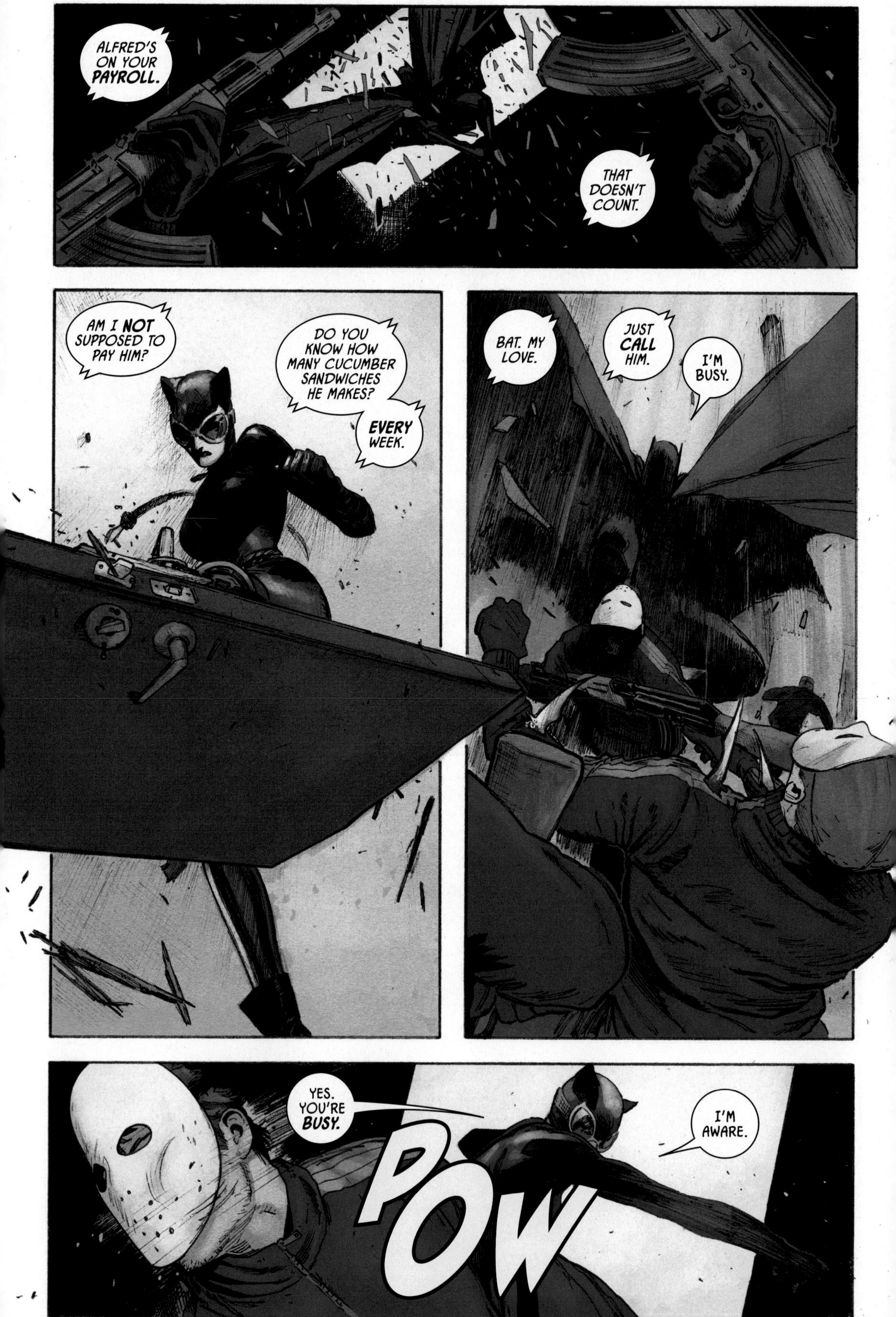
ALFRED'S ON YOUR PAYROLL.
THAT DOESN'T COUNT.
AM I NOT SUPPOSED TO PAY HIM?
DO YOU KNOW HOW MANY CUCUMBER SANDWICHES HE MAKES?
EVERY WEEK.
BAT. MY LOVE.
JUST CALL HIM.
I'M BUSY.
YES. YOU'RE BUSY.
I'M AWARE.
POW

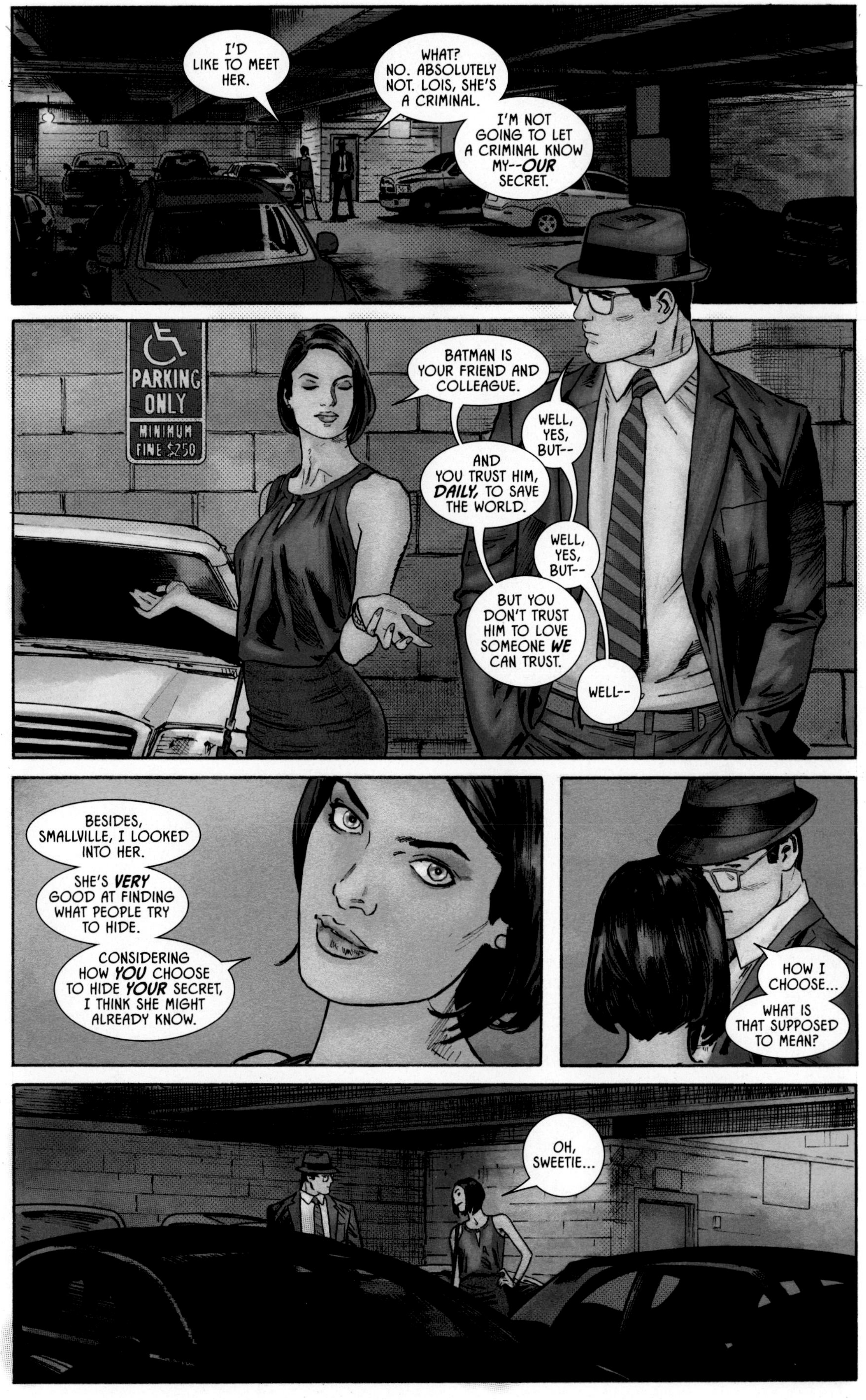
I'D LIKE TO MEET HER.
WHAT? NO. ABSOLUTELY NOT. LOIS, SHE'S A CRIMINAL.
I'M NOT GOING TO LET A CRIMINAL KNOW MY--*OUR* SECRET.
PARKING ONLY
MINIMUM FINE $250
BATMAN IS YOUR FRIEND AND COLLEAGUE.
WELL, YES, BUT--
AND YOU TRUST HIM, *DAILY,* TO SAVE THE WORLD.
WELL, YES, BUT--
BUT YOU DON'T TRUST HIM TO LOVE SOMEONE *WE* CAN TRUST.
WELL--
BESIDES, SMALLVILLE, I LOOKED INTO HER.
SHE'S *VERY* GOOD AT FINDING WHAT PEOPLE TRY TO HIDE.
CONSIDERING HOW *YOU* CHOOSE TO HIDE *YOUR* SECRET, I THINK SHE MIGHT ALREADY KNOW.
HOW I CHOOSE...
WHAT IS THAT SUPPOSED TO MEAN?
OH, SWEETIE...

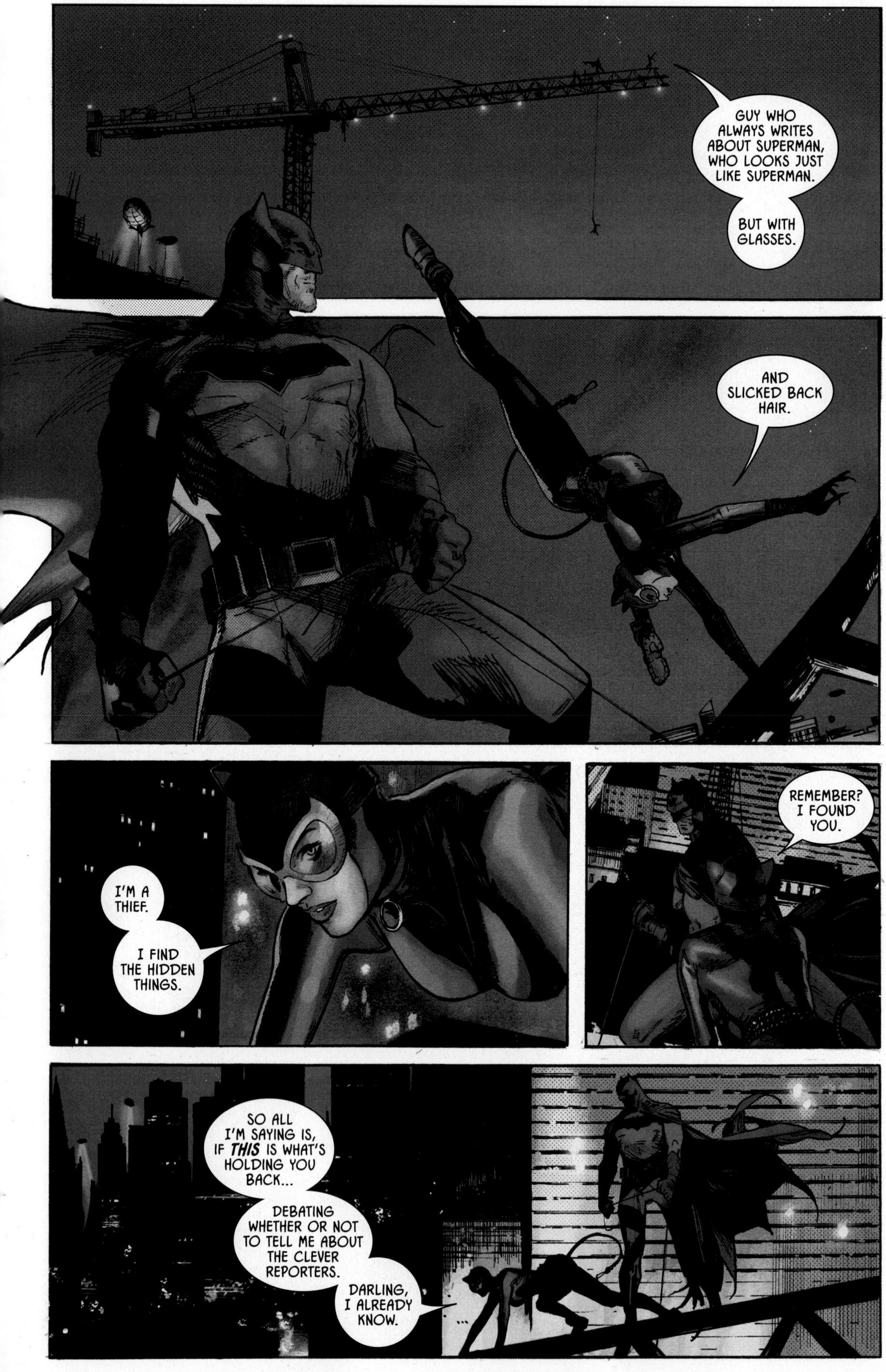
GUY WHO ALWAYS WRITES ABOUT SUPERMAN, WHO LOOKS JUST LIKE SUPERMAN.
BUT WITH GLASSES.
AND SLICKED BACK HAIR.
I'M A THIEF.
I FIND THE HIDDEN THINGS.
REMEMBER? I FOUND YOU.
SO ALL I'M SAYING IS, IF THIS IS WHAT'S HOLDING YOU BACK...
DEBATING WHETHER OR NOT TO TELL ME ABOUT THE CLEVER REPORTERS.
DARLING, I ALREADY KNOW.
...

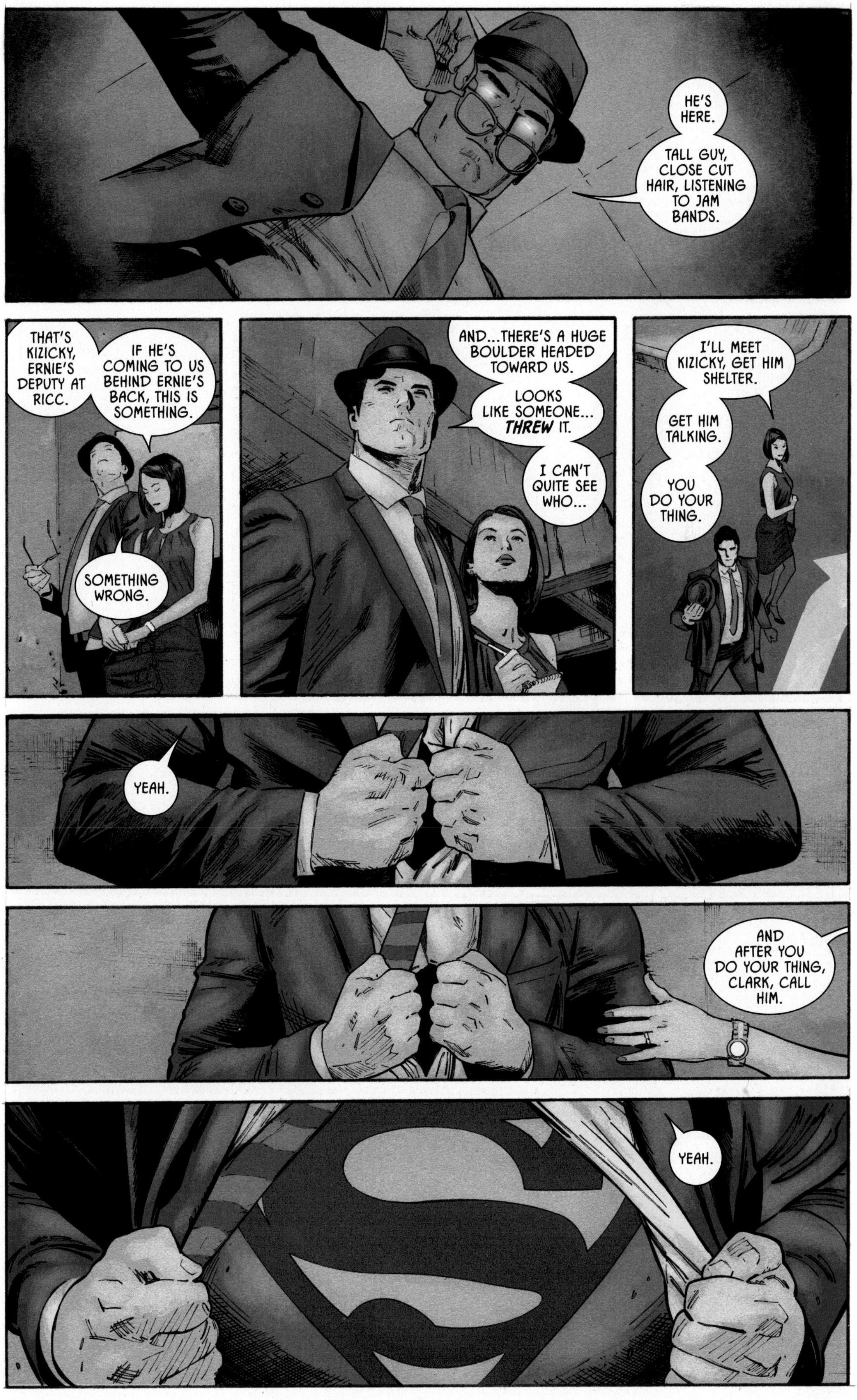
HE'S HERE.
TALL GUY, CLOSE CUT HAIR, LISTENING TO JAM BANDS.
THAT'S KIZICKY, ERNIE'S DEPUTY AT RICC.
IF HE'S COMING TO US BEHIND ERNIE'S BACK, THIS IS SOMETHING.
SOMETHING WRONG.
AND...THERE'S A HUGE BOULDER HEADED TOWARD US.
LOOKS LIKE SOMEONE... THREW IT.
I CAN'T QUITE SEE WHO...
I'LL MEET KIZICKY, GET HIM SHELTER.
GET HIM TALKING.
YOU DO YOUR THING.
YEAH.
AND AFTER YOU DO YOUR THING, CLARK, CALL HIM.
YEAH.

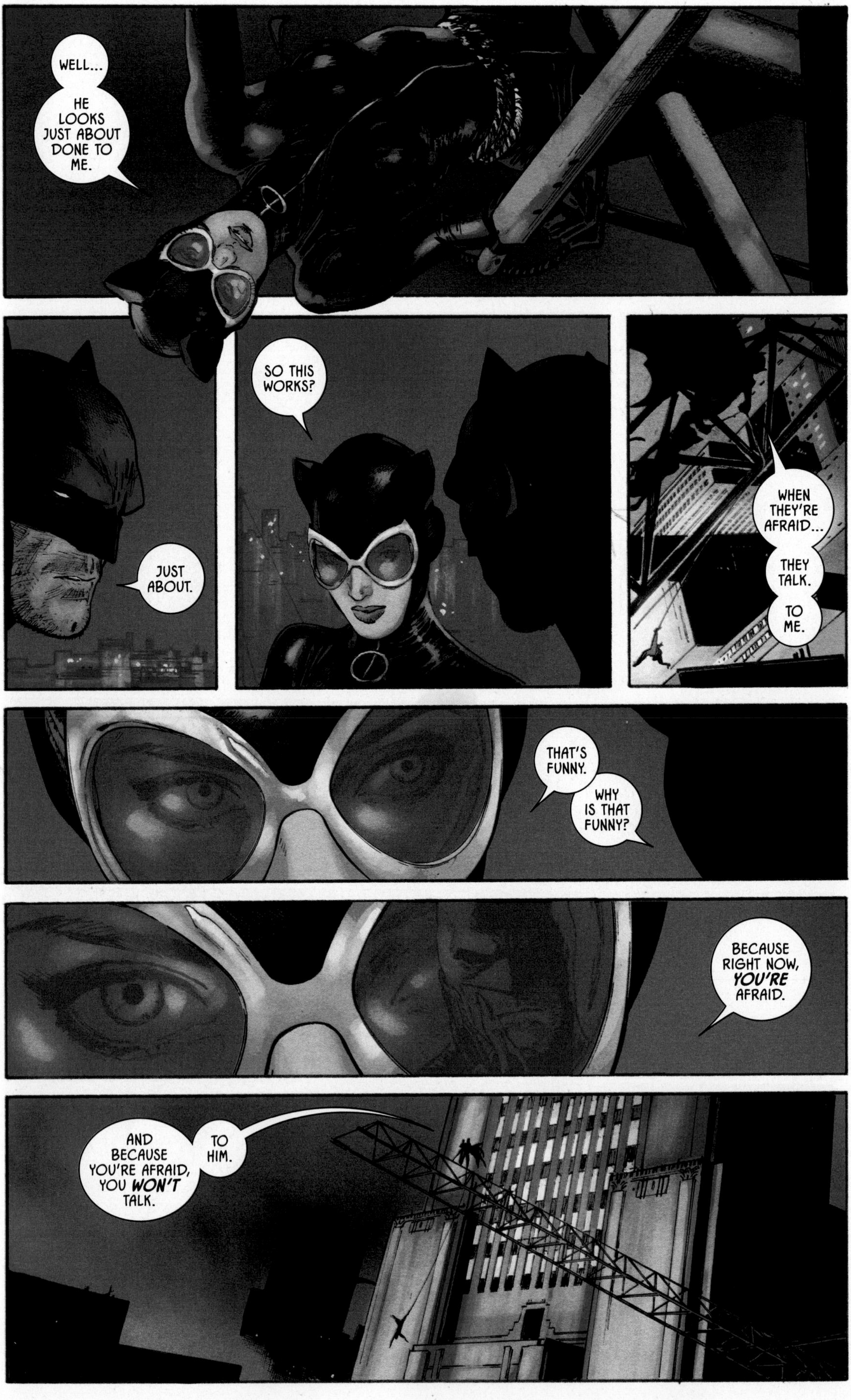
WELL...
HE LOOKS JUST ABOUT DONE TO ME.
JUST ABOUT.
SO THIS WORKS?
WHEN THEY'RE AFRAID...
THEY TALK.
TO ME.
THAT'S FUNNY.
WHY IS THAT FUNNY?
BECAUSE RIGHT NOW, ***YOU'RE*** AFRAID.
AND BECAUSE YOU'RE AFRAID, YOU ***WON'T*** TALK.
TO HIM.

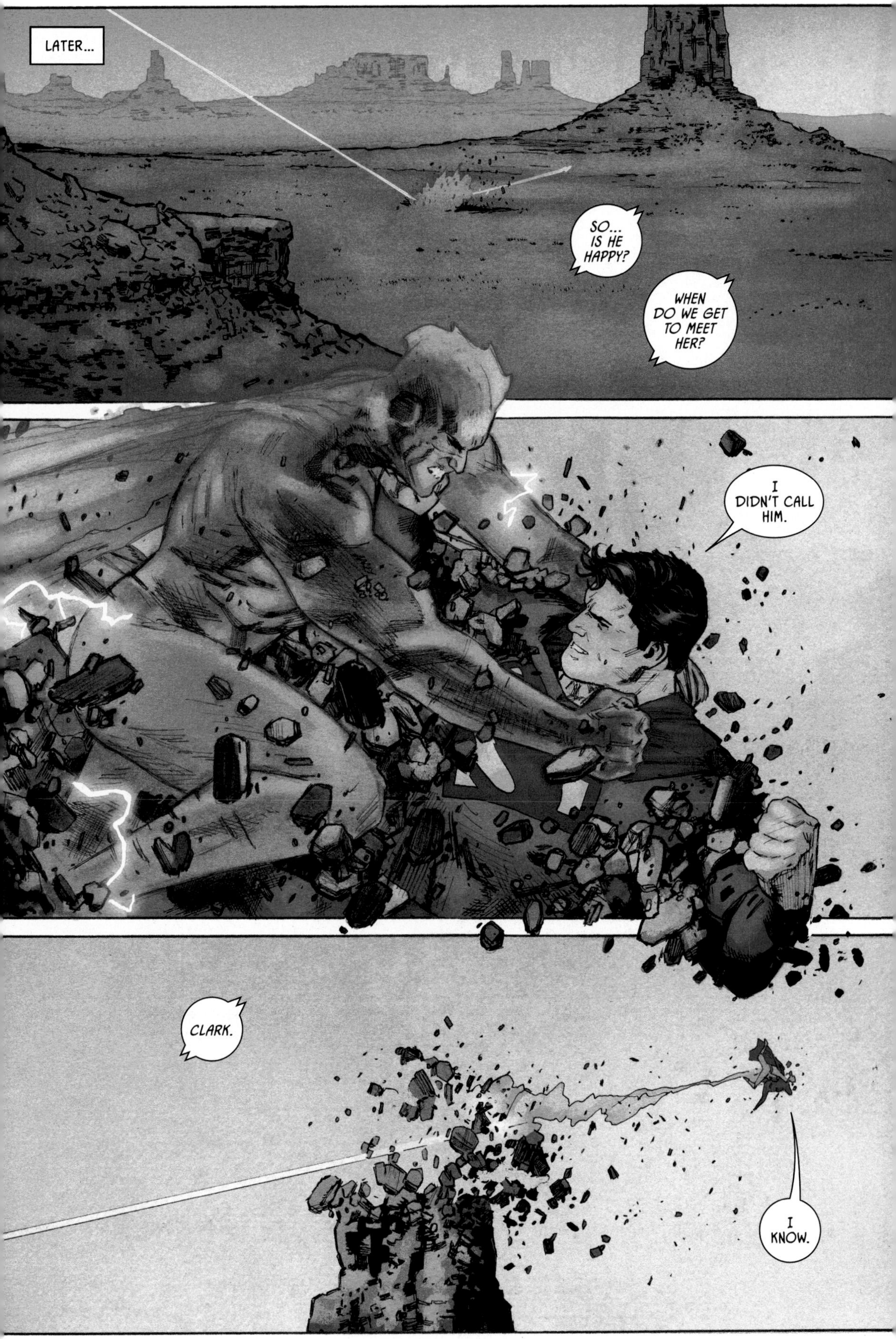
LATER...
SO... IS HE HAPPY?
WHEN DO WE GET TO MEET HER?
I DIDN'T CALL HIM.
CLARK.
I KNOW.

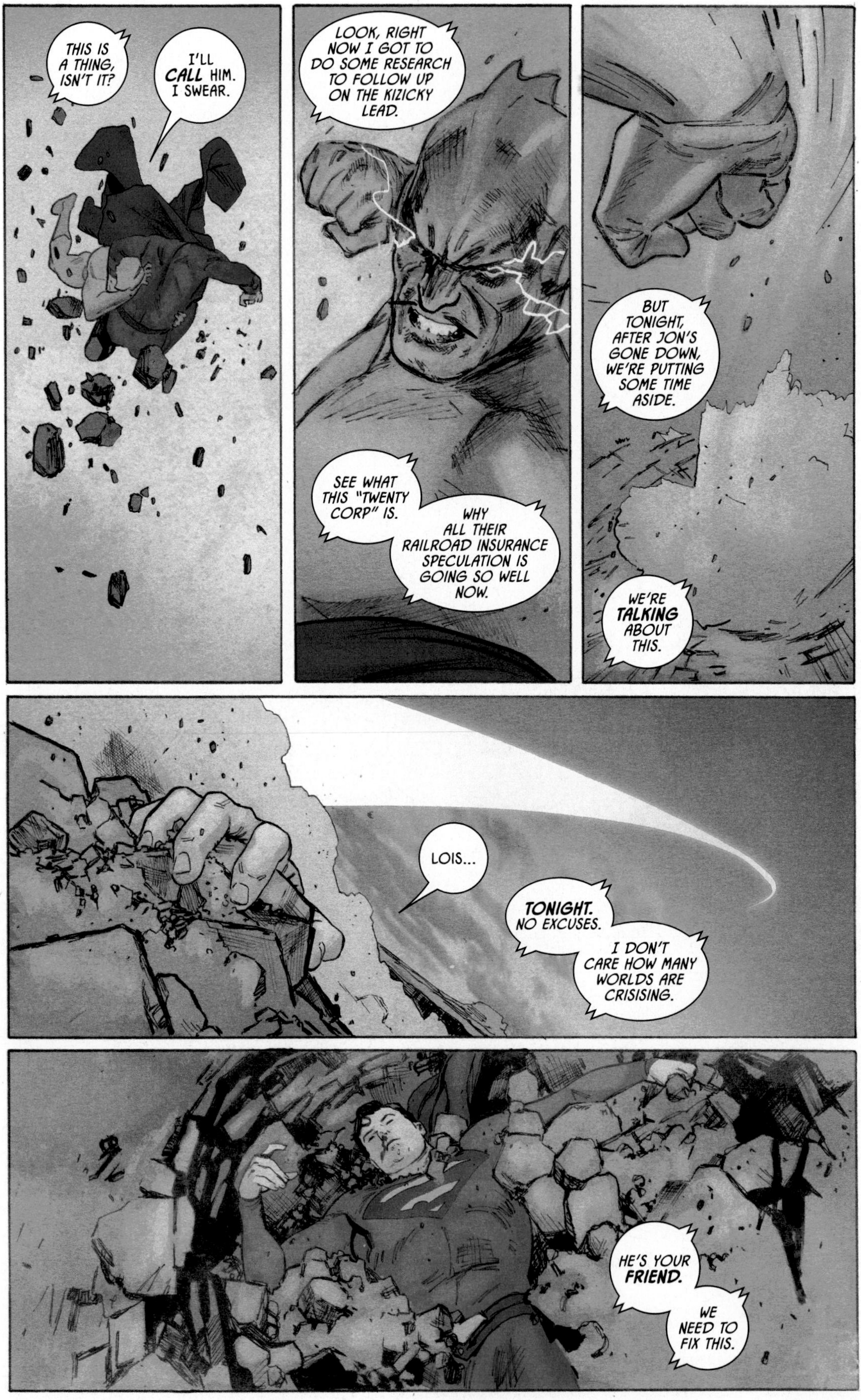
THIS IS A THING, ISN'T IT?
I'LL CALL HIM. I SWEAR.
LOOK, RIGHT NOW I GOT TO DO SOME RESEARCH TO FOLLOW UP ON THE KIZICKY LEAD.
SEE WHAT THIS "TWENTY CORP" IS.
WHY ALL THEIR RAILROAD INSURANCE SPECULATION IS GOING SO WELL NOW.
BUT TONIGHT, AFTER JON'S GONE DOWN, WE'RE PUTTING SOME TIME ASIDE.
WE'RE TALKING ABOUT THIS.
LOIS...
TONIGHT. NO EXCUSES.
I DON'T CARE HOW MANY WORLDS ARE CRISISING.
HE'S YOUR FRIEND.
WE NEED TO FIX THIS.

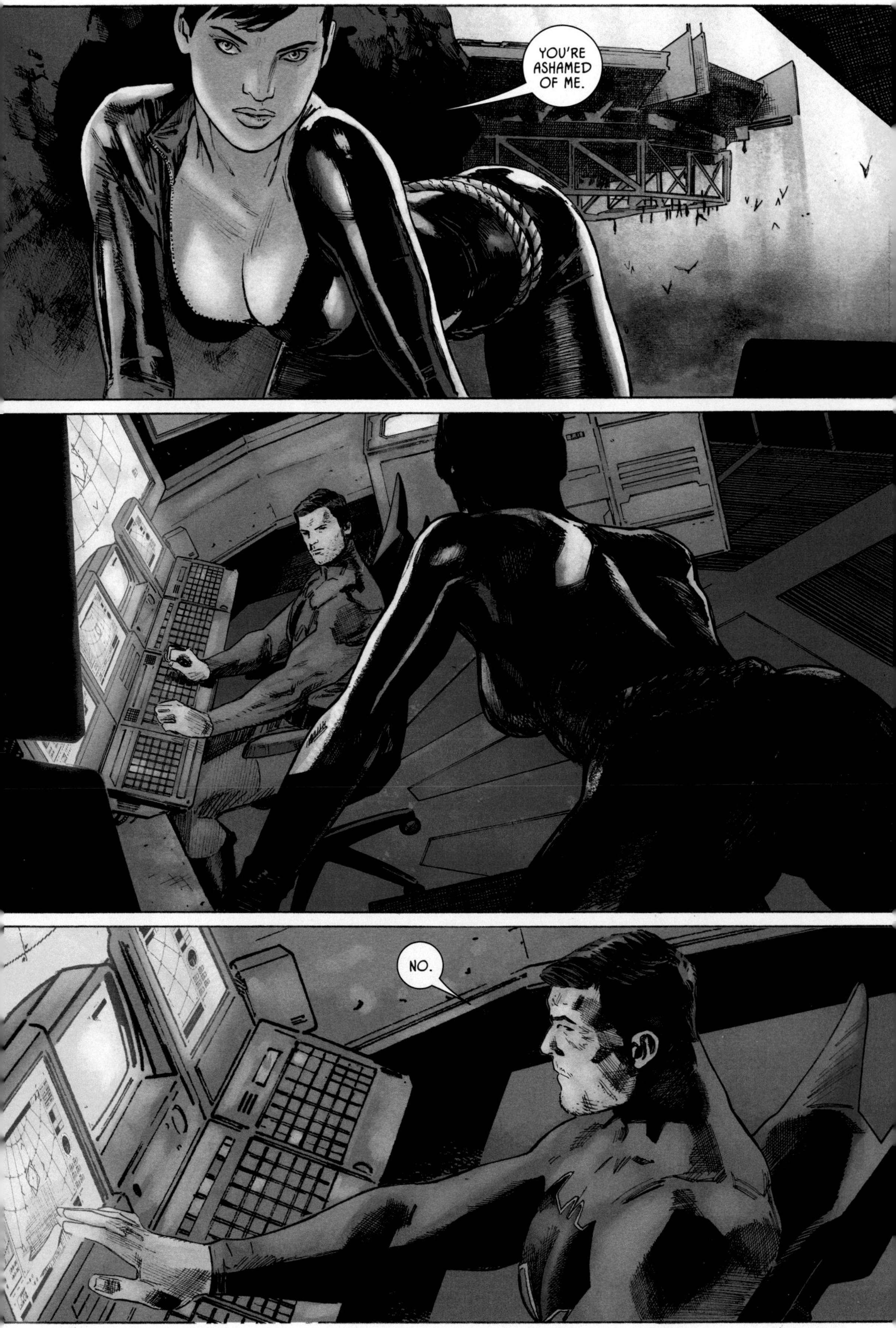
YOU'RE ASHAMED OF ME.
NO.

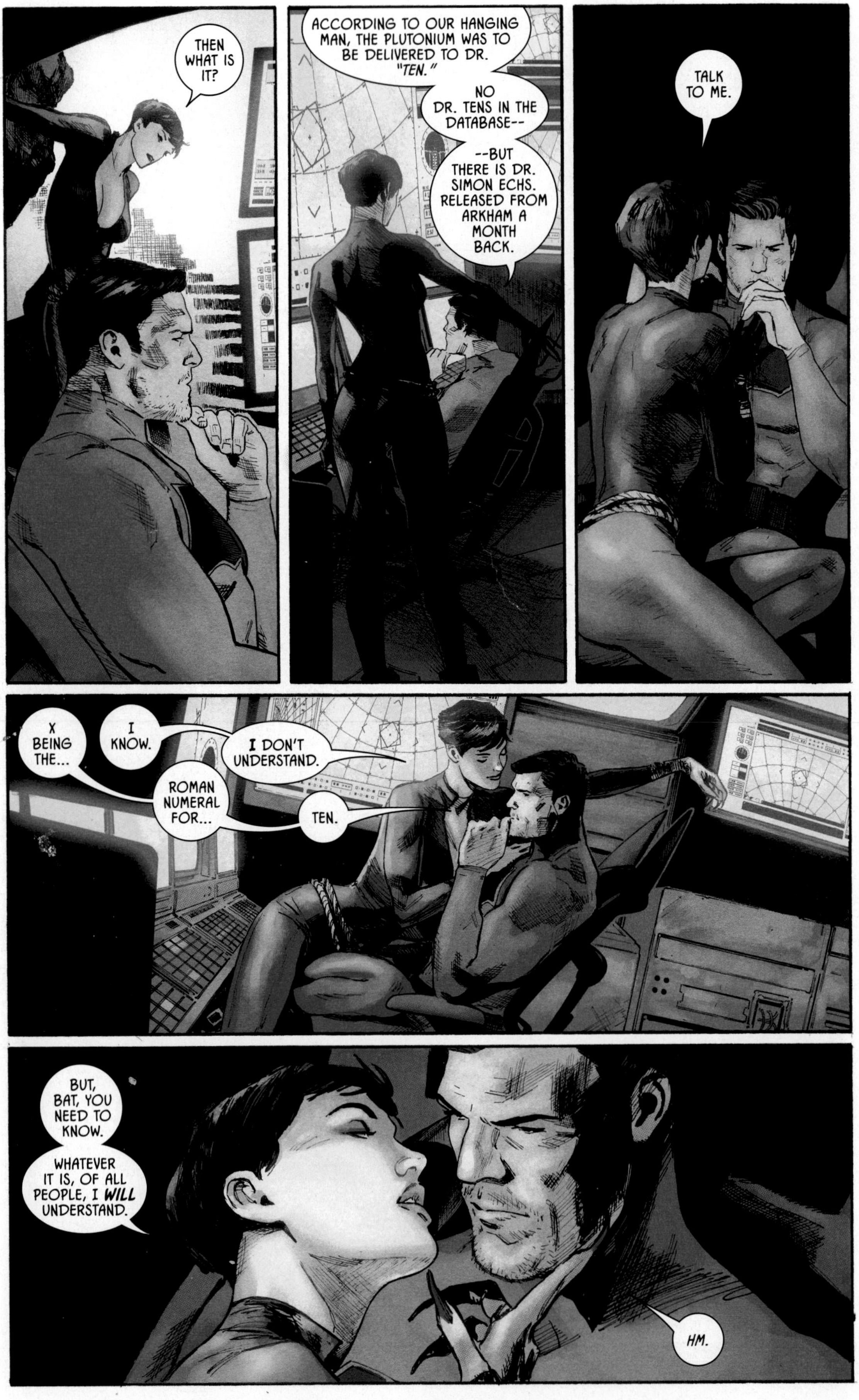
THEN WHAT IS IT?
ACCORDING TO OUR HANGING MAN, THE PLUTONIUM WAS TO BE DELIVERED TO DR. "TEN."
NO DR. TENS IN THE DATABASE--
--BUT THERE IS DR. SIMON ECHS. RELEASED FROM ARKHAM A MONTH BACK.
TALK TO ME.
X BEING THE...
ROMAN NUMERAL FOR...
TEN.
I KNOW.
I DON'T UNDERSTAND.
BUT, BAT, YOU NEED TO KNOW.
WHATEVER IT IS, OF ALL PEOPLE, I WILL UNDERSTAND.
HM.

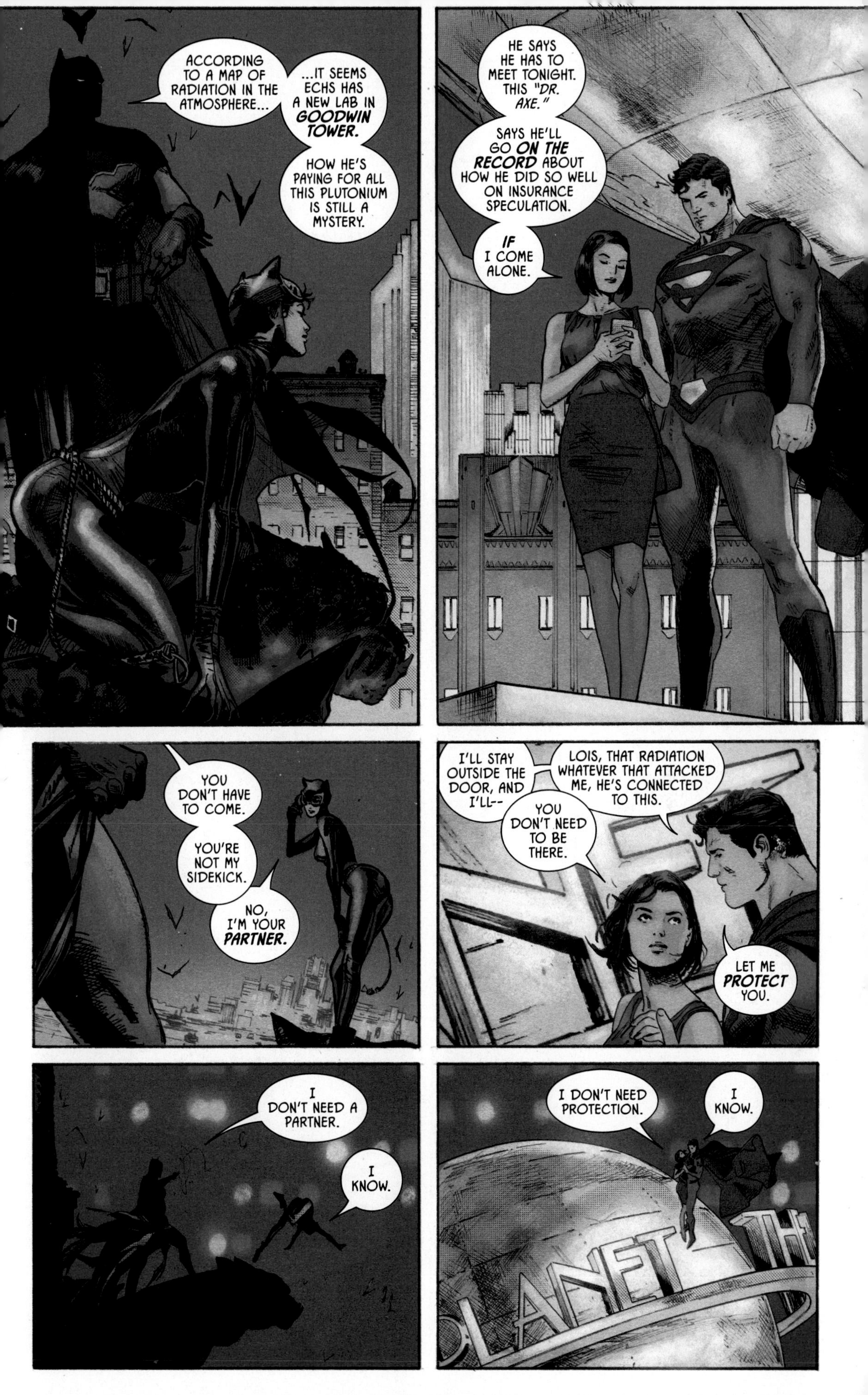
ACCORDING TO A MAP OF RADIATION IN THE ATMOSPHERE...
...IT SEEMS ECHS HAS A NEW LAB IN **GOODWIN TOWER.**
HOW HE'S PAYING FOR ALL THIS PLUTONIUM IS STILL A MYSTERY.
HE SAYS HE HAS TO MEET TONIGHT. THIS *"DR. AXE."*
SAYS HE'LL GO **ON THE RECORD** ABOUT HOW HE DID SO WELL ON INSURANCE SPECULATION.
IF I COME ALONE.
YOU DON'T HAVE TO COME.
YOU'RE NOT MY SIDEKICK.
NO, I'M YOUR ***PARTNER.***
I'LL STAY OUTSIDE THE DOOR, AND I'LL--
LOIS, THAT RADIATION WHATEVER THAT ATTACKED ME, HE'S CONNECTED TO THIS.
YOU DON'T NEED TO BE THERE.
LET ME ***PROTECT*** YOU.
I DON'T NEED A PARTNER.
I KNOW.
I DON'T NEED PROTECTION.
I KNOW.
LANET THE

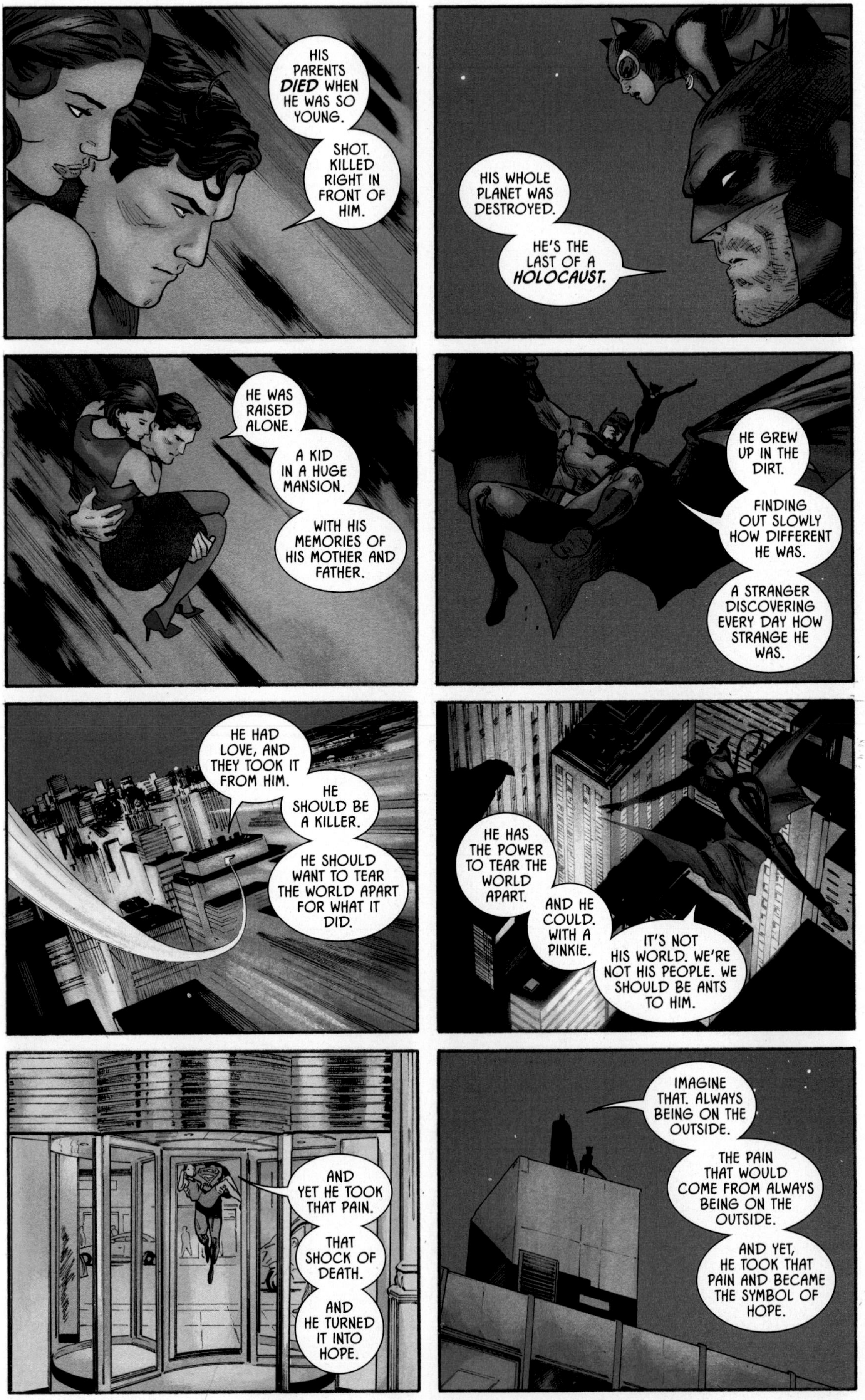
HIS PARENTS DIED WHEN HE WAS SO YOUNG.
SHOT. KILLED RIGHT IN FRONT OF HIM.
HIS WHOLE PLANET WAS DESTROYED.
HE'S THE LAST OF A HOLOCAUST.
HE WAS RAISED ALONE.
A KID IN A HUGE MANSION.
WITH HIS MEMORIES OF HIS MOTHER AND FATHER.
HE GREW UP IN THE DIRT.
FINDING OUT SLOWLY HOW DIFFERENT HE WAS.
A STRANGER DISCOVERING EVERY DAY HOW STRANGE HE WAS.
HE HAD LOVE, AND THEY TOOK IT FROM HIM.
HE SHOULD BE A KILLER.
HE SHOULD WANT TO TEAR THE WORLD APART FOR WHAT IT DID.
HE HAS THE POWER TO TEAR THE WORLD APART.
AND HE COULD. WITH A PINKIE.
IT'S NOT HIS WORLD. WE'RE NOT HIS PEOPLE. WE SHOULD BE ANTS TO HIM.
AND YET HE TOOK THAT PAIN.
THAT SHOCK OF DEATH.
AND HE TURNED IT INTO HOPE.
IMAGINE THAT. ALWAYS BEING ON THE OUTSIDE.
THE PAIN THAT WOULD COME FROM ALWAYS BEING ON THE OUTSIDE.
AND YET, HE TOOK THAT PAIN AND BECAME THE SYMBOL OF HOPE.

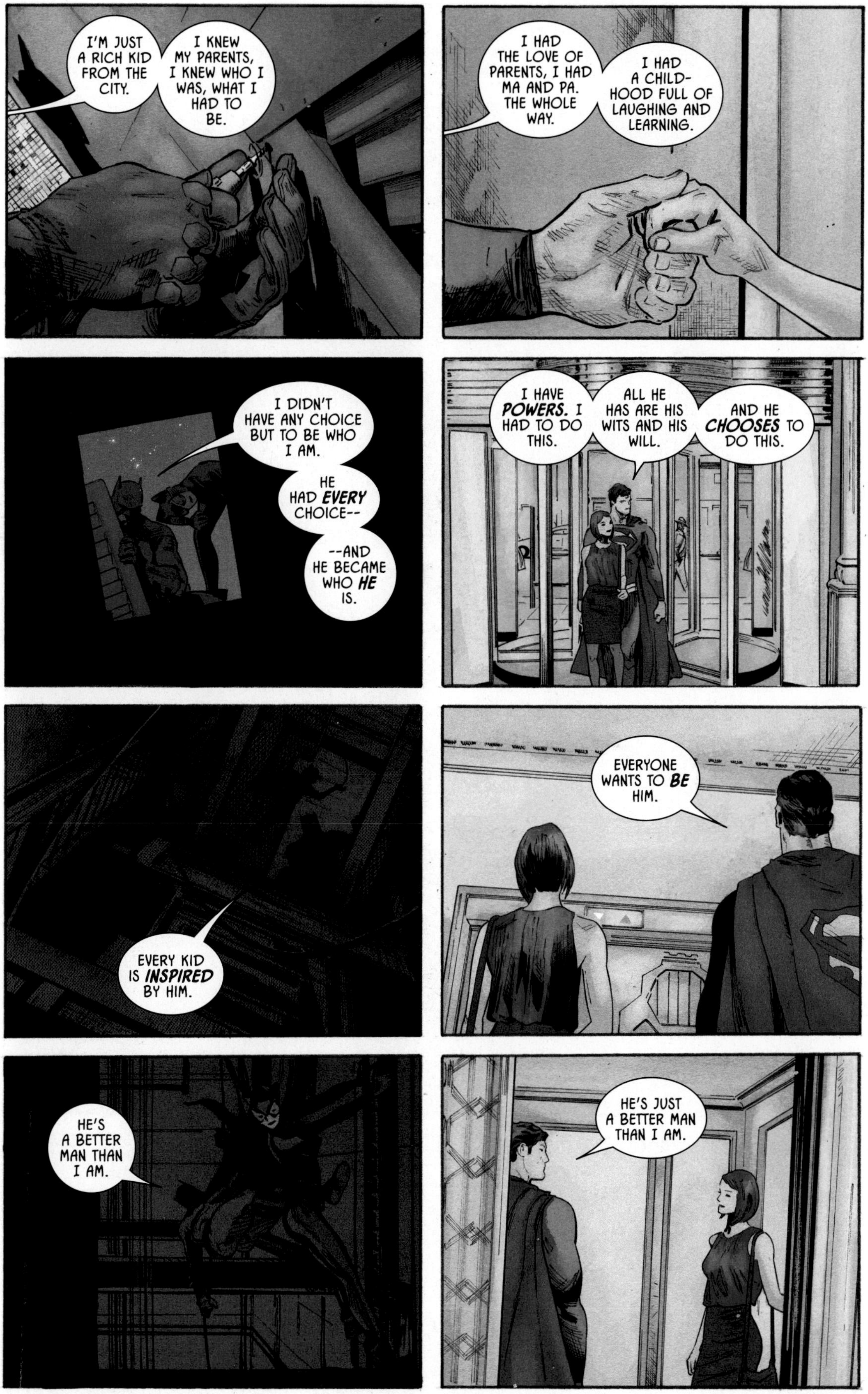
I'M JUST A RICH KID FROM THE CITY.
I KNEW MY PARENTS, I KNEW WHO I WAS, WHAT I HAD TO BE.
I HAD THE LOVE OF PARENTS, I HAD MA AND PA. THE WHOLE WAY.
I HAD A CHILDHOOD FULL OF LAUGHING AND LEARNING.
I DIDN'T HAVE ANY CHOICE BUT TO BE WHO I AM.
HE HAD EVERY CHOICE--
--AND HE BECAME WHO HE IS.
I HAVE POWERS. I HAD TO DO THIS.
ALL HE HAS ARE HIS WITS AND HIS WILL.
AND HE CHOOSES TO DO THIS.
EVERY KID IS INSPIRED BY HIM.
EVERYONE WANTS TO BE HIM.
HE'S A BETTER MAN THAN I AM.
HE'S JUST A BETTER MAN THAN I AM.

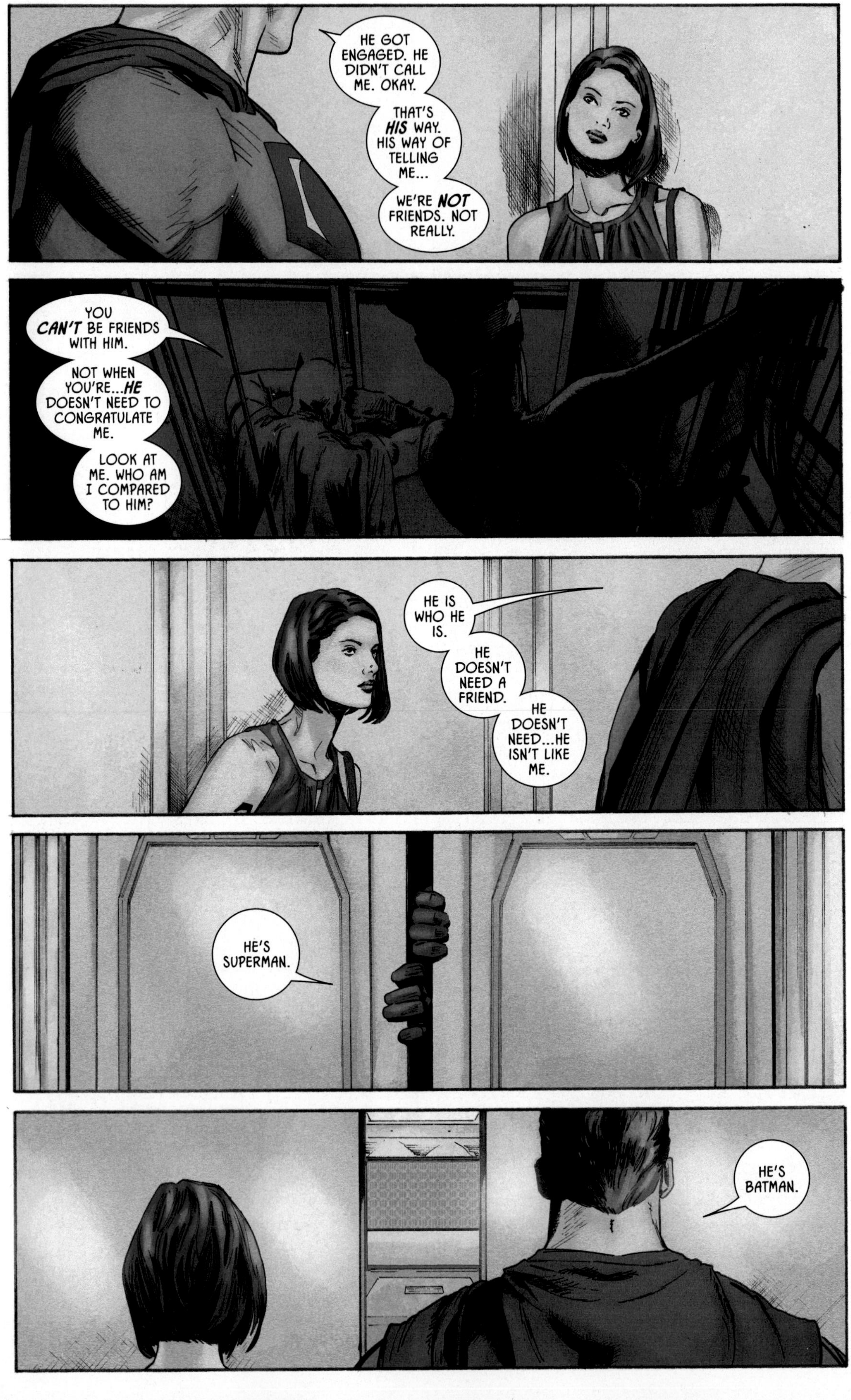
HE GOT ENGAGED. HE DIDN'T CALL ME. OKAY.
THAT'S ***HIS*** WAY. HIS WAY OF TELLING ME...
WE'RE ***NOT*** FRIENDS. NOT REALLY.
YOU ***CAN'T*** BE FRIENDS WITH HIM.
NOT WHEN YOU'RE...***HE*** DOESN'T NEED TO CONGRATULATE ME.
LOOK AT ME. WHO AM I COMPARED TO HIM?
HE IS WHO HE IS.
HE DOESN'T NEED A FRIEND.
HE DOESN'T NEED...HE ISN'T LIKE ME.
HE'S SUPERMAN.
HE'S BATMAN.

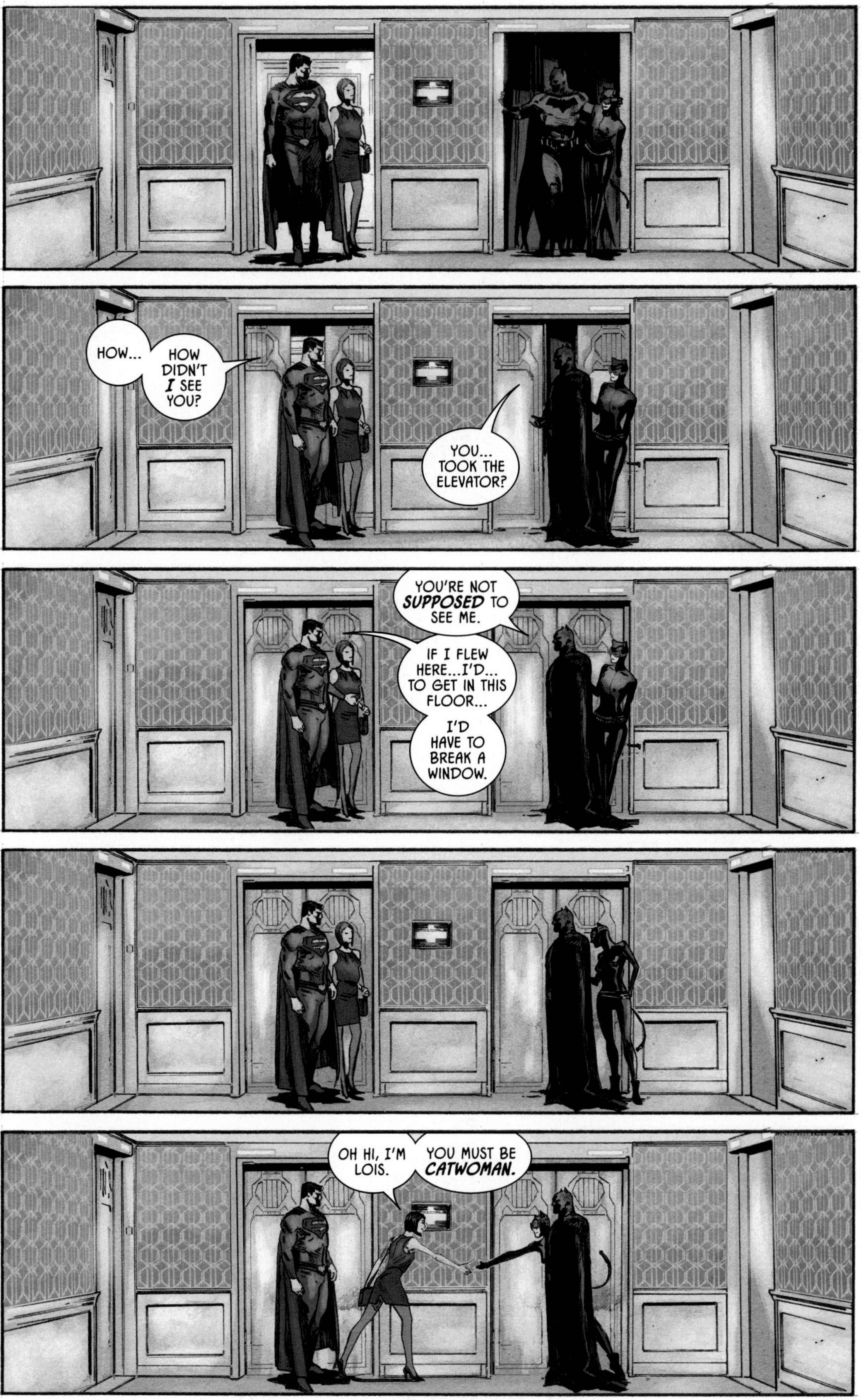
HOW...
HOW DIDN'T I SEE YOU?
YOU... TOOK THE ELEVATOR?
YOU'RE NOT SUPPOSED TO SEE ME.
IF I FLEW HERE...I'D... TO GET IN THIS FLOOR...
I'D HAVE TO BREAK A WINDOW.
OH HI, I'M LOIS.
YOU MUST BE CATWOMAN.

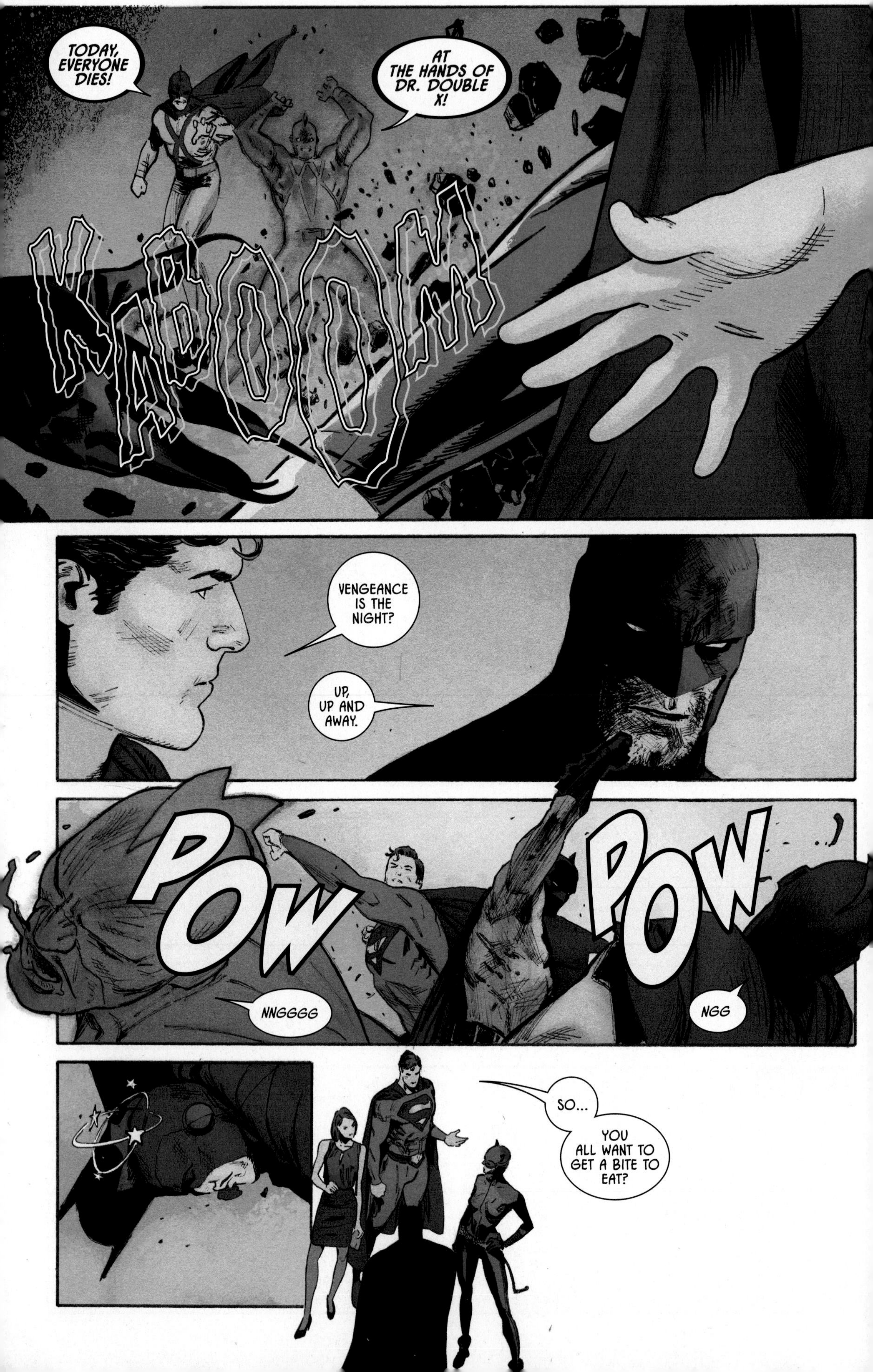
TODAY, EVERYONE DIES!
AT THE HANDS OF DR. DOUBLE X!
KABOOM
VENGEANCE IS THE NIGHT?
UP, UP AND AWAY.
POW
POW
NNGGGG
NGG
SO...
YOU ALL WANT TO GET A BITE TO EAT?

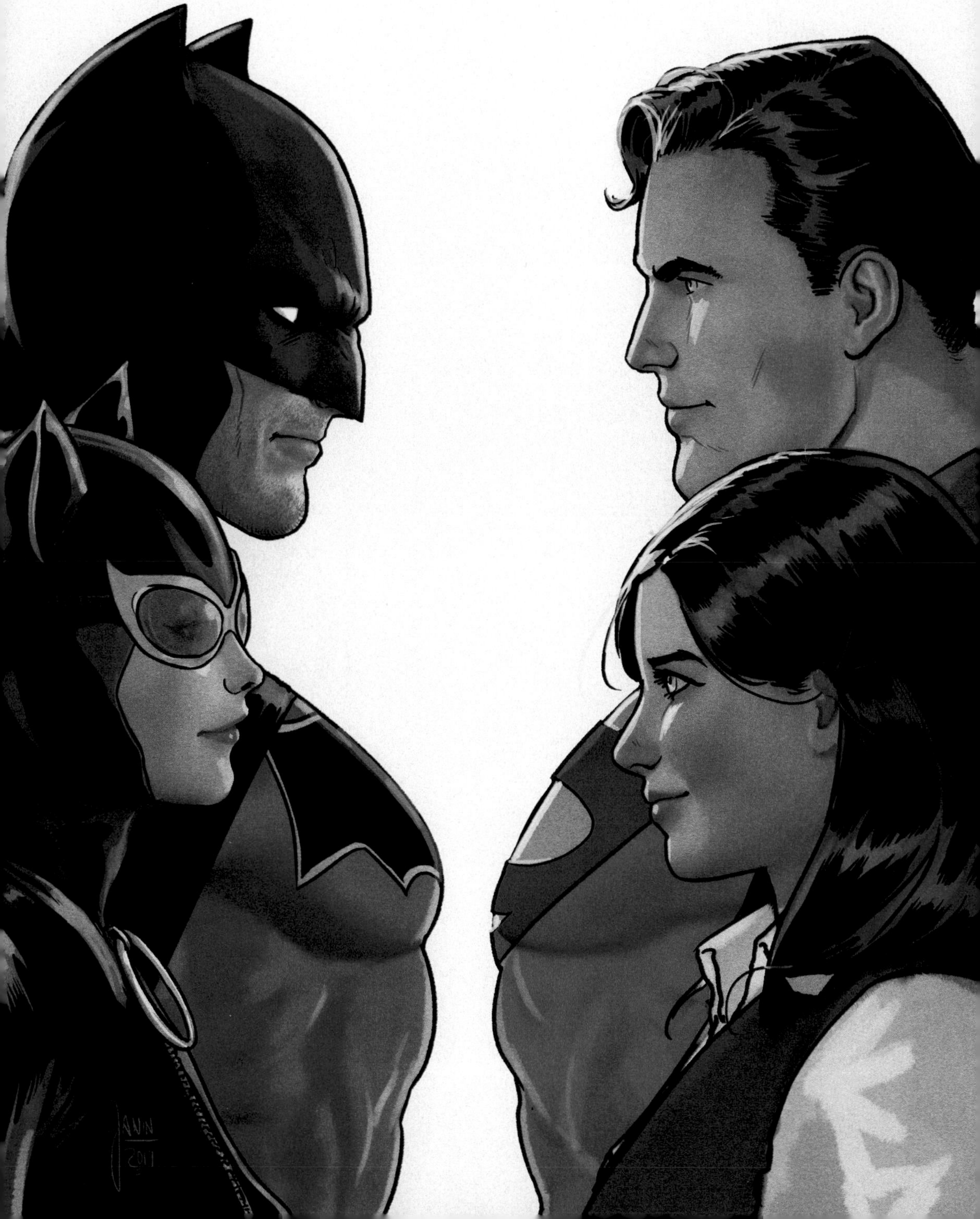

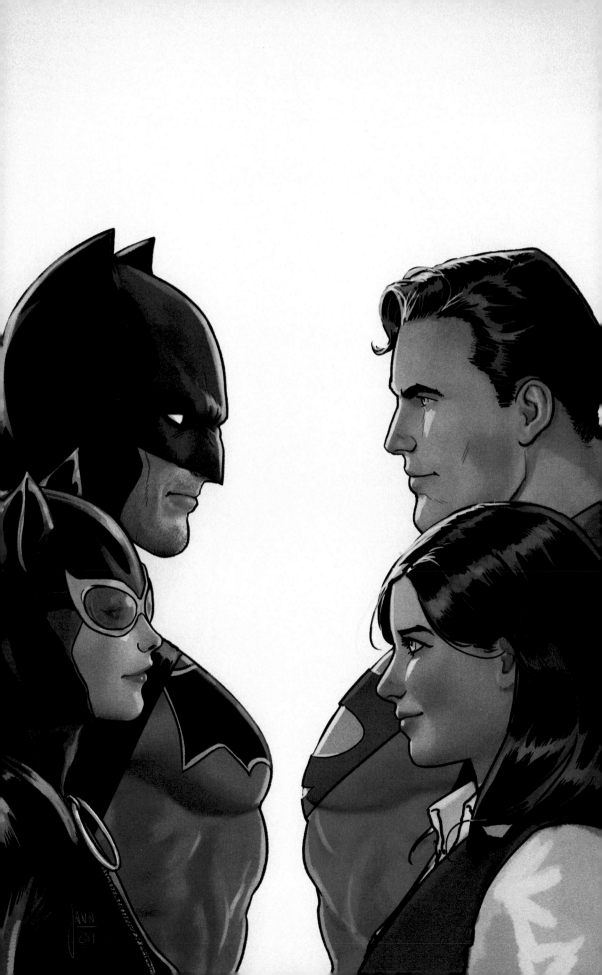

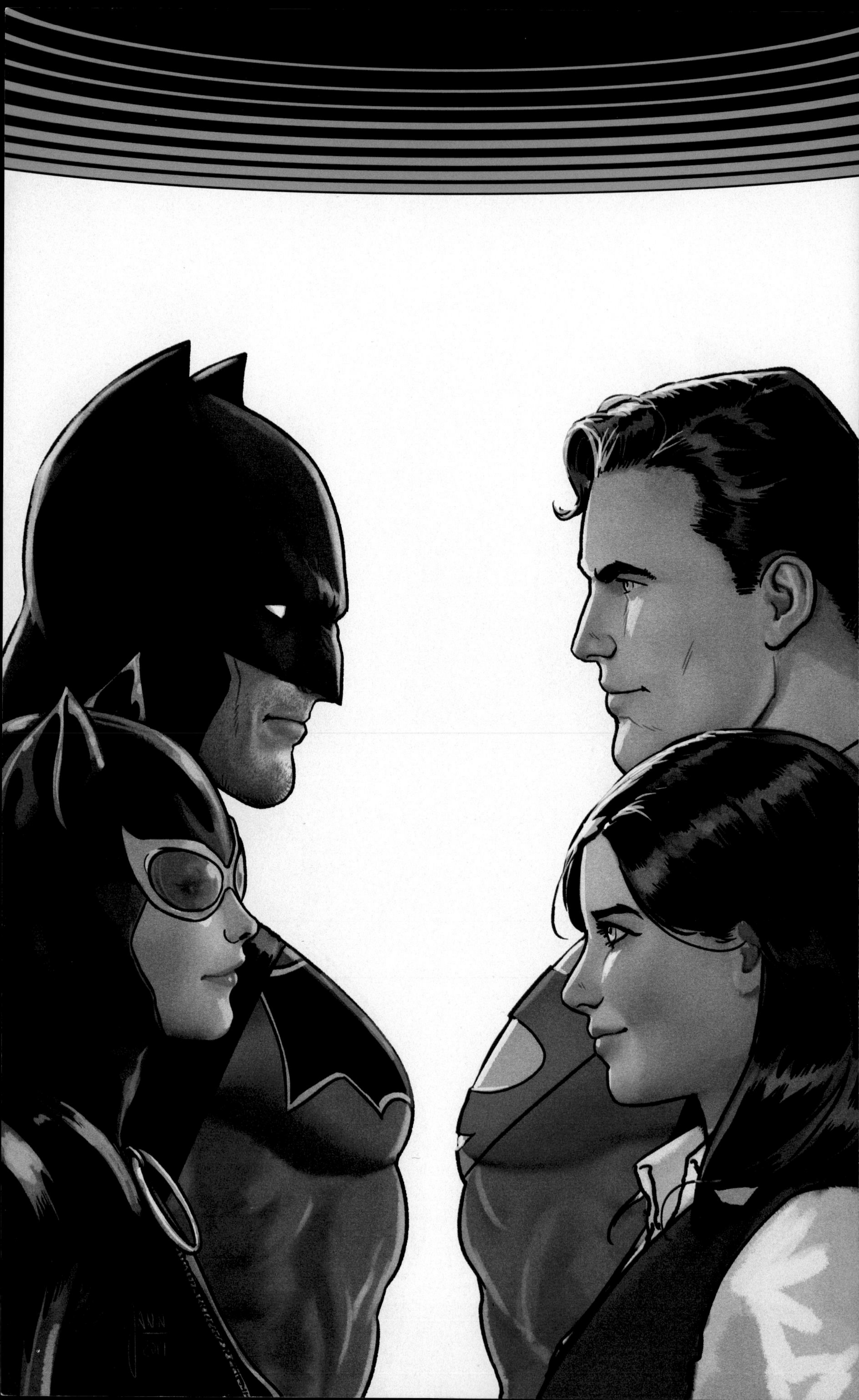

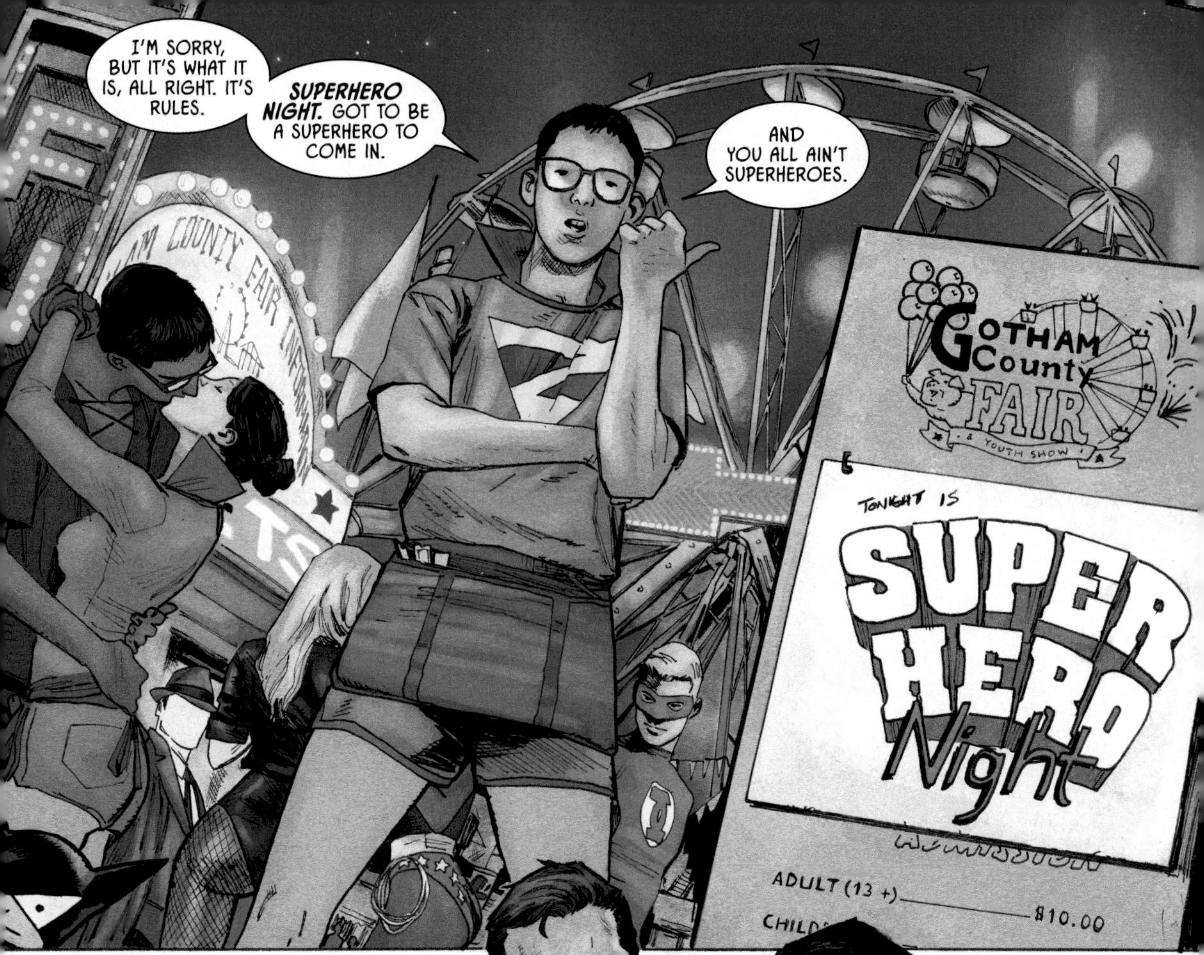
I'M SORRY, BUT IT'S WHAT IT IS, ALL RIGHT. IT'S RULES.
SUPERHERO NIGHT. GOT TO BE A SUPERHERO TO COME IN.
AND YOU ALL AIN'T SUPERHEROES.
GOTHAM County FAIR
TONIGHT IS
SUPER HERO Night
ADULT (13 +) $10.00

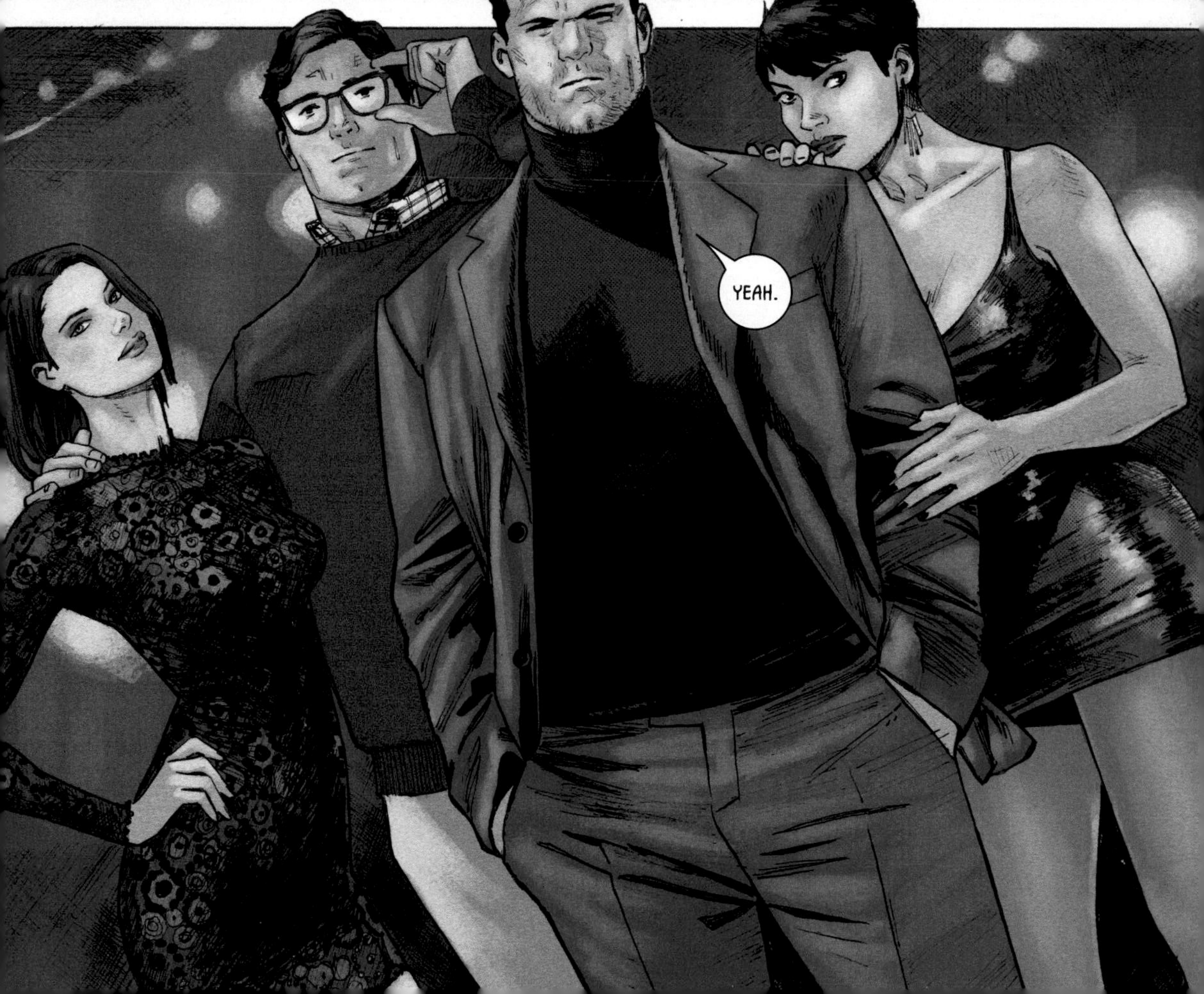
YEAH.

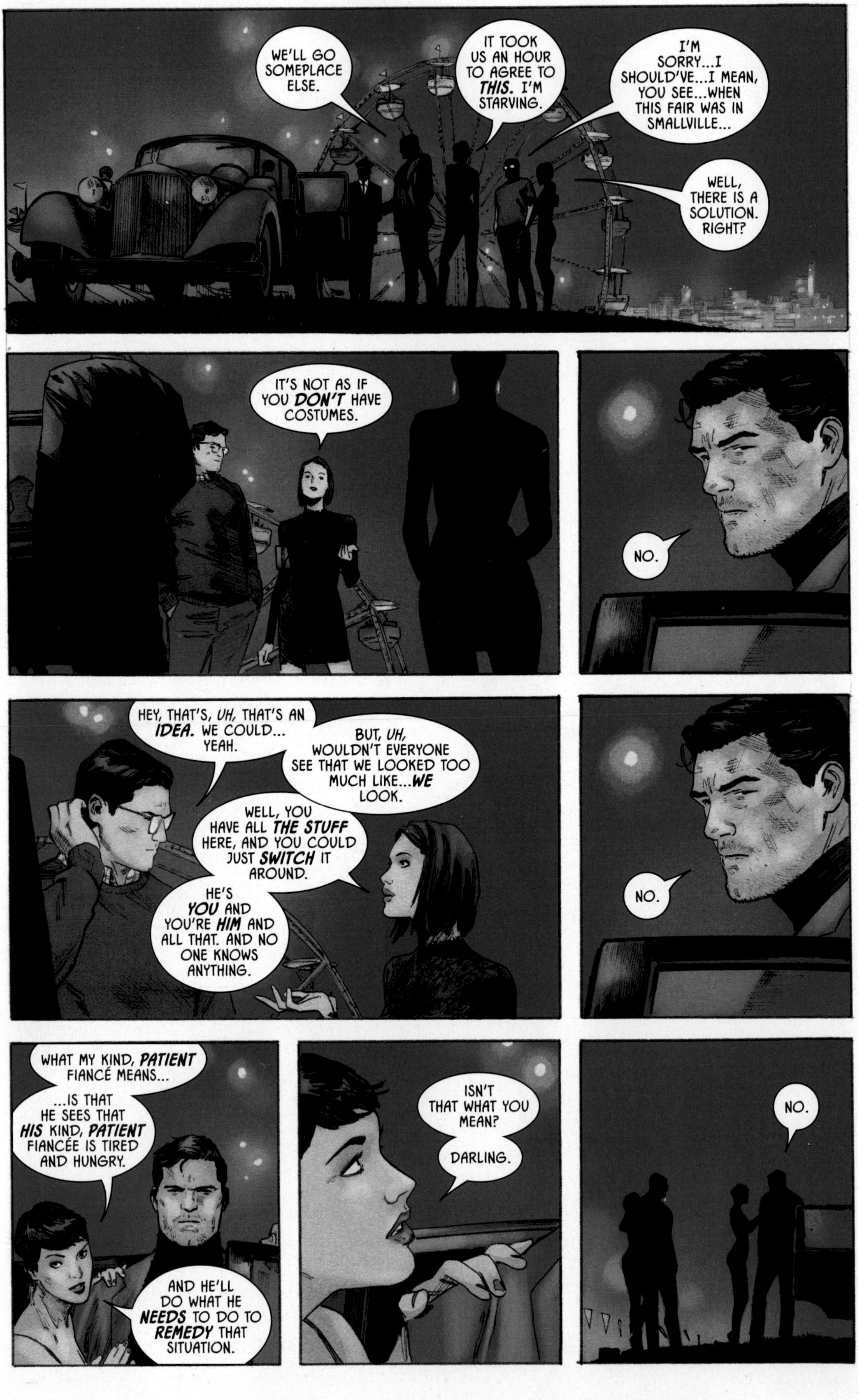
WE'LL GO SOMEPLACE ELSE.
IT TOOK US AN HOUR TO AGREE TO THIS. I'M STARVING.
I'M SORRY...I SHOULD'VE...I MEAN, YOU SEE...WHEN THIS FAIR WAS IN SMALLVILLE...
WELL, THERE IS A SOLUTION. RIGHT?
IT'S NOT AS IF YOU DON'T HAVE COSTUMES.
NO.
HEY, THAT'S, UH, THAT'S AN IDEA. WE COULD... YEAH.
BUT, UH, WOULDN'T EVERYONE SEE THAT WE LOOKED TOO MUCH LIKE...WE LOOK.
WELL, YOU HAVE ALL THE STUFF HERE, AND YOU COULD JUST SWITCH IT AROUND.
HE'S YOU AND YOU'RE HIM AND ALL THAT. AND NO ONE KNOWS ANYTHING.
NO.
WHAT MY KIND, PATIENT FIANCÉ MEANS...
...IS THAT HE SEES THAT HIS KIND, PATIENT FIANCÉE IS TIRED AND HUNGRY.
AND HE'LL DO WHAT HE NEEDS TO DO TO REMEDY THAT SITUATION.
ISN'T THAT WHAT YOU MEAN?
DARLING.
NO.

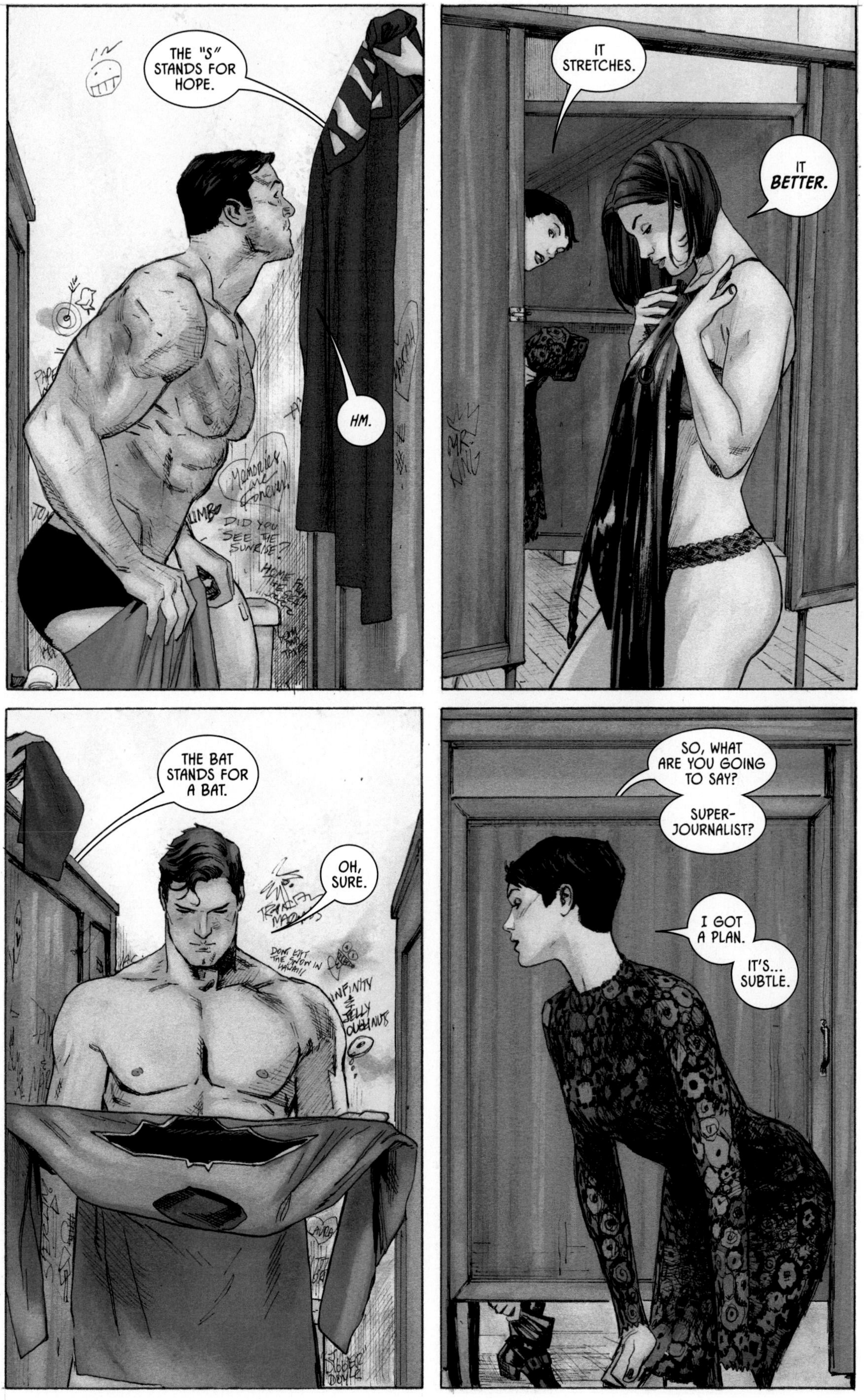

THE "S" STANDS FOR HOPE.
HM.
IT STRETCHES.
IT *BETTER.*
THE BAT STANDS FOR A BAT.
OH, SURE.
SO, WHAT ARE YOU GOING TO SAY?
SUPER-JOURNALIST?
I GOT A PLAN.
IT'S... SUBTLE.

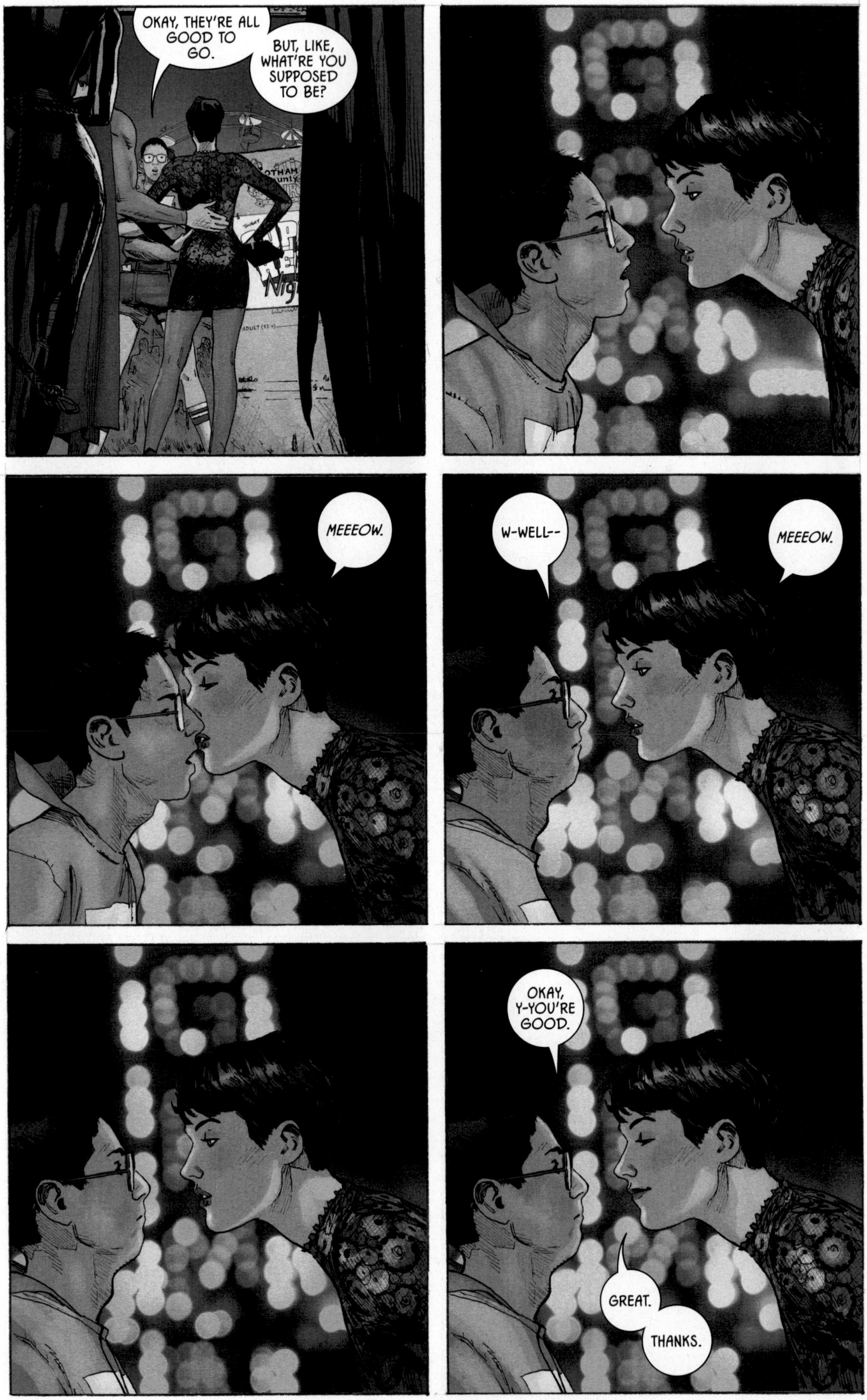
OKAY, THEY'RE ALL GOOD TO GO.
BUT, LIKE, WHAT'RE YOU SUPPOSED TO BE?
MEEEOW.
W-WELL--
MEEEOW.
OKAY, Y-YOU'RE GOOD.
GREAT.
THANKS.

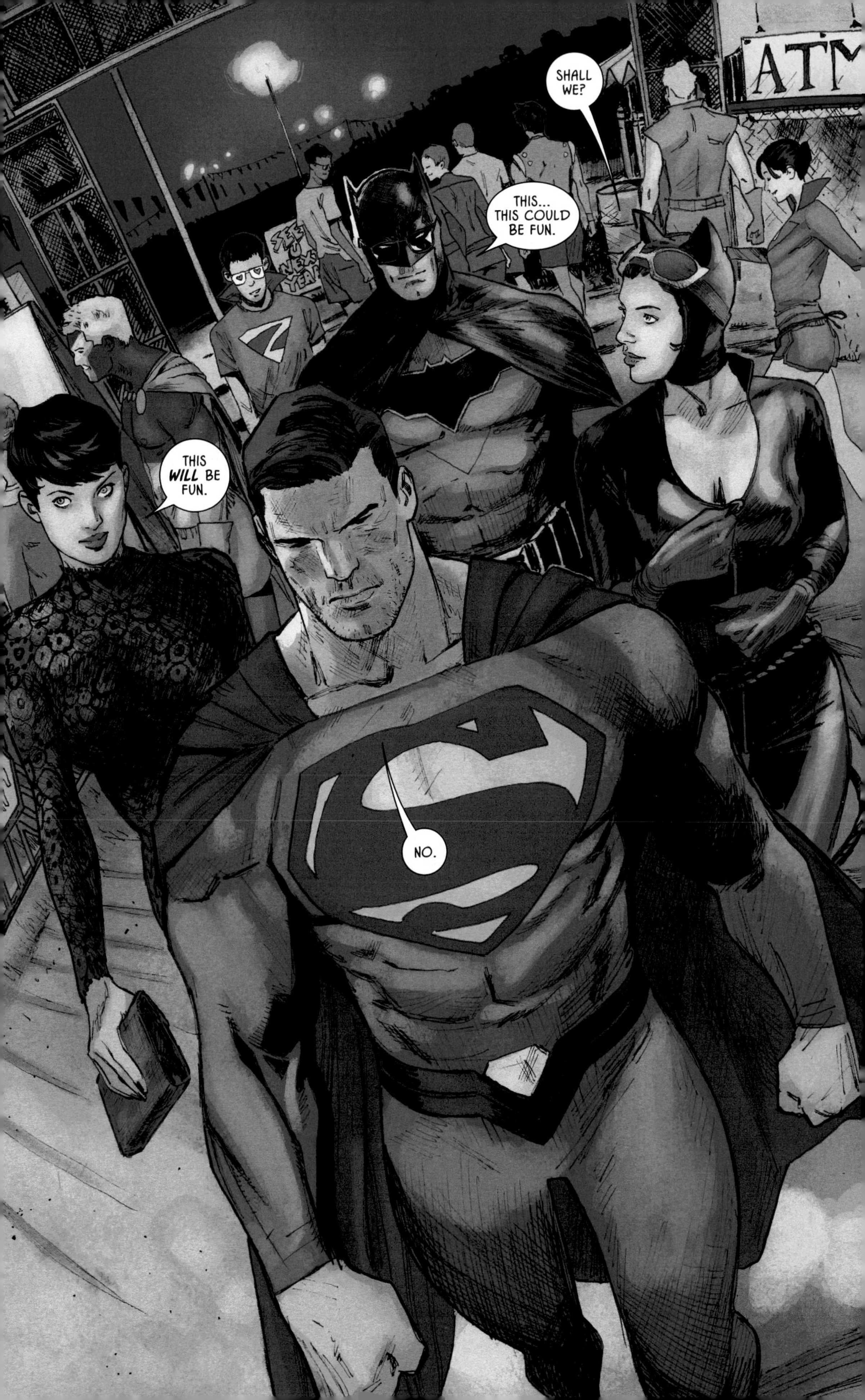
SHALL WE?
THIS... THIS COULD BE FUN.
THIS WILL BE FUN.
NO.

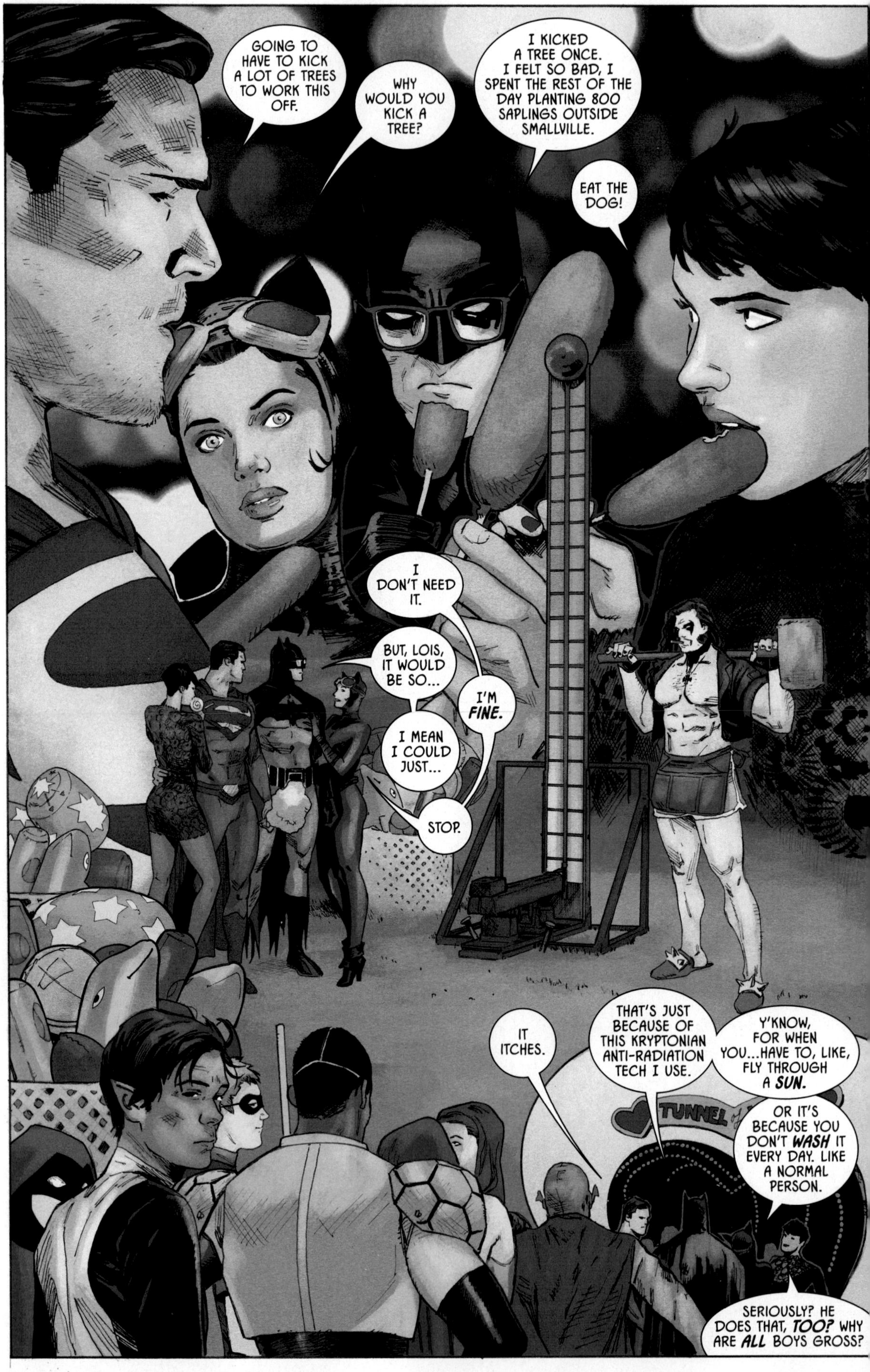
GOING TO HAVE TO KICK A LOT OF TREES TO WORK THIS OFF.
WHY WOULD YOU KICK A TREE?
I KICKED A TREE ONCE. I FELT SO BAD, I SPENT THE REST OF THE DAY PLANTING 800 SAPLINGS OUTSIDE SMALLVILLE.
EAT THE DOG!
I DON'T NEED IT.
BUT, LOIS, IT WOULD BE SO...
I'M FINE.
I MEAN I COULD JUST...
STOP.
IT ITCHES.
THAT'S JUST BECAUSE OF THIS KRYPTONIAN ANTI-RADIATION TECH I USE.
Y'KNOW, FOR WHEN YOU...HAVE TO, LIKE, FLY THROUGH A SUN.
TUNNEL
OR IT'S BECAUSE YOU DON'T WASH IT EVERY DAY. LIKE A NORMAL PERSON.
SERIOUSLY? HE DOES THAT, TOO? WHY ARE ALL BOYS GROSS?

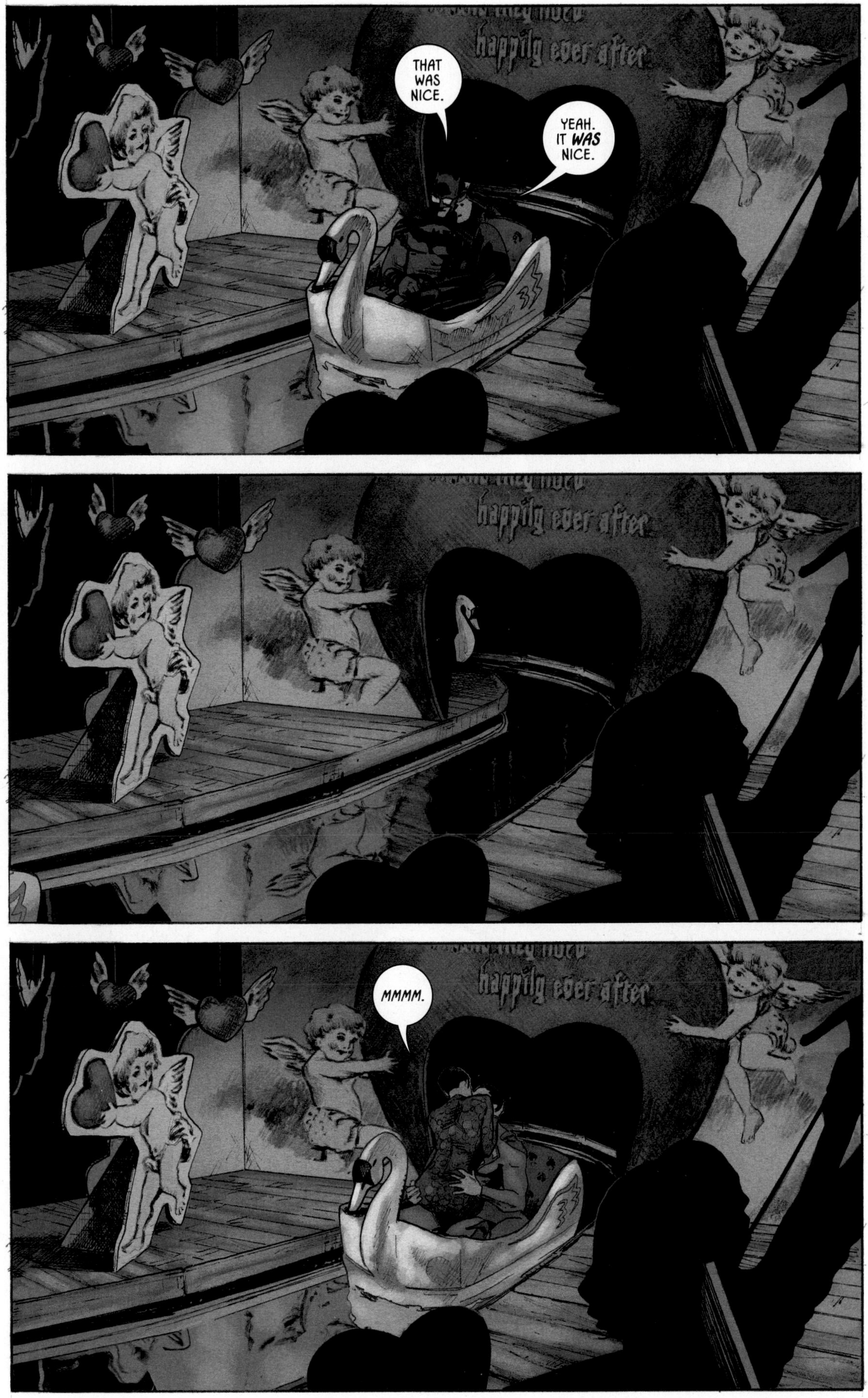
happily ever after
THAT WAS NICE.
YEAH. IT *WAS* NICE.
happily ever after
happily ever after
MMMM.

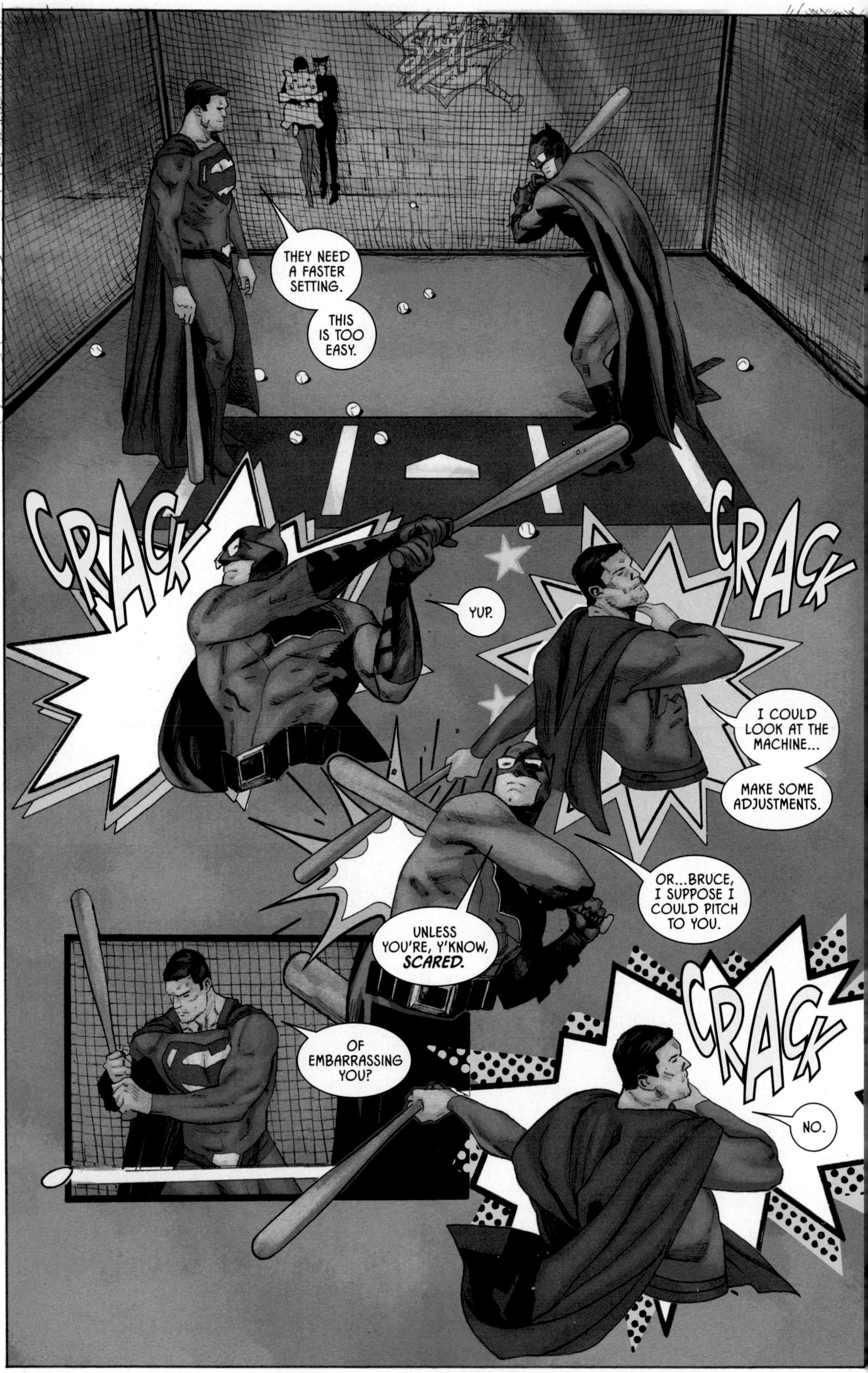
THEY NEED A FASTER SETTING.
THIS IS TOO EASY.
CRACK
YUP.
CRACK
I COULD LOOK AT THE MACHINE...
MAKE SOME ADJUSTMENTS.
OR...BRUCE, I SUPPOSE I COULD PITCH TO YOU.
UNLESS YOU'RE, Y'KNOW, *SCARED.*
CRACK
OF EMBARRASSING YOU?
NO.

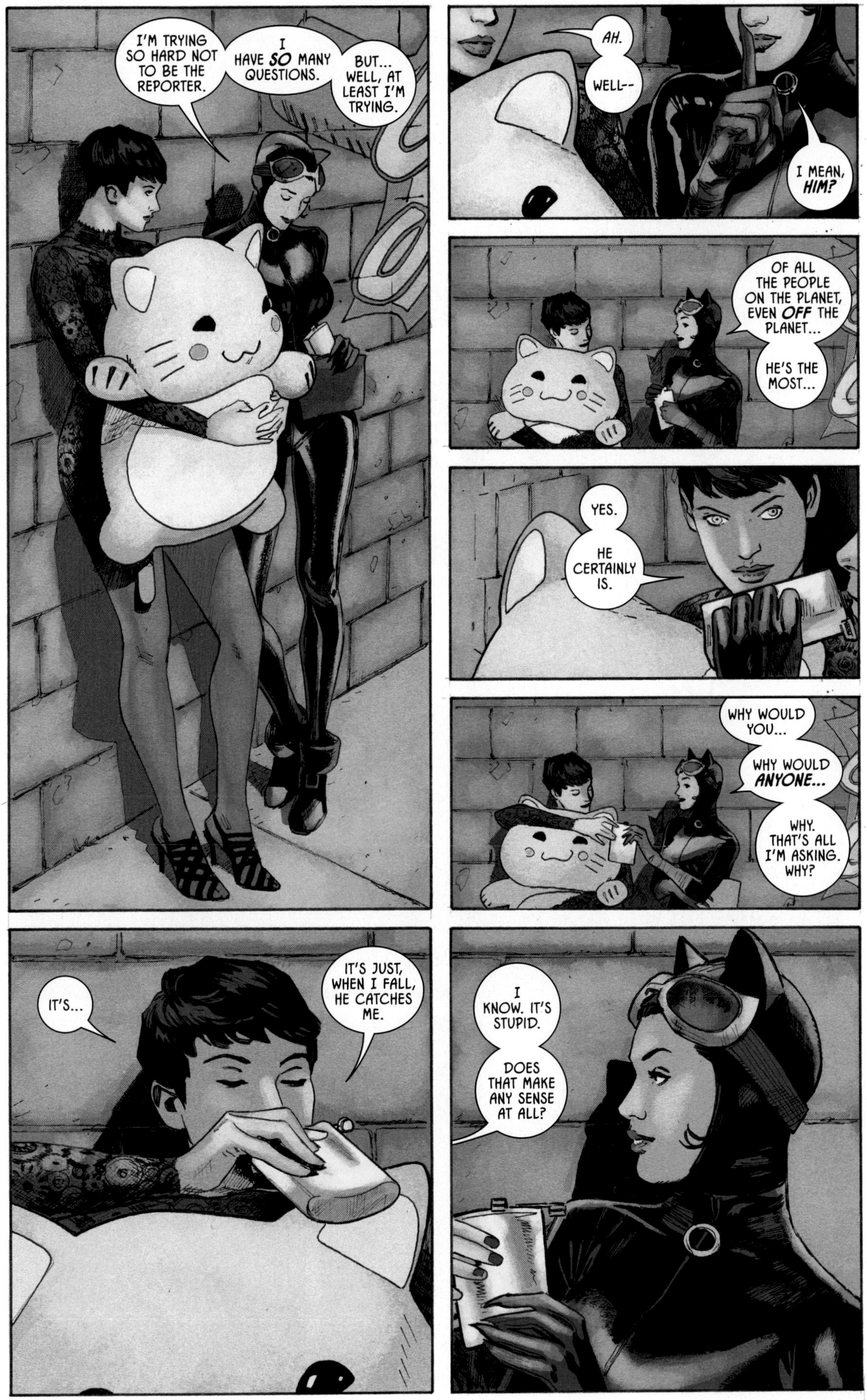
I'M TRYING SO HARD NOT TO BE THE REPORTER.
I HAVE SO MANY QUESTIONS.
BUT... WELL, AT LEAST I'M TRYING.
AH.
WELL--
I MEAN, HIM?
OF ALL THE PEOPLE ON THE PLANET, EVEN OFF THE PLANET...
HE'S THE MOST...
YES.
HE CERTAINLY IS.
WHY WOULD YOU...
WHY WOULD ANYONE...
WHY. THAT'S ALL I'M ASKING. WHY?
IT'S...
IT'S JUST, WHEN I FALL, HE CATCHES ME.
I KNOW. IT'S STUPID.
DOES THAT MAKE ANY SENSE AT ALL?

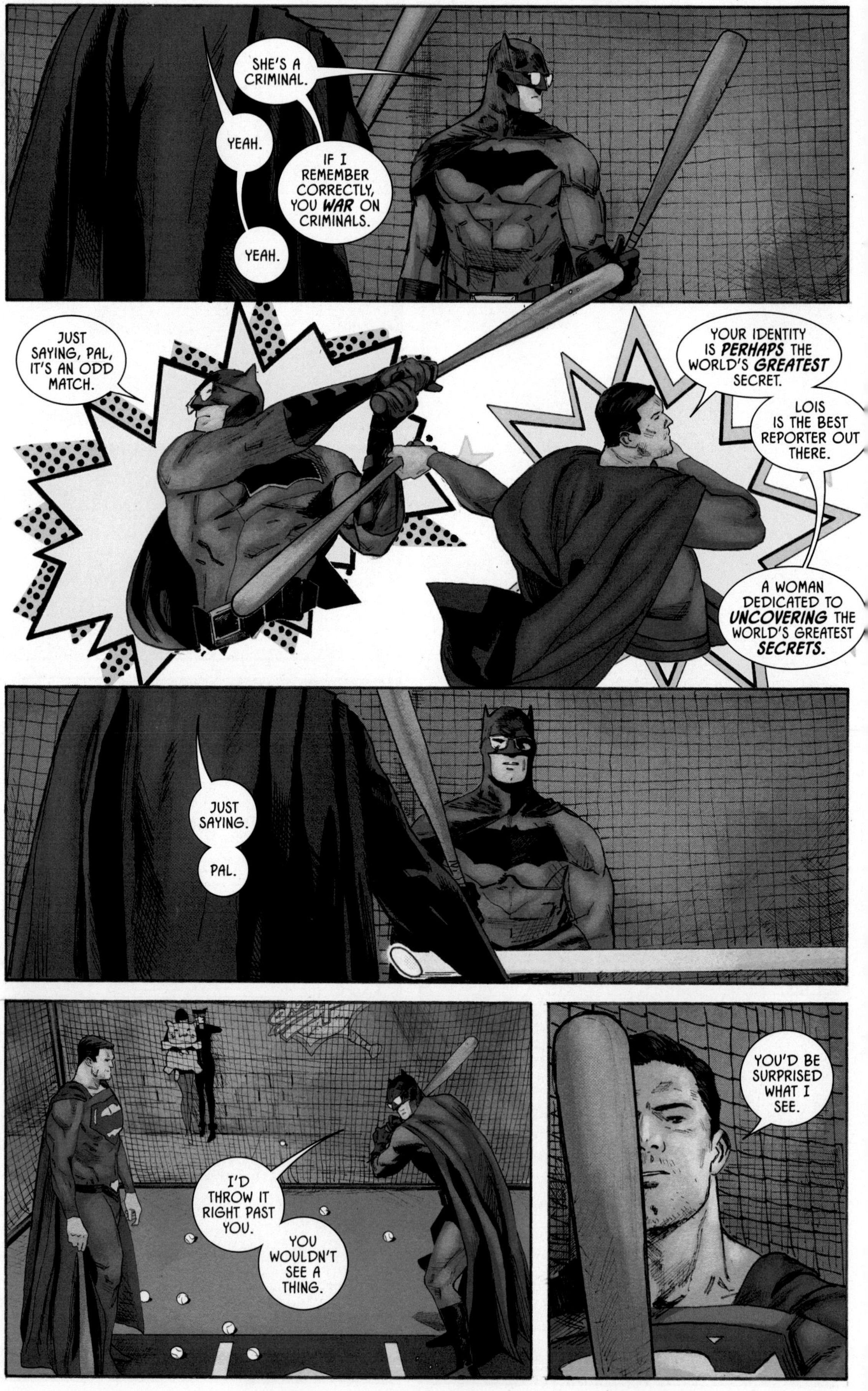
SHE'S A CRIMINAL.
YEAH.
IF I REMEMBER CORRECTLY, YOU WAR ON CRIMINALS.
YEAH.
JUST SAYING, PAL, IT'S AN ODD MATCH.
YOUR IDENTITY IS PERHAPS THE WORLD'S GREATEST SECRET.
LOIS IS THE BEST REPORTER OUT THERE.
A WOMAN DEDICATED TO UNCOVERING THE WORLD'S GREATEST SECRETS.
JUST SAYING.
PAL.
I'D THROW IT RIGHT PAST YOU.
YOU WOULDN'T SEE A THING.
YOU'D BE SURPRISED WHAT I SEE.

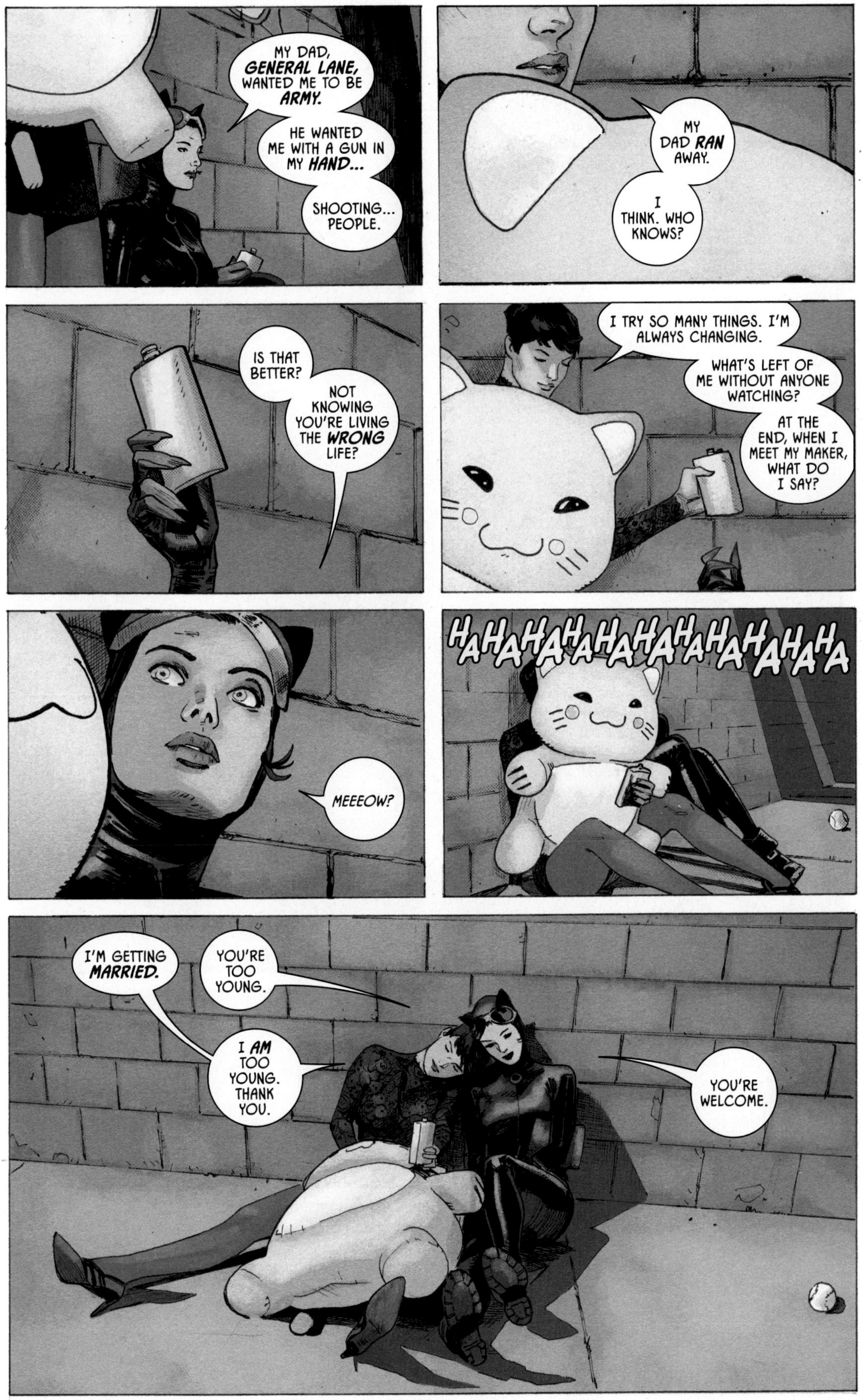
MY DAD, **GENERAL LANE,** WANTED ME TO BE **ARMY.**
HE WANTED ME WITH A GUN IN MY **HAND...**
SHOOTING... PEOPLE.
MY DAD **RAN** AWAY.
I THINK. WHO KNOWS?
IS THAT BETTER?
NOT KNOWING YOU'RE LIVING THE **WRONG** LIFE?
I TRY SO MANY THINGS. I'M ALWAYS CHANGING.
WHAT'S LEFT OF ME WITHOUT ANYONE WATCHING?
AT THE END, WHEN I MEET MY MAKER, WHAT DO I SAY?
MEEEOW?
HAHAHAHAHAHAHAHAHAHAHAHAHAHA
I'M GETTING **MARRIED.**
YOU'RE TOO YOUNG.
I **AM** TOO YOUNG. THANK YOU.
YOU'RE WELCOME.

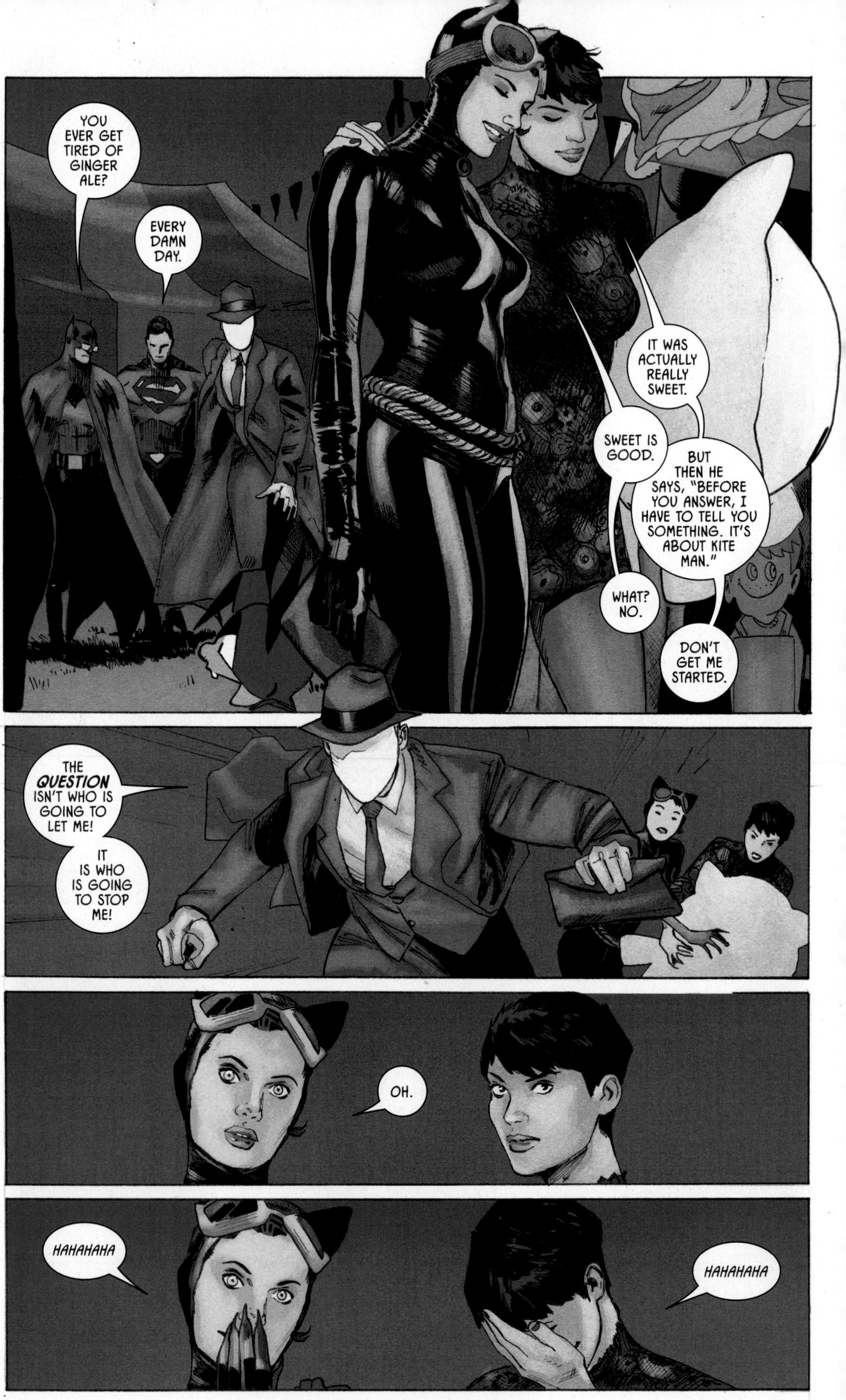
YOU EVER GET TIRED OF GINGER ALE?
EVERY DAMN DAY.
IT WAS ACTUALLY REALLY SWEET.
SWEET IS GOOD.
BUT THEN HE SAYS, "BEFORE YOU ANSWER, I HAVE TO TELL YOU SOMETHING. IT'S ABOUT KITE MAN."
WHAT? NO.
DON'T GET ME STARTED.
THE QUESTION ISN'T WHO IS GOING TO LET ME!
IT IS WHO IS GOING TO STOP ME!
OH.
HAHAHAHA
HAHAHAHA

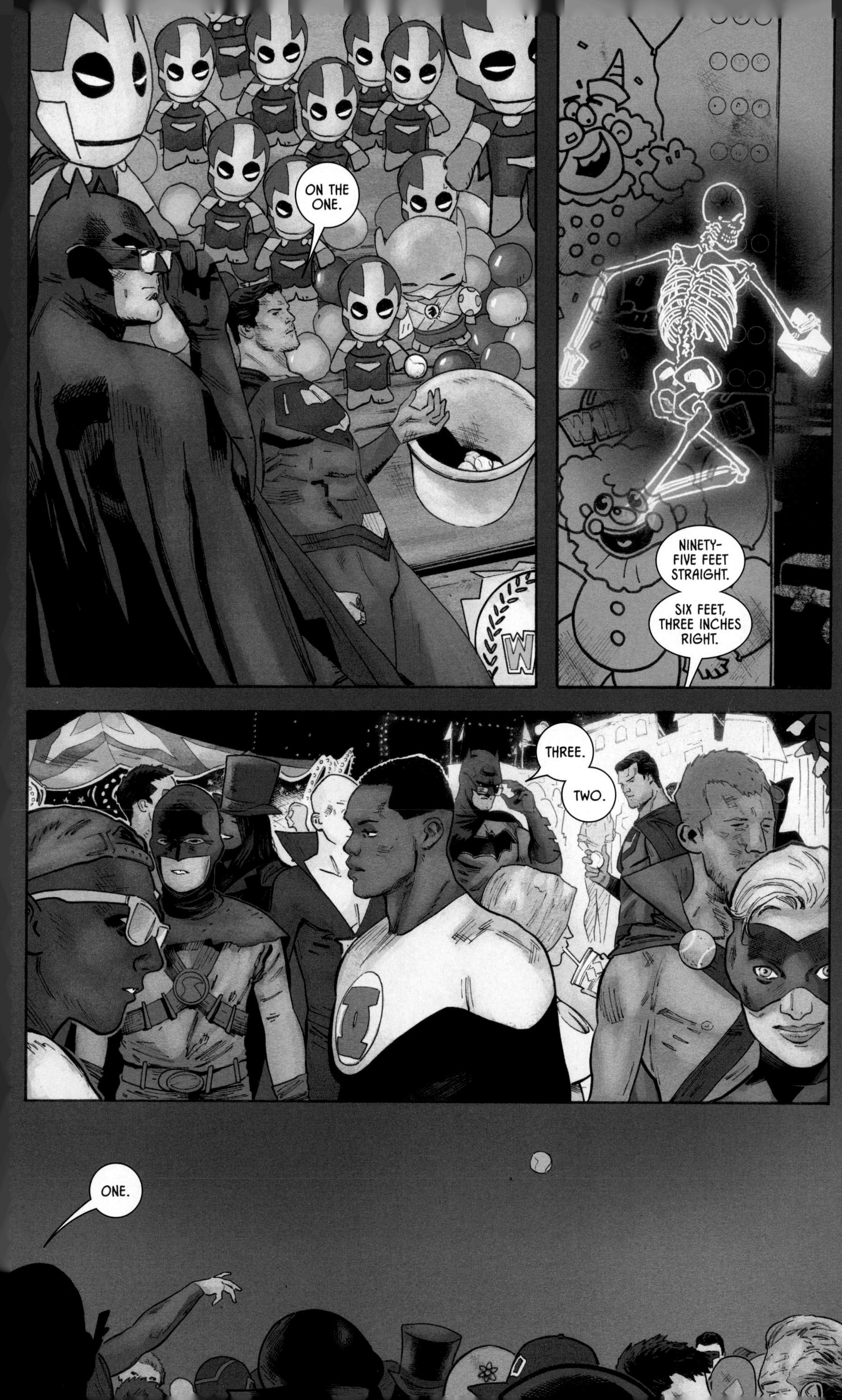
ON THE ONE.
NINETY-FIVE FEET STRAIGHT.
SIX FEET, THREE INCHES RIGHT.
THREE.
TWO.
ONE.

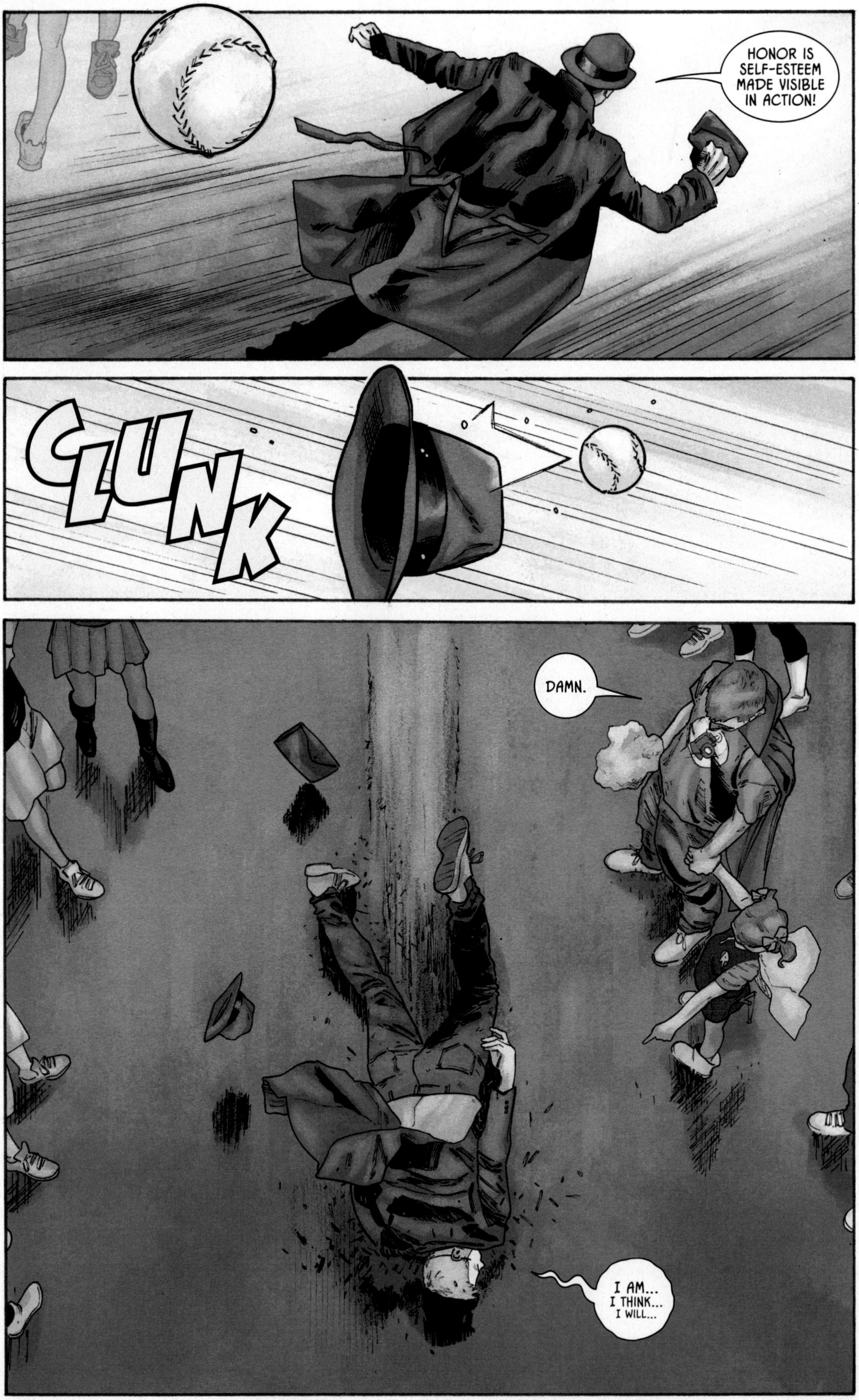
HONOR IS SELF-ESTEEM MADE VISIBLE IN ACTION!
CLUNK
DAMN.
I AM... I THINK... I WILL...

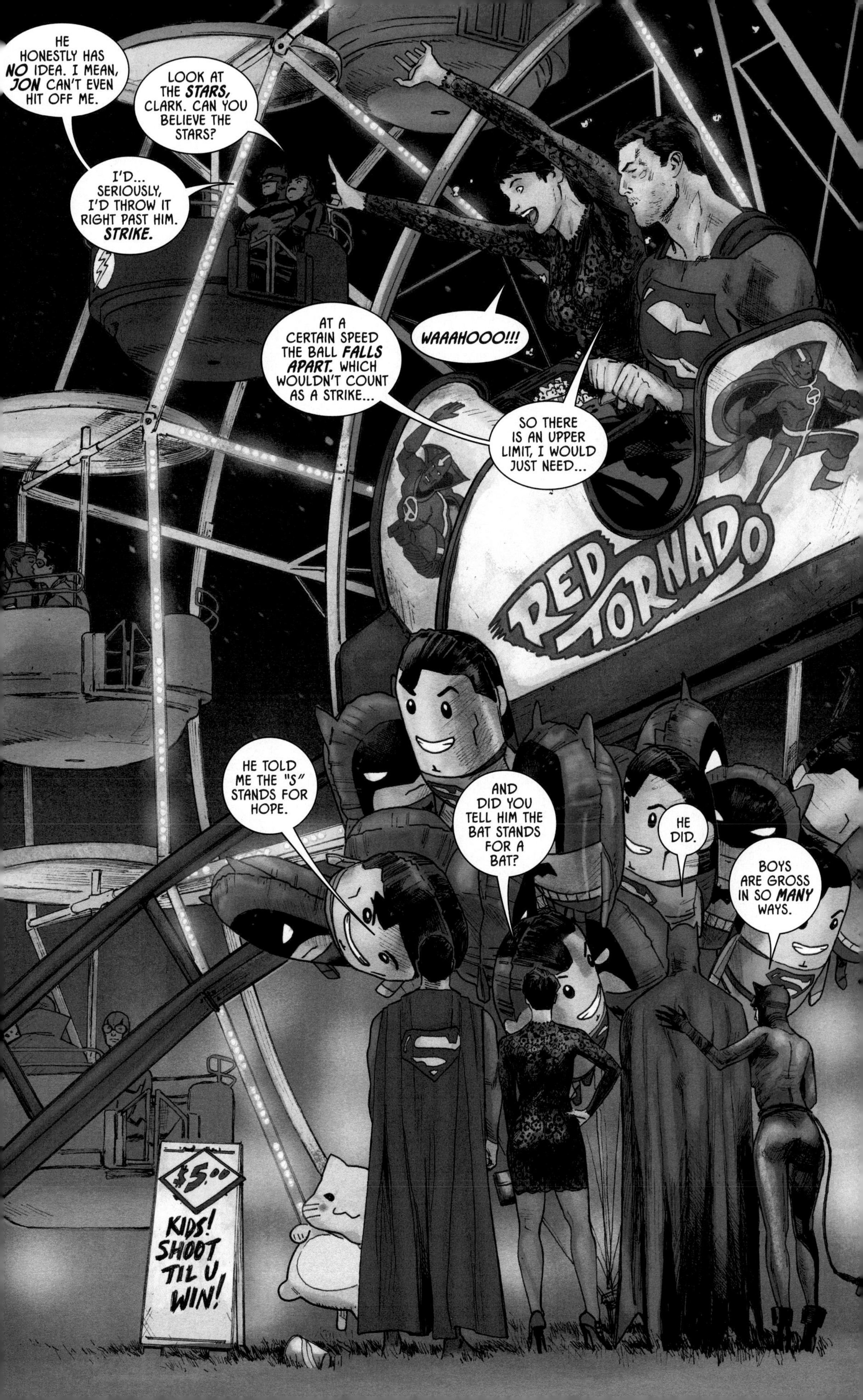
HE HONESTLY HAS **NO** IDEA. I MEAN, **JON** CAN'T EVEN HIT OFF ME.
LOOK AT THE **STARS,** CLARK. CAN YOU BELIEVE THE STARS?
I'D... SERIOUSLY, I'D THROW IT RIGHT PAST HIM. **STRIKE.**
WAAAHOOO!!!
AT A CERTAIN SPEED THE BALL **FALLS APART.** WHICH WOULDN'T COUNT AS A STRIKE...
SO THERE IS AN UPPER LIMIT, I WOULD JUST NEED...
RED TORNADO
HE TOLD ME THE "S" STANDS FOR HOPE.
AND DID YOU TELL HIM THE BAT STANDS FOR A BAT?
HE DID.
BOYS ARE GROSS IN SO **MANY** WAYS.
$5.00
KIDS! SHOOT TIL U WIN!

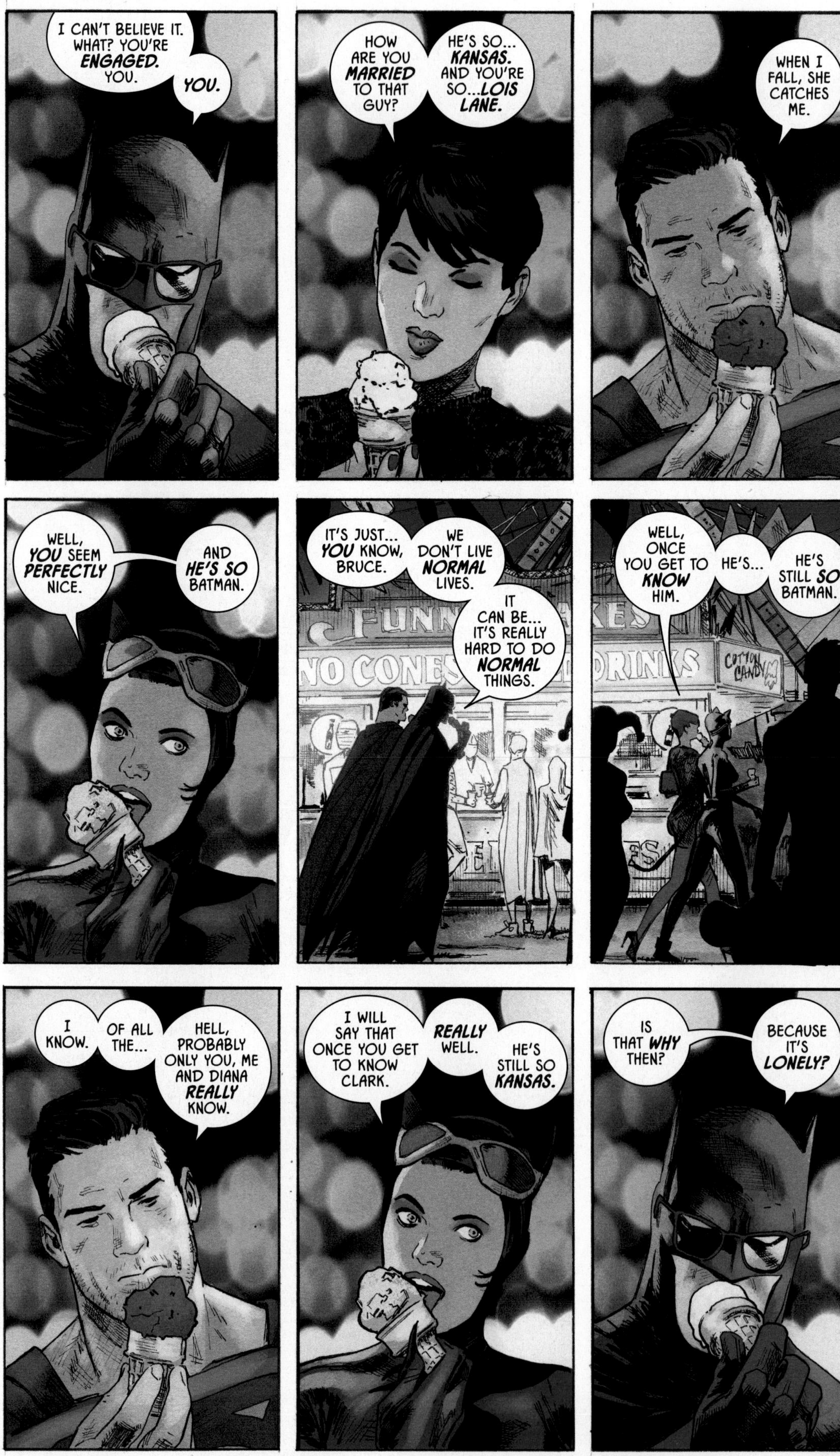

I CAN'T BELIEVE IT. WHAT? YOU'RE ENGAGED. YOU.
YOU.
HOW ARE YOU MARRIED TO THAT GUY?
HE'S SO... KANSAS. AND YOU'RE SO...LOIS LANE.
WHEN I FALL, SHE CATCHES ME.
WELL, YOU SEEM PERFECTLY NICE.
AND HE'S SO BATMAN.
IT'S JUST... YOU KNOW, BRUCE.
WE DON'T LIVE NORMAL LIVES.
IT CAN BE... IT'S REALLY HARD TO DO NORMAL THINGS.
FUNN
KES
NO CONES
DRINKS
COTTON CANDY
WELL, ONCE YOU GET TO KNOW HIM.
HE'S...
HE'S STILL SO BATMAN.
I KNOW.
OF ALL THE...
HELL, PROBABLY ONLY YOU, ME AND DIANA REALLY KNOW.
I WILL SAY THAT ONCE YOU GET TO KNOW CLARK.
REALLY WELL.
HE'S STILL SO KANSAS.
IS THAT WHY THEN?
BECAUSE IT'S LONELY?

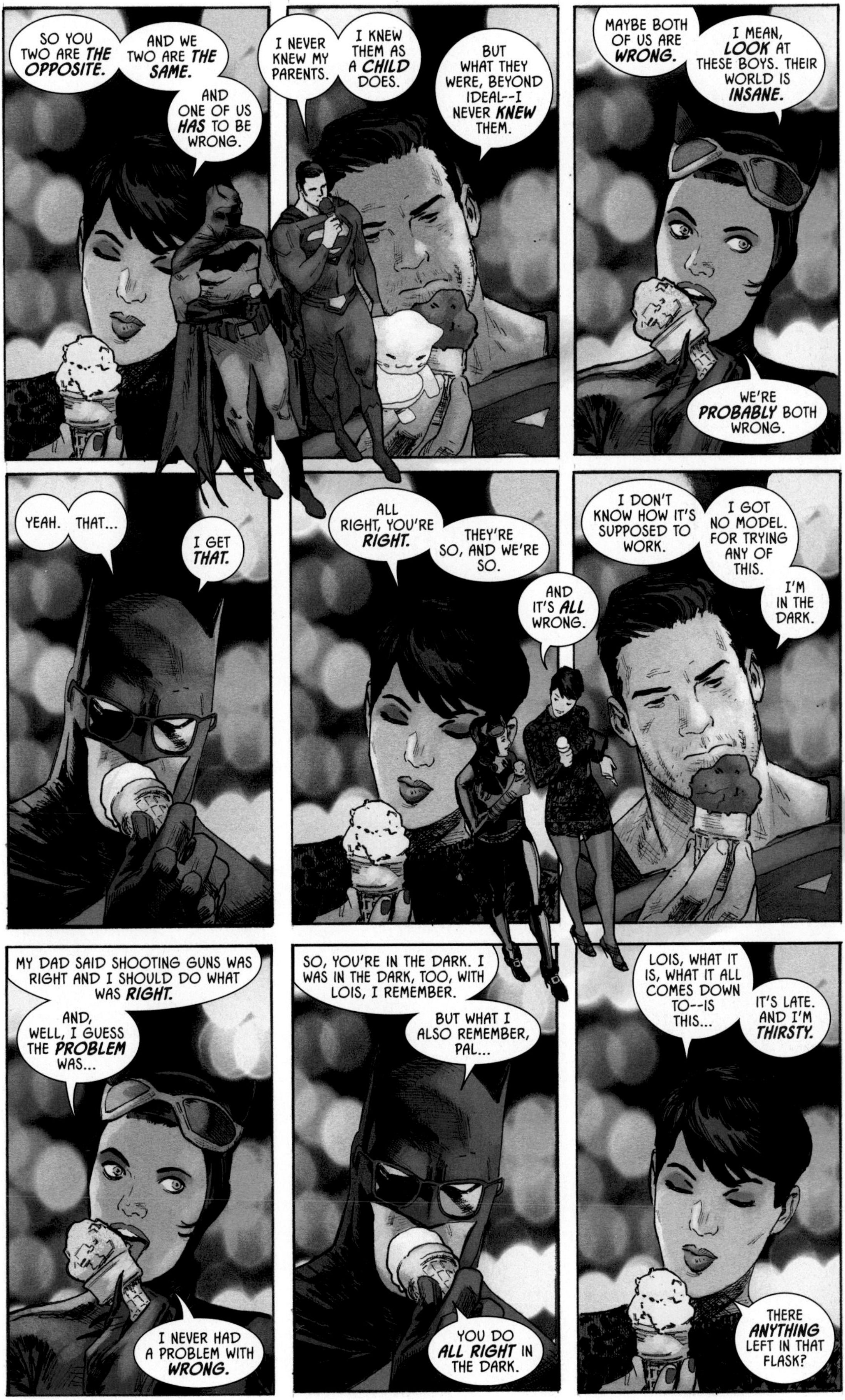
SO YOU TWO ARE THE OPPOSITE.
AND WE TWO ARE THE SAME.
AND ONE OF US HAS TO BE WRONG.
I NEVER KNEW MY PARENTS.
I KNEW THEM AS A CHILD DOES.
BUT WHAT THEY WERE, BEYOND IDEAL--I NEVER KNEW THEM.
MAYBE BOTH OF US ARE WRONG.
I MEAN, LOOK AT THESE BOYS. THEIR WORLD IS INSANE.
WE'RE PROBABLY BOTH WRONG.
YEAH.
THAT...
I GET THAT.
ALL RIGHT, YOU'RE RIGHT.
THEY'RE SO, AND WE'RE SO.
AND IT'S ALL WRONG.
I DON'T KNOW HOW IT'S SUPPOSED TO WORK.
I GOT NO MODEL. FOR TRYING ANY OF THIS.
I'M IN THE DARK.
MY DAD SAID SHOOTING GUNS WAS RIGHT AND I SHOULD DO WHAT WAS RIGHT.
AND, WELL, I GUESS THE PROBLEM WAS...
I NEVER HAD A PROBLEM WITH WRONG.
SO, YOU'RE IN THE DARK. I WAS IN THE DARK, TOO, WITH LOIS, I REMEMBER.
BUT WHAT I ALSO REMEMBER, PAL...
YOU DO ALL RIGHT IN THE DARK.
LOIS, WHAT IT IS, WHAT IT ALL COMES DOWN TO--IS THIS...
IT'S LATE. AND I'M THIRSTY.
THERE ANYTHING LEFT IN THAT FLASK?

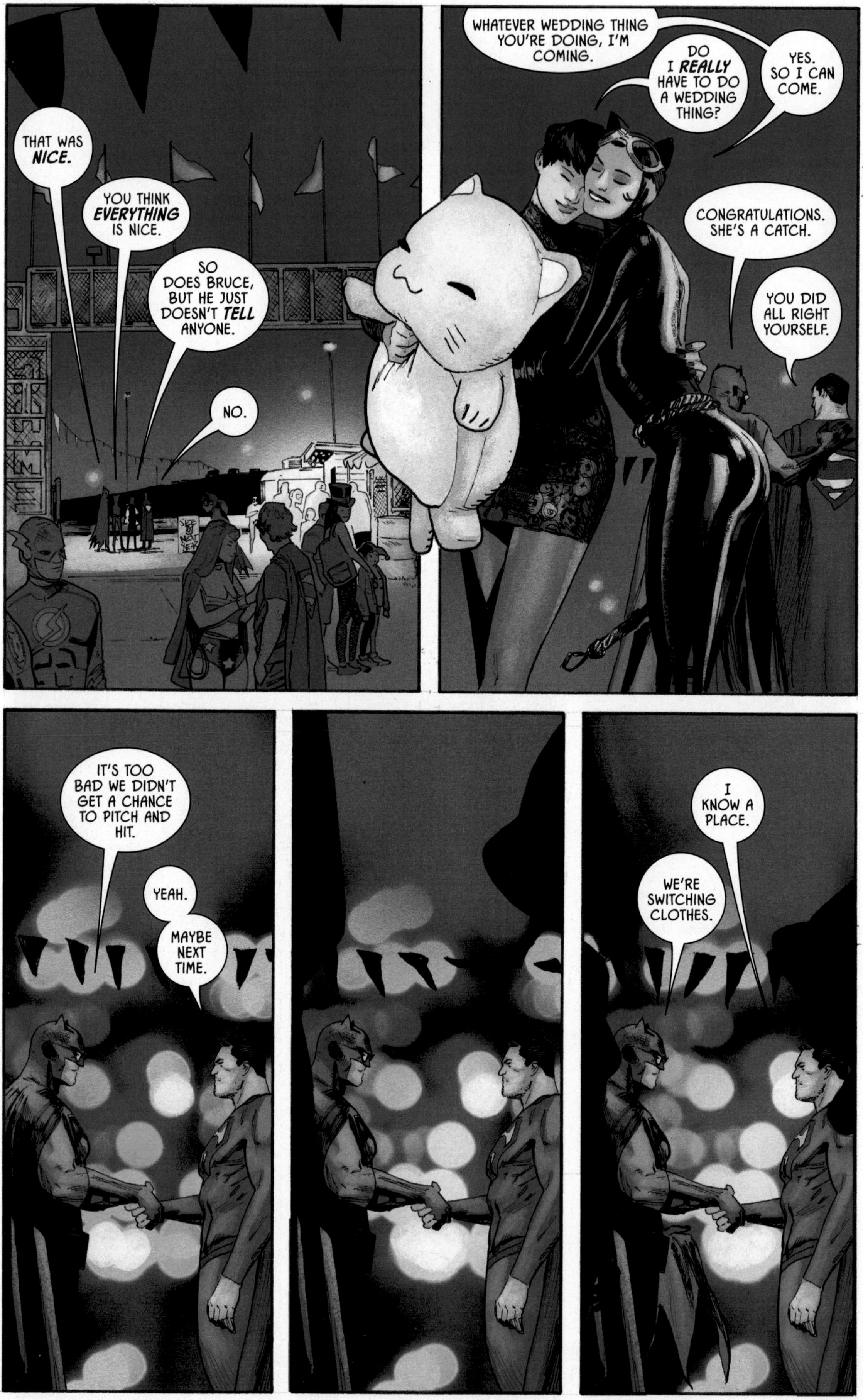
THAT WAS NICE.
YOU THINK EVERYTHING IS NICE.
SO DOES BRUCE, BUT HE JUST DOESN'T TELL ANYONE.
NO.
WHATEVER WEDDING THING YOU'RE DOING, I'M COMING.
DO I REALLY HAVE TO DO A WEDDING THING?
YES. SO I CAN COME.
CONGRATULATIONS. SHE'S A CATCH.
YOU DID ALL RIGHT YOURSELF.
IT'S TOO BAD WE DIDN'T GET A CHANCE TO PITCH AND HIT.
YEAH.
MAYBE NEXT TIME.
I KNOW A PLACE.
WE'RE SWITCHING CLOTHES.

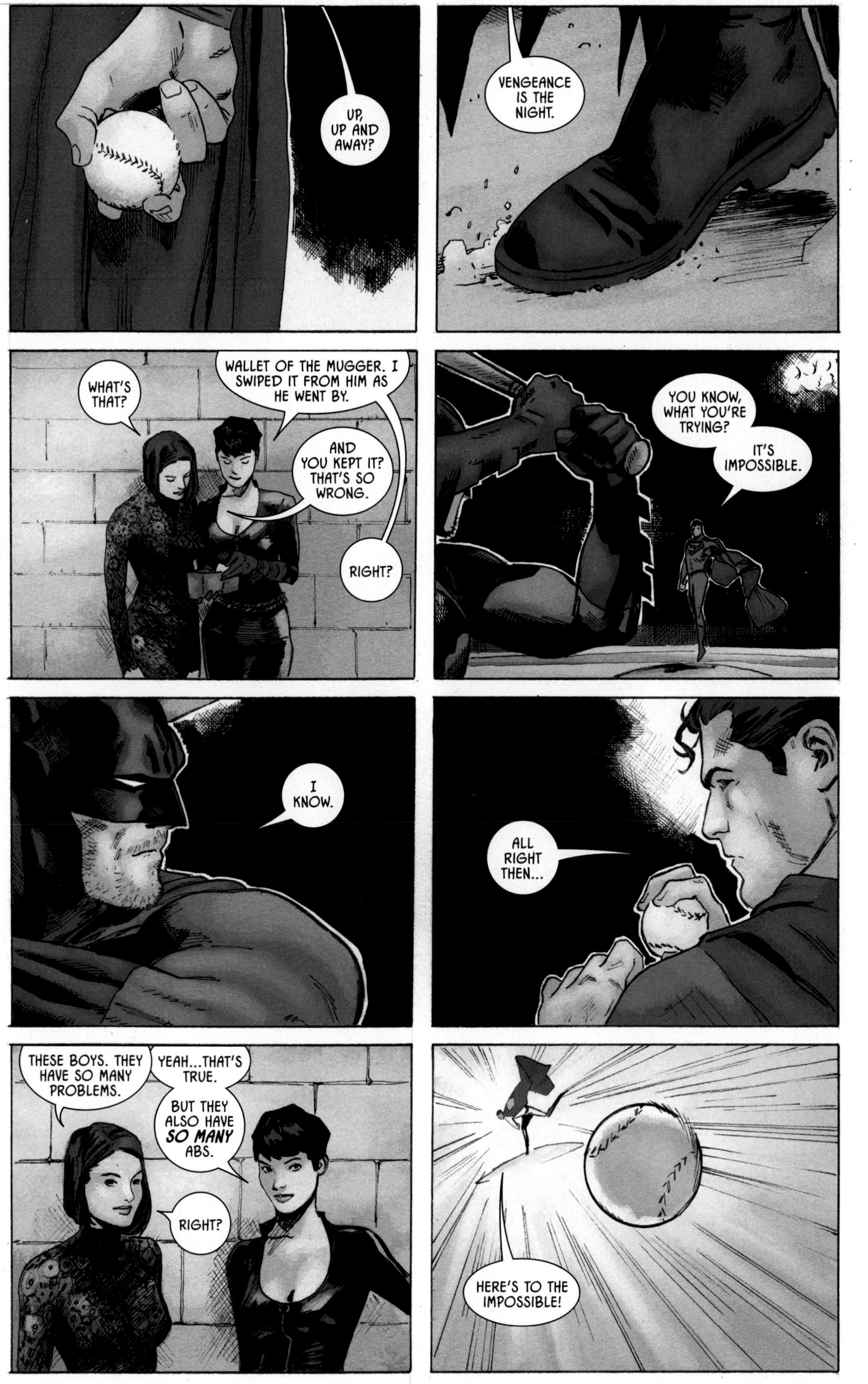
UP, UP AND AWAY?
VENGEANCE IS THE NIGHT.
WHAT'S THAT?
WALLET OF THE MUGGER. I SWIPED IT FROM HIM AS HE WENT BY.
AND YOU KEPT IT? THAT'S SO WRONG.
RIGHT?
YOU KNOW, WHAT YOU'RE TRYING?
IT'S IMPOSSIBLE.
I KNOW.
ALL RIGHT THEN...
THESE BOYS. THEY HAVE SO MANY PROBLEMS.
YEAH...THAT'S TRUE.
BUT THEY ALSO HAVE ***SO MANY*** ABS.
RIGHT?
HERE'S TO THE IMPOSSIBLE!

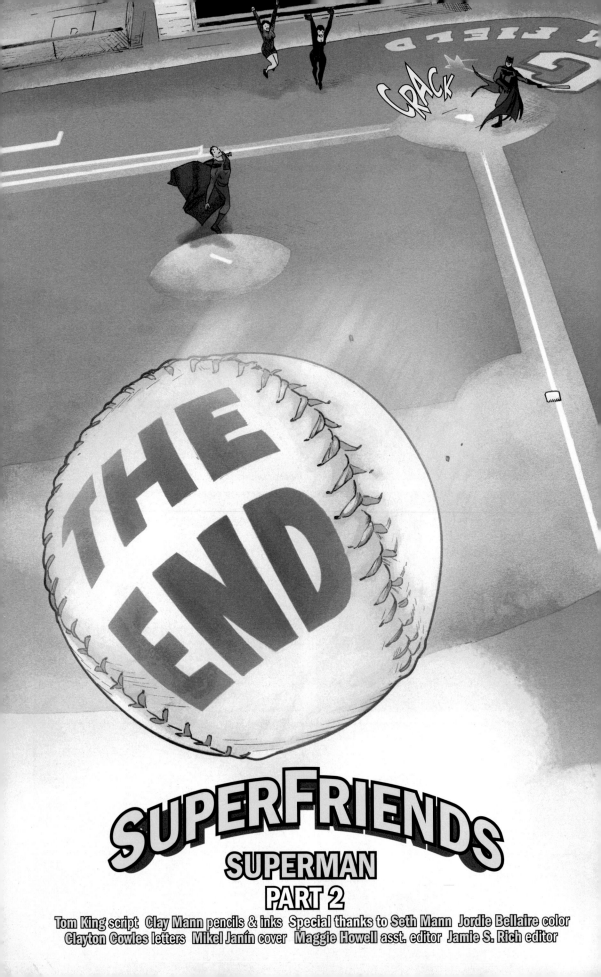

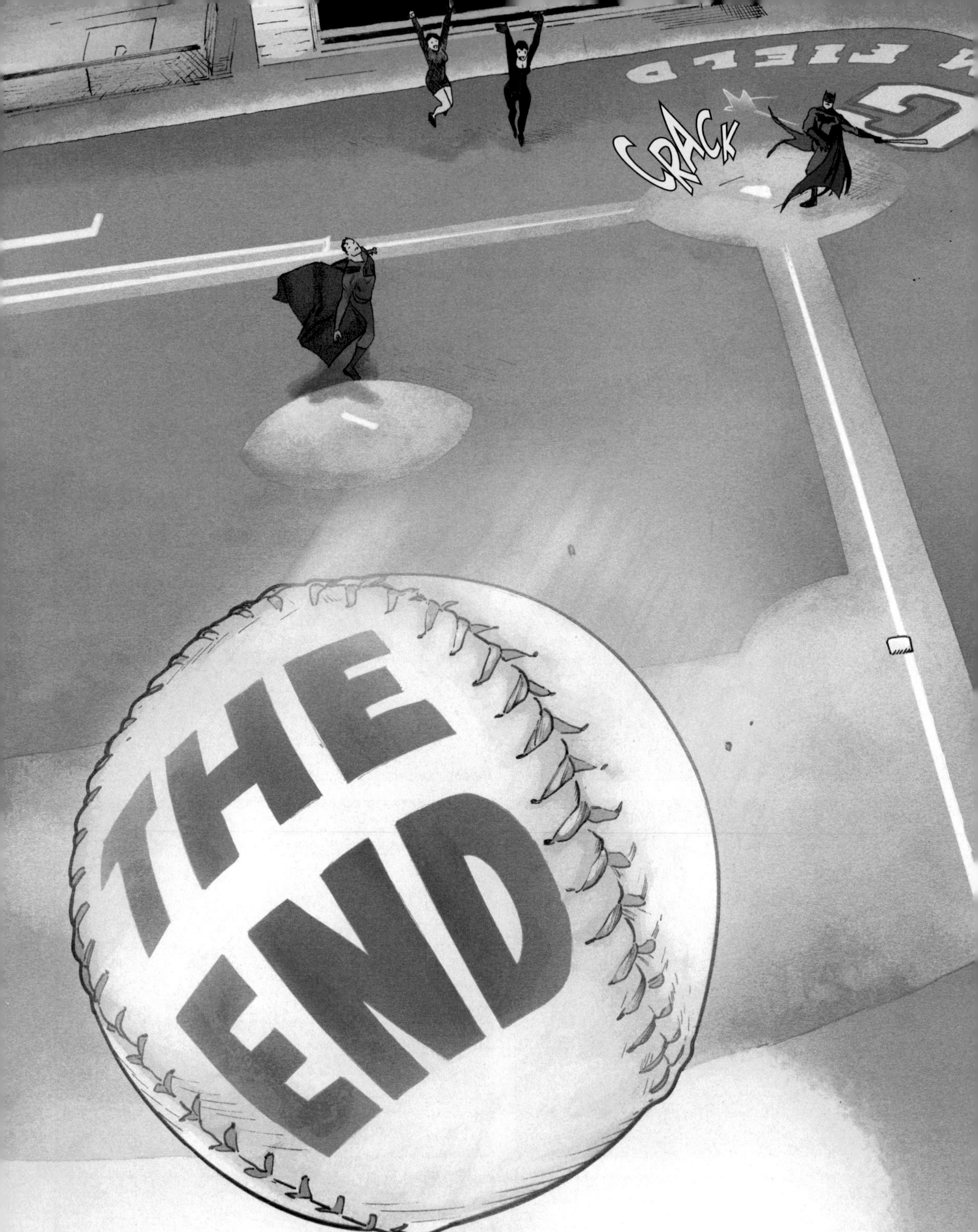
CRACK
THE END

SUPERFRIENDS

SUPERMAN

PART 2

Tom King script Clay Mann pencils & inks Special thanks to Seth Mann Jordie Bellaire color
Clayton Cowles letters Mikel Janín cover Maggie Howell asst. editor Jamie S. Rich editor

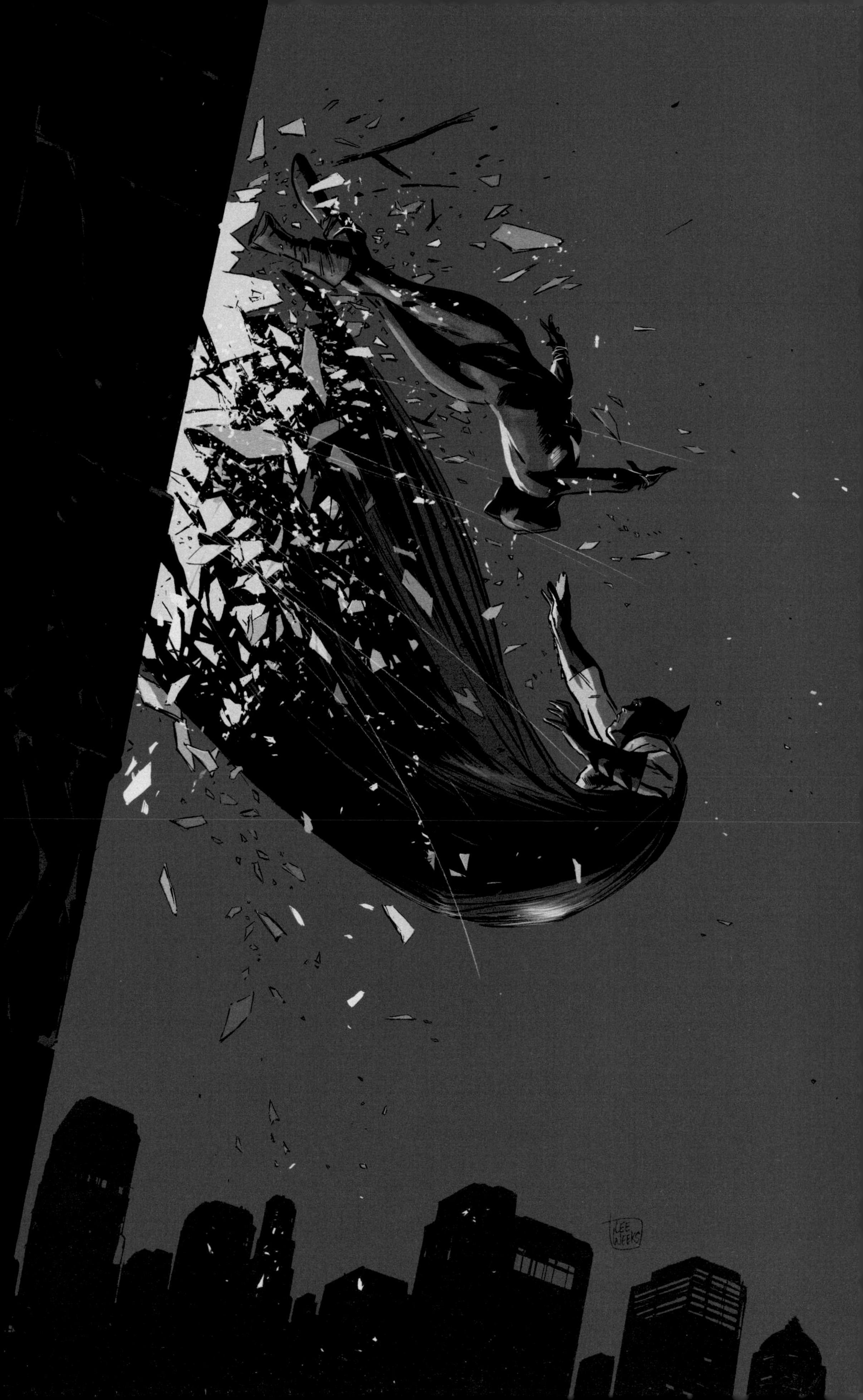
LEE WEEKS

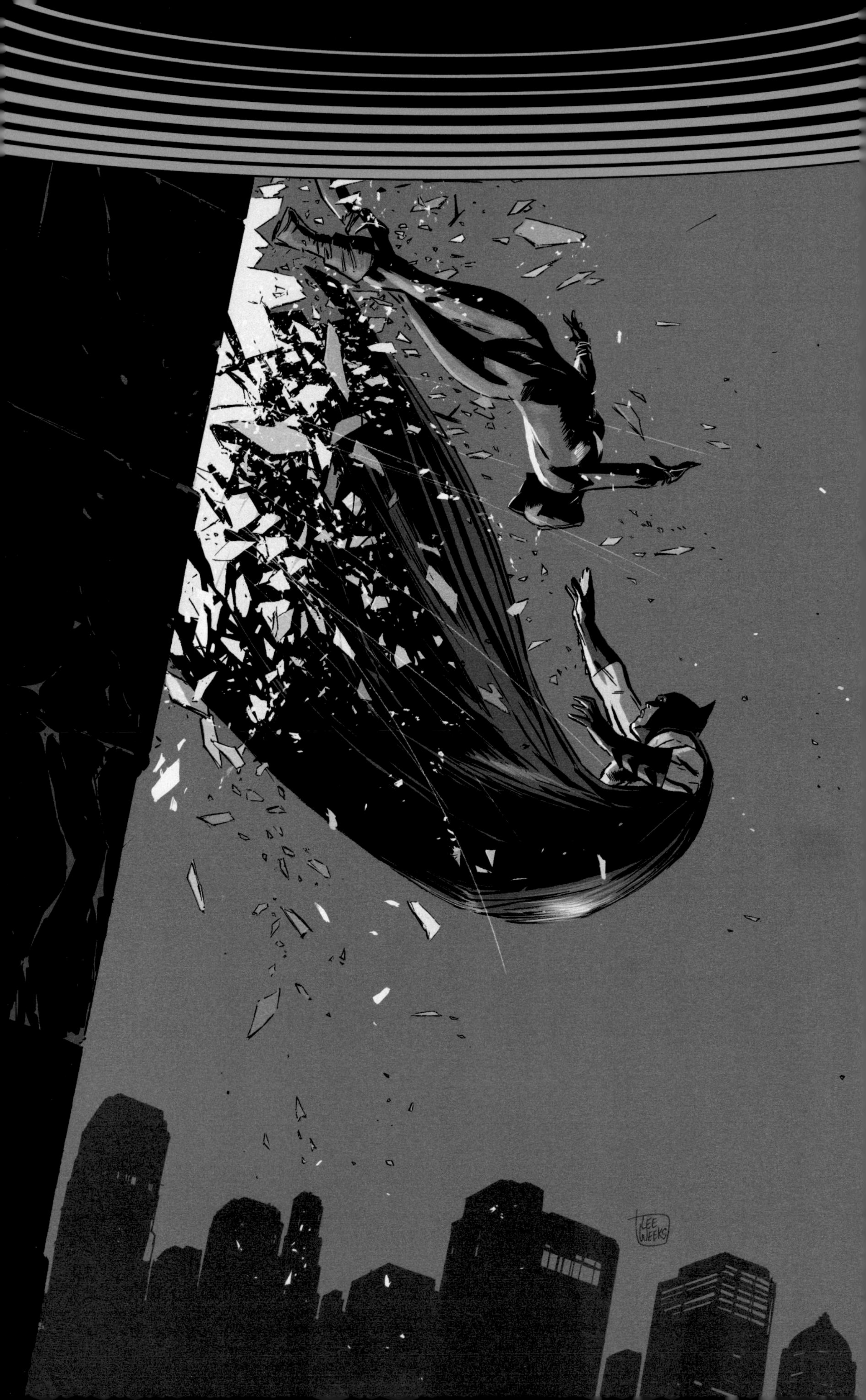
LEE WEEKS

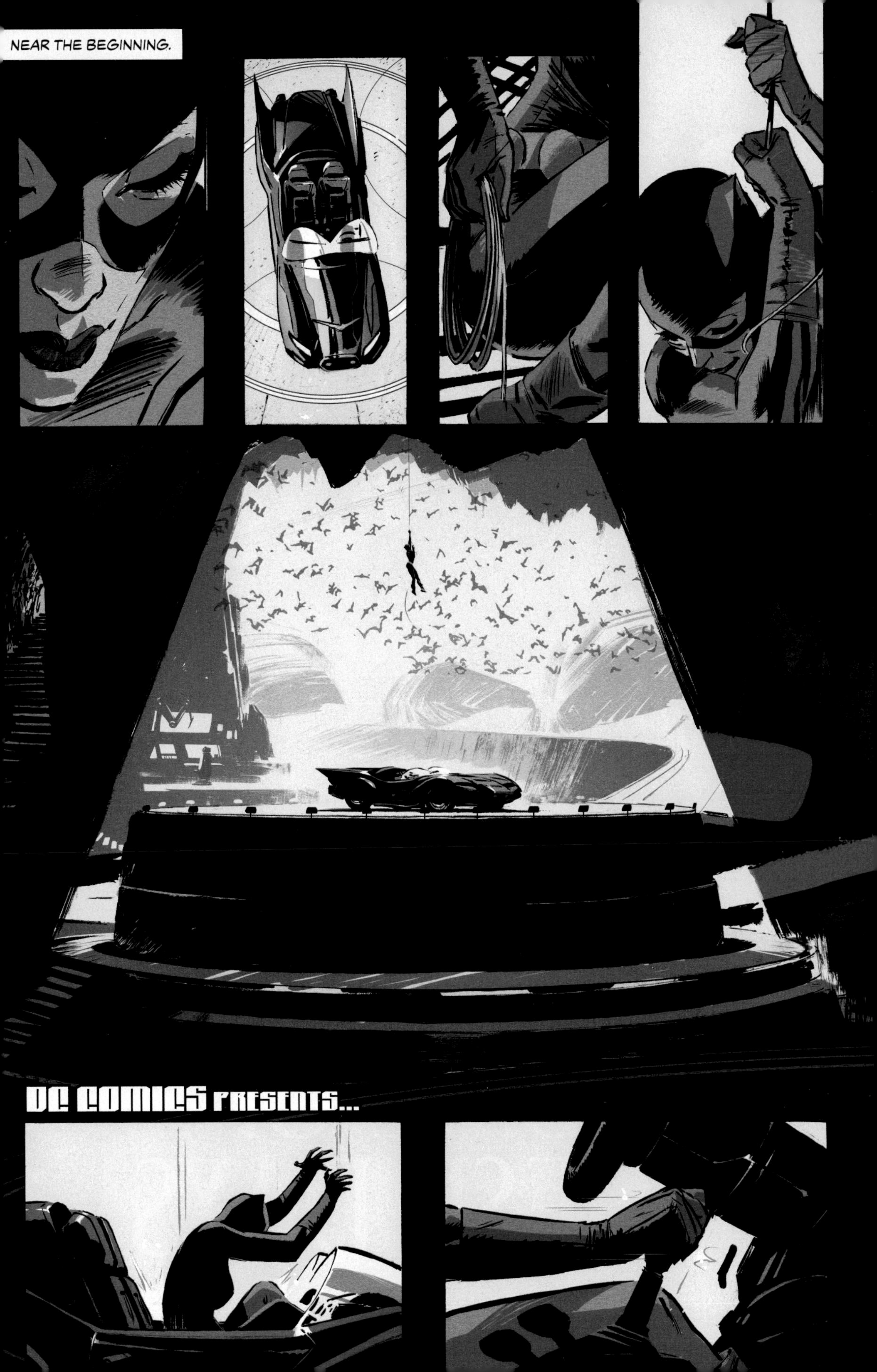
NEAR THE BEGINNING.
DC COMICS PRESENTS...

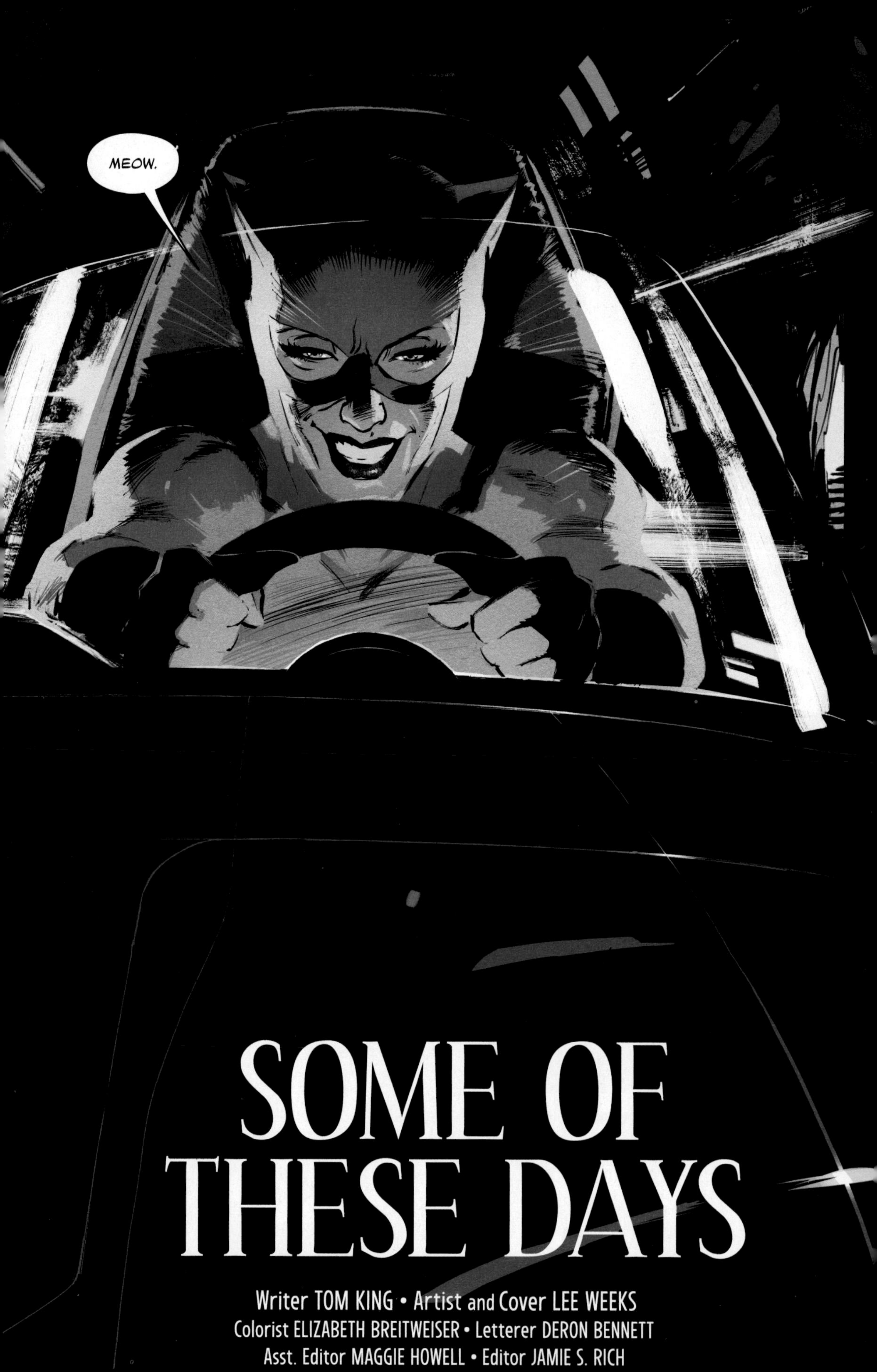
MEOW.
SOME OF THESE DAYS
Writer TOM KING • Artist and Cover LEE WEEKS
Colorist ELIZABETH BREITWEISER • Letterer DERON BENNETT
Asst. Editor MAGGIE HOWELL • Editor JAMIE S. RICH

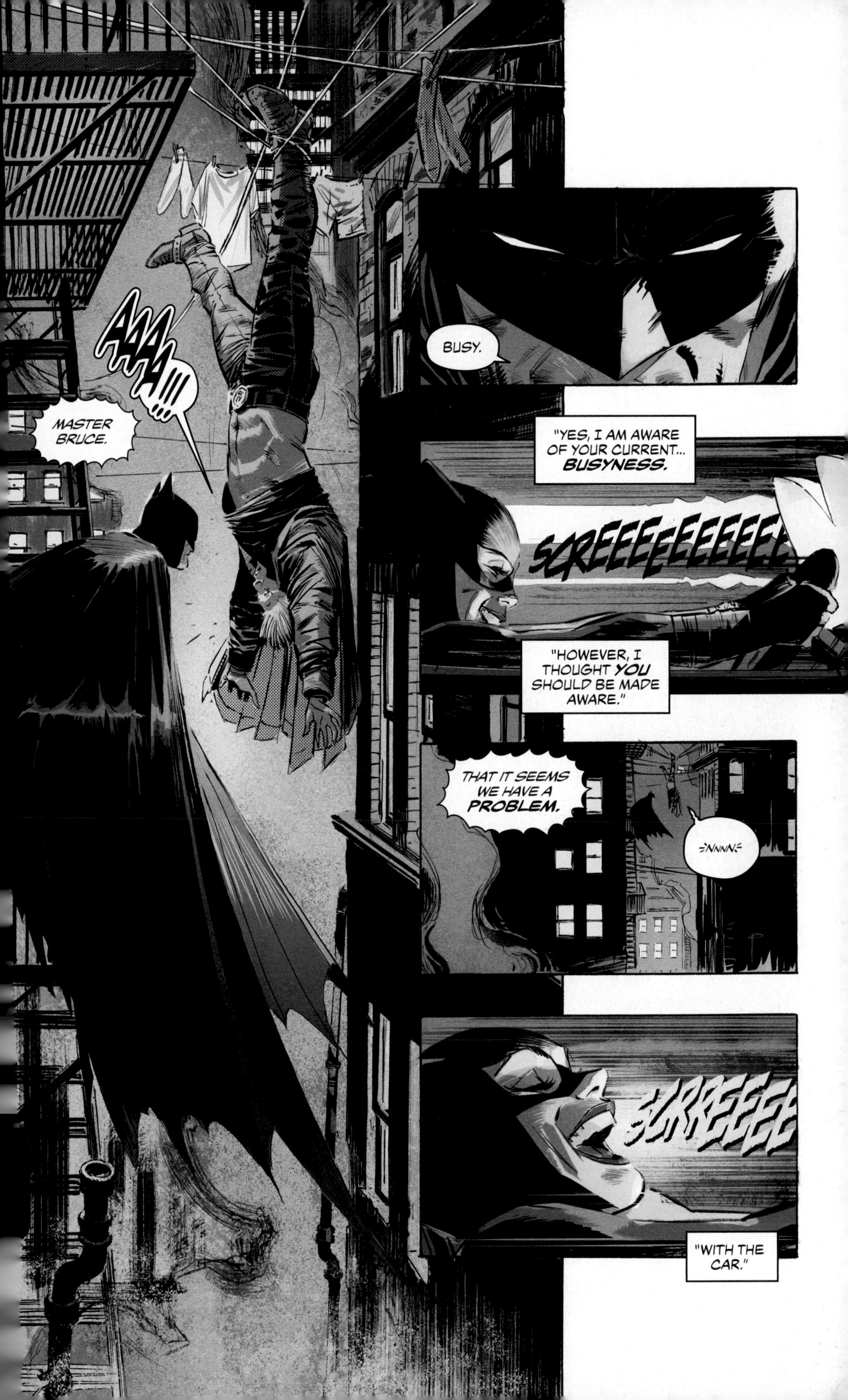
AAAA!!!
MASTER BRUCE.
BUSY.
"YES, I AM AWARE OF YOUR CURRENT... **BUSYNESS.**
SCREEEEEEEEEE
"HOWEVER, I THOUGHT **YOU** SHOULD BE MADE AWARE."
THAT IT SEEMS WE HAVE A **PROBLEM.**
NNNN
SCREEEE
"WITH THE CAR."

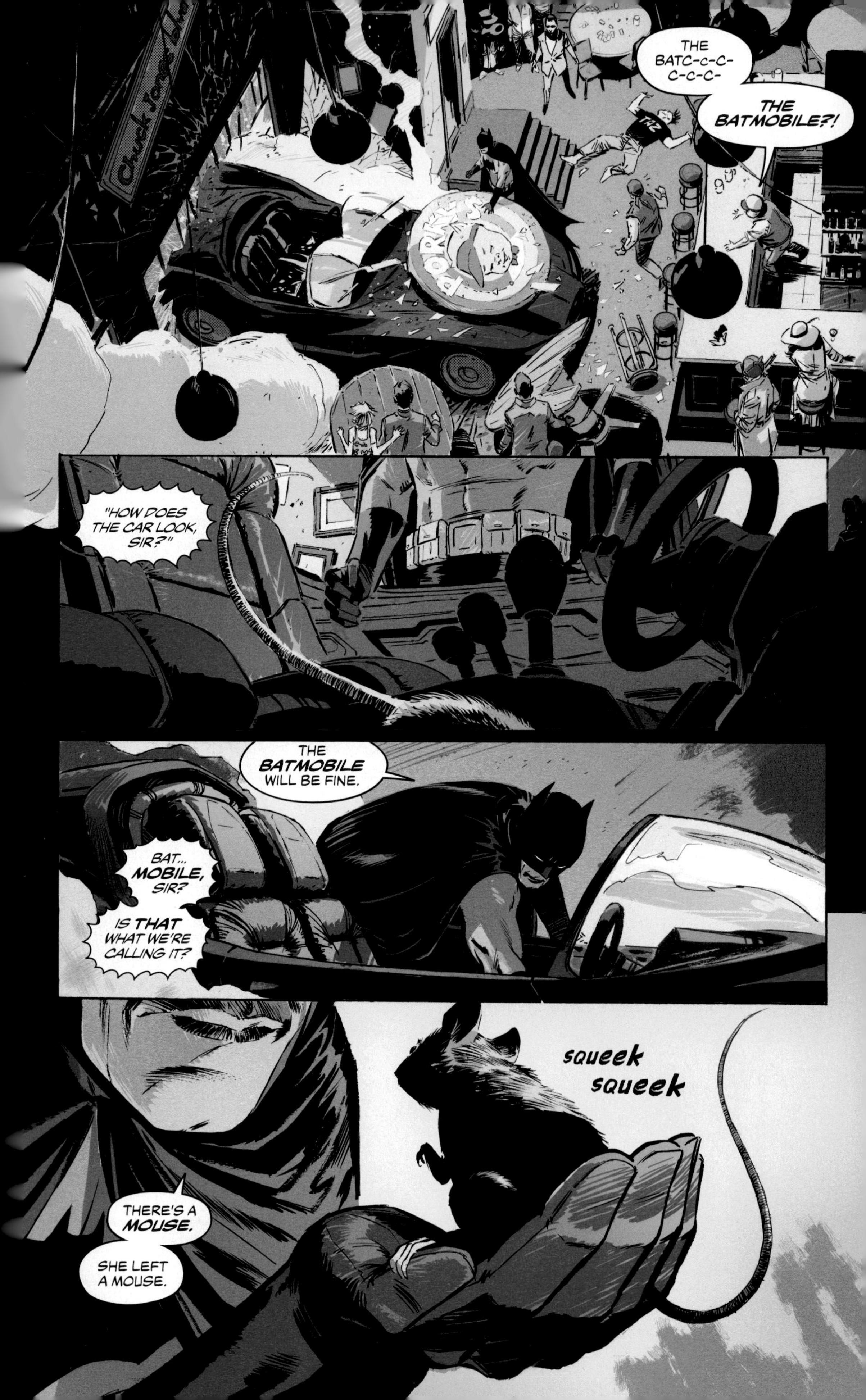

THE BATC-c-C-C-c-C-
THE BATMOBILE?!
"HOW DOES THE CAR LOOK, SIR?"
THE BATMOBILE WILL BE FINE.
BAT... MOBILE, SIR?
IS THAT WHAT WE'RE CALLING IT?
squeek squeek
THERE'S A MOUSE.
SHE LEFT A MOUSE.

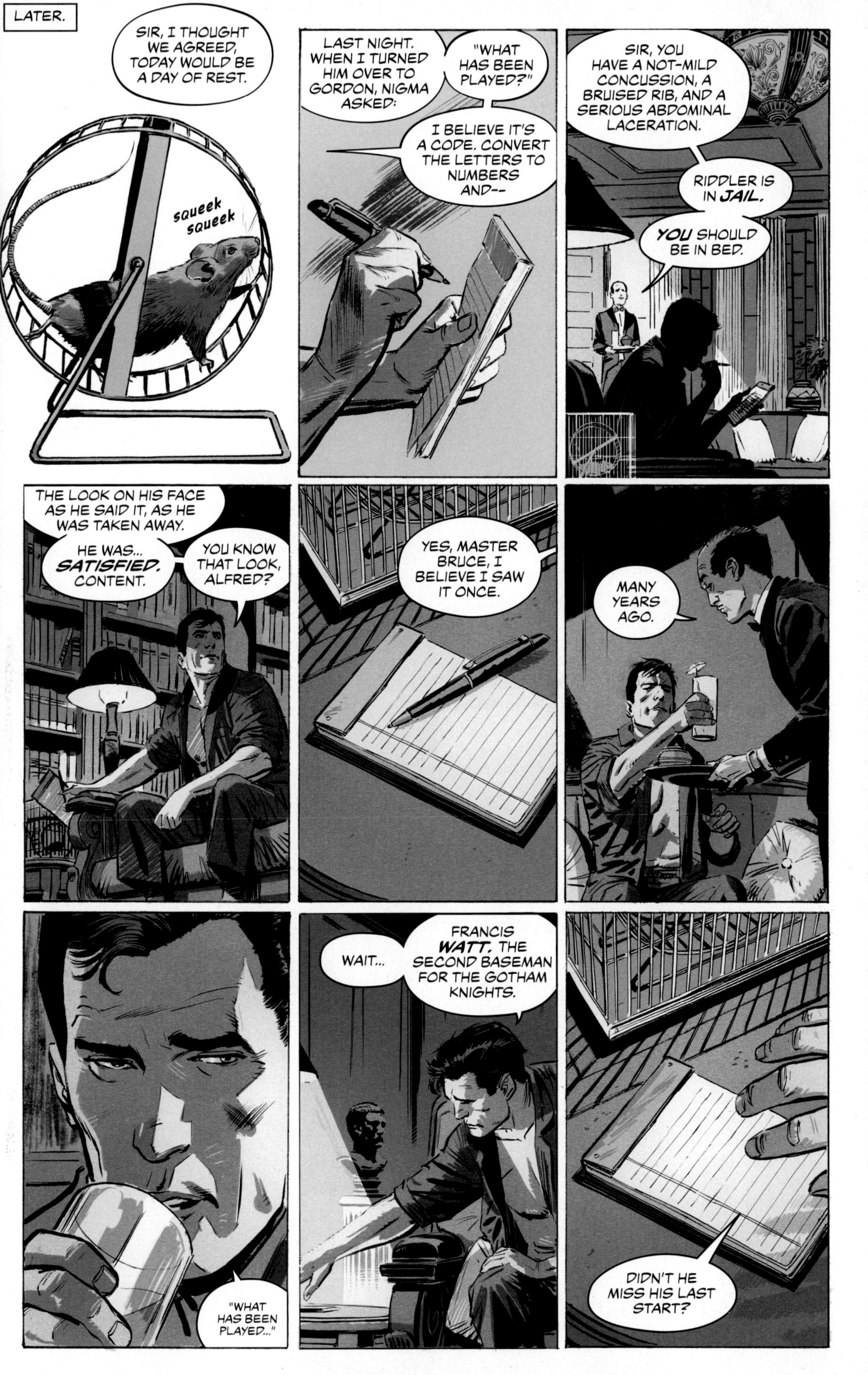
LATER.
SIR, I THOUGHT WE AGREED, TODAY WOULD BE A DAY OF REST.
squeek squeek
LAST NIGHT. WHEN I TURNED HIM OVER TO GORDON, NIGMA ASKED:
"WHAT HAS BEEN PLAYED?"
I BELIEVE IT'S A CODE. CONVERT THE LETTERS TO NUMBERS AND--
SIR, YOU HAVE A NOT-MILD CONCUSSION, A BRUISED RIB, AND A SERIOUS ABDOMINAL LACERATION.
RIDDLER IS IN JAIL.
YOU SHOULD BE IN BED.
THE LOOK ON HIS FACE AS HE SAID IT, AS HE WAS TAKEN AWAY.
HE WAS... SATISFIED. CONTENT.
YOU KNOW THAT LOOK, ALFRED?
YES, MASTER BRUCE, I BELIEVE I SAW IT ONCE.
MANY YEARS AGO.
"WHAT HAS BEEN PLAYED..."
WAIT...
FRANCIS WATT. THE SECOND BASEMAN FOR THE GOTHAM KNIGHTS.
DIDN'T HE MISS HIS LAST START?

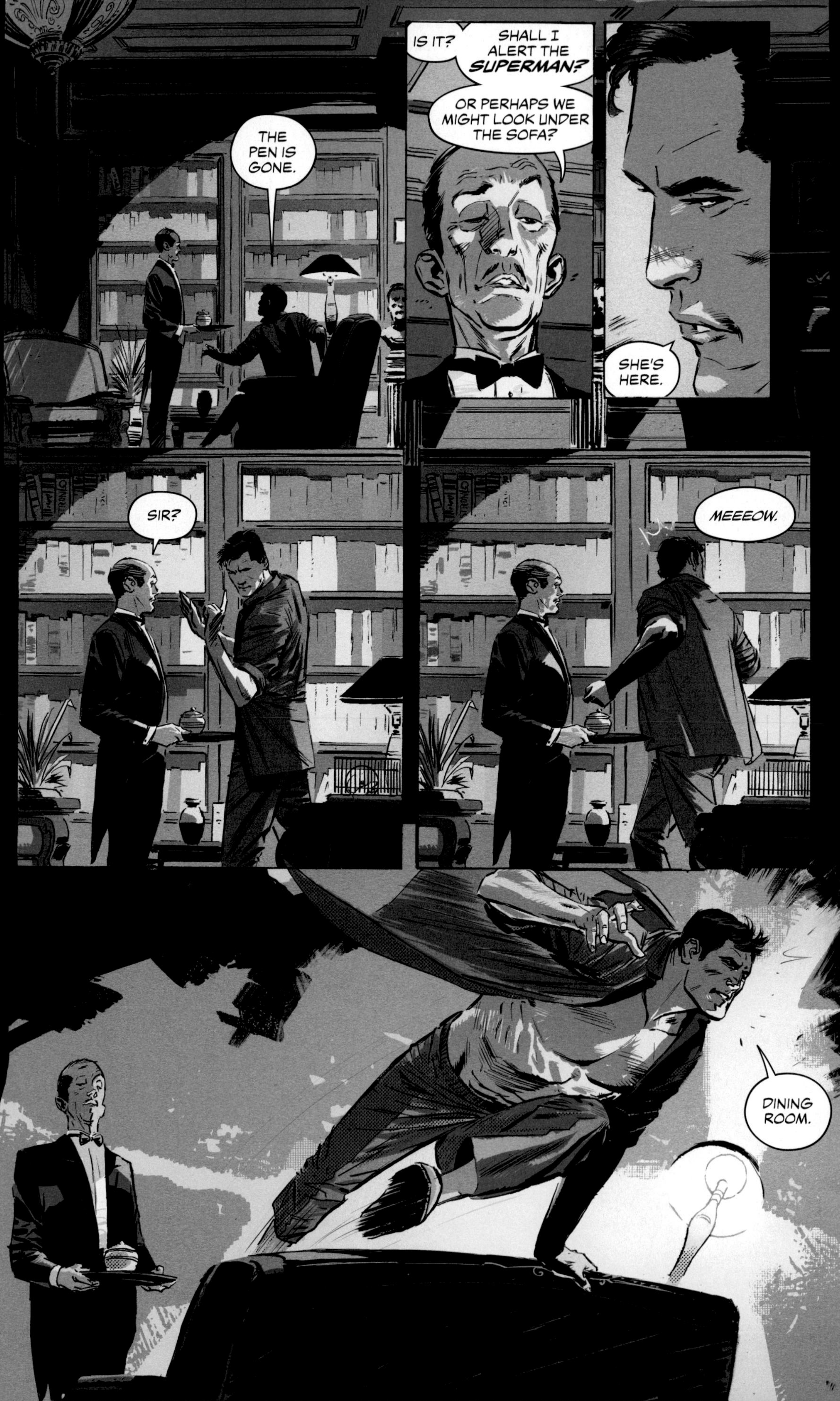
THE PEN IS GONE.
IS IT?
SHALL I ALERT THE SUPERMAN?
OR PERHAPS WE MIGHT LOOK UNDER THE SOFA?
SHE'S HERE.
SIR?
MEEEOW.
DINING ROOM.

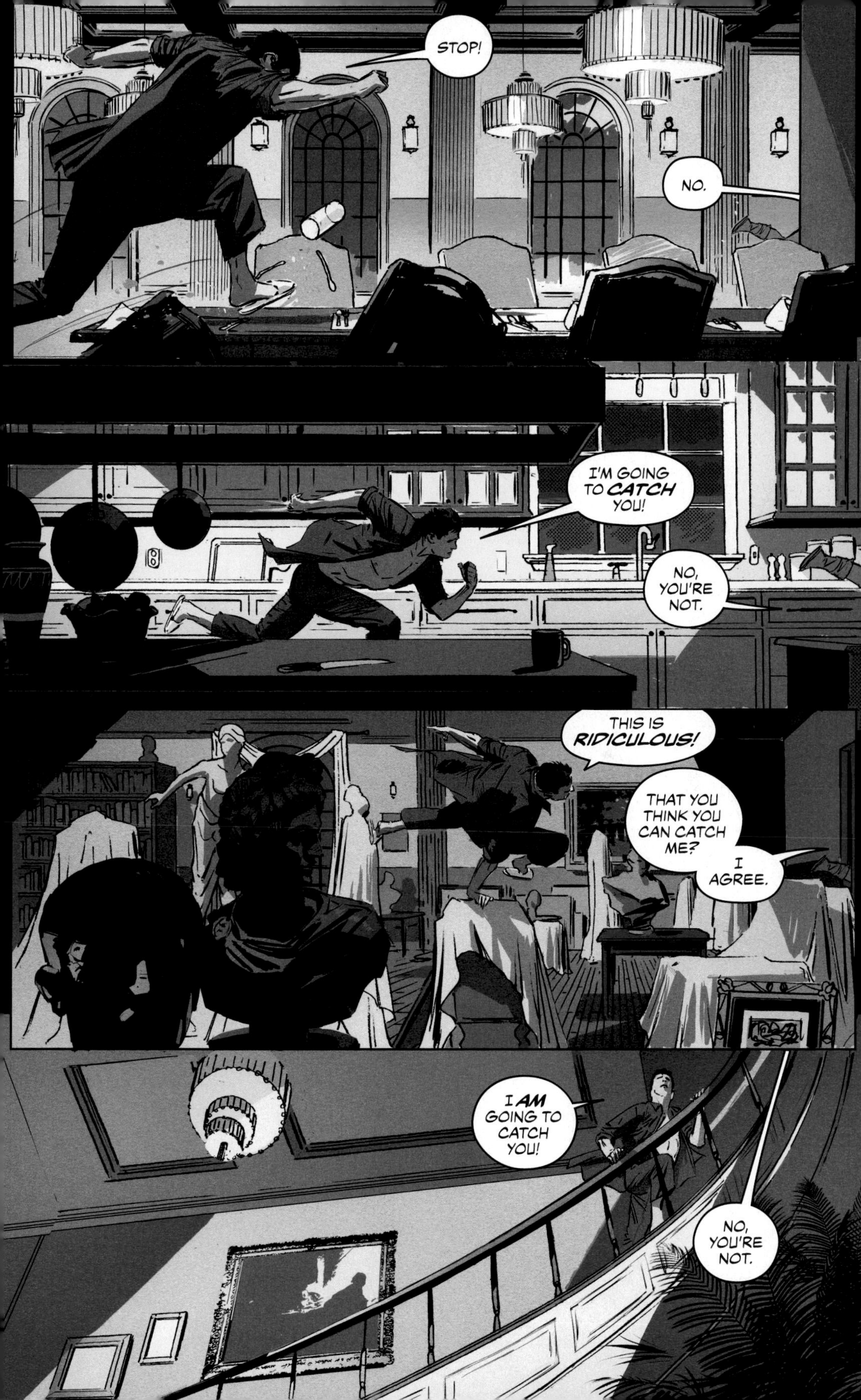
STOP!
NO.
I'M GOING TO CATCH YOU!
NO, YOU'RE NOT.
THIS IS RIDICULOUS!
THAT YOU THINK YOU CAN CATCH ME?
I AGREE.
I AM GOING TO CATCH YOU!
NO, YOU'RE NOT.

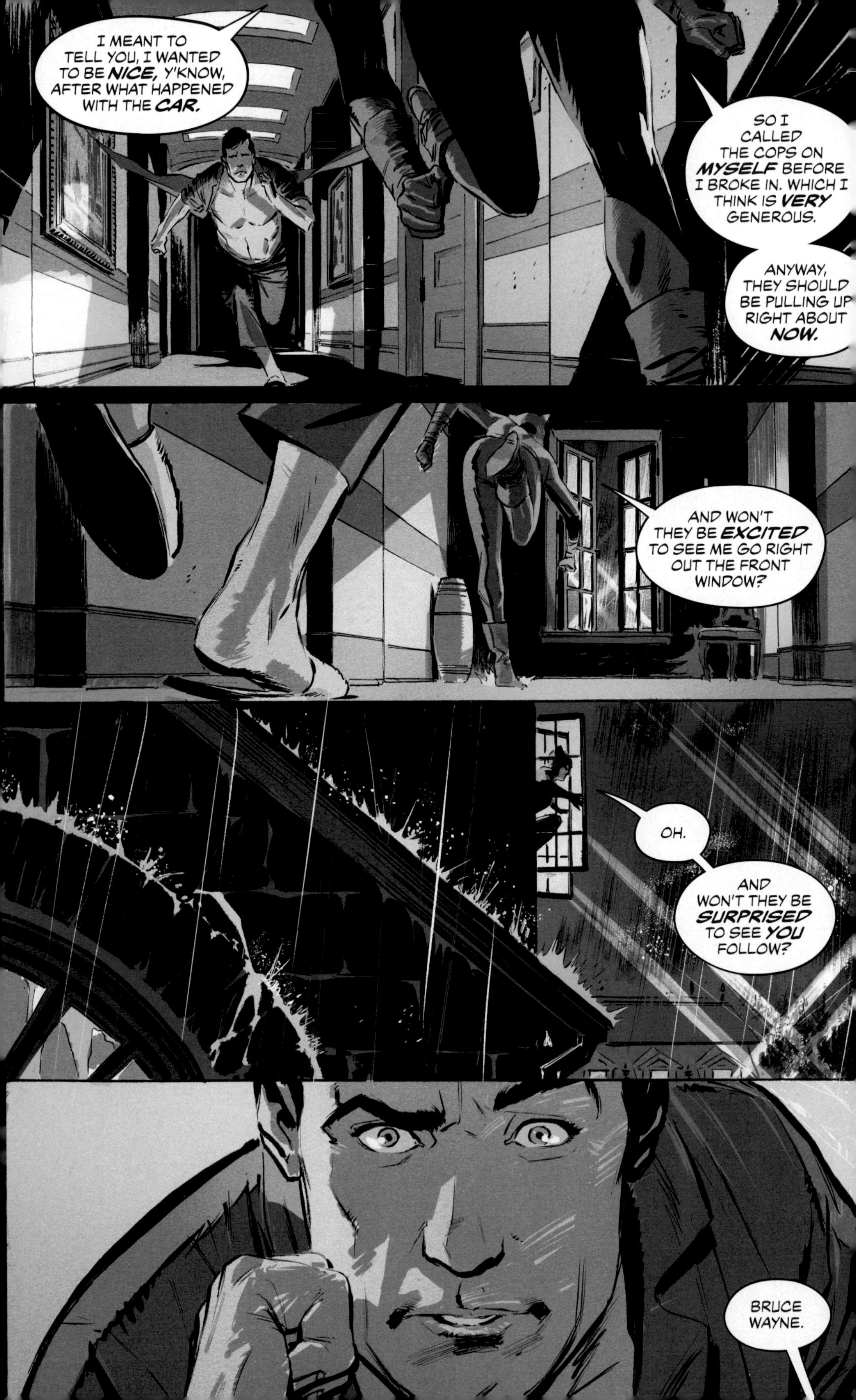
I MEANT TO TELL YOU, I WANTED TO BE NICE, Y'KNOW, AFTER WHAT HAPPENED WITH THE CAR.
SO I CALLED THE COPS ON MYSELF BEFORE I BROKE IN. WHICH I THINK IS VERY GENEROUS.
ANYWAY, THEY SHOULD BE PULLING UP RIGHT ABOUT NOW.
AND WON'T THEY BE EXCITED TO SEE ME GO RIGHT OUT THE FRONT WINDOW?
OH.
AND WON'T THEY BE SURPRISED TO SEE YOU FOLLOW?
BRUCE WAYNE.

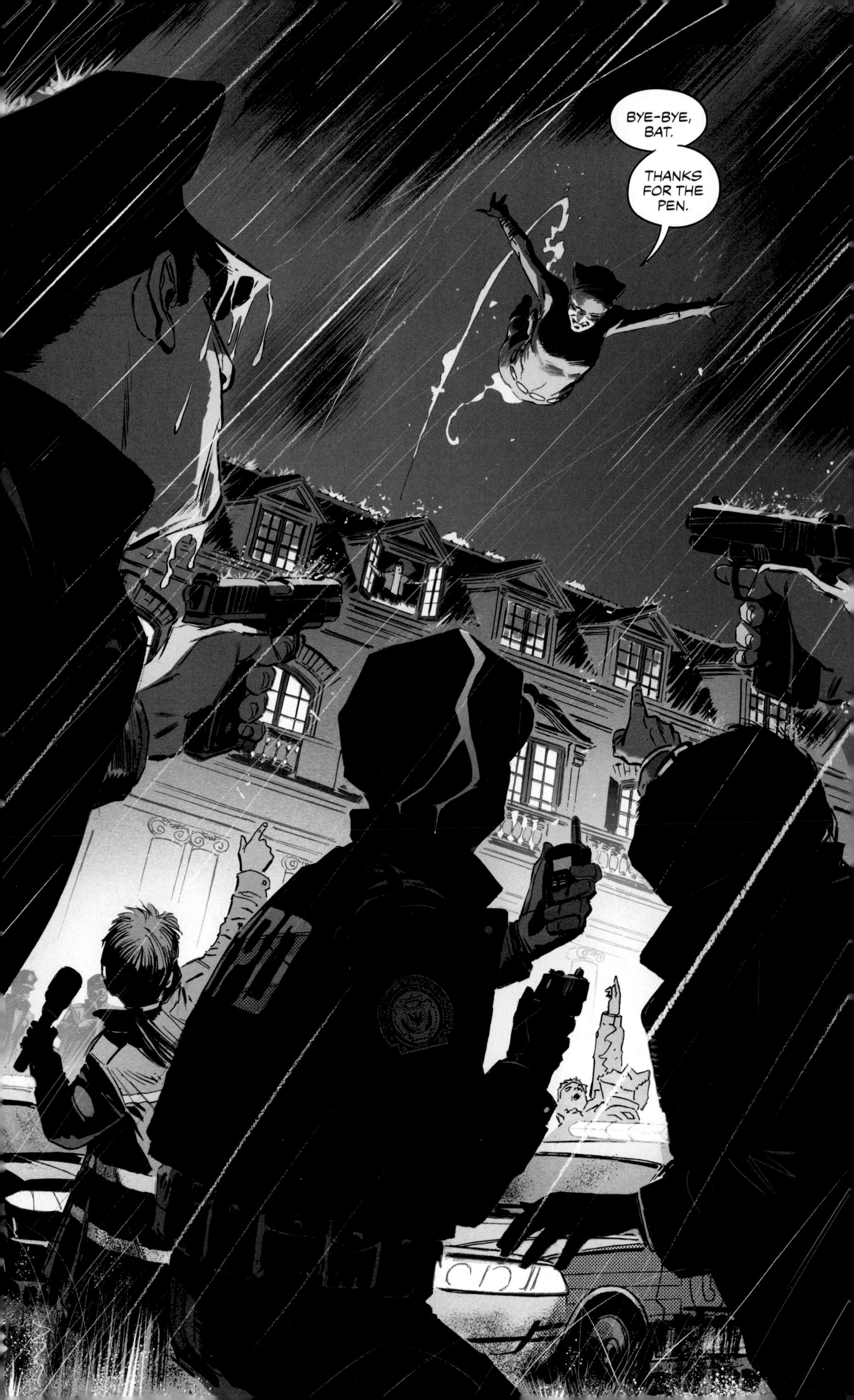
BYE-BYE, BAT.
THANKS FOR THE PEN.

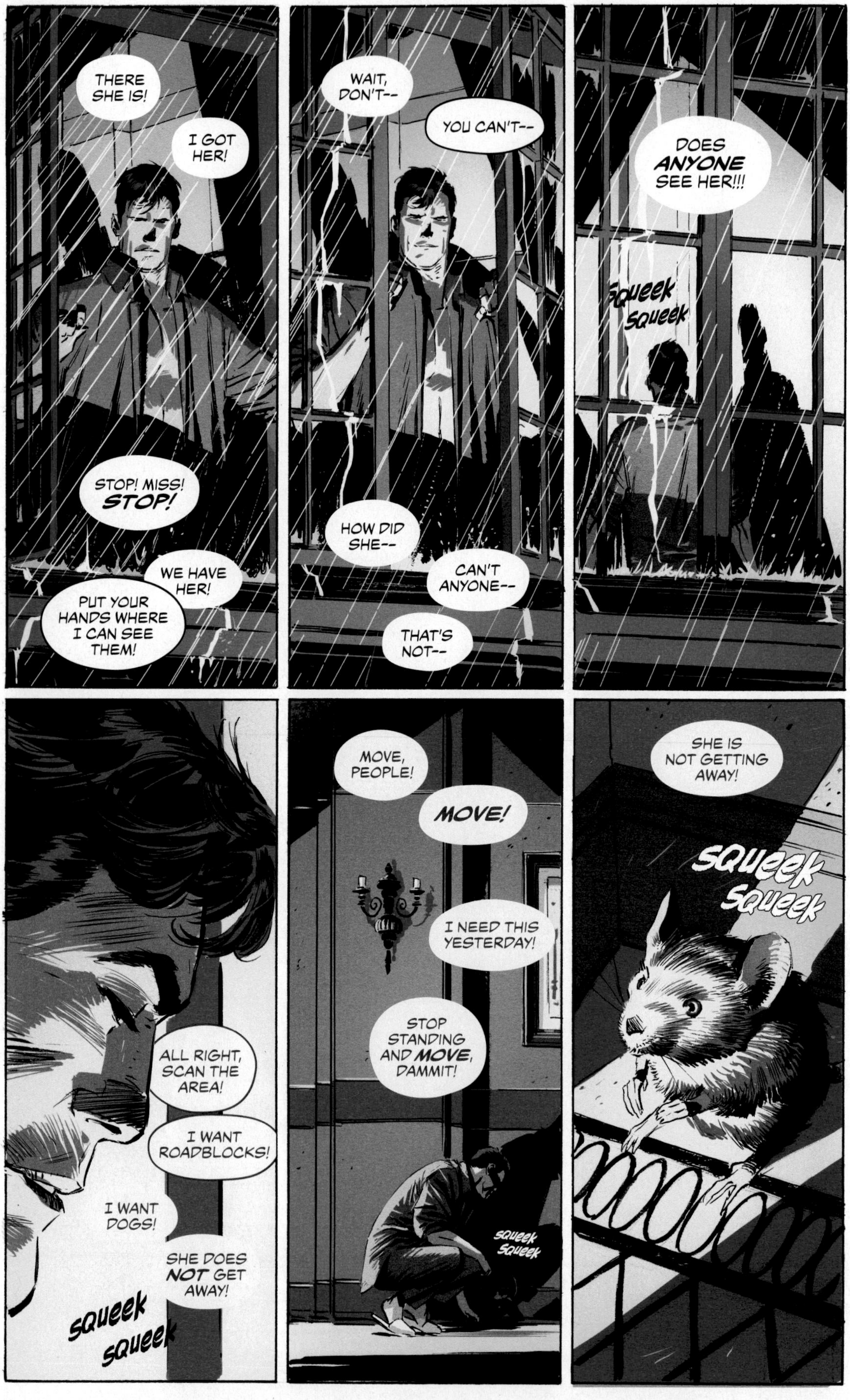
THERE SHE IS!
I GOT HER!
STOP! MISS! STOP!
WE HAVE HER!
PUT YOUR HANDS WHERE I CAN SEE THEM!
WAIT, DON'T--
YOU CAN'T--
HOW DID SHE--
CAN'T ANYONE--
THAT'S NOT--
DOES ANYONE SEE HER!!!
SQUEEK SQUEEK
ALL RIGHT, SCAN THE AREA!
I WANT ROADBLOCKS!
I WANT DOGS!
SHE DOES NOT GET AWAY!
SQUEEK SQUEEK
MOVE, PEOPLE!
MOVE!
I NEED THIS YESTERDAY!
STOP STANDING AND MOVE, DAMMIT!
SQUEEK SQUEEK
SHE IS NOT GETTING AWAY!
SQUEEK SQUEEK

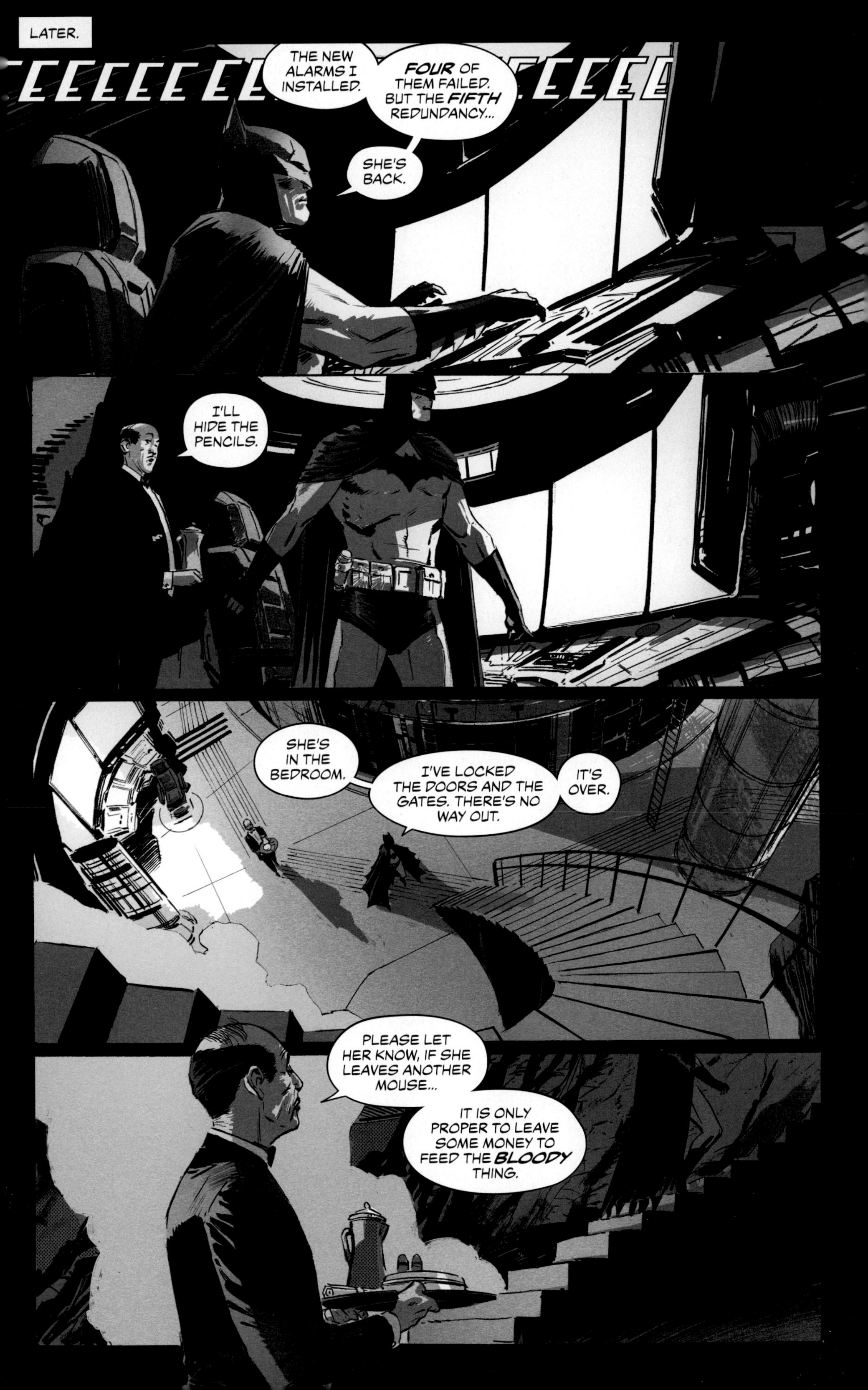
LATER.
EEEEEEEEEEEEEEEE
THE NEW ALARMS I INSTALLED.
FOUR OF THEM FAILED. BUT THE FIFTH REDUNDANCY...
SHE'S BACK.
I'LL HIDE THE PENCILS.
SHE'S IN THE BEDROOM.
I'VE LOCKED THE DOORS AND THE GATES. THERE'S NO WAY OUT.
IT'S OVER.
PLEASE LET HER KNOW, IF SHE LEAVES ANOTHER MOUSE...
IT IS ONLY PROPER TO LEAVE SOME MONEY TO FEED THE BLOODY THING.

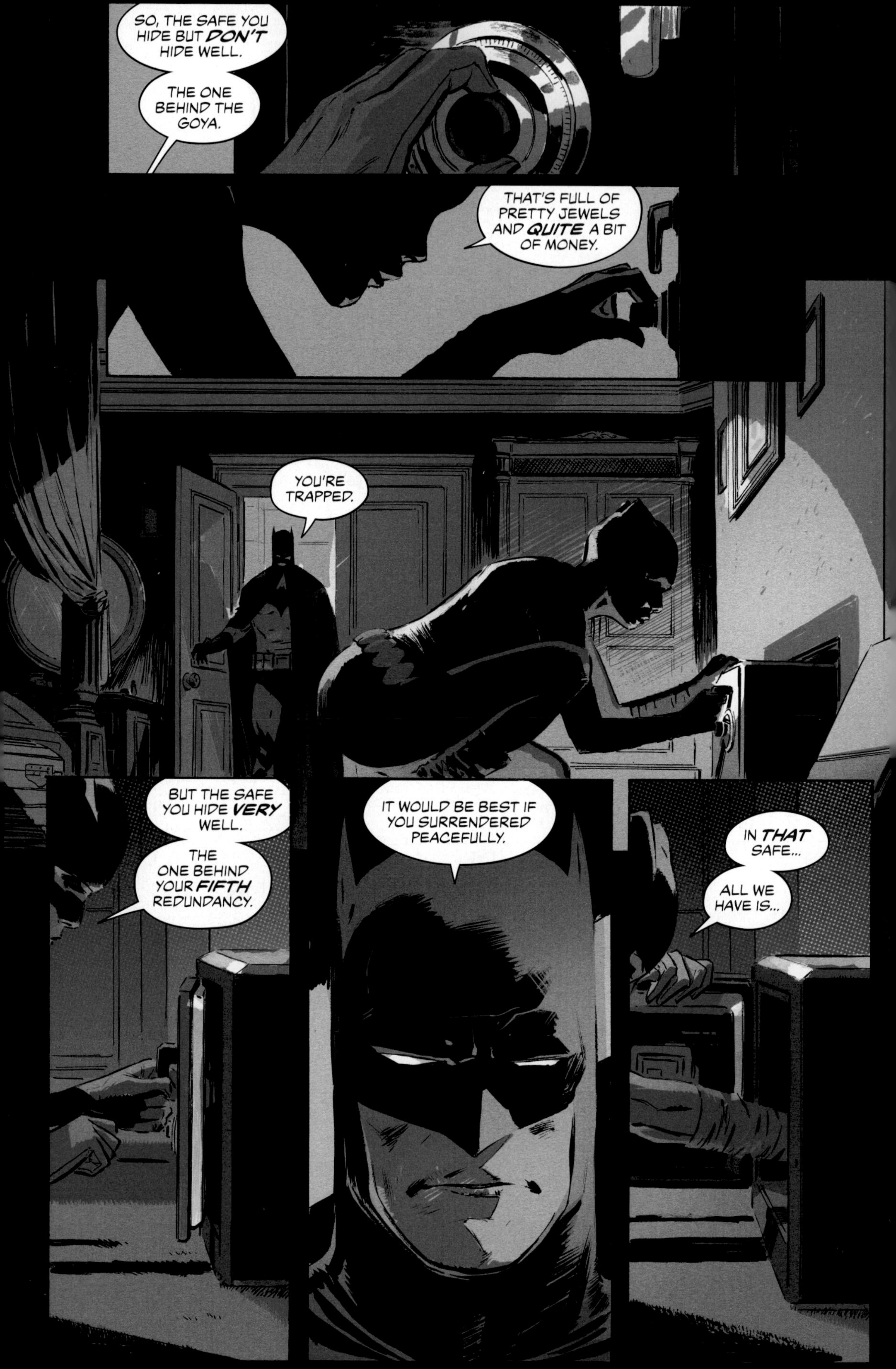

SO, THE SAFE YOU HIDE BUT *DON'T* HIDE WELL.
THE ONE BEHIND THE GOYA.
THAT'S FULL OF PRETTY JEWELS AND *QUITE* A BIT OF MONEY.
YOU'RE TRAPPED.
BUT THE SAFE YOU HIDE *VERY* WELL.
THE ONE BEHIND YOUR *FIFTH* REDUNDANCY.
IT WOULD BE BEST IF YOU SURRENDERED PEACEFULLY.
IN *THAT* SAFE...
ALL WE HAVE IS...

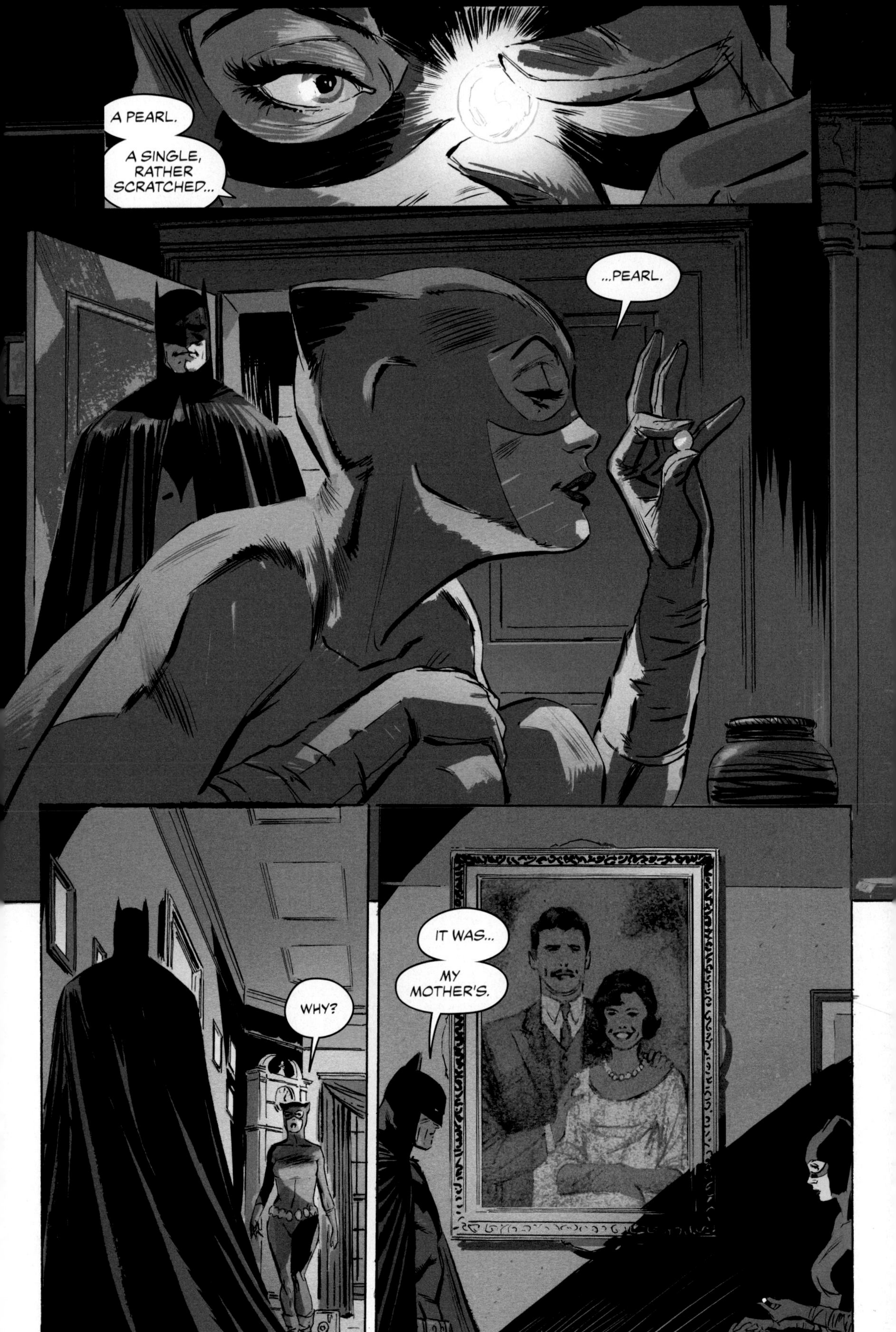
A PEARL.
A SINGLE, RATHER SCRATCHED...
...PEARL.
WHY?
IT WAS...
MY MOTHER'S.

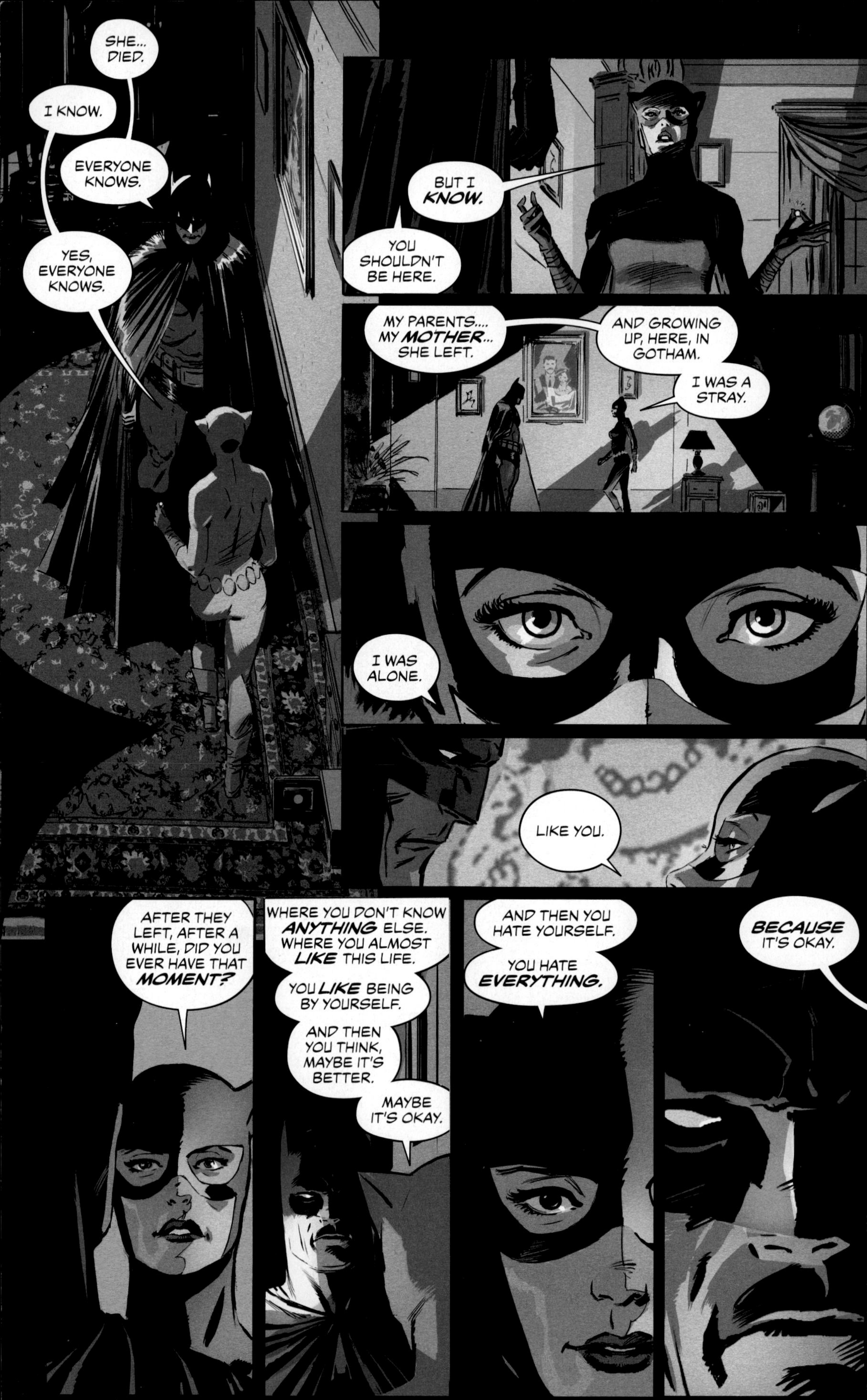
SHE... DIED.
I KNOW.
EVERYONE KNOWS.
YES, EVERYONE KNOWS.
BUT I KNOW.
YOU SHOULDN'T BE HERE.
MY PARENTS.... MY MOTHER... SHE LEFT.
AND GROWING UP, HERE, IN GOTHAM.
I WAS A STRAY.
I WAS ALONE.
LIKE YOU.
AFTER THEY LEFT, AFTER A WHILE, DID YOU EVER HAVE THAT MOMENT?
WHERE YOU DON'T KNOW ANYTHING ELSE. WHERE YOU ALMOST LIKE THIS LIFE.
YOU LIKE BEING BY YOURSELF.
AND THEN YOU THINK, MAYBE IT'S BETTER.
MAYBE IT'S OKAY.
AND THEN YOU HATE YOURSELF.
YOU HATE EVERYTHING.
BECAUSE IT'S OKAY.

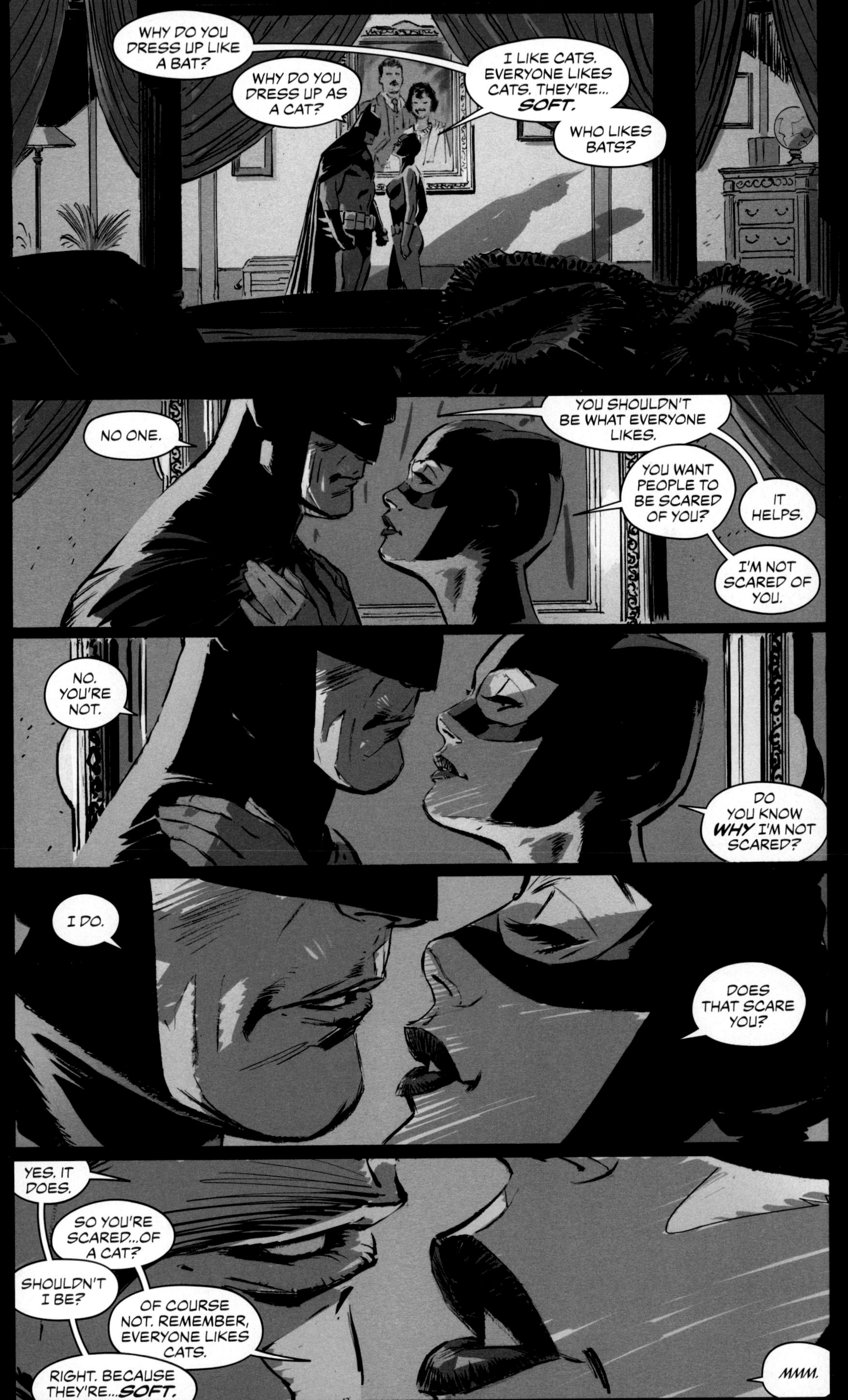
WHY DO YOU DRESS UP LIKE A BAT?
WHY DO YOU DRESS UP AS A CAT?
I LIKE CATS. EVERYONE LIKES CATS. THEY'RE... SOFT.
WHO LIKES BATS?
NO ONE.
YOU SHOULDN'T BE WHAT EVERYONE LIKES.
YOU WANT PEOPLE TO BE SCARED OF YOU?
IT HELPS.
I'M NOT SCARED OF YOU.
NO. YOU'RE NOT.
DO YOU KNOW WHY I'M NOT SCARED?
I DO.
DOES THAT SCARE YOU?
YES. IT DOES.
SO YOU'RE SCARED...OF A CAT?
SHOULDN'T I BE?
OF COURSE NOT. REMEMBER, EVERYONE LIKES CATS.
RIGHT. BECAUSE THEY'RE...SOFT.
MMM.

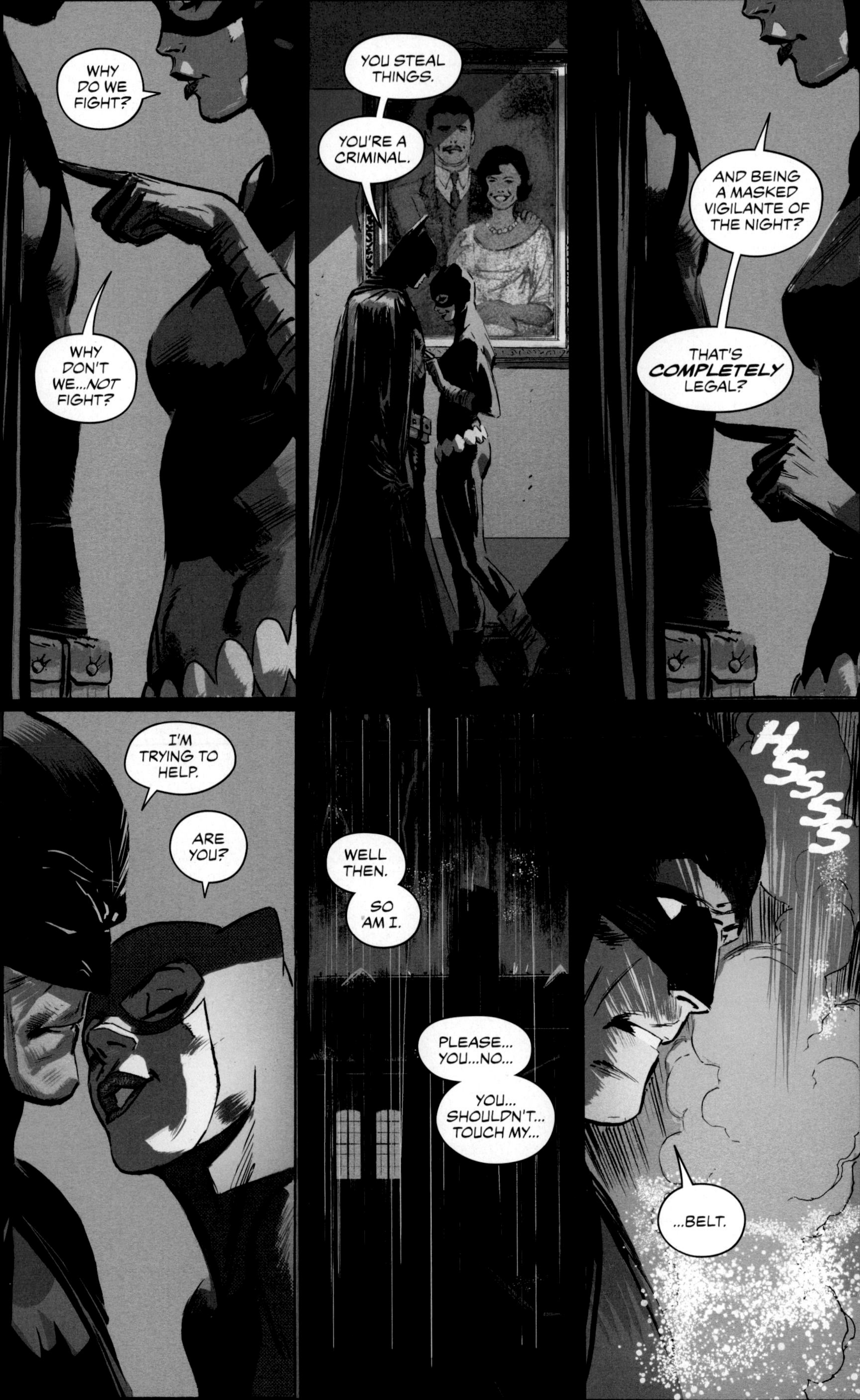
WHY DO WE FIGHT?
WHY DON'T WE...NOT FIGHT?
YOU STEAL THINGS.
YOU'RE A CRIMINAL.
AND BEING A MASKED VIGILANTE OF THE NIGHT?
THAT'S COMPLETELY LEGAL?
I'M TRYING TO HELP.
ARE YOU?
WELL THEN.
SO AM I.
PLEASE... YOU...NO...
YOU... SHOULDN'T... TOUCH MY...
HSSSS
...BELT.

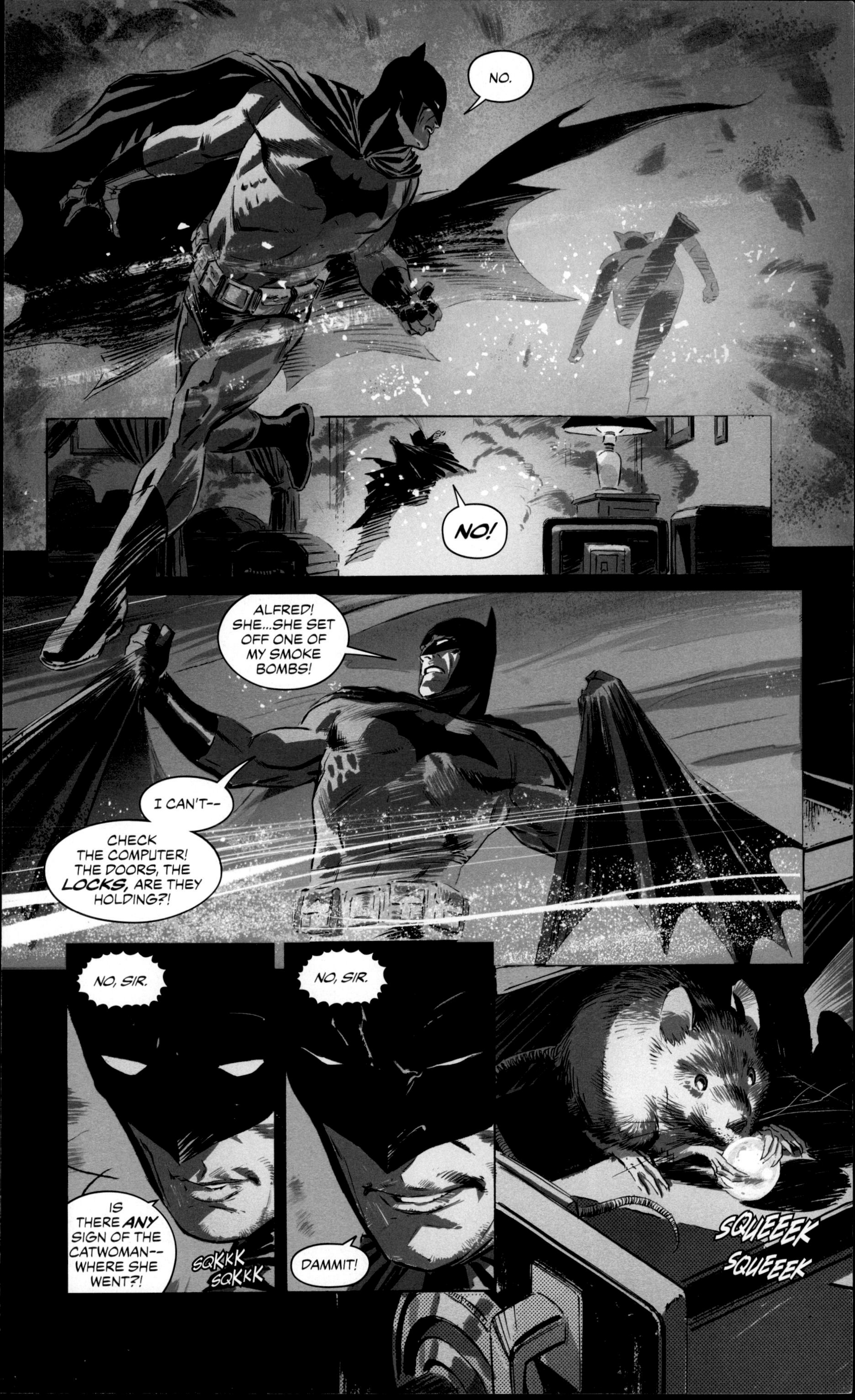
NO.
NO!
ALFRED! SHE...SHE SET OFF ONE OF MY SMOKE BOMBS!
I CAN'T--
CHECK THE COMPUTER! THE DOORS, THE LOCKS, ARE THEY HOLDING?!
NO, SIR.
IS THERE ANY SIGN OF THE CATWOMAN-- WHERE SHE WENT?!
SQKKK SQKKK
NO, SIR.
DAMMIT!
SQUEEEK SQUEEEK

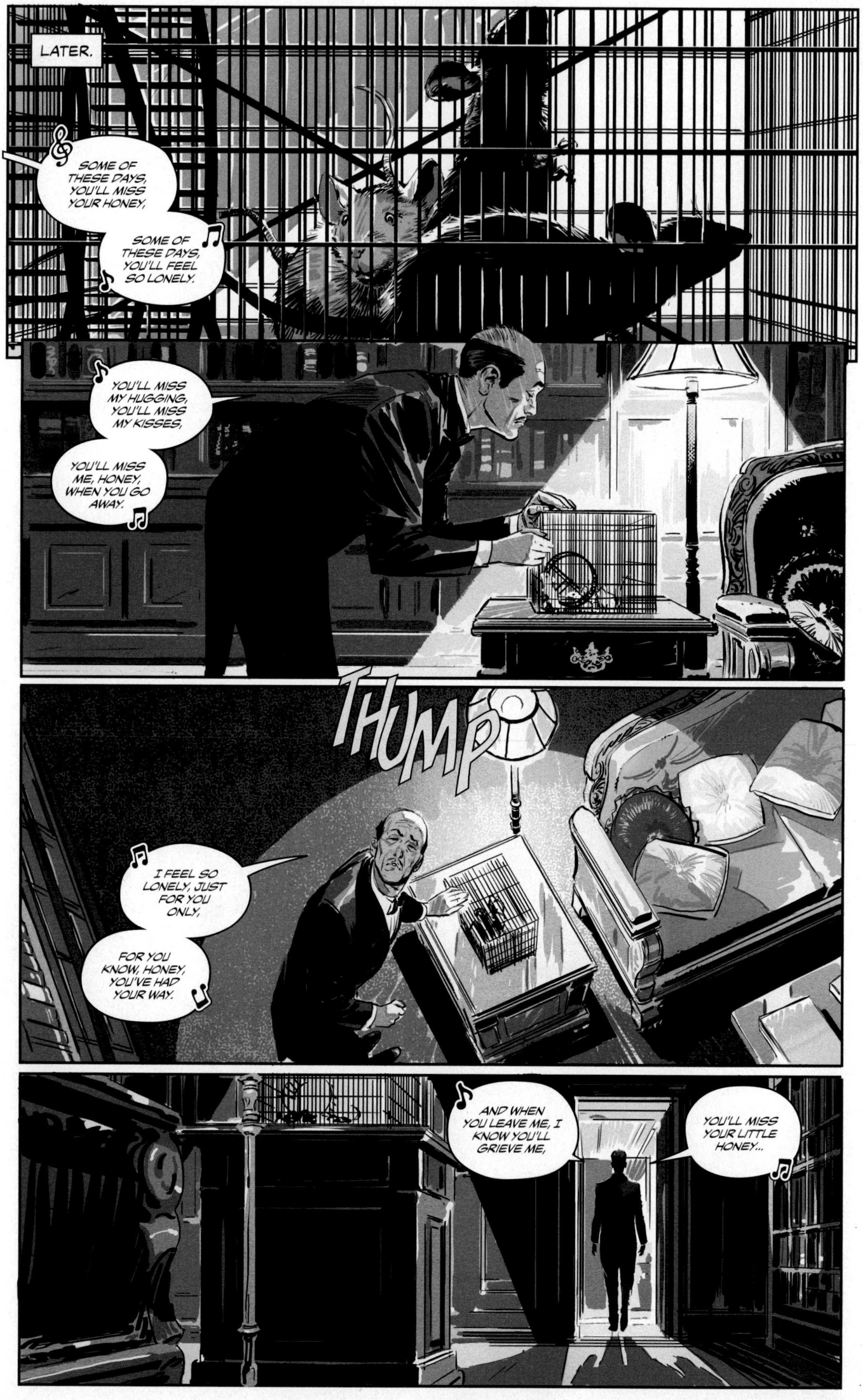
LATER.
SOME OF THESE DAYS, YOU'LL MISS YOUR HONEY,
SOME OF THESE DAYS, YOU'LL FEEL SO LONELY.
YOU'LL MISS MY HUGGING, YOU'LL MISS MY KISSES,
YOU'LL MISS ME, HONEY, WHEN YOU GO AWAY.
THUMP
I FEEL SO LONELY, JUST FOR YOU ONLY,
FOR YOU KNOW, HONEY, YOU'VE HAD YOUR WAY.
AND WHEN YOU LEAVE ME, I KNOW YOU'LL GRIEVE ME,
YOU'LL MISS YOUR LITTLE HONEY...

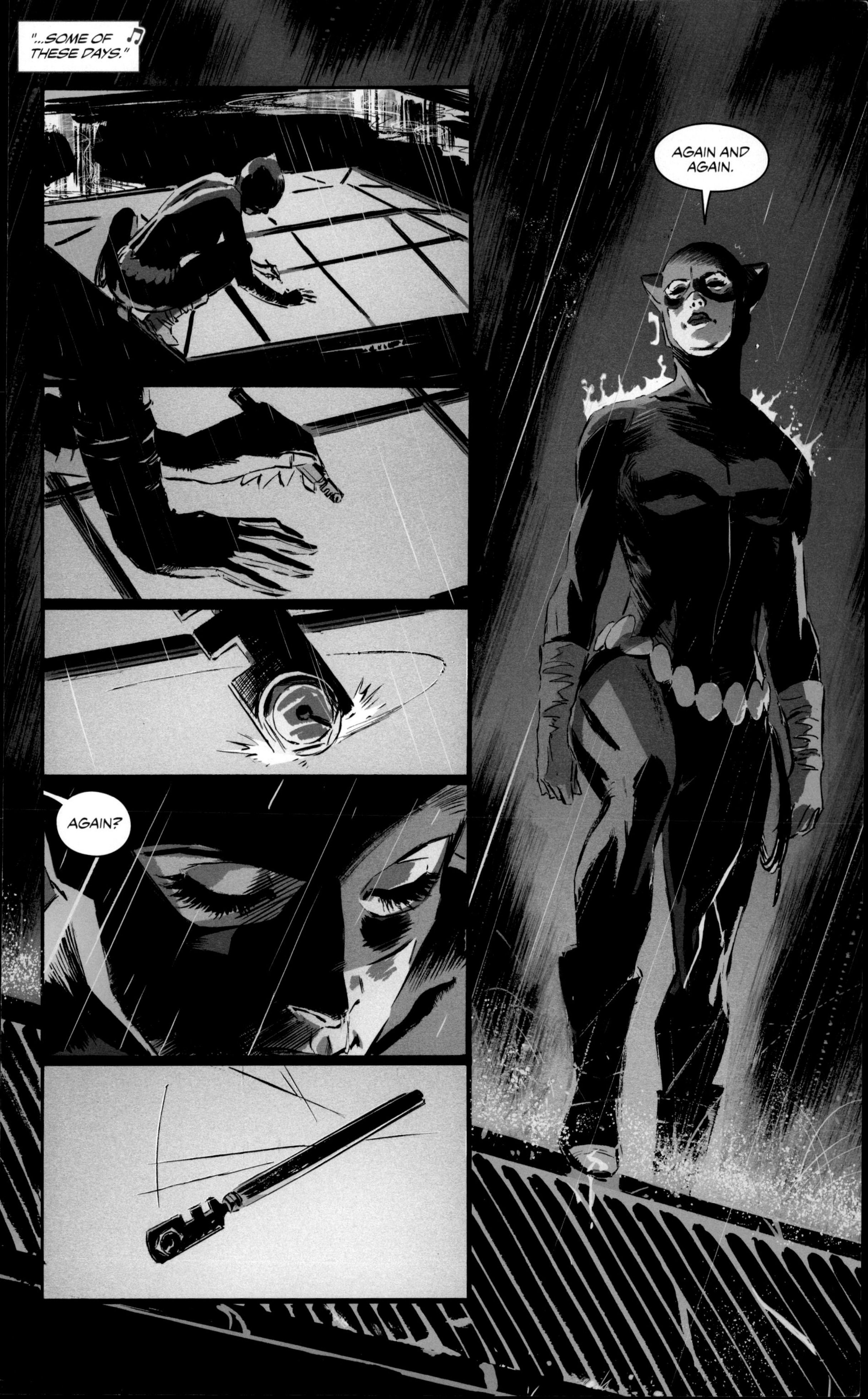
"...SOME OF THESE DAYS."
AGAIN?
AGAIN AND AGAIN.

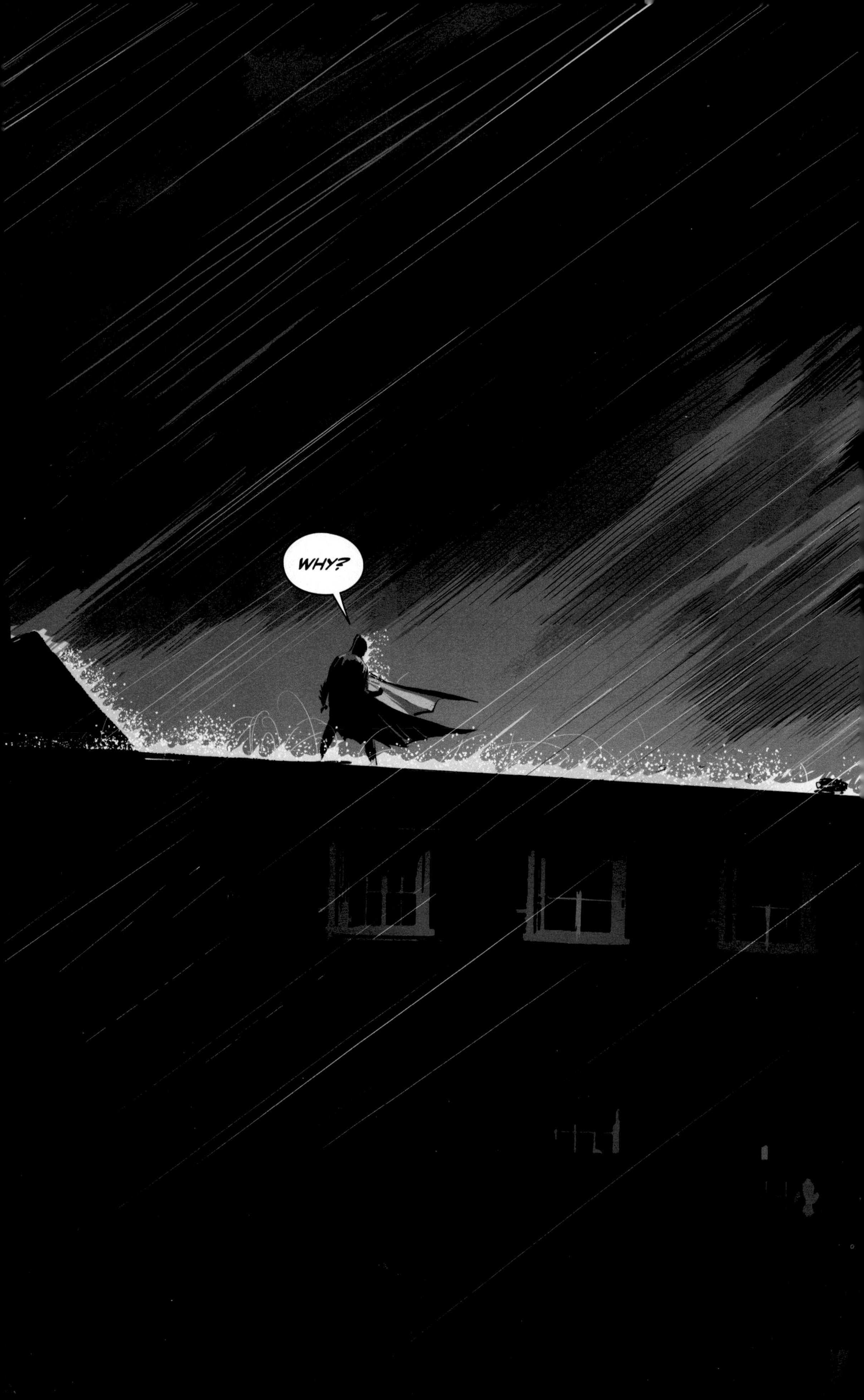
WHY?

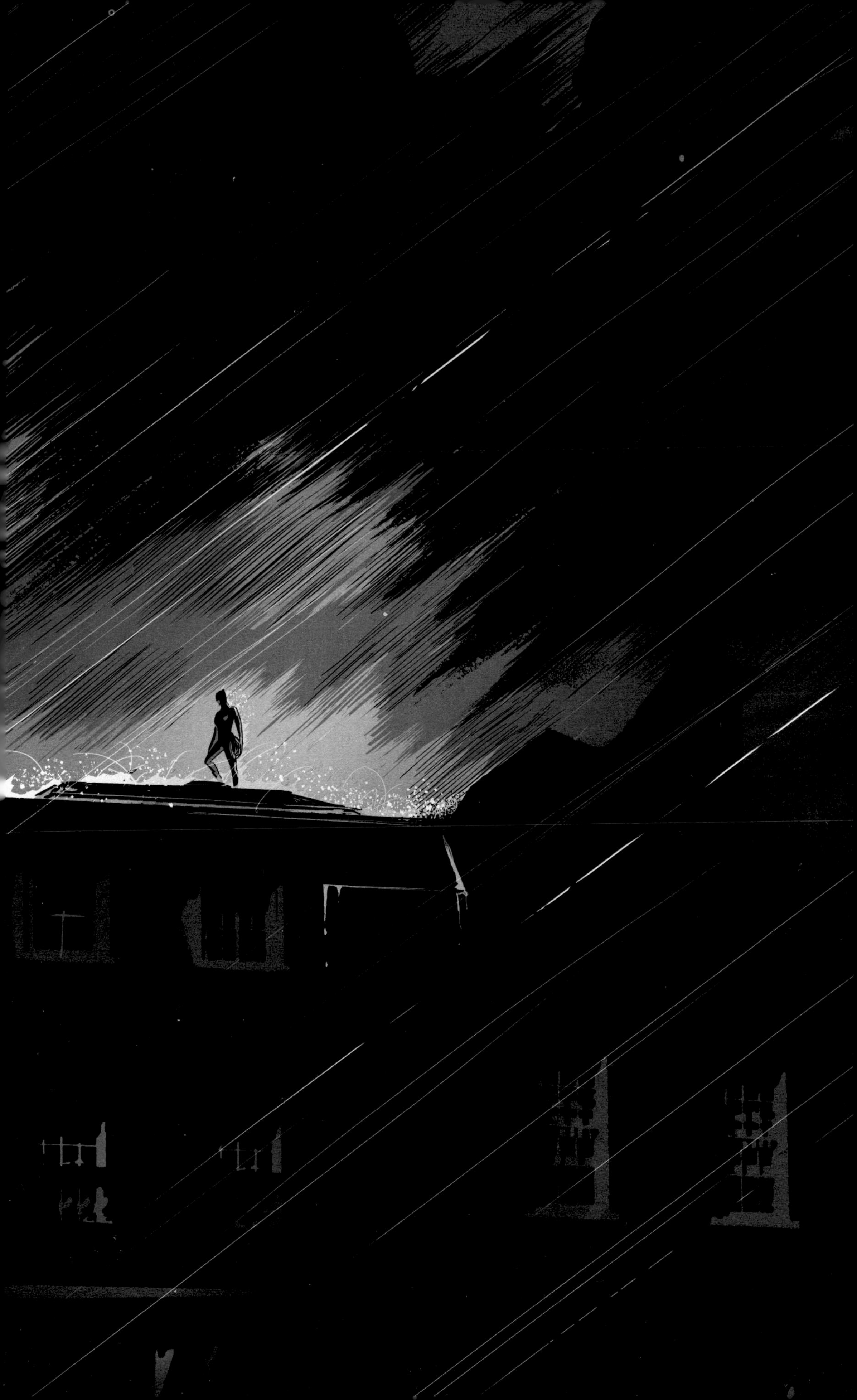

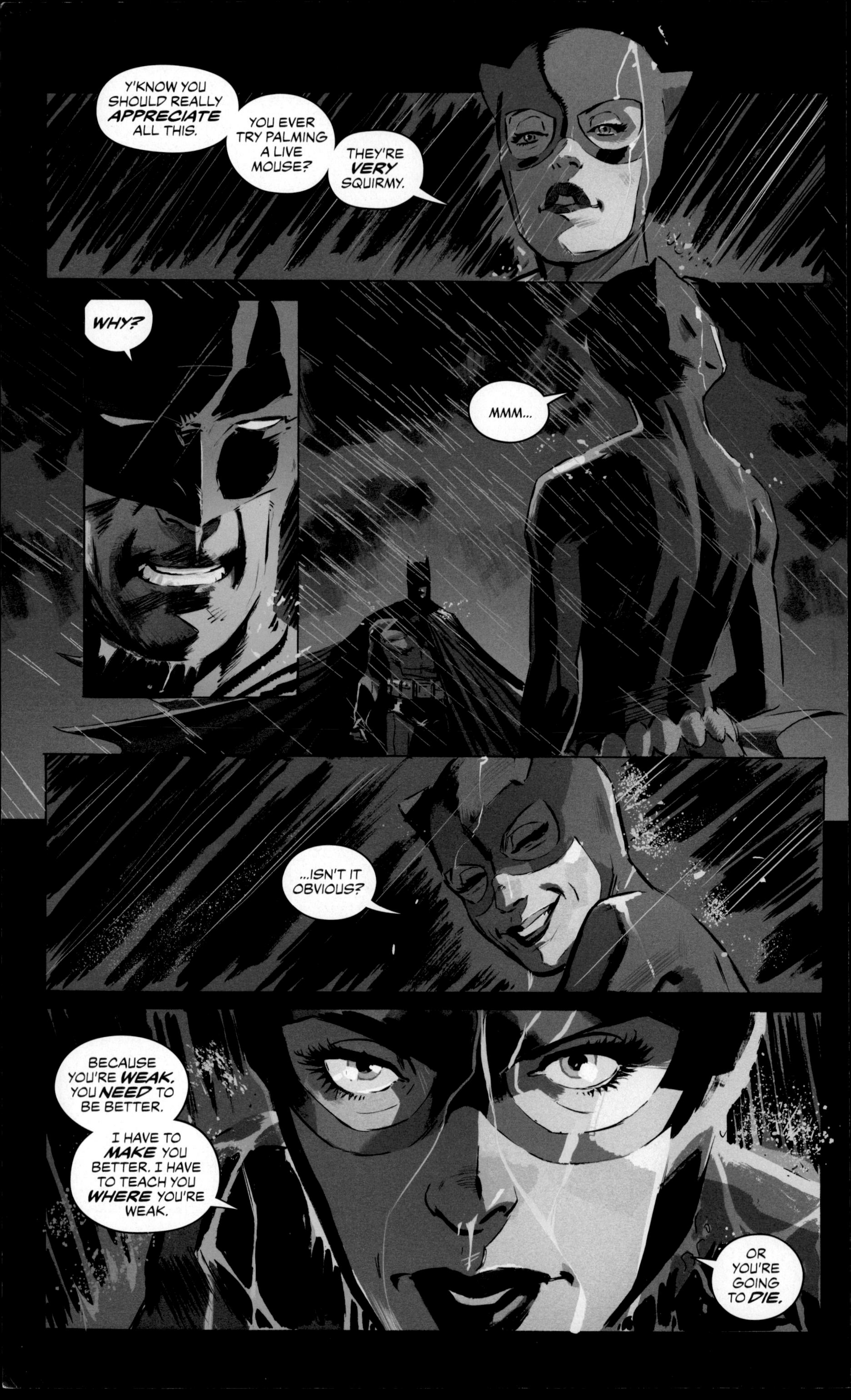
Y'KNOW YOU SHOULD REALLY APPRECIATE ALL THIS.
YOU EVER TRY PALMING A LIVE MOUSE?
THEY'RE VERY SQUIRMY.
WHY?
MMM...
...ISN'T IT OBVIOUS?
BECAUSE YOU'RE WEAK. YOU NEED TO BE BETTER.
I HAVE TO MAKE YOU BETTER. I HAVE TO TEACH YOU WHERE YOU'RE WEAK.
OR YOU'RE GOING TO DIE.

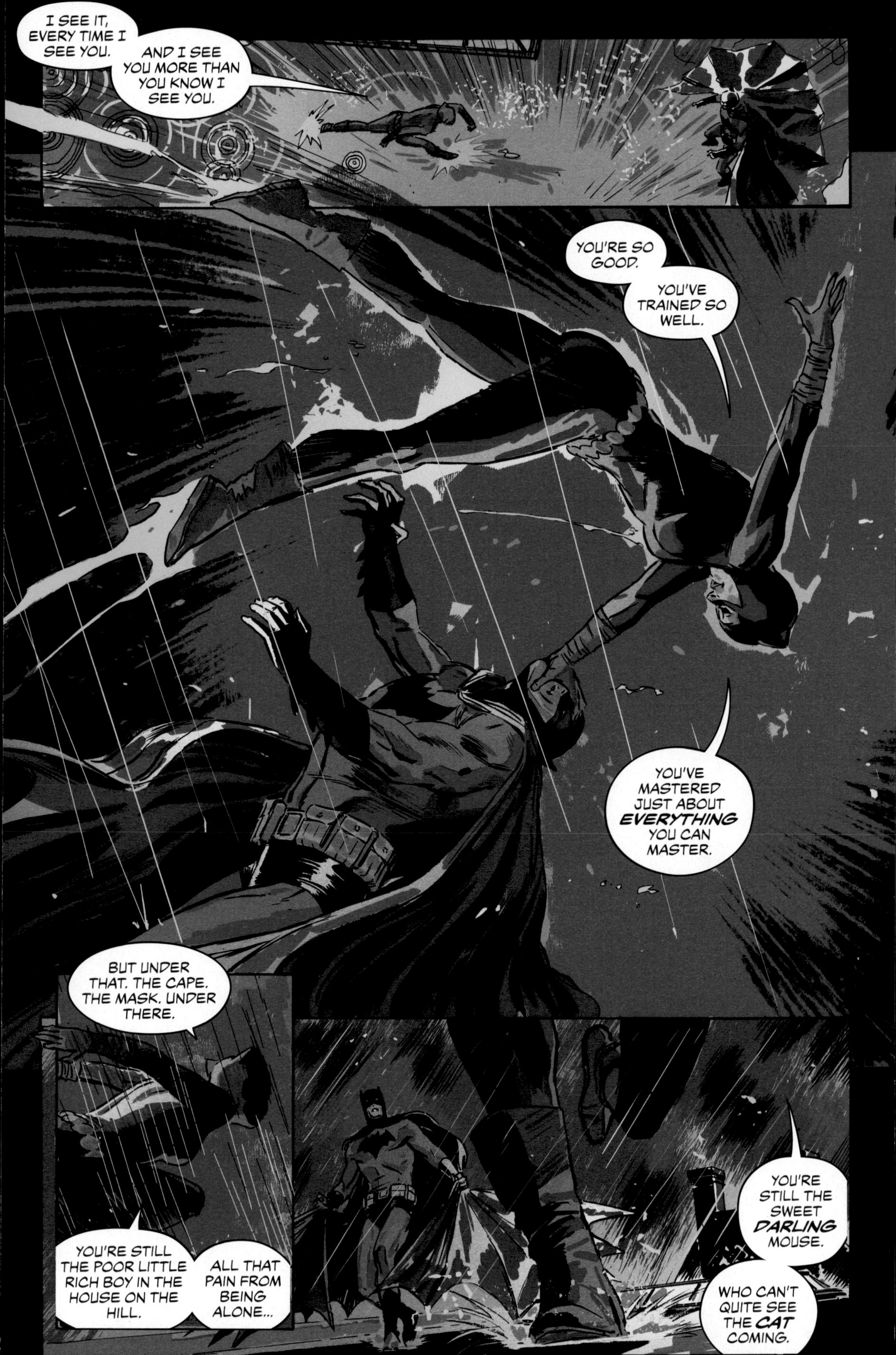
I SEE IT, EVERY TIME I SEE YOU.
AND I SEE YOU MORE THAN YOU KNOW I SEE YOU.
YOU'RE SO GOOD.
YOU'VE TRAINED SO WELL.
YOU'VE MASTERED JUST ABOUT EVERYTHING YOU CAN MASTER.
BUT UNDER THAT. THE CAPE. THE MASK. UNDER THERE.
YOU'RE STILL THE POOR LITTLE RICH BOY IN THE HOUSE ON THE HILL.
ALL THAT PAIN FROM BEING ALONE...
YOU'RE STILL THE SWEET DARLING MOUSE.
WHO CAN'T QUITE SEE THE CAT COMING.

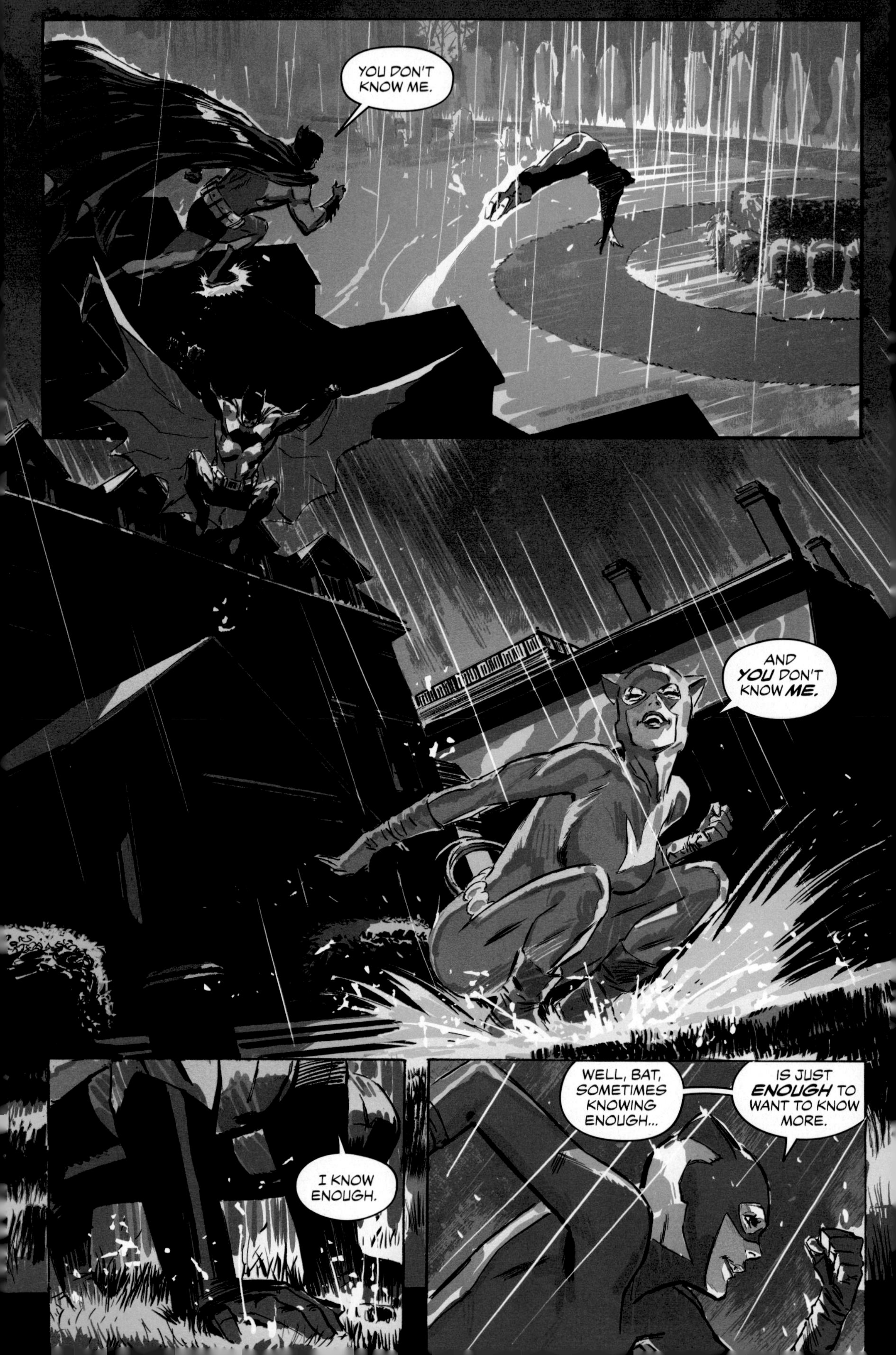
YOU DON'T KNOW ME.
AND YOU DON'T KNOW ME.
I KNOW ENOUGH.
WELL, BAT, SOMETIMES KNOWING ENOUGH...
IS JUST ENOUGH TO WANT TO KNOW MORE.

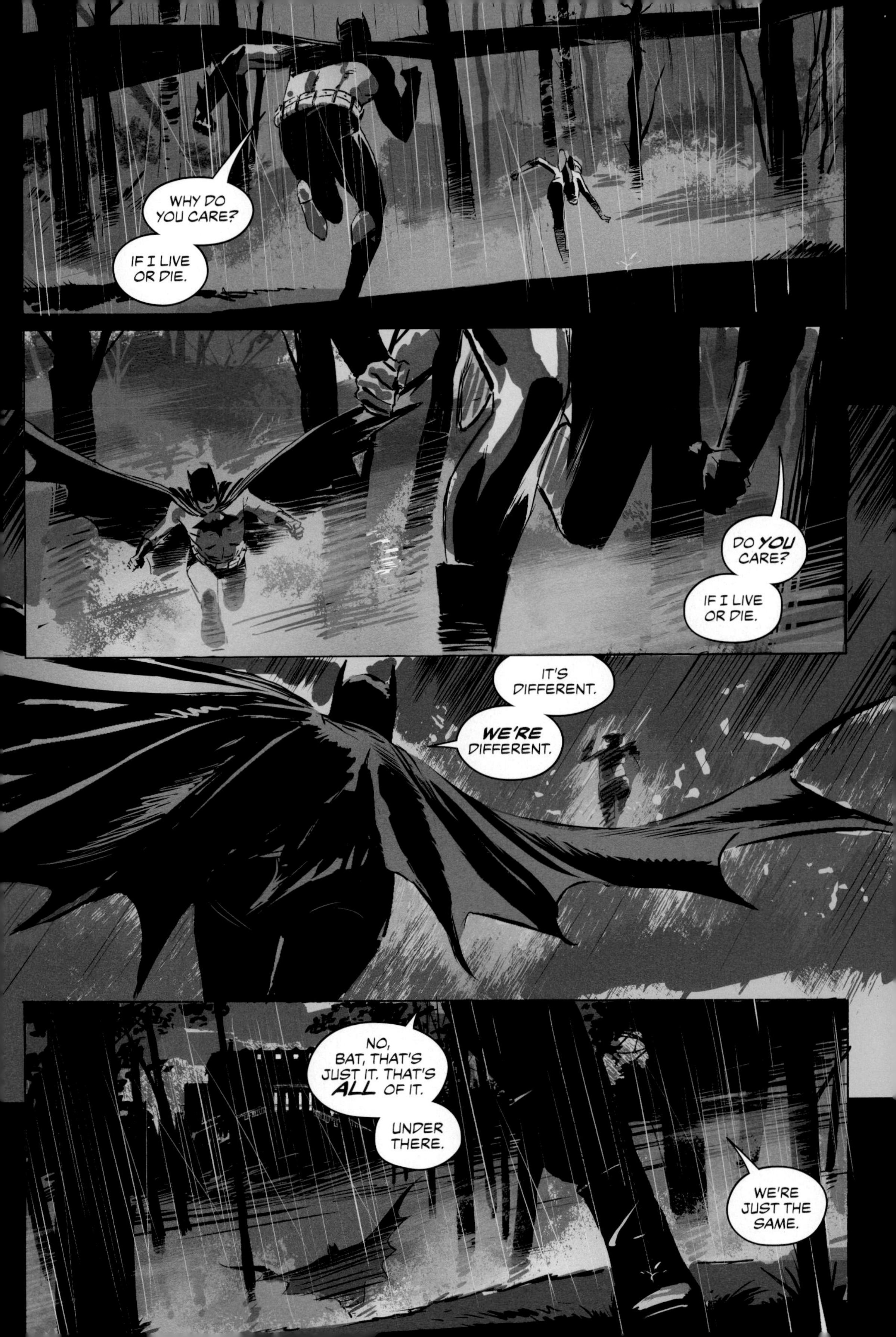
WHY DO YOU CARE?
IF I LIVE OR DIE.
DO YOU CARE?
IF I LIVE OR DIE.
IT'S DIFFERENT.
WE'RE DIFFERENT.
NO, BAT, THAT'S JUST IT. THAT'S ALL OF IT.
UNDER THERE.
WE'RE JUST THE SAME.

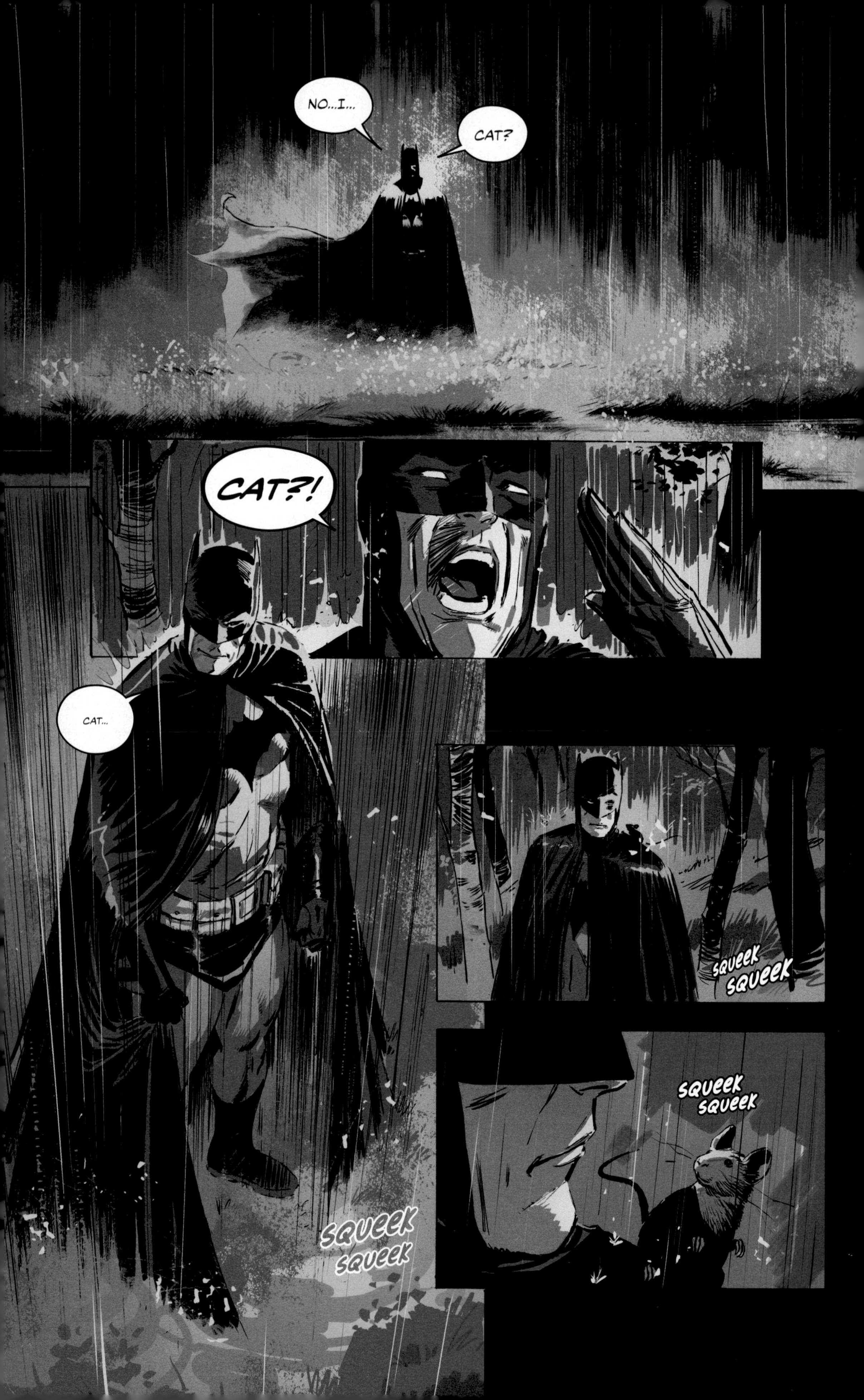
NO...I...
CAT?
CAT?!
CAT...
SQUEEK
SQUEEK
SQUEEK
SQUEEK
SQUEEK
SQUEEK

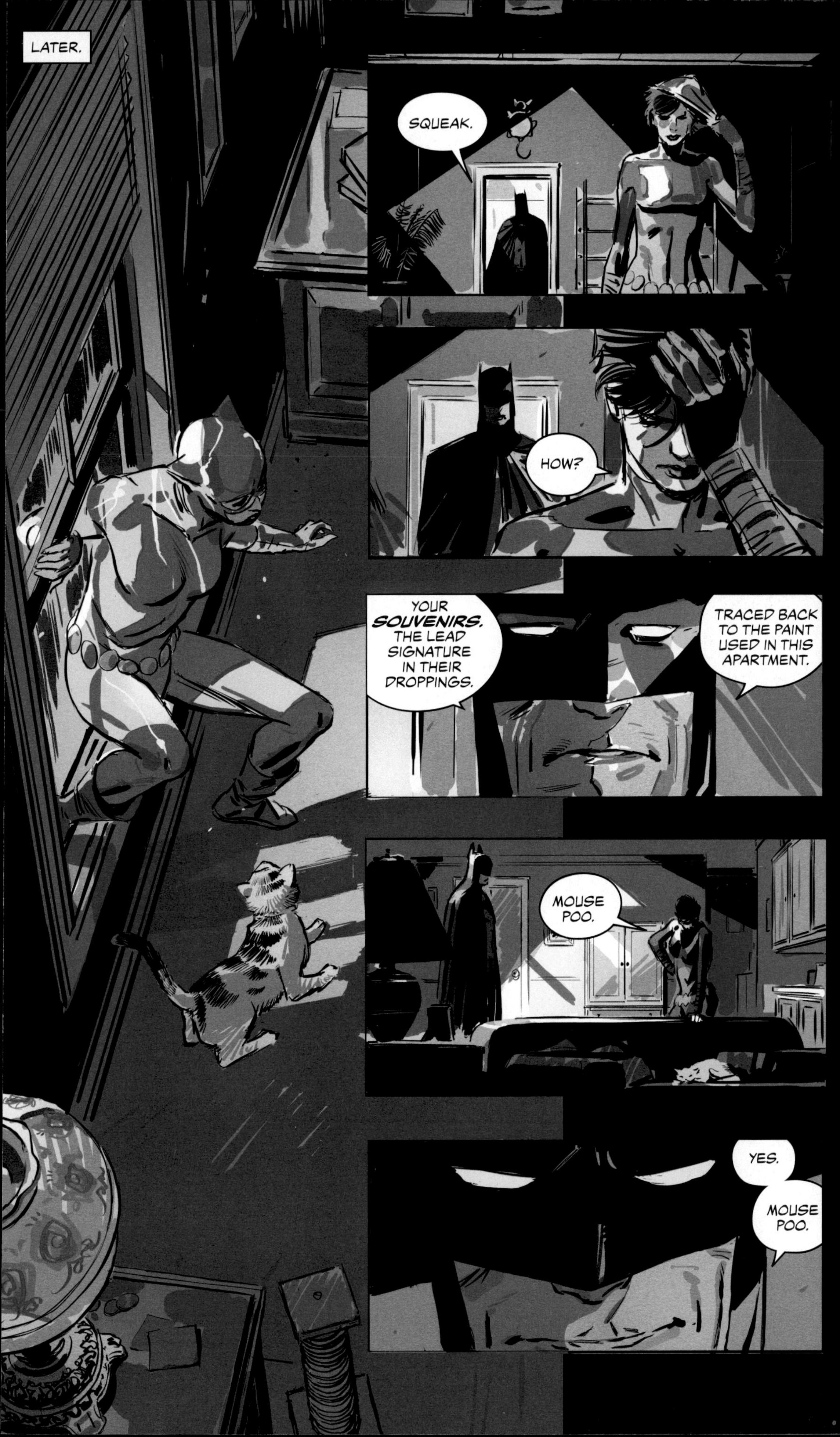
LATER.
SQUEAK.
HOW?
YOUR SOUVENIRS. THE LEAD SIGNATURE IN THEIR DROPPINGS.
TRACED BACK TO THE PAINT USED IN THIS APARTMENT.
MOUSE POO.
YES.
MOUSE POO.

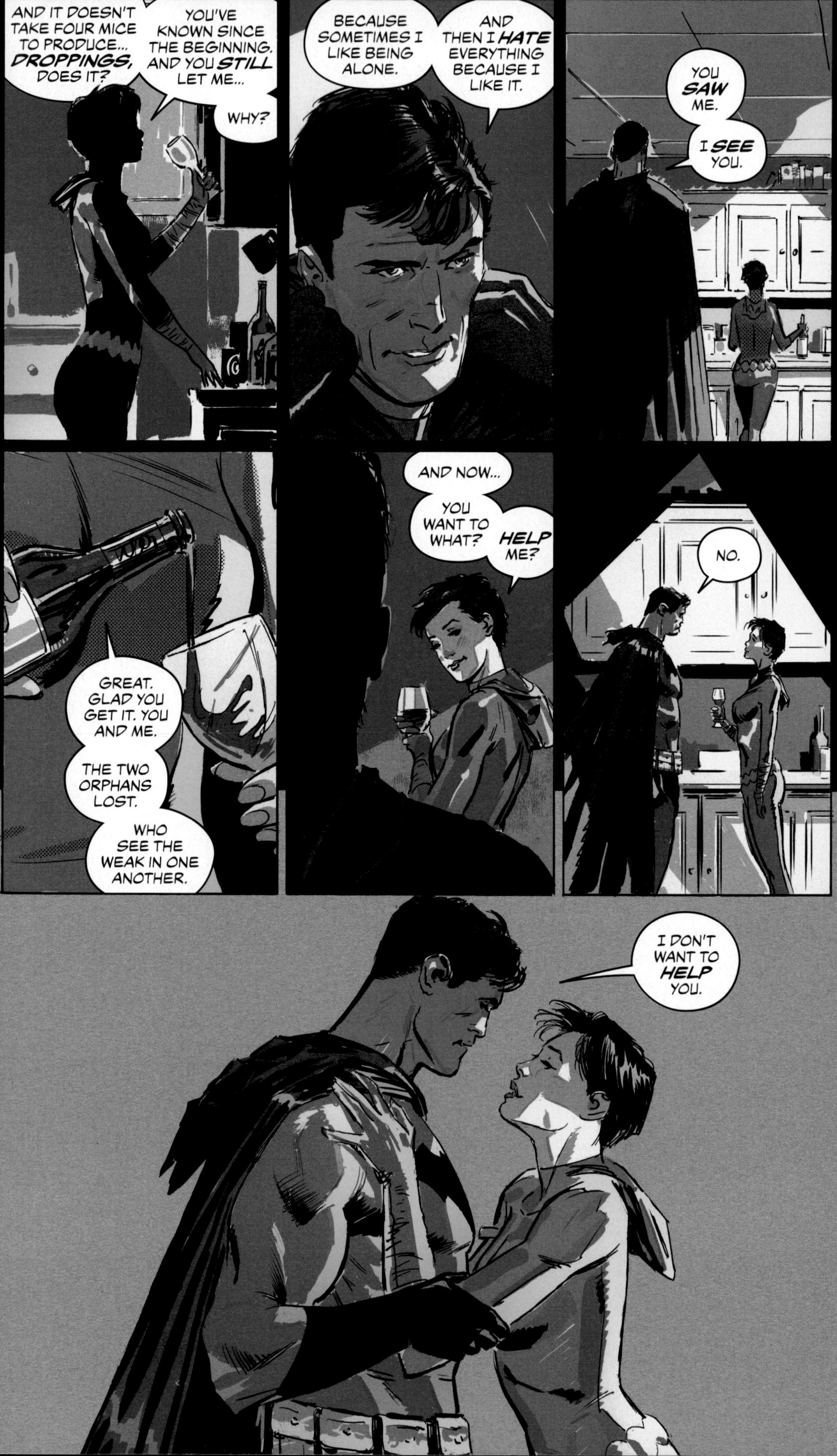
AND IT DOESN'T TAKE FOUR MICE TO PRODUCE... DROPPINGS, DOES IT?
YOU'VE KNOWN SINCE THE BEGINNING. AND YOU STILL LET ME...
WHY?
BECAUSE SOMETIMES I LIKE BEING ALONE.
AND THEN I HATE EVERYTHING BECAUSE I LIKE IT.
YOU SAW ME.
I SEE YOU.
GREAT. GLAD YOU GET IT. YOU AND ME.
THE TWO ORPHANS LOST.
WHO SEE THE WEAK IN ONE ANOTHER.
AND NOW...
YOU WANT TO WHAT?
HELP ME?
NO.
I DON'T WANT TO HELP YOU.

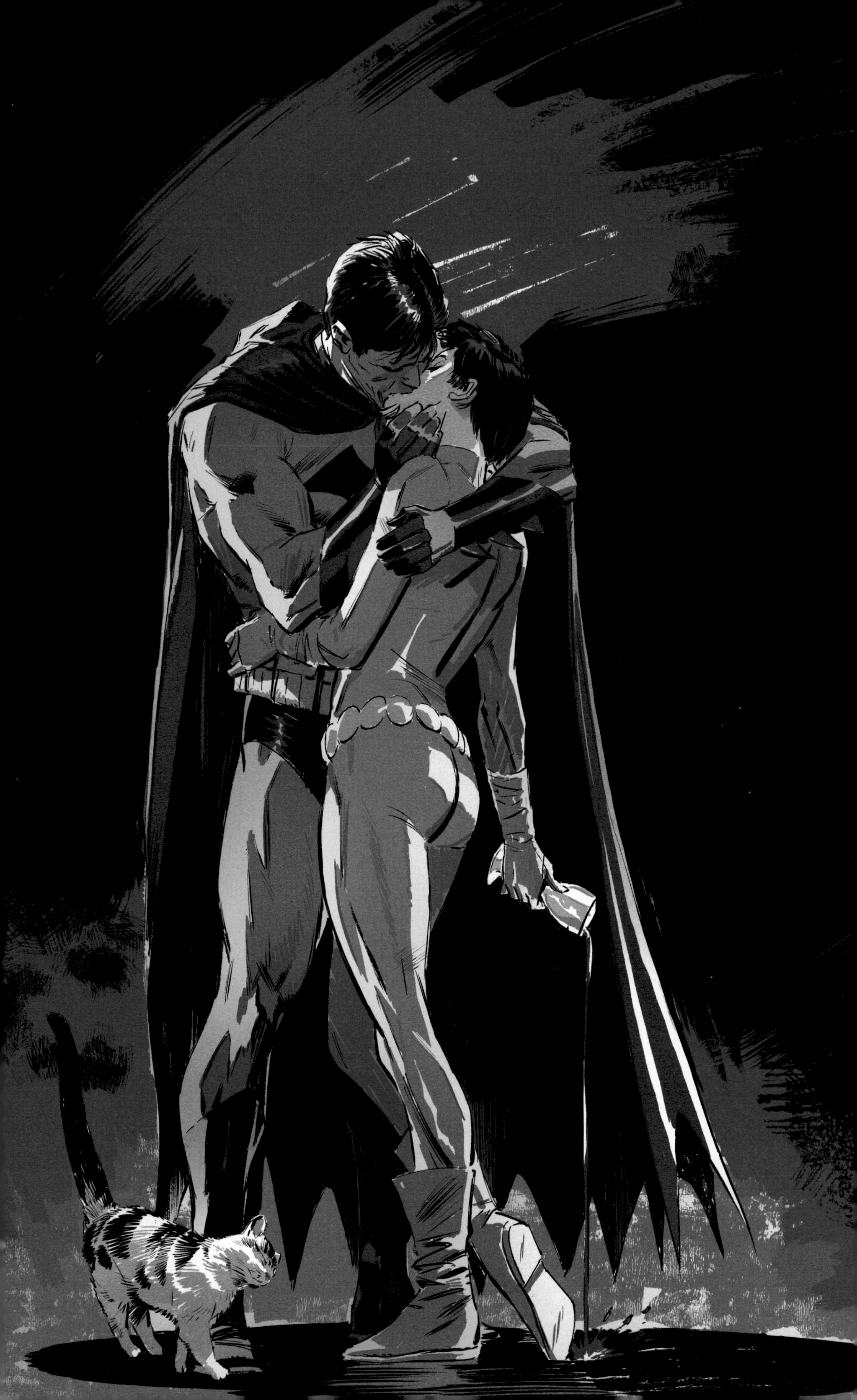

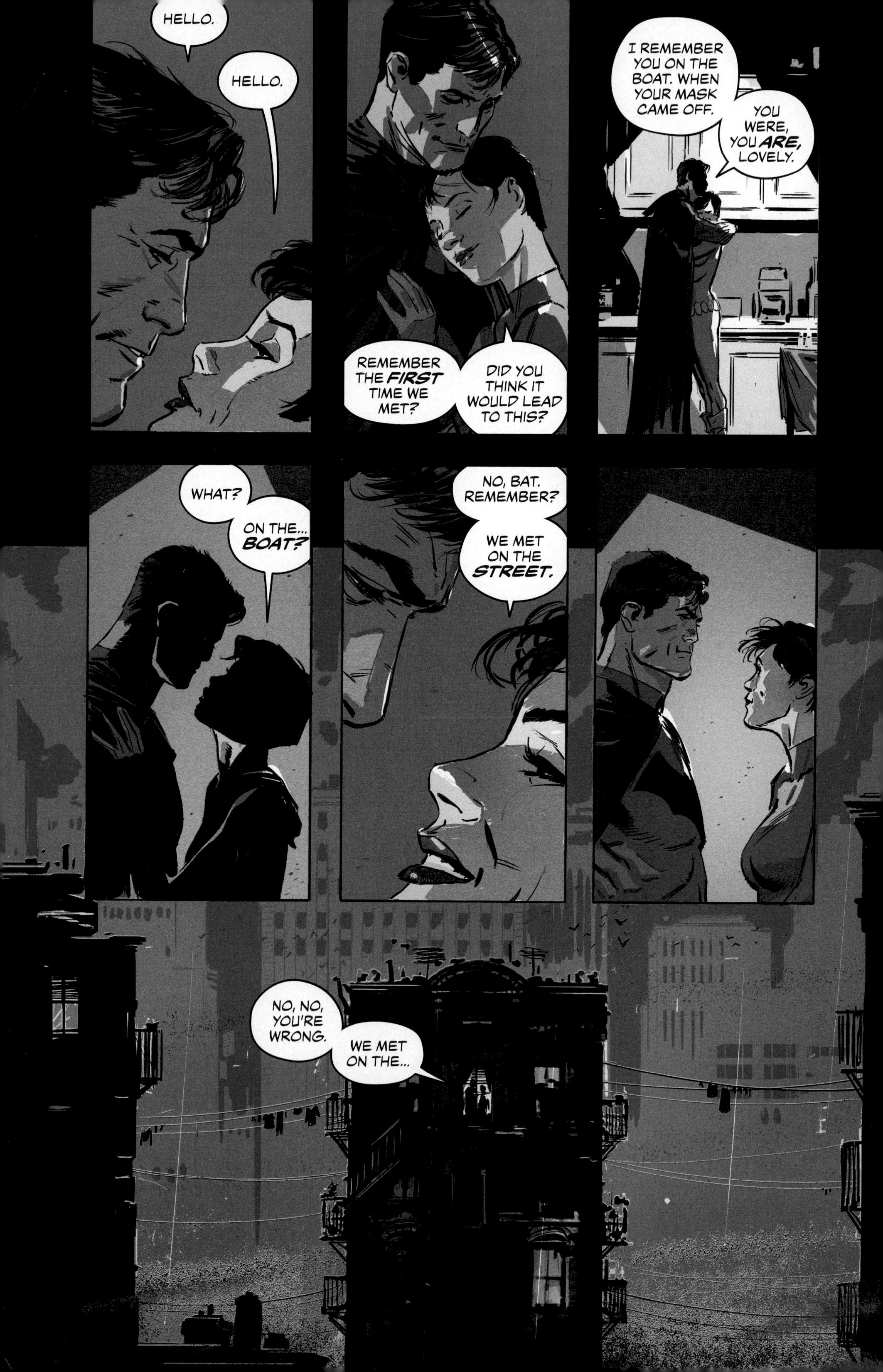
HELLO.
HELLO.
REMEMBER THE FIRST TIME WE MET?
DID YOU THINK IT WOULD LEAD TO THIS?
I REMEMBER YOU ON THE BOAT. WHEN YOUR MASK CAME OFF.
YOU WERE, YOU ARE, LOVELY.
WHAT?
ON THE... BOAT?
NO, BAT. REMEMBER?
WE MET ON THE STREET.
NO, NO, YOU'RE WRONG.
WE MET ON THE...

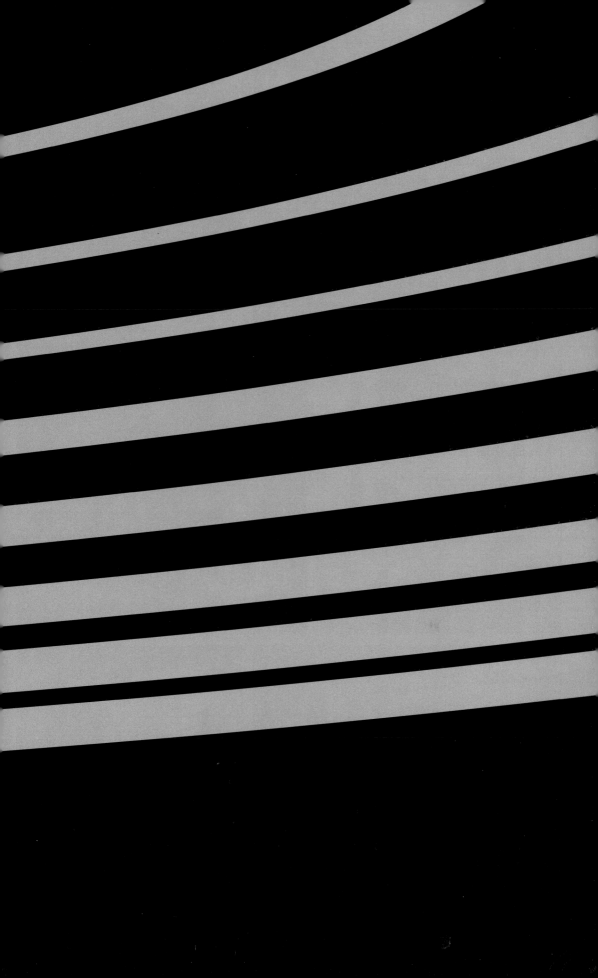

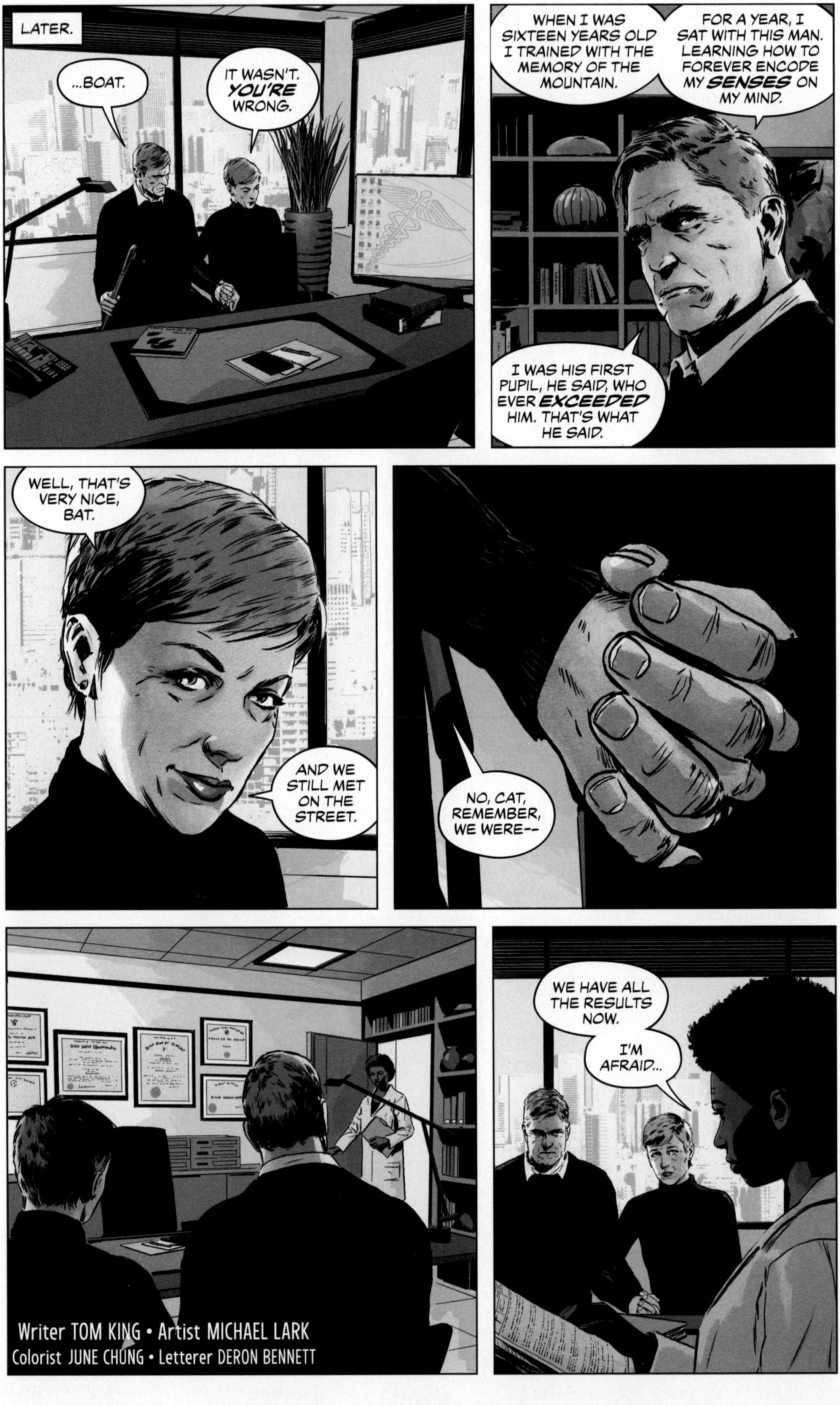
LATER.
...BOAT.
IT WASN'T. YOU'RE WRONG.
WHEN I WAS SIXTEEN YEARS OLD I TRAINED WITH THE MEMORY OF THE MOUNTAIN.
FOR A YEAR, I SAT WITH THIS MAN. LEARNING HOW TO FOREVER ENCODE MY SENSES ON MY MIND.
I WAS HIS FIRST PUPIL, HE SAID, WHO EVER EXCEEDED HIM. THAT'S WHAT HE SAID.
WELL, THAT'S VERY NICE, BAT.
AND WE STILL MET ON THE STREET.
NO, CAT, REMEMBER, WE WERE--
WE HAVE ALL THE RESULTS NOW.
I'M AFRAID...
Writer TOM KING • Artist MICHAEL LARK
Colorist JUNE CHUNG • Letterer DERON BENNETT

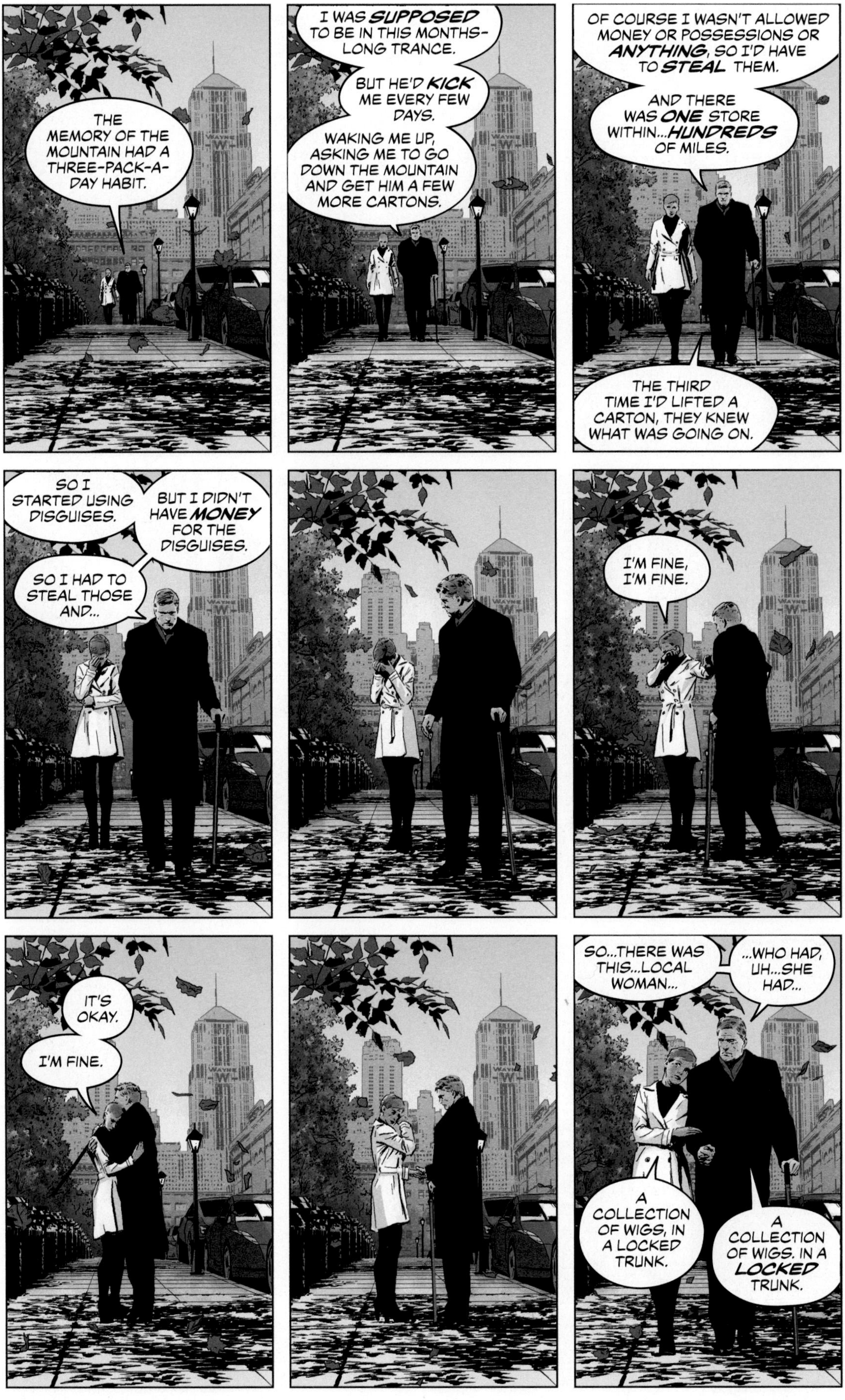
THE MEMORY OF THE MOUNTAIN HAD A THREE-PACK-A-DAY HABIT.
I WAS SUPPOSED TO BE IN THIS MONTHS-LONG TRANCE.
BUT HE'D KICK ME EVERY FEW DAYS.
WAKING ME UP, ASKING ME TO GO DOWN THE MOUNTAIN AND GET HIM A FEW MORE CARTONS.
OF COURSE I WASN'T ALLOWED MONEY OR POSSESSIONS OR ANYTHING, SO I'D HAVE TO STEAL THEM.
AND THERE WAS ONE STORE WITHIN...HUNDREDS OF MILES.
THE THIRD TIME I'D LIFTED A CARTON, THEY KNEW WHAT WAS GOING ON.
SO I STARTED USING DISGUISES.
BUT I DIDN'T HAVE MONEY FOR THE DISGUISES.
SO I HAD TO STEAL THOSE AND...
I'M FINE, I'M FINE.
IT'S OKAY.
I'M FINE.
SO...THERE WAS THIS...LOCAL WOMAN...
...WHO HAD, UH...SHE HAD...
A COLLECTION OF WIGS, IN A LOCKED TRUNK.
A COLLECTION OF WIGS. IN A LOCKED TRUNK.

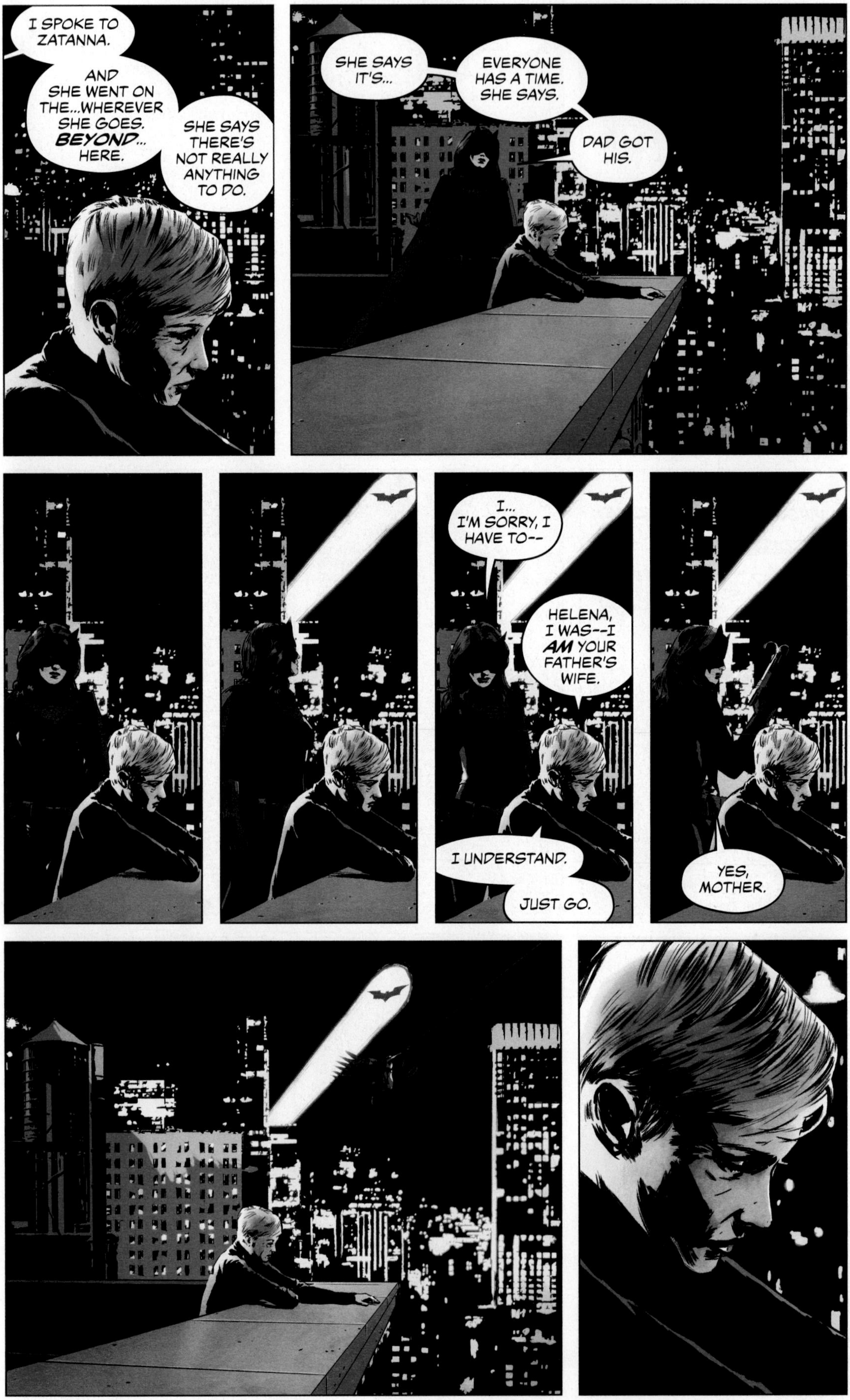
I SPOKE TO ZATANNA.
AND SHE WENT ON THE...WHEREVER SHE GOES. BEYOND... HERE.
SHE SAYS THERE'S NOT REALLY ANYTHING TO DO.
SHE SAYS IT'S...
EVERYONE HAS A TIME. SHE SAYS.
DAD GOT HIS.
I... I'M SORRY, I HAVE TO--
HELENA, I WAS--I AM YOUR FATHER'S WIFE.
I UNDERSTAND.
JUST GO.
YES, MOTHER.

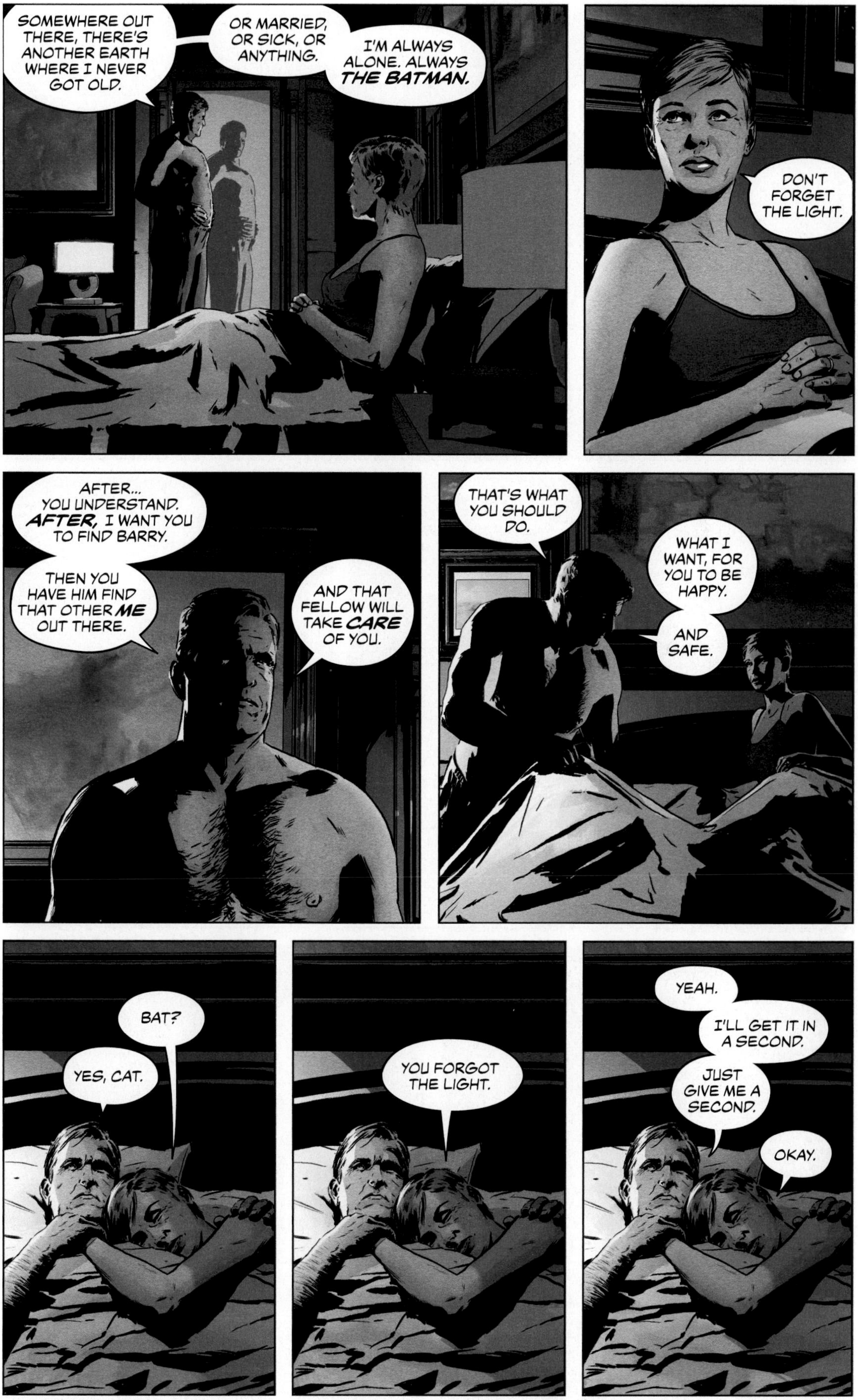
SOMEWHERE OUT THERE, THERE'S ANOTHER EARTH WHERE I NEVER GOT OLD.
OR MARRIED, OR SICK, OR ANYTHING.
I'M ALWAYS ALONE. ALWAYS **THE BATMAN.**
DON'T FORGET THE LIGHT.
AFTER... YOU UNDERSTAND. ***AFTER,*** I WANT YOU TO FIND BARRY.
THEN YOU HAVE HIM FIND THAT OTHER ***ME*** OUT THERE.
AND THAT FELLOW WILL TAKE ***CARE*** OF YOU.
THAT'S WHAT YOU SHOULD DO.
WHAT I WANT, FOR YOU TO BE HAPPY.
AND SAFE.
BAT?
YES, CAT.
YOU FORGOT THE LIGHT.
YEAH.
I'LL GET IT IN A SECOND.
JUST GIVE ME A SECOND.
OKAY.

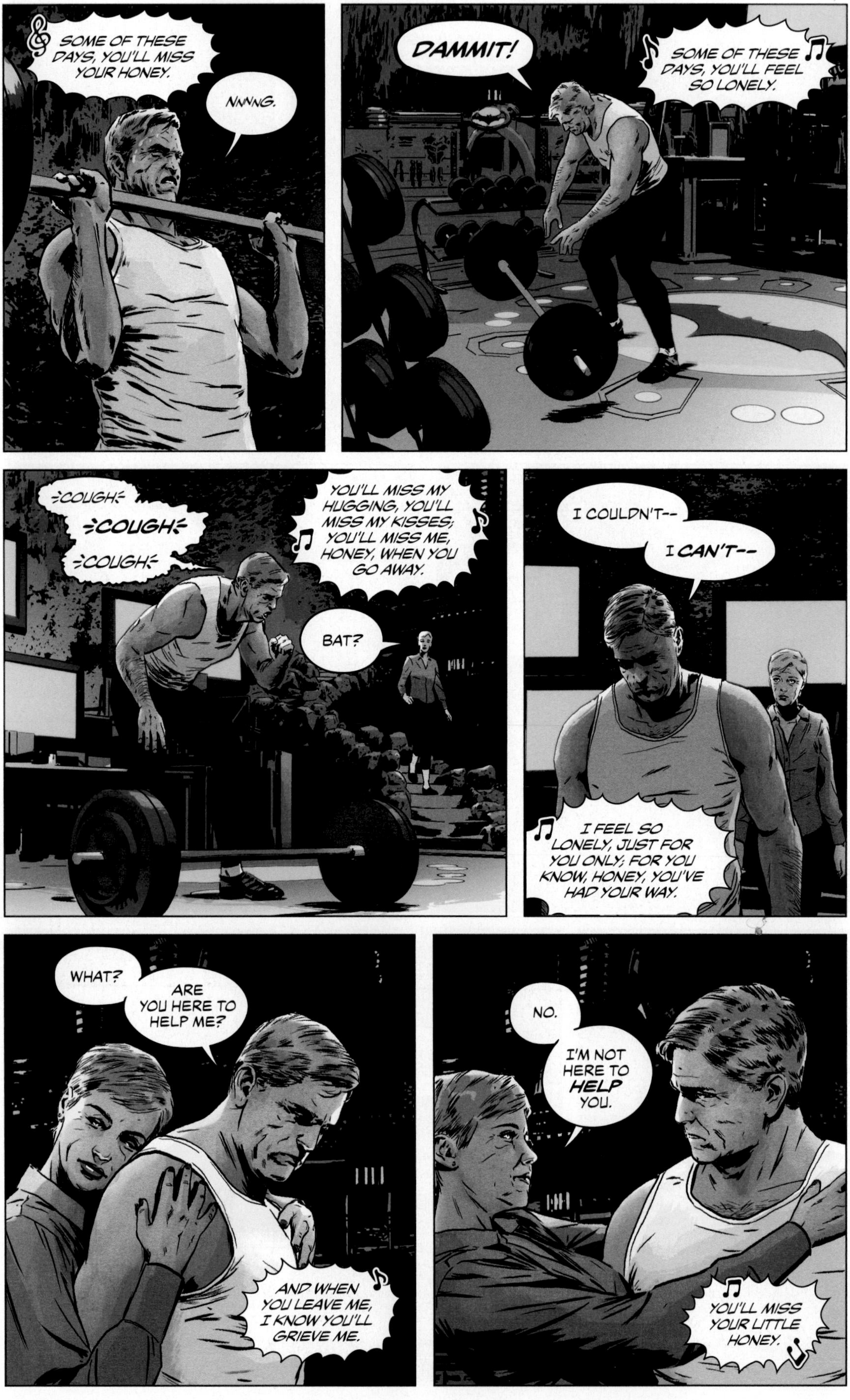
SOME OF THESE DAYS, YOU'LL MISS YOUR HONEY.
NNNNG.
DAMMIT!
SOME OF THESE DAYS, YOU'LL FEEL SO LONELY.
COUGH
COUGH
COUGH
YOU'LL MISS MY HUGGING, YOU'LL MISS MY KISSES; YOU'LL MISS ME, HONEY, WHEN YOU GO AWAY.
BAT?
I COULDN'T--
I CAN'T--
I FEEL SO LONELY, JUST FOR YOU ONLY; FOR YOU KNOW, HONEY, YOU'VE HAD YOUR WAY.
WHAT?
ARE YOU HERE TO HELP ME?
AND WHEN YOU LEAVE ME, I KNOW YOU'LL GRIEVE ME.
NO.
I'M NOT HERE TO HELP YOU.
YOU'LL MISS YOUR LITTLE HONEY.

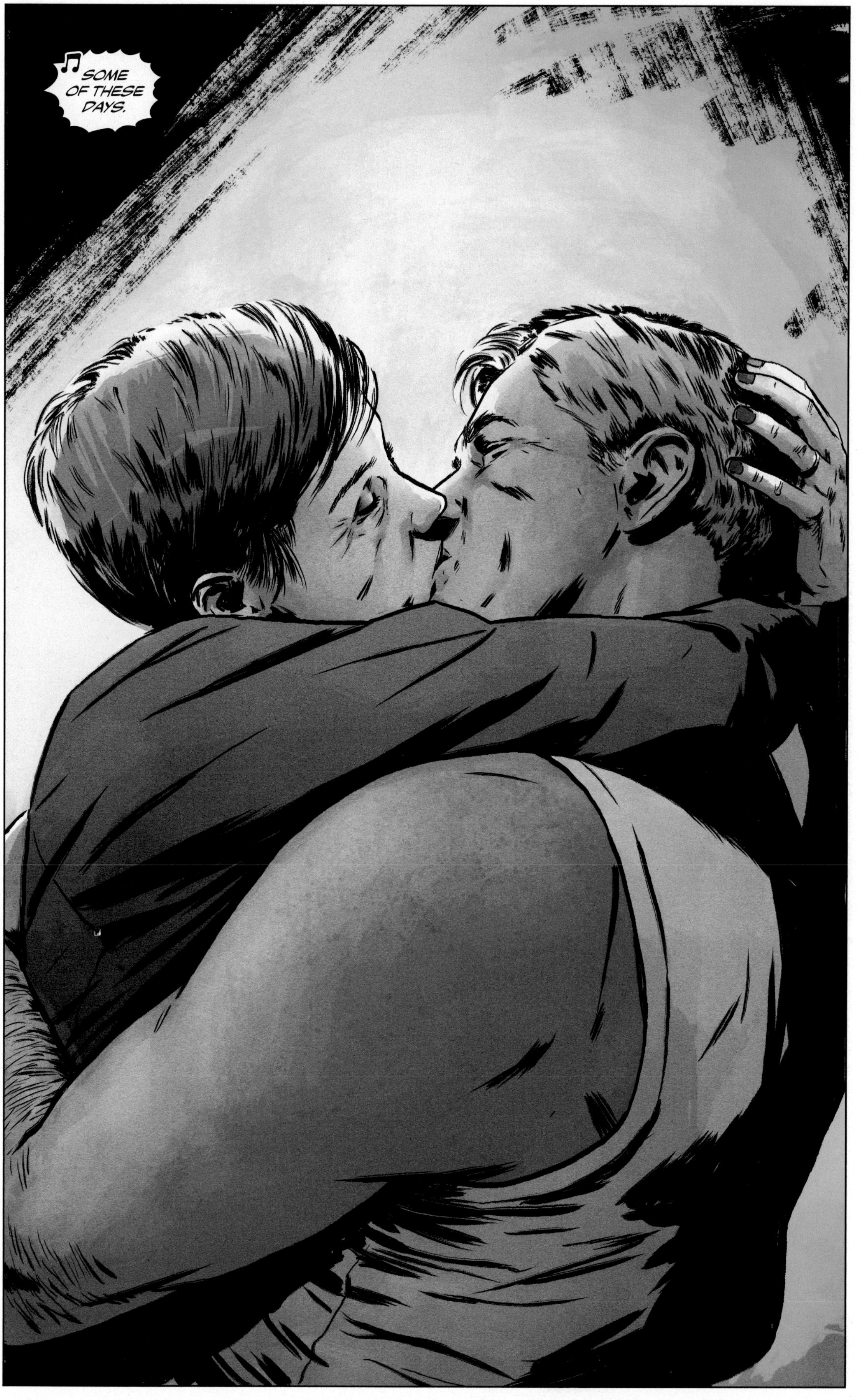
♫ SOME OF THESE DAYS.

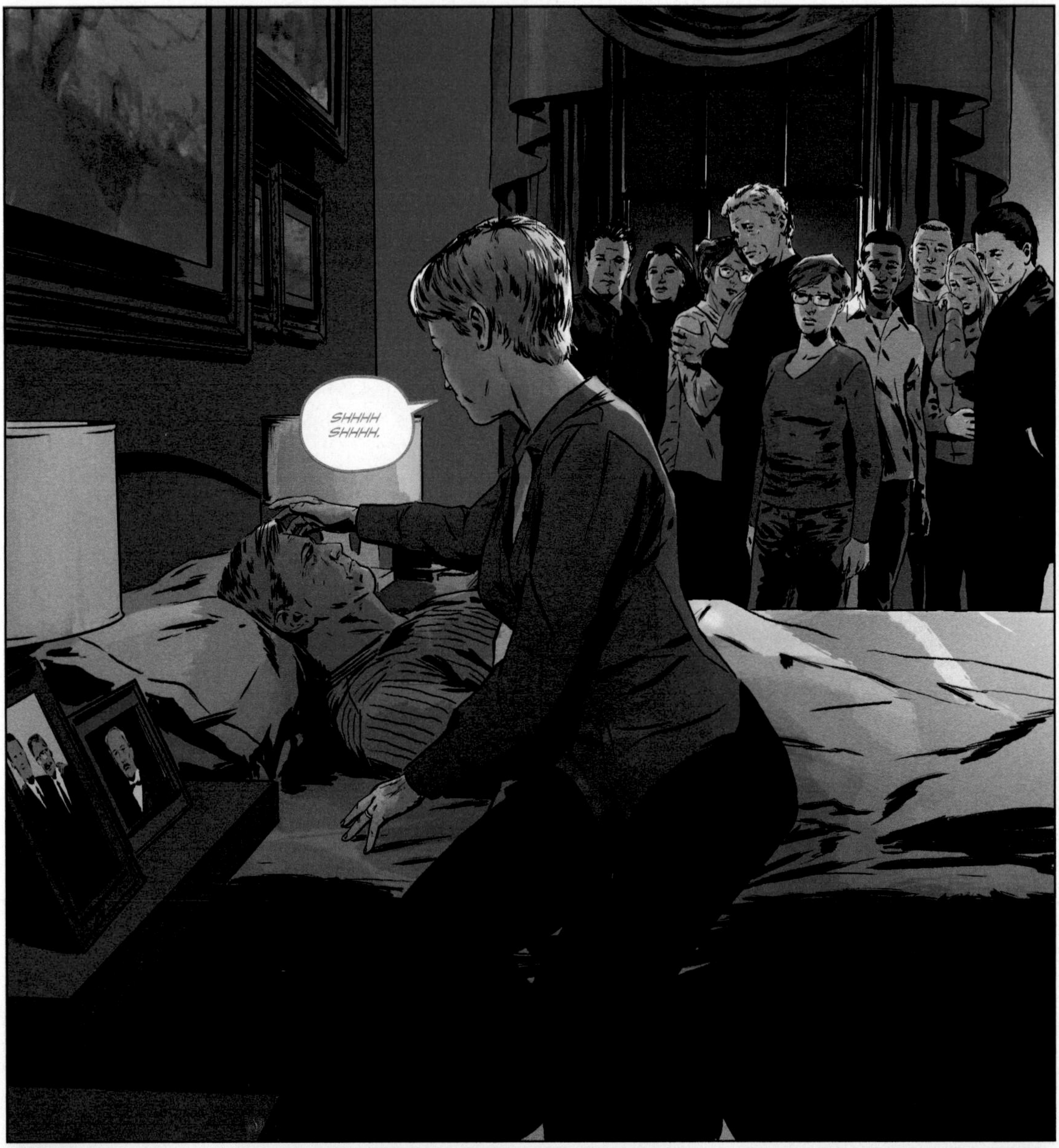
SHHHH
SHHHH.

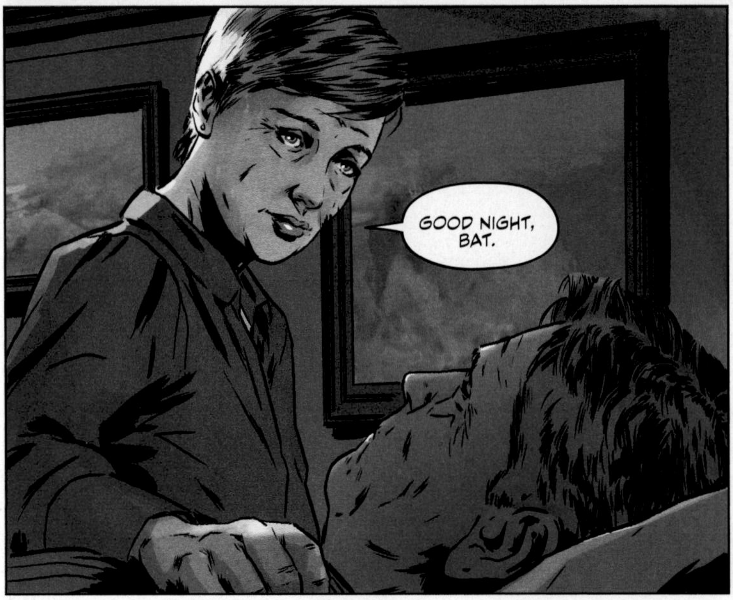
GOOD NIGHT,
BAT.

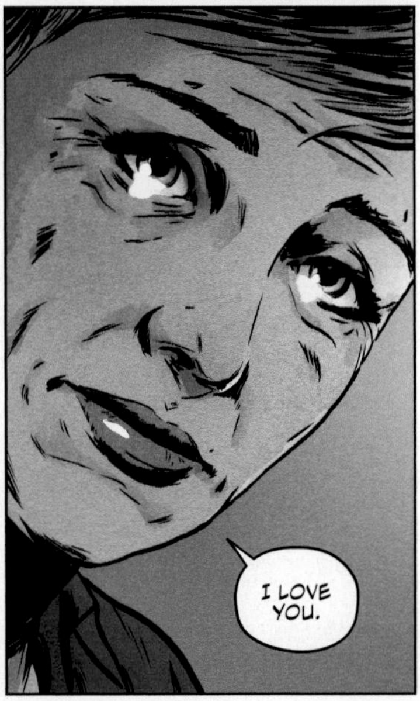
I LOVE
YOU.

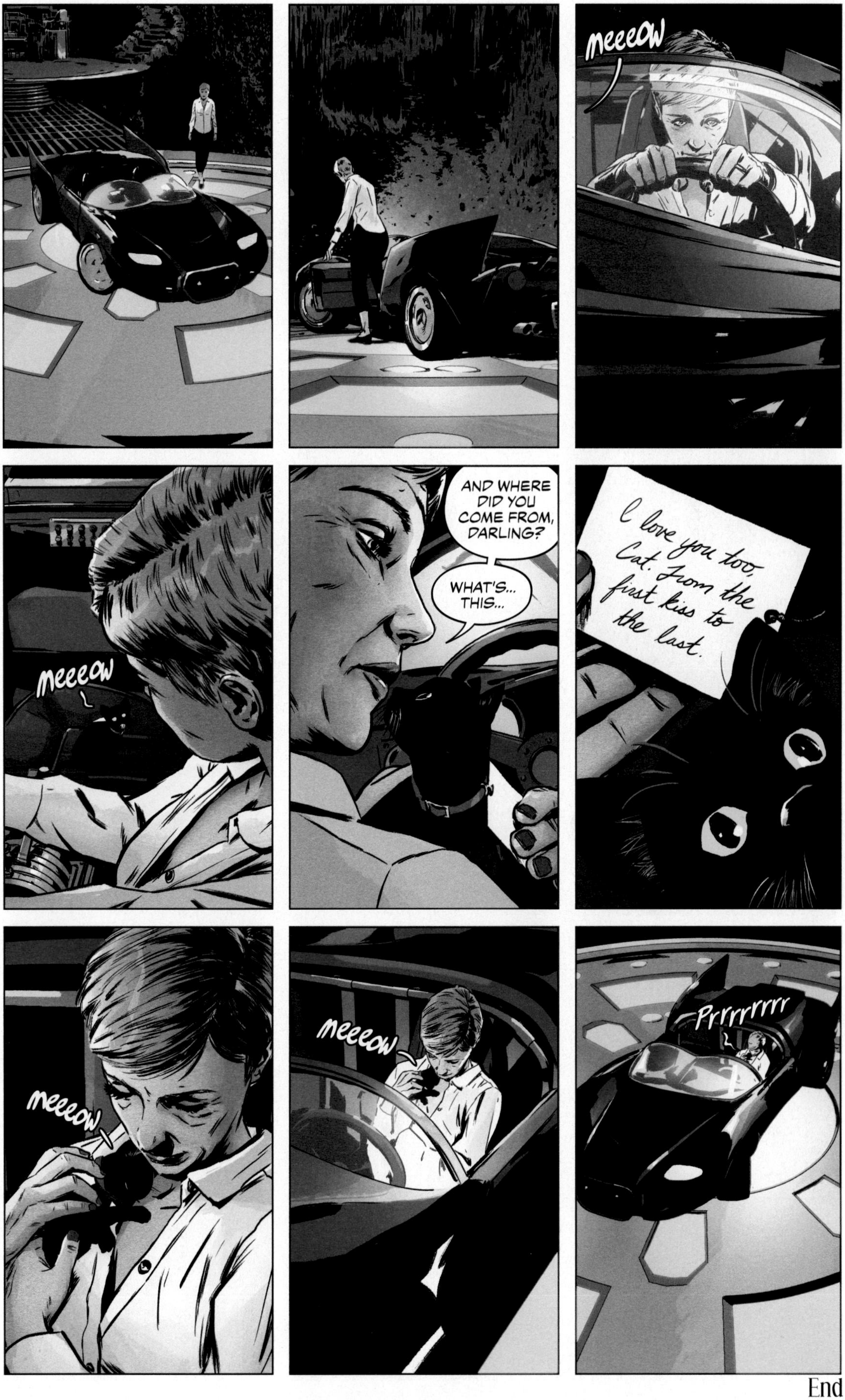
meeeow
meeeow
AND WHERE DID YOU COME FROM, DARLING?
WHAT'S... THIS...
I love you too, Cat. From the first kiss to the last.
meeeow
meeeow
Prrrrrrr

End

BATMAN #33 variant cover by OLIVIER COIPEL and DAVE STEWART

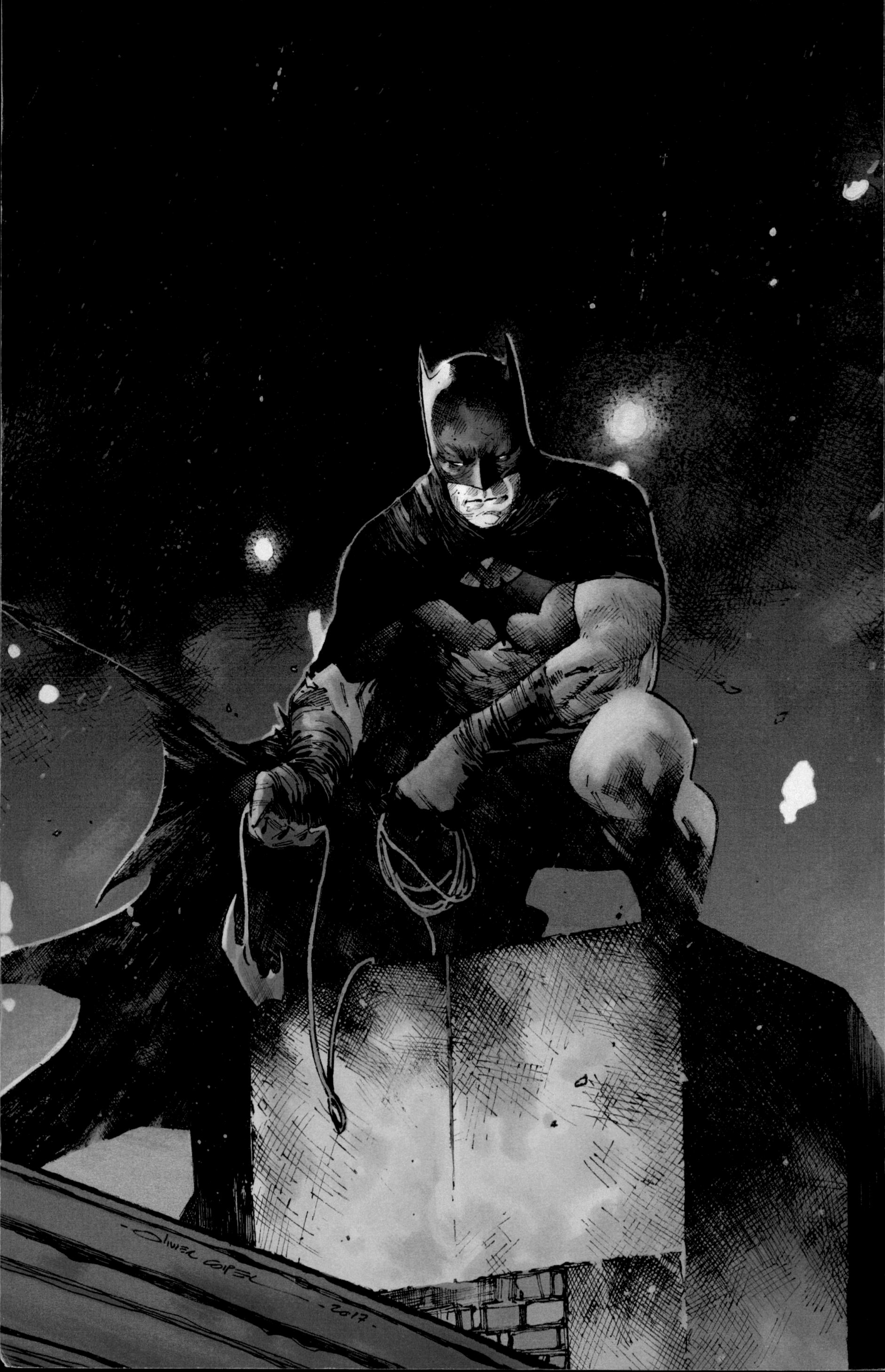

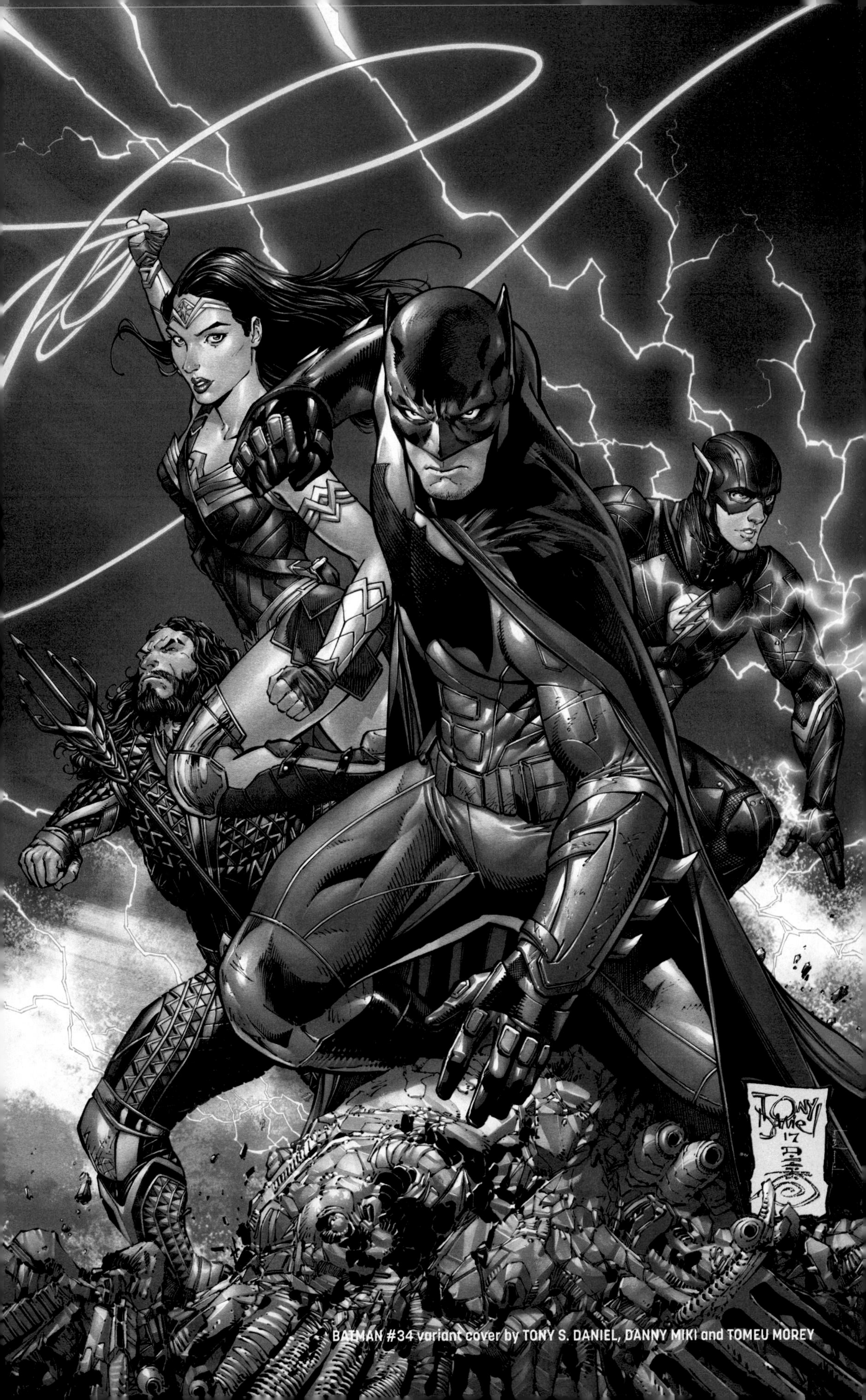

BATMAN #34 variant cover by TONY S. DANIEL, DANNY MIKI and TOMEU MOREY

BATMAN #35 variant cover by TONY S. DANIEL and TOMEU MOREY

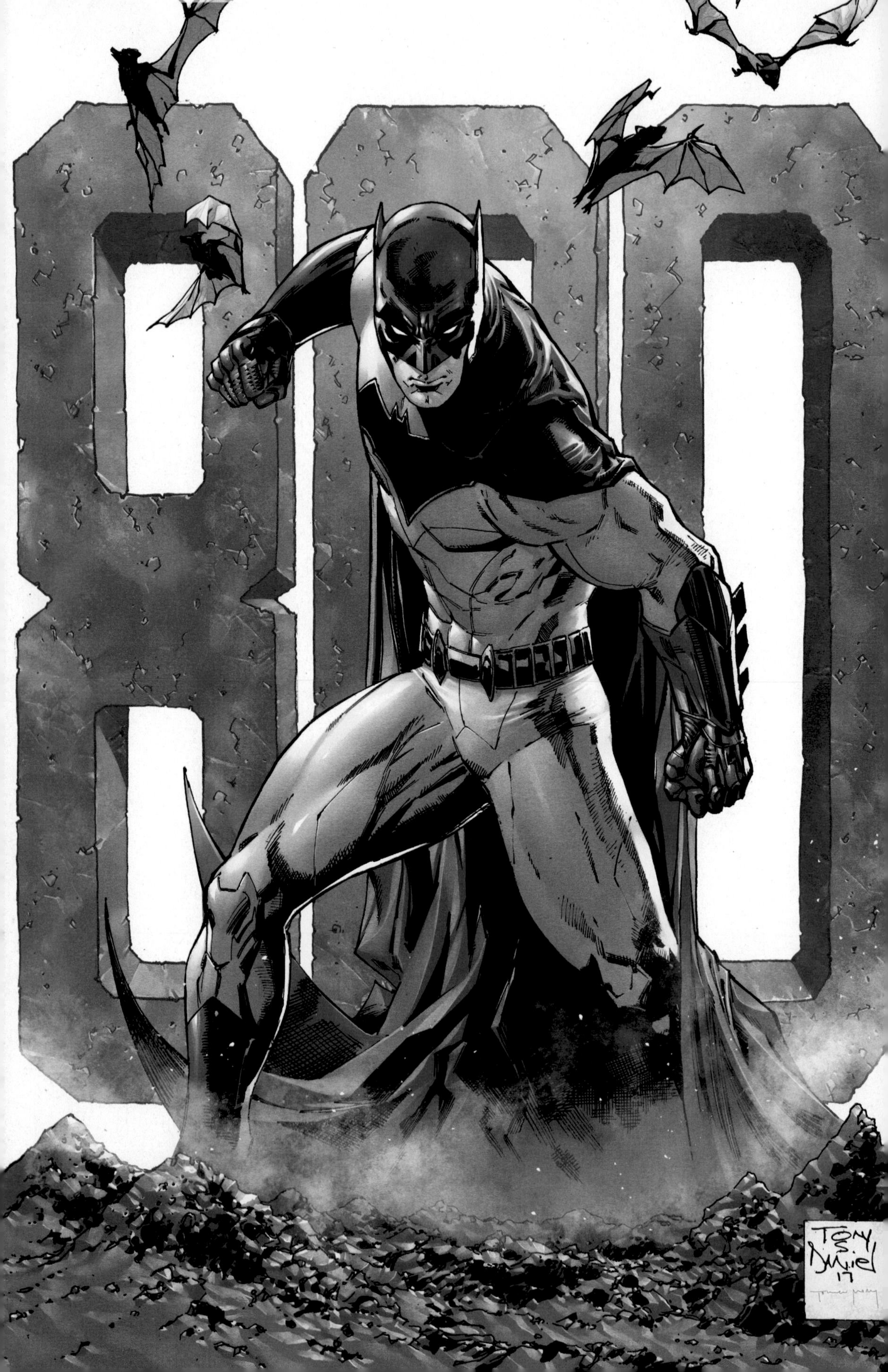

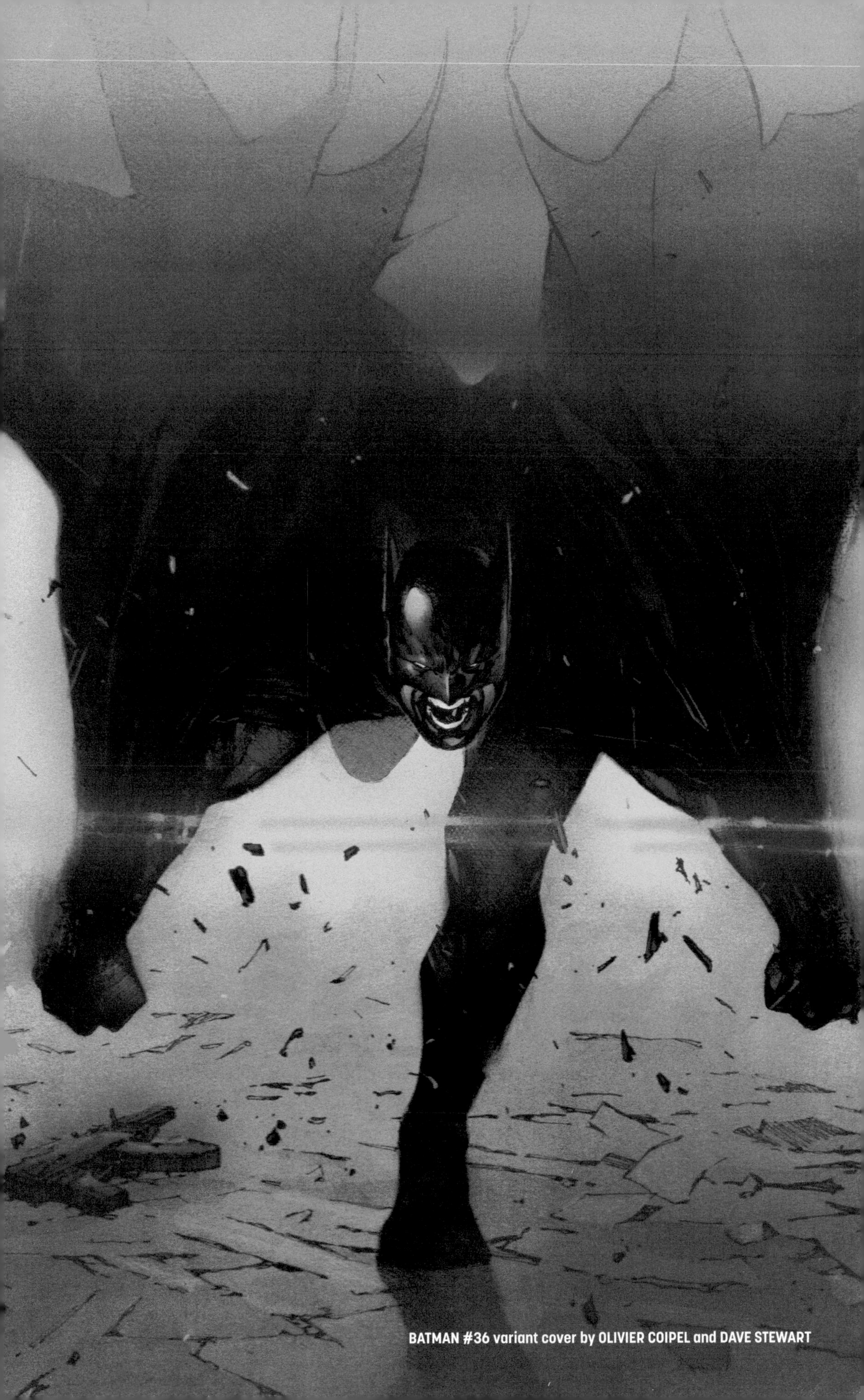

BATMAN #36 variant cover by OLIVIER COIPEL and DAVE STEWART

BATMAN #37 variant cover by OLIVIER COIPEL and DAVE STEWART

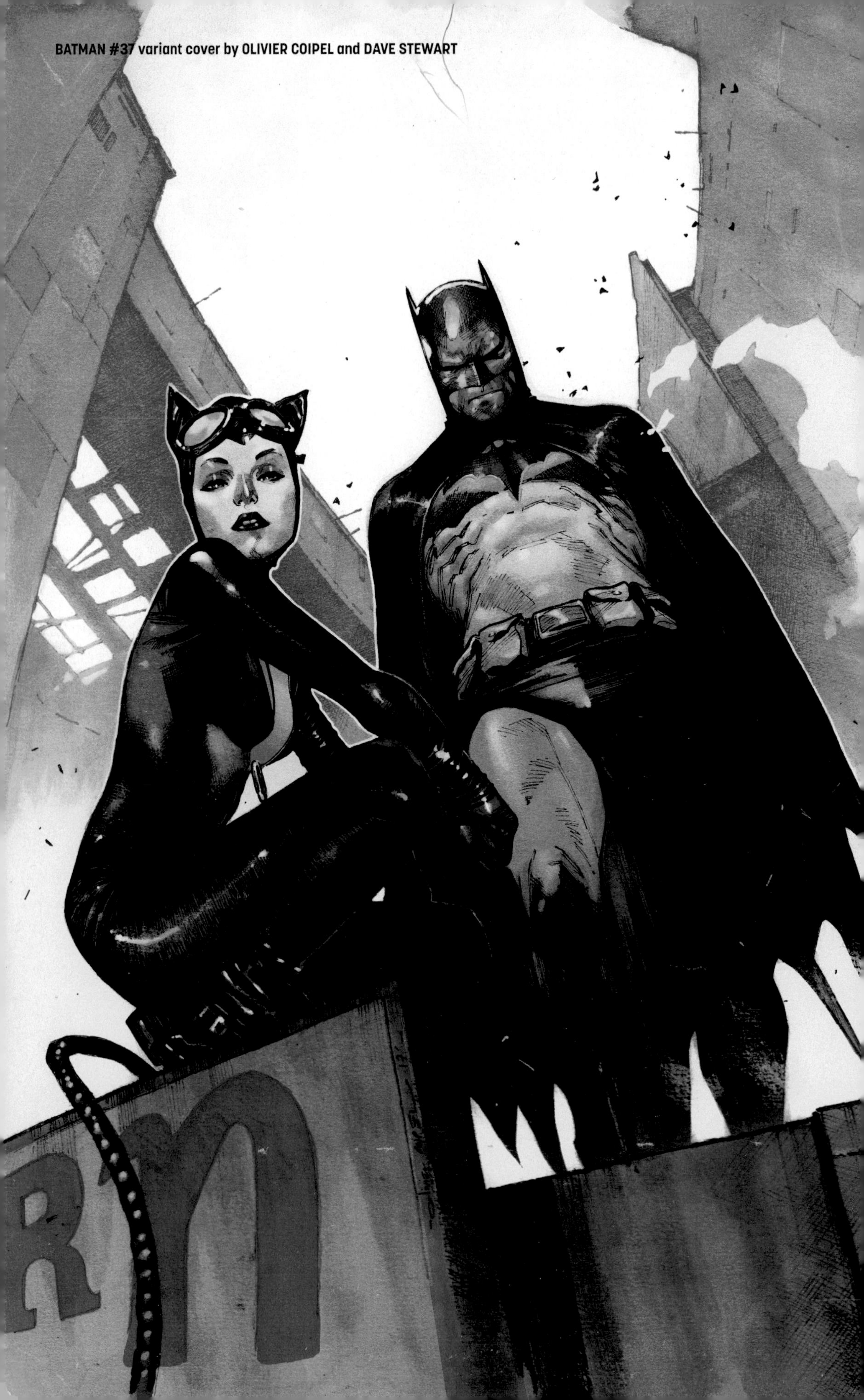